Operations Strategy

DAVID WALTERS

palgrave
macmillan

First published 2002 by
PALGRAVE MACMILLAN
Houndmills, Basingstoke, Hampshire RG21 6XS and
175 Fifth Avenue, New York, N.Y. 10010
Companies and representatives throughout the world

PALGRAVE MACMILLAN is the global academic imprint of the Palgrave Macmillan division of St. Martin's Press, LLC and of Palgrave Macmillan Ltd. Macmillan® is a registered trademark in the United States, United Kingdom and other countries. Palgrave is a registered trademark in the European Union and other countries.

ISBN 0–333–96112–9

This book is printed on paper suitable for recycling and made from fully managed and sustained forest sources.

A catalogue record for this book is available from the British Library.

Library of Congress Catalog Card Number: 2002075742.

10   9   8   7   6   5   4   3   2
11   10   09   08   07   06   05   04   03

Printed and bound in Great Britain by
Creative Print & Design (Ebbw Vale), Wales

Contents

Acknowledgements   ix

PART 1   DEVELOPING A VIEW OF STRATEGIC OPERATIONS MANAGEMENT

Introduction: new economy – new business models   2
Why a different approach?   2
The value chain: integrated demand and supply chains   5
Operations strategy: profile and definitions   7
References   11

**1 Emerging characteristics of value and value creation
      and delivery**   13
A time of change   13
Value creation and value delivery   19
Summary   22
References   24

2 Perspectives of value   25
Introduction   25
A customer value model   27
Approaches to defining value   28
Summary   34
References   35

3 Value as a business concept   36
Introduction: revisiting basic concepts   36
Value strategy decisions: strategic effectiveness and
      operational efficiency   46
A conceptual approach to a value strategy model   49
Summary   58
References   58

v

4 Value based organisations: the growth of flexible response
  and virtual organisations   59
  Introduction   59
  Where we came from   63
  Some constructs   64
  More recent events   69
  Where we may be heading   70
  Some directives for the future: the virtual organisation   78
  Summary   83
  References   84

5 Supply chains and value chains: definitions, characteristics,
  differences and directions   86
  Introduction   86
  The value chain perspective   92
  Current perspectives   99
  Implications: a value strategy   102
  Summary   103
  References   103

6 Value based organisations: the value chain approach   105
  Introduction   105
  Organisational issues   117
  Summary   120
  References   120

7 Strategic and operational characteristics and components   122
  Introduction   122
  A generic approach   124
  A generic value chain   129
  Key issues and questions for value chain decisions   135
  Adding value in the value chain   138
  The value chain: organisational profile characteristics: an
    emphasis on value for the customer and the shareholder   139
  Value chain: decisions and processes   144
  Summary   150
  References   152

8 Corporate value, performance management, coordination
  and control: issues and options   154
  Introduction   154
  The stakeholder approach   155
  Using added value as a performance measure   160
  The balanced scorecard   162
  Developing a strategic operations management performance
    planning, coordination and control model   165

Summary   174
References   174

9 Managing customer value and the value proposition   176
   Introduction   176
   A customer value model   178
   Components of customer value   182
   The value delivery gap   188
   Positioning: the value proposition   193
   Creating a value proposition: a case study   195
   Summary   198
   References   198

10 Core competencies, key success factors, value/cost drivers
   and process management   200
   Introduction   200
   Core competencies/capabilities   201
   Competencies and capabilities   202
   Key success factors   209
   Value drivers   212
   Core competencies/capabilities, key success factors and
      value drivers   215
   Business processes: a conduit for value chain operations   217
   Core competencies/capabilities and key success factors:
      Li and Fung continued   222
   Summary   224
   References   224

11 Where value strategy and value operations meet   226
   Introduction   226
   A framework for integrating value strategy and value production 227
   The value chain: organisation profile   233
   The value chain: processes, activities and decisions   234
   Implementing value production: Li and Fung continued   238
   Summary   243
   References   244

PART 2   EXISTING VALUE CHAINS

   Introduction   248

12 Industry value chains   250
   The Prato (Italy) value chain   250
   The automotive industry   254
   Summary   263
   References   264

13 Corporate value chains 265
The McKesson HBOC Corporation 265
IKEA 273
Summary 279
References 280

14 Value and value chains in healthcare 281
Introduction: value chains and a healthcare application 281
A value chain study at Queen Elizabeth Hospital 283
Value chain processes 293
Summary 297
References 297

15 Value chains in education 298
Introduction 298
A new business model for education? 300
What are the implications of value chains for universities? 303
Summary 306
References 310

PART 3 CONFIGURING THE VALUE CHAIN STRUCTURE AND PERFORMANCE

Introduction 312

16 Configuring the value chain: 1 314
Introduction: concepts and issues for the future 314
Revisiting value positioning and competitive advantage strategy 318
Exploring the interfaces 322
Intra- and inter-organisational processes 324
Performance planning and measurement in the value chain 326
Value chain planning and control 336
Summary 339
References 341

17 Configuring the value chain: 2 343
Introduction 343
Creating a value chain design 346
Summary 360
References 361

18 Case study exercises 362
Introduction 362
A value chain 'audit model': questions requiring answers 362
Case study 1: Caterpillar Inc 367
Case study 2: value chains in broadcasting 372
Case study 3: Wal-Mart – a model fmcg retail value chain? 374
Case study 4: Dell Computer Corporation 377

Index 383

Acknowledgements

As any author knows no book can be written without a great deal of help from colleagues. This has been no exception. Thanks are owed to Margaret Wiseman and Monica Byrnes who together word-processed and proof-read the chapters.

My thanks are also due to Dr Peter Jones and the Clinical and Nursing staff of the Queen Elizabeth Hospital in Rotorua for the time and effort given to me in researching and writing Chapter 14. My colleague Professor Tony Adams was responsible for the material on current and future developments in international education in Chapter 15.

Special thanks to Lynda, my wife, for listening and in particular for improving my computer skills, especially for introducing me to the draw toolbar; an instrument of torture that eventually became a friend!!

part one
Developing a view of strategic operations management

Introduction: New Economy – New Business Models

WHY A DIFFERENT APPROACH?

Recent changes have occurred to traditional competition. Competitive advantages have become competitive necessities. Figure I.1 identifies the changing nature of competition over recent years. It also suggests the changing response of business organisations. The traditional marketing approach has evolved: 'customer centricity' has developed from a product-led marketing philosophy. Senior academics have commented on the role of value creation and delivery in strategic management.

Value is an interesting concept. The underlying motivation for changes in customer expectations is a shift in the consumer perspective of value which has moved away from a combination of benefits dominated by price towards a range of benefits in which price, for some customer segments, has very little impact. Value is assumed to be the benefits received from a product choice less their costs of acquisition.

Porter (1996) offers a view of the role of 'value' in a strategic context:

> A company can outperform rivals only if it can establish a difference that it can preserve. It must deliver greater value to customers or create comparable value at lower cost or do both. The arithmetic of superior profitability then follows: delivering greater value allows a company to charge higher average unit prices; greater efficiency results in lower average costs.

Current academic and industry perspectives of the changes affecting new approaches to business models are represented by:

> The supply chain is dead ... A supply chain is all the assets, information, and processes that provide supply. A demand chain is all the assets, information, and processes that define demand. A value chain is a joining of the two for mutual benefit ... new business techniques are replacing traditional ways of managing assets and information in the supply chain ... inventory management has moved

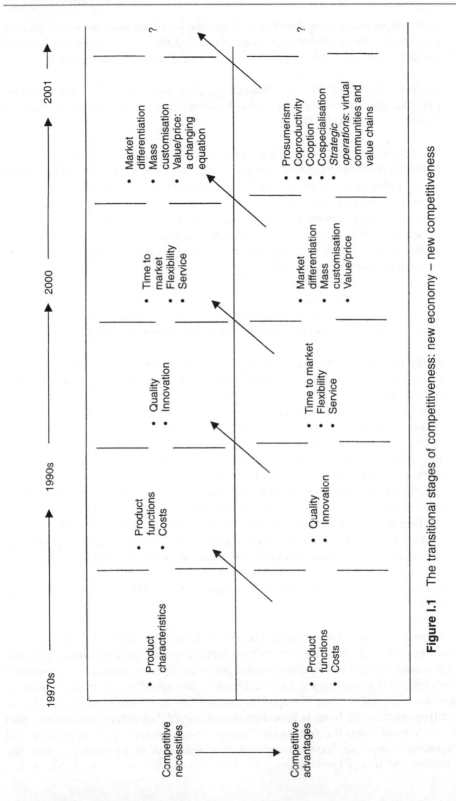

Figure I.1 The transitional stages of competitiveness: new economy – new competitiveness

from simply exchanging data between companies to integration (where information systems are tied together), and on to collaboration (where entire organisations are tied together) . . . the supply chain is becoming more of a value chain.

Andrew White, (VP Product Strategy, Logility and member of the Voluntary Interindustry Commerce Standards Association) commenting in *Transport & Distribution*, October 2000.

What we are starting to see is that different elements of new value chains display different economics, skill sets, and so on, forcing them to think and subsequently organise along new organisational boundaries. And contrary to the old hierarchies, supplementing their organisations with networks of, for example, suppliers to offer a better or cheaper product, the new value chains do not start with existing organisations and their capabilities, but rather with market opportunities. On the basis of these opportunities, products and services are designed and the necessary web of value providers is assembled.

Bornheim *et al* (2001), p. 23.

And in the Australian wine industry we see evidence of this approach:

In the rapidly evolving wine industry, Foster's will have to be careful it remains competitive with the emerging virtual winemakers operating without heavy investment in vineyards.

Relying instead on purchased, bulk wine, they invest in capable management and brand building.

The cost advantage can be significant, with one industry source saying the virtual winery might invest only 50c for each $1 of sales compared to $2 or even $2.50 of capital for the more traditional winemaker.

To be fair to Foster's, the virtual winemaking concept was one of the key attractions of Beringer, where the Zinfandel product is completely outsourced.

Chief financial officer Trevor O'Hoy likes to call it 'chateau cash flow'.

Wine traditionalists might blanch, but the reality is the myth and magic surrounding the wine industry is fast being replaced by a focus on shareholder value.

Richard Gluyas, 'Foster's winery is no small beer', *The Australian*, 29 October 2001.

Clearly business now operates in an environment which is both dynamic and challenging: globalisation, falling tariff barriers, all-embracing technology, information and communication sciences, excess capacity and product customisation expectations from customers are rapidly becoming norms. A new formula for success is apparent among the successful companies. Competitive advantage, here, is based on a new set of distinctive capabilities that have evolved from the companies' unique relationships with suppliers and customers, their understanding and management of technology, and the creation and use of knowledge.

A report by International Market Assessment and Ernst and Young (1998) identified a number of companies who are reaching well beyond their traditional role in manufacturing: managing upstream and downstream, processes and transactions as they adopt a value-chain perspective.

A typical response from companies facing declining profitability and productivity has been to cut costs or expand revenues by finding more business. Measures such as cutting costs and increasing efficiency have inherent attractions for companies: they are easy to understand, to communicate and to implement. However, focussing on efficiency alone does not build long-term value for customers, nor does it create or extend competitive advantage. Customer-focussed companies create additional value for their customers by building value chains to service customer needs. They create a multi-enterprise organisation that integrates supply chain efficiencies with a demand chain strategy. *Strategic operations* are an approach that identifies the activities of all organisations in the value chain. It seeks to identify where and who can perform activities to greatest effect to create competitive advantage. Cooperation is essential, not competition and certainly not conflict.

Operations strategy has five key features:

- a visionary who sees how 'putting pieces together' can create a more effective business model;
- core processes that are inter-organisational rather than intra-organisational;
- a supporting infrastructure that facilitates integration;
- the customer as an integral part of the chain, a major stakeholder;
- an inter-organisational performance planning system.

The result is an overall approach with five distinctive characteristics:

- distributed assets (such as manufacturing and distribution facilities as well as inventories) located so as to achieve strategic effectiveness and operating efficiencies;
- distributed processes (the design, production, marketing and service maintenance processes) located so as to achieve flexibility, quality, time and cost objectives by specialist participants in the value chain;
- flexible systems providing flexibility in product-service delivery;
- communication, co-operation and co-ordination between processes;
- synchronised networks of virtual entities – the virtual organisation.

THE VALUE CHAIN: INTEGRATED DEMAND AND SUPPLY CHAINS

Supply chain management has focussed on moving products and services *downstream* towards the customer. Typically the supply chain is coordinated by manufacturing companies or dominant resellers who use in-house manufacturing and distribution facilities to achieve market-based objectives such as market share volumes and customer penetration. Demand chain management shifts the emphasis towards 'customisation', directing product and service offers towards specific customers or customer groups sharing particular characteristics. The preference is to outsource rather than own the functions and processes that facilitate and deliver value. Focus is on asset leverage and communication through distributed assets and outsourcing. There is a large incentive to integrate supply and demand chains – it provides new opportunities for creating market value. Working together results in more specific and manageable value propositions and increases the returns to the value-chain participants. There is an interdependent relationship between supply and demand: companies need to understand customer demand so that they can manage it, create future demand and, of course, meet the level of desired customer satisfaction. Demand defines the supply-chain target, while supply-side capabilities support, shape and sustain demand.

Processes rather than functions

A feature shared by a large number of organisations is the way they consider each business process as a discreet function. Departments operate in isolation, unaware of the impact of their performance on that of others. A business process is: '. . . a set of logically related tasks performed to achieve a defined business outcome' (Davenport and Short, 1990). These authors suggest that a set of processes form a business system – or a value chain. They also suggest processes have two important characteristics. Processes have defined business outcomes for which there are recipients that may be either internal or external to the organisation. They also cross organisational boundaries; that is they normally occur across or between organisational (either intra or inter) boundaries and are independent of formal organisational structures. Performance measurements used vary and often result in conflicting goals. Within the supply chain, trading partners can (and do) operate in strategic and operational isolation. Effort is duplicated and systems cannot interact: the outcome is competition not cooperation.

Effective organisations work together to identify core processes across the demand and supply chains. They explore the implications of locating these core processes within specialist, partnership organisations.

Generic core processes of the value chain include design and development, 'production', 'procurement', 'marketing' and 'service'. Logistics is the support process that provides the infrastructure vital to manage the 'stocks and flows' of products, materials and components and information throughout the value chain. Each core process in the demand chain comprises numerous activities, the importance of which varies across industries. Often similar sections of industry differ in their infrastructure. Where they do not differ is in the integration of core processes and activities with the shared goal of maximising strategic effectiveness and operating efficiencies.

Knowledge management

Knowledge and knowledge management are integral components in strategic operations management. Knowledge management can be defined as *the organisational capability which identifies, locates (creates or acquires), transfers, converts and distributes knowledge into competitive advantage.* For example, knowledge management influences R and D investment strategy and the application of experience-based knowledge to emphasise commercial abilities. Knowledge is a resource, in the same context as financial, human and other resources. Knowledge management within strategic operations enables an 'organisation' to make more effective decisions about how to structure value chain operations to maximise customer satisfaction. In a broader context, we use the knowledge base to identify what additional knowledge is required to increase competitive advantage: to develop a knowledge strategy.

Technology management

Another underlying influence in strategic operations management is technology management. It is broader in scope than manufacturing/operations strategy: *the integration of process and product technology to address the planning, development and implementation of technological capabilities and capacities to meet the strategic and operational objectives of an organisation or combination of organisations.* Technology management can enhance the value delivered by planning manufacturing responses that deliver market volume and product and service delivery characteristics. It develops an asset structure that meets cost and plant utilisation goals *and* customer value specifications. A technology strategy may be derived by deciding upon the *combined* manufacturing and logistics support needed to meet market demand.

Relationship management

Relationship management is the managerial activity which *identifies, establishes, maintains and reinforces economic relationships with customers, suppliers and other partners with complementary (and supplementary) capabilities and capacities so that the objectives of the organisation and those of all other partners may be met by agreeing and implementing mutually acceptable strategies.* Relationship management can influence positioning and strategy by identifying, developing and maintaining partnerships that achieve the product service objectives needed to meet customer expectations. Relationship management moves the organisation towards cross-functional decision-making and control and is clearly an important component in strategic operations management.

OPERATIONS STRATEGY: PROFILE AND DEFINITIONS

Normann and Ramirez (1993) suggest:

> ... strategy is primarily the art of positioning a company in the right place on the value chain – the right business, the right segments, the right products and market segments, the right value-adding activities.

and:

> The focus of strategic analysis is not the company or even the industry, but the value creating system itself, within which different economic actors – suppliers, business partners, allies, customers – work together to coproduce value. Their key strategic task is the reconfiguration of roles and relationships among this constellation of actors in order to mobilise the creation of value in new forms and by new players . . . their underlying strategic goal is to create an ever improving fit between competencies and customers . . .

Strategic operations, viewed this way, become an integral component in the strategy process, extending upstream and downstream to ensure an optimum response to the end-users' requirements. Furthermore, it is proactive, seeking to identify customer-led opportunities and to source and integrate the competencies and inputs required, creating a value proposition that meets the opportunity.

Figure I.2 illustrates this change and serves to identify the theme to be adopted by this text. Subsequent chapters will explore the concepts and their application. However some explanation or description of them is required:

- *Customer value expectations:* customers 'value' specific criteria. Product/service quality and reliability, service guarantees and so on are attributes that represent value to customers. Customers incur real costs (and opportunity costs) when acquiring product/services and these are important elements of the customer value model. *Customer value drivers* are derived from this model.
- *Cost analysis of value drivers:* value drivers are specific to end user customers. Value drivers are 'the things that are important to customers' and reflect customer priorities such that they will pay a premium for them or switch suppliers. Value drivers reinforce competitive advantage BUT meeting value drivers has cost implications for the business.
- *Core capabilities, processes and assets profile:* each industry (and market sector) requires its participants to have specific resources and skills, processes and assets if it is to be successful. The value model chain permits a structured partnership approach, each partner contributing unique competencies.
- *Partner/value chain stakeholders' expectations:* value chain participants are stakeholders, each of whom has specific expectations. Unless these are met the success of the value chain is in doubt.
- *Value proposition:* using aggregate capabilities, skills and resources, the value chain identifies what is to be delivered to the customer and by what means; the benefits and costs to the customer; and the internal processes necessary to produce the value.
- *Value positioning and strategy for competitive advantage:* a value strategy states how the value proposition will be produced and delivered. The roles of knowledge, technology and relationship management in value

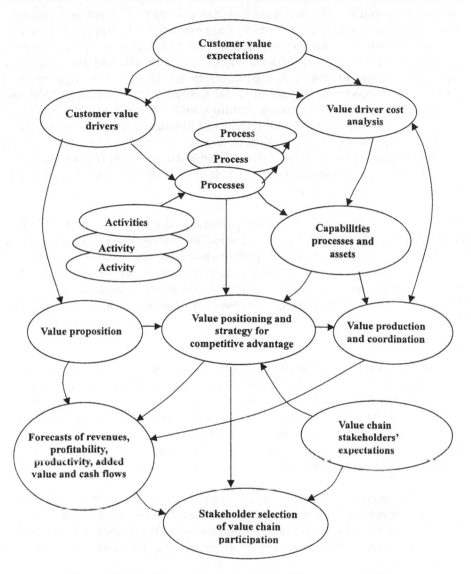

Figure I.2 Profiling value chain stakeholder core capabilities, assets, processes and expectations

production, communication and delivery are explored with a view to creating sustainable competitive advantage.

- *Value production and coordination:* successful value delivery is based upon an understanding of 'stakeholder interests' and their management as well as the effective management of 'operations' (defined as production, logistics and service).

There can be little doubt that the changes that have occurred in the business environment have brought about fundamental shifts in the response of businesses. Both philosophy and structure are undergoing significant changes. Increasingly alliances and partnerships are extended. The importance of 'distributed operations' (and therefore assets); the notion that core processes may be inter-organisational rather than intra-organisational; and the increasing frequency of the inclusion of customers in the design, development and production of products, suggest the need to expand the concept and the role of operations management into a planning and coordinating role. The issue that needs to be addressed is not where and how large should a manufacturing or logistics facility be; but rather, do we need to own the facility(ies) at all!

Clearly some lessons have been available (if not learnt) and issues for consideration have been identified. Boulton *et al* (2000) make a useful contribution when they contend:

> The encompassing challenge that companies face in this new environment is how to identify and leverage all sources of value, not just the assets that appear on the traditional balance sheet. These important assets including customers, brands, suppliers, employees, patents, and ideas – are at the core of creating a successful business now and in the future . . . But what assets are most important in the New Economy? How do we leverage these assets to create value for our own organisations in a changing business environment? What new strategies are required for us to create value?

The authors continue by making the point that the new business models comprise asset portfolios whose success is influenced by the interaction of the assets. Furthermore, in the new economy business model, asset portfolios are far more diversified than those of traditional organisations and include intangible assets such as relationships, intellectual property and leadership. They suggest that new business models are becoming commonplace in 'every industry' in the new economy:

> In these emerging models intangible assets such as relationships, knowledge, people, brands and systems are taking center stage. The companies that successfully combine and leverage these intangible assets in the creation of their business models are the same companies that are creating the most value for their stakeholders.

In an attempt at establishing a 'model' to identify assets that create value the authors propose five core categories of assets: physical, financial, employee and supplier, customer and organisation. Examples are given of companies that have focussed on a specific asset group to create above average value.

For Boulton *et al* it is clear that '. . . the ultimate success of each of these companies depends not on its ability to make the most of just one or two assets, but on its skill in optimising all assets that make up the business model'. They broaden the definition of an asset in the following way:

● Assets are tangible and intangible and extend beyond the balance sheet. They should be located where they will be strategically effective.

- Assets are, therefore, both owned and leased, controlled and uncontrolled. They offer sources of value that are within an organisation's control and outwith it.
- Assets are sources of both financial and non-financial benefits. Intangible assets such as customers provide information as well as cash from sales revenues.
- Employees provide skills and ideas and, over a period of time, knowledge and learning. Organisations provide processes and systems.
- Assets have distinct lifecycles.
- Assets include internal and external sources of value. The asset base of the virtual organisation includes numerous external relationships.

Pebler (2000) in describing the development of virtual organisation structures in the oil industry offers a prescription for the future virtual organisation:

> The virtual enterprise of the future will be much more dynamic and sensitive to the need for tuning operational parameters of the enterprise as a whole, including capital spending for both producers and service companies, optimising the whole chain of value creation. The future world will be characterised by knowledge management and collaborative decision-making by way of virtual teams. Virtual enterprises will be empowered by a willingness to do business in more productive ways and by information technologies that eliminate barriers between stakeholders and radically improve work processes.

It is arguable that the changes that have occurred are all due to the 'new economy'. However there can be little doubt that the changes have brought with them a response from corporate thinkers. Whittington *et al* (2000) comment:

> Increasingly competition, new information technologies, the rise of the knowledge economy, and extended global scope are all forcing many large companies to experiment with new forms of organising themselves. The concepts vary – they are seeking to become networked, virtual, horizontal or project based. But all these concepts express a need at the dawn of a new century to develop flatter, more flexible and intelligent forms of organising.

REFERENCES

Bornheim, S., J. Weppler and O. Ohlen (2001), *e-road mapping: digital strategizing for the new economy*, Palgrave, Basingstoke.

Boulton, R. E. S., B. D. Libert and S. M. Samek (2000), 'A business model for the new economy', *The Journal of Business Strategy*, July/August.

Davenport, T. H. and J. E. Short (1990), 'The new industrial engineering: information technology and business process design', *Sloan Management Review*, Summer.

Normann, R. and R. Ramirez (1993), 'From value chain to value constellation: designing interactive strategy', *Harvard Business Review*, July/August.

Pebler, R. P. (2000), 'The virtual oil company: capstone of integration', *Oil & Gas Journal*, 6 March.

Porter, M. E. (1996), 'What is strategy?' *Harvard Business Review*, November/December.

Whittington, R., A. Pettigrew and W. Ruigrok (2000), 'New notions of organizational "fit"', in *Mastering Strategy*, *Financial Times*/Prentice-Hall, London.

chapter 1

Emerging Characteristics of Value Creation and Delivery

A TIME OF CHANGE

During the 1990s customer focus became more a reality rather than an ideology. Band (1991) reported on anticipatory comments by North American managers and consultants suggesting that successful businesses would be those which moved closer towards their customers.

At the beginning of the period markets began to show trends that, by the end of the decade, were well-established drivers in the business environment. Many of these were new; others were established trends that accelerated. Recalling some of the comments made at that time provides an interesting background to current and future business strategy and structure decisions.

For example, R.C. Inglis, president of a Canadian consulting company, commenting on price as a competitive weapon, concluded that price reductions did increase market share, but only temporarily and that subsequently market shares returned to about the same after a price war as they were before. He suggested that consumers see products as much the same as each other and consequently price is of short-term effect but customer service (and quality) are likely to be main factors in deciding who gets the order. 'A company can outperform rivals only if it can establish a difference that it can preserve. It must deliver greater value to customers or create comparable value at lower cost or do both. The arithmetic of superior profitability then follows: delivering greater value allows a company to charge higher average unit prices; greater efficiency results in lower average costs.' The events of the late 1990s suggest this to be the case, possibly reinforcing the impact of service in developing customer loyalty.

Global manufacturing and distribution have made virtually all products available on a broadcast basis. The exclusive channels decision is no longer an option for any other than a few distinctive brands. Rapidly changing technology, shortening product life cycles, market fragmentation and the demand for customised products were suggested by Band as likely to be important trends and events have proven this to be the case. A senior advertising executive was reported by Band as opining that consumer choice could, for the individual, polarise. The consumer will prefer to have the best, if it is in a category that is important to the consumer, or will want the cheapest of the 'good-enoughs' if it is not. Band was led to conclude at the time that 'To come out on top, businesses will have to operate from strategies based on organisational flexibility, an unrelenting drive to create and deliver the value, and constant attention to the detail of the customer's demands.' (Band: 1991)

To describe the change that was occurring (and which continued) during the 1990s the term 'market turbulence' has been popular. Glazer (1991) defines turbulence as 'more events per unit of time'. Pine (1993) expands this to suggest that the increasing number and magnitude of market events requiring an organisation's attention per unit of time creates difficulties. He suggests that market turbulence creates more difficulties for *mass producers* because they need time to respond to market changes. Pine's work on mass customisation is significant to this discussion because he identifies not only the process technology changes that have occurred, but also the attitude shifts by management as the 'new economy' and its ground rules became accepted. He identifies differences in demand and structural factors that occur as market turbulence increases. Before we consider these we should review the context.

The implications of changes in the business environment

It is suggested (Pine: 1993; Ashkenas *et al*: 1995 and Day: 1999) that market turbulence has resulted in changing the competitive nature of industrial and consumer markets. Dominant effects are consumer/customer related, such as changing demographics, changing socio-economics and socio-cultural influences, resulting in changing customer attitudes and expectations. The underlying motivation for changes in customer expectations is a shift in the consumer perspective of value which has moved away from a combination of benefits dominated by price towards a range of benefits in which price, for some customer segments, has very little impact. Value is assumed to be the benefits received from a product choice less their costs of acquisition. There would appear to be an agreement among these and other commentators, that the consumer shift in expectations is one of a number of elements in the dynamics of market turbulence, but one which has had an important influence.

Returning to Pine's analysis of demand and structural factors and the differences between low and high market turbulence, changes in customer value expectations are summarised by changes in the characteristics of the demand factors, while changes in structural factors represent 'market' induced changes. The issue is to consider how an effective response is being made to both. Pine is suggesting that among both, significant differences can be observed:

Low market turbulence		High market turbulence
	Demand factors	
Stable and predictable demand levels	become	Unstable and unpredictable
Necessities	become	Luxuries
Easily defined needs and wants	become	Uncertain needs and wants
Slowly changing needs and wants	become	Rapidly changing needs and wants
Low price consciousness	becomes	High price consciousness
Low quality concerns	become	Concerns for high quality
Low fashion consciousness	becomes	High fashion consciousness
Low level service requirements	become	High level service requirements
	Structural factors	
Low buyer power	becomes	High buyer power
Low competitive intensity	becomes	High competitive intensity
Low/medium levels of saturation	become	High levels of saturation
Long, predictable product life cycles	become	Short and unpredictable cycles
Low rates of technological change	become	High rates
Narrowly defined marketing channels	become	Broadly defined channels
Local markets for sourcing and sales	become	Global markets
Slow/medium responses to orders	become	Requests for rapid response
Predictable order volumes	become	Unpredictable volumes
Large frequent customer orders	become	Smaller and less frequent orders
A stable number of order delivery points	become	Points unstable and varying in number

Adapted from Pine (1993)

Ashkenas *et al* (1995) adopt a similar approach and argument. They compare the critical factors that influenced organisational success in the twentieth century with that seen as necessary for the future:

Old success factors	New success factors
Size	Speed
Role clarity	Flexibility
Specialisation	Integration
Control	Innovation

Ashkenas and his co-authors, in proposing a response to changes that are occurring, are defining the generic key factors necessary for successful survival: sustainable competitive advantage requires one further factor – *coordination*.

Speed considers response to customer requirements and to the 'time-to-market' aspects of new product development. *Flexibility* refers to a multi-skilled work force, the ability to take on new skills and an ability to move to new locations as well as service new customers in new ways. *Integration* implies organisational ability to create mechanisms that pull together diverse activities as they are needed. The new organisation focuses more on developing relevant processes and less on specialist production. Specialists remain essential but the critical ability is to be able to identify, locate, and source resources and then collaborate with the resource owners to create an integrated value offer. Organisations that succeed during rapid change (or extreme market turbulence) find *innovation* essential. They create innovative networks, processes and products and organisation structures and transactions systems that stimulate creativity. While the authors infer *coordination* as the characteristic binding these factors into a successful holistic structure it is an essential skill, or perhaps role, that results in sustainable competitive advantage. Coordination will be seen to have a dominant role in the emerging response structures.

Day (1999) identifies five 'transitions' that are having (or will have) disruptive effects. These include *more supply and less differentiation* (or excess capacity for commodity type products) which results in product-service imitation. Day cites the athletic shoe market as an example for which imitation reaches well beyond products and into delivery methods. The Net based shopping offers of the major UK food retailers are another example. Globalisation, *more global and less local* trends are another important transition. Globalisation is being fuelled by the convergence, or homogenisation, of customer needs, trade liberalisation and the opportunities offered by international trends in deregulation. Day refers to the move from a 'marketplace' to a 'marketspace' perspective (a concept introduced by Rayport and Sviokla). Day suggests this is a new emphasis not only on marketing communications, but also on product-service characteristics and transaction payment systems. The marketspace removes the need for dominant location: '... customers can shop across the globe or country, dramatically cutting the advantage of local presence that is the mainstay of many retailers'. *More competition and more collaboration* imply a shift away from self-damaging behaviour (such as that inflicted by price competition) towards a more collaborative approach to customer satisfaction. Day identifies an arrangement between Sony and Philips who are working together to develop common optical media standards and supplying components for one another. Collaboration in the European automotive industry has resulted in shared diesel engine developments. As Day comments: 'There are many markets in which a firm can be a customer, supplier and rival at the same time.'

The preference among most organisations for long term customer relationships rather than expanding the 'new customer base' is identified by Day as *more relating and less transacting*, reflecting the move towards customer retention, and points to the organisational changes occurring in many companies whereby they organise around customers rather than products or sales districts. The adoption of customer profitability and retention are becoming important as performance measures. Day's final 'transition' concerns response to customer requirements. Again this considers both strategic and operational aspects. *More sense-and-respond and less make-and-sell* suggests an increasing application of computer aided design and manufacturing systems and a departure from traditional make-to-forecast manufacturing and response based logistics systems based upon economies of scale and vertical control structures. *Economies of integration,* the coordination of capacities and capabilities on an inter-organisational basis are rapidly replacing economies of scale in manufacturing strategy.

Day offers *market orientation* (or being market driven) as a means of dealing with market turbulence and proposes a model in which there are 'three elements of successful market driven organisations'. These are:

- an *externally oriented culture* with dominant beliefs, values and behaviour emphasising superior customer value and a continual quest for new sources of advantage. (Porter (1996) has suggested that this often results in operational/short term benefits which are soon imitated by competitors);
- *distinctive capabilities* in market sensing, market relating and anticipatory strategic thinking. In other words market driven organisations are better educated about their markets and better able to form close relationships with valued customers. Clear strategic thinking enables them to devise proactive marketing strategies that *involve* suppliers and customers, thereby increasing the value obtained by all participants in the value creation, production and delivery process;
- a *configuration* that enables the entire organisation to anticipate and respond to changing customer requirements and market conditions. *This includes all the other capabilities for delivering customer value from product design to order fulfillment, plus an adaptive organisation design together with a supporting infrastructure. All of these aspects of the configuration are aligned with the development of a superior value proposition.*

Competitive responses

There are a number of interesting responses reported by companies to these demand and structural changes identified by these and other authors. However, before reviewing them we should explore one aspect of the changes in more detail, the characteristics of customer value expectations. Traditionally we have considered form, possession, and time and place utilities as drivers of consumer utility satisfaction. *Form utility* has been provided by a company's production function. This was centralised, and finished product reaches the market through a distribution process which provides *possession utility* created by marketing activities, creating awareness of a product or service and facilitating transactions. Logistics create *time and place utilities.* However, as Rayport and Sviokla (1994) suggest, the move towards digital products changes the entire value creation, production, communication, and delivery and service process. Furthermore, customer expectations themselves have created new aspects of utility such as *convenience, choice, information, communication and 'experience'*. In a recent comment on the *Tomorrow Project*, a view of the future of relationships in the UK, Worsley (2000) identifies another dimension of value, that of *fit*. Worsley argues that if the consumer can now purchase clothes to meet an individual specification, can buy CDs with 'individualised' tracks, there is good reason to believe that the view: ' "It must fit me exactly" will become the defining outlook and expectation of the next few decades.' Evidence already exists to this effect. Toffler (1980) coined the term *prosumer* to identify consumer involvement in product design and manufacture and, if we consider the IKEA approach, we can include logistics. Nike offers customers the facility to design their own shoes using the Nike website. Customers in the US can choose between a cross trainer or a runner, select their shoe size, desired colour combinations and add personalised identification. The customer can view their 'creation' in three dimensions and when satisfied consummate the transaction by providing credit card details. A fee of US$10 is charged for this customised service, together with a delivery charge, both of which are added to the retail price. Delivery takes two to three weeks and if the shoes are not satisfactory they can be returned to a Nike store. (Hannen: 1999). Levi-Strauss (Day, *op cit*) offers a similar service. *Personal Pair* is a service in which jeans for women are made to their exact specifications. Day also cites *Custom Foot*, which offers to make shoes to order from a choice of 10,000 variations for women and 7800 for men. Dell Computers' build-to-order approach is well documented and requires no detailed comment but does offer a customised product with short delivery time.

The utility, or value characteristics, of the *experience economy* are of interest. Pine and Gilmore (1998) extend the difference between service products and 'experiences'. They argue that as goods and services become 'commoditised' experiences will become a distinct (differentiated) offering. In the *experience economy* the value delivered is a structured combination of memorable sensations that are *staged* rather than simply manufactured or sold. The value (or utility) is a memorable event individual to the person who is: '. . . engaged on an emotional, physical, intellectual or even spiritual level'. Pine and Gilmore suggest that 'outsourced' children's birthday parties are an example of this type of value. Theme based restaurants such as the Hard Rock Café are another example of *experience based value*. In other situations experience can be used to add 'live' explanation to an event. For example, Stirling Jail (Stirling, Scotland) uses actors who play roles in order to add reality for visitors to the museum. The authors forecast developments such that a company may be able to charge admission to what is essentially a merchandise based offer. They suggest that experience based value has two dimensions. The first is *customer participation* that may involve passive participation, in which the customer has no part to play, through to active participation in which customers assume key roles. The second dimension is *connection*, or environmental relationships, in which the involvement varies from absorption to immersion. The attempts by Asda, the UK superstore multiple to introduce 'singles' nights' into regular shopping visits is an example of connection. Customers seeking partners were expected to get involved (immersed) in the activity.

Four experience value products emerge from the authors' discussion: entertainment, education, aesthetics and escapism. They argue that experience value offers opportunity for premium pricing through distinctive differentiation.

VALUE CREATION AND VALUE DELIVERY

This review of recent trends suggests some changes are also occurring in the views held by some organisations. Judging by their strategy and structure decisions, they view the characteristics of customer expectation and subsequent satisfaction as different to those of the past and clearly very important. Perhaps they share the view expressed by Peter Drucker: 'The business of business is getting and keeping customers'. The point to be taken is that for decisions to be effective they require a managerial framework within which alternatives may be identified, evaluated and subsequently implemented.

Day identifies fundamental differences between the traditional organisation (self centred as identified by Day) and market driven organisations. These differences describe the philosophy expressed by Drucker's statement. They are:

Market driven organisations	*Self centred (traditional) organisations*
All decisions start with the customer and opportunities for advantage	We sell to whoever will buy
Quality is customer defined	Quality is conformance to internal standards
The best ideas come from living with the customer	Customers do not know what they want
Knowledge about customers is a valuable asset (as is the knowledge they possess)	Customer data are a control mechanism
Marketing channels are value adding partners	Marketing channels are conduits
Customer loyalty is the key to profitability	New customer accounts are what matter
There are no sacred cows; check, change and adjust the value offered	Protect the existing structures and revenues
Learn from mistakes	Avoid mistakes
Market research is decision insurance	Market research justifies decisions
Paranoia about competitors is healthy	We can live without our competitors
The behaviour of competitors can be anticipated and influenced	Competitors are unpredictable
We know more than the competition	If the competition does it, it must be right

Adapted from Day (1999)

An emerging emphasis on value

Day refers to the value chain in the context of organisation structure and this is relevant to our discussion:

> These organisations are also highly tuned to changes in customer requirements and priorities or signs of value migrating to different parts of the value chain, and keep modifying their value propositions with these changes in mind.

Day (1999) is acknowledging the need for the market driven organisation to be flexible and responsive. Here Day shares the views of Ashkenas and his colleagues concerning what we might call generic key success factors, that is, speed, flexibility, integration, innovation, and the added feature, coordination.

Porter (1996) offers a view of the role of 'value' in a strategic context:

> ... the quest for productivity, quality and speed has spawned a remarkable number of management tools and techniques and bit by bit, almost imperceptibly [these] management tools have taken the place of strategy. As managers push to improve on all fronts, they move farther away from viable competitive positions.

He develops an argument to differentiate between strategy and what he labels *operational effectiveness*:

> A company can outperform rivals only if it can establish a difference that it can preserve. It must deliver greater value to customers or create comparable value at lower cost or do both. The arithmetic of superior profitability then follows: delivering greater value allows a company to charge higher average unit prices; greater efficiency results in lower average costs.

Operational effectiveness alone is insufficient for long term competitive success:

> [competitive strategy] is about being different ... the essence of strategy is in the activities – choosing to perform activities differently or to perform different activities to rivals.

In essence Porter is suggesting that strategic effectiveness is about doing the right things; operational effectiveness is doing the right things right!!

Porter offers a simple model of a productivity frontier in which *non-price buyer value delivered* is compared with a *relative cost position*. The higher/more value delivered the higher the relative cost position. The model does not address the entire issue, however. The *productivity frontier*, rather than being: '... the sum of all practices at any given time, the maximum value that a company delivering a particular good or service can create at a given cost ...', may be considered as a coordinated value creating process in which value is optimised within a set of constraints imposed by the necessity to deliver long term stakeholder value. In other words the value produced satisfies the target customers' expectations *and, at the same time,* meets the objectives of each of the stakeholder organisations involved in its creation, production and delivery. Operational effectiveness is achieved by extending value creation into the implementation of the customer value delivery, either by coproduction processes with the customer or, possibly, with supplier organisations. Clearly the possibility of one organisation undertaking all of the 'value' processes depends much upon its competence portfolio and the transaction cost profile comparison of internal versus external processes. This takes us back to Day's view of the market oriented organisation which monitors the value creation and production process throughout the value chain and uses the observations to modify the value proposition (as and when necessary) and the value chain configuration (as and when required).

The value chain as a basis for planning overall strategy

Value and competitive advantage are compatible concepts. A value based competitive advantage can be established by identifying those benefits or value attributes expected (by the customer) which offer an opportunity to increase the attractiveness of their market offer to target customers. What differs between the view taken by Day's 'market driven organisation' and that of the 'self centred (traditional) organisation' is that both profitability and competitive advantage may be enhanced by collaboration with suppliers, customers *and* competitors!

Others share this view. Slywotzky and Morrison (1997) introduce the term 'customer-centric thinking'. They consider the traditional value chain, which begins with the company's core competencies and its assets and then moves to consider other inputs and materials, to a product offering through marketing channels and then finally to the end user, to be redundant. In customer-centric thinking the modern value chain reverses the approach. The customer becomes the first link and everything follows. This approach changes the traditional chain such that it takes on a customer driven perspective. These authors suggest:

> In the old economic order, the focus was on the immediate customer. Today business no longer has the luxury of thinking about just the immediate customer. To find and keep customers our perspective has to be radically expanded. In a value migration world, our vision must include two, three, or even four customers along the value chain. So, for example, a component supplier must understand the economic motivations of the manufacturer who buys the components, the distributor who takes the manufacturer's products to sell and the end-user consumer.

The organisation's value chain becomes merged with those of other value chain members in an attempt to create and deliver exclusivity to the customer. Normann and Ramirez (1993) have also dealt with this. They see the value chain as an analytical tool that facilitates strategy:

> ... strategy is primarily the art of positioning a company in the right place on the value chain – the right business, the right segments, the right products and market segments, the right value-adding activities.

and:

> The focus of strategic analysis is not the company or even the industry, but the value creating system itself, within which different economic actors – suppliers, business partners, allies, customers – work together to coproduce value. Their key strategic task is the reconfiguration of roles and relationships among this constellation of actors in order to mobilise the creation of value in new forms and by new players . . . their underlying strategic goal is to create an ever improving fit between competencies and customers . . .

SUMMARY

Strategic operations, viewed this way, becomes an integral component in the strategy process extending upstream and downstream to ensure an optimum response to the end users' requirements. Furthermore, it is proactive, seeking to identify customer-led opportunities and to source and integrate the competencies and inputs required to create a value proposition that meets the opportunity. Porter's approach is valid here; his productivity frontier offers a basic model to explore the value production alternatives. Non-price value delivered forms the basis of a value based strategy. It identifies positioning and delivery tasks. The relative cost position identifies the financially viable alternative value production and delivery options. Given a value strategy and positioning we can use operational effectiveness as a means by which we identify cost-efficient ways in which the value strategy can best be implemented.

An example from food distribution can be used to explain this proposition.

In the UK the product-market strategies of the leading companies do not differ to any great extent. Marketing activities can, and do, create a value proposition and its positioning. Profitability, productivity and cash flow are enhanced by operational effectiveness. For example, customers expect choice and this varies between product categories (and between companies). To meet the customers' expectations *and* to meet shareholder objectives requires an efficient operations infrastructure. It is at this point that we begin to see supply chain management assume importance. Given the product-market and service objectives that have evolved from customer expectations it is only by efficient management of inventories and deliveries that both the customers' expectations and those of the shareholder can be met. It follows that unless we deploy the relevant 'management tools and techniques' (Porter: 1996) these cannot be met. But here is an important consideration: the techniques currently used (JIT, VMI, ECR, QR, and so on) should only be seen for what they are, a means to an end not the end in themselves. It is also one of the reasons why the supply chain is a reactive, but very efficient, means of optimising the costs of manufacturing and delivering products. Increasingly there is an argument made for assuming a *demand*, or *value chain* approach. Supporters of this view suggest that the supply chain works within a prescribed demand situation, whereas the value chain, being proactive, seeks opportunities and configures a structure to take full advantage of the opportunity. It can be used to explore opportunities and alternative value delivery methods. For example Beech (1998) comments: 'There is an interdependent relationship between supply and demand: companies need to understand customer demand so that they can manage it, create future demand and, of course, meet the level of desired customer satisfaction. Demand defines the supply-chain target, while supply-side capabilities support, shape and sustain demand.'

Observation in the business environment suggests there is evidence to support this view. Ford have made some interesting acquisitions during the past two years, which would appear to have been motivated by their view of where industry profits are being made together with a revised view of customer expectations and their requirements for a 'complete' product range. The vehicle range has been broadened by the purchase of Jaguar and other marques but the automotive industry *total* product range is far more extensive. It includes maintenance, financial and insurance services, car rental and (in the not too distant future) vehicle disposal. Hence it should come as no surprise to see Ford acquire Kwikfit (tyres and exhaust services) and in the US a vehicle recycling company. In Australia they have been experimenting with investment in the equity of large distributors. Clearly there are considerations concerning critical mass and economies of scale but equally there is the suggestion that there are concerns to ensure product and production capacity coverage. Capacity coverage at a local cost base is essential for global operations: it ensures that price competitiveness can be maintained, and if this can be achieved through partnership agreements then capital commitment is avoided.

Another, more recent example, concerns Unilever's entry into the domestic services business. Norton (2000) reports the company's launch of 'myhome', a home cleaning, laundering and, eventually a gardening business. Aware of its lack of competencies, Unilever has acquired 'Mrs McMopp', a home cleaning business, and 'Palace Laundry', both London based businesses. Services will be expanded to include home repairs and security as well as gardening. The attraction for Unilever is the estimated four billion pounds sterling per year spent on home services and the potential growth it offers. Competition exists, but is not national, so the attraction includes a fragmented market which offers huge potential for partnerships within a value chain structure.

These examples provide us with sufficient evidence to question existing structures. Strategy decisions have always involved an intra-company approach. Increasingly we need to adopt not only an inter-organisational approach but also an extra-organisational view that involves the end user and the suppliers, our distributors, our employees, investors and peripheral groups that may have influence in this larger market. A strategic operations approach would ensure that opportunities are identified, that the relevant value is created, produced, delivered and serviced. It will also ensure that the appropriate competencies are sourced, integrated and coordinated to ensure the interests of *all* stakeholders are met.

REFERENCES •••••••••••••••••••••••••••••••••

Ashkenas, R. D. U., J. Todd and S. Kerr (1995), *The Boundaryless Organisation*, Jossey-Bass, San Francisco.

Band, W. A. (1991), *Creating Value for Customers*, Wiley, New York.

Beech, J. (1998), 'The supply-demand nexus: from integration to synchronization' in *Strategic Supply Chain Alignment*, edited by Gattorna J., Gower, London.

Day, G. (1999), *The Market Driven Organisation*, The Free Press, New York.

Drucker, P. (1985), *Innovation and Entrepreneurship*, Heinemann, London.

Glazer, R. (1991), 'Marketing in an information-intensive environment: strategic implications of knowledge as an asset', *Journal of Marketing*, October.

Hannen, M. (1999), in *Business Review Weekly*, 10 December.

Normann, R. and R. Ramirez (1993), 'From value chain to value constellation: designing interactive strategy', *Harvard Business Review*, July/August.

Norton, C. (2000), 'Big business plugs into four billion (sterling) chores goldmine', *The Independent*, 14 March.

Pine III, B. J. (1993), *Mass Customisation: The New Frontier in Business Competition*, Harvard Business School Press, Boston.

Pine III, B. J. and J. H. Gilmore (1998), 'Welcome to the experience economy'. *Harvard Business Review*, July/August.

Porter, M. E. (1996), 'What is strategy?', *Harvard Business Review*, November/December.

Rayport, J. F. and J. J. Sviokla (1994), 'Managing in the marketspace', *Harvard Business Review*, November/December.

Slywotzky, A. J. and D. J. Morrison (1997), *The Profit Zone*, Wiley, New York.

Toffler, A. (1980), *The Third Wave*, Morrow, New York.

Worsley, R. (2000), 'Our society is geared to the search for pleasure', (Podium) *The Independent*, 10 March.

chapter 2

Perspectives of Value

LEARNING OUTCOMES

The student will be able to:

- understand the importance of defining value in precise and 'useable' terms;
- use the concept of 'value-in-use' as a value-planning tool;
- identify and map customers' 'consumption chains';
- develop a model for analysing customer value preferences and expectations.

INTRODUCTION

Value is a term frequently used but infrequently understood and for which numerous interpretations exist. In a business context, value implies stakeholder satisfaction, which is a broader consideration than simply customer satisfaction. Stakeholder satisfaction ensures that not only are customers' expectations met, but also those of employees, suppliers, shareholders, the investment market influencers, the community and government. It follows that stakeholder satisfaction presents the business with a broader range of decisions and, typically, a larger number of ways in which satisfaction can be delivered.

Value is not a new concept. It will be recalled that Adam Smith introduced the notion of 'value in use' in 1776. He argued for two aspects of value. He was of the view that value was determined by labour costs (subsequently modified to 'production costs'). Smith also argued that 'value in use' from a user's point of view is important. It is only when it is *used* that the full costs and benefits of a product-service may be identified. A number of companies use the 'value in use' concept to arrive at pricing decisions. The notion that an end-user should consider all aspects of a product-service purchase, not simply the price to be paid, enables both vendors and purchasers to identify all of the elements of the procurement – installation – operation – maintenance

25

– replacement continuum. The process encourages both parties to look for trade-off situations such as high acquisition costs with low operating and maintenance costs, together with relevant supplier services packages. This approach introduces the possibility of integrated activities in which the supplier-customer relationship expands from a one-to-one relationship into a fragmented, but economically viable, value delivery system.

This situation is currently more the exception than the rule. Value creation (for that is what stakeholder value actually is about) has a history of development. Band (1991) traces the history of value creation, comparing North American interpretations with those of Japanese management philosophies which, ultimately, defines what it is the customer is offered and how this is accomplished, by whom, how, when and, of course why (which is usually the reference to corporate/stakeholder objectives). Band suggests that during a whole range of changes occurring in the 1980s: 'Executives who got the quality and service "religion" . . . failed to remember that quality and service are the means, but *value for the customer* is the end'. Band interprets this simply and succinctly: 'The idea of creating value may, indeed, be reduced to a concept as simple as striving to become ever more "useful" to customers'. And:

> But of course good intentions must be transformed into practical reality. The businesses that will succeed in the decades ahead are not those with advantages defined in terms of internal functions, but those that can become truly market focussed – that is, able to profitably deliver sustainable superior value to their customers.

This means being able to do the following:

- choose the target customer and combination of benefits and price that to the customer would constitute superior value, and
- manage all functions rigorously to reflect this choice of benefits and prices so that the business actually provides and communicates this chosen value, and does so at a cost allowing adequate returns.

Looking more closely at the question of user value, the following characteristics are found:

- quality – expressed in terms of features of products or services that are consistently valued by customers;
- cost – the 'sacrifice' required of the user (in terms of money, time, risk or self esteem);
- schedule – the delivery of user-valued features in the correct quantity, time and place.

It follows that it is management's responsibility to identify what is valued by the end-user and indeed other 'customer groups' and to create, monitor and modify organisational systems that add value to the product-service. Thus, for Band, the assertion is that creating and delivering value is much more than 'a passing business fad'. Rather it is an approach to strategic management that can be used to ensure that organisations respond to customer expectations, doing so with organisational structures that are flexible. Value creation, he suggests, is *strategic* (because it entails both organisational and behavioural change), and it is *continuous* (because the challenge of delivering customer satisfaction in a dynamic marketplace requires unrelenting attention to achieving higher and higher levels of performance).

A CUSTOMER VALUE MODEL

Utility and value

Band has suggested there exist some basic criteria or a *customer value model* that has a basis in economics. In Chapter 1 the concepts of utility and value were introduced. The economists' concept of utility is similar to that of value in a business context. It will be recalled that to form, possession, time and place utilities were added convenience, choice, information (and communication) and 'experience' as aspects of utility that are important in customer satisfaction. It follows that during any purchasing situation certain attributes of a product or service will represent utility or value to the purchaser. Furthermore, it is likely that one particular combination of attributes will represent more value to a customer than does another. A customer value criterion may be defined as:

> An attribute (or characteristic) of a product or service considered by a purchaser to be a primary reason for selecting a *specific* product (or service) because it enhances the value of the purchaser's output (business to business customers) or improves their lifestyle (consumer product-service customers).

Customer value criteria, therefore, represent extensions of the basic economic utility characteristics of form, ownership, time, convenience, and so on. Such features may be expressed as generic customer value criteria:

- *security*: warranties, price guarantees
- *convenience*: reduced 'preparation' times, availability
- *performance*: quality features that enhance the customer's own market advantage, time advantage
- *economy*: relative price advantage – initially or over the life cycle of the product-service
- *aesthetics*: design leadership
- *reliability*: durability in use, spaced maintenance periods

Customer expectations and the value proposition

It follows that value is determined by the utility combination of benefits delivered to the customer, but there is a cost to the customer of acquiring such benefits. *Value* then is a preferred combination of benefits compared with acquisition costs. From an organisation's perspective, the response to customer expectations is a *value proposition*, which is a statement of what value is to be delivered to the customer. Externally, the value statement is the means by which the organisation 'positions' the offer to the target customer. Internally, the value statement identifies how the value is to be produced, communicated, delivered and maintained. The internal statement specifies processes, responsibilities, volumes and costs to be achieved if the customer and each of the other stakeholders is to receive satisfaction. Webster (1994) suggests: 'The value proposition should be the firm's single most important organising principle', and implies that the traditional perspective of marketing with its transaction based approach has shifted: 'Our definition of marketing is built around the concept of the value chain. Marketing is the process of defining, developing and delivering value'.

The economists' perspective of value

Bowman and Ambrosini (2000) offer a theoretical approach to value, from a business strategy perspective. They address value creation and value capture and the role of value in strategy. They suggest two aspects to value: use value and exchange value. *Use value* is subjectively assessed by customers, who base their evaluation of value on their perceptions of the usefulness of the product. Hence the total monetary value is the amount the customer is *prepared* to pay for the product. *Exchange value* is realised when the product is sold. It is the amount paid by the buyer to the producer for the perceived use value.

The authors use the economists' concept of *consumer surplus* to explain the consumer/customer view of value. The price the customer is prepared to pay is 'price + consumer surplus'. Consumer surplus in a business context is equivalent to the benefits the product or service delivers. Exchange value, the price realised, and costs of producing the product or service determine the profit made. Clearly profit is only made if the exchange value exceeds the costs of the input resources. The authors argue that: '. . . Profit can only be attributed to the actions of organisational members as their labour is the only input into the production process that has the capacity to create new use values, which are the source of the realised exchange value. So . . . labour performed by organisational members is the source of the firm's profit'. This assumption is arguable and despite the definition of categories of labour and acknowledgment of entrepreneurial skill, the assumption does require debate.

Bowman and Ambrosini contend that profitability is determined by comparisons customers make between the firm's product, their needs and feasible competitive offers, and the comparisons resource suppliers make of the opportunity costs occurring among alternative customers. Hence the authors conclude that the extent of value capture and the realisation of the exchange value is determined by the bargaining relationships between buyers and sellers, the availability of substitutes, the bargaining power between suppliers and customers, and sustaining costs.

The arguments presented and conclusions reached by the authors have logic but may need closer scrutiny when applied to industrial situations. The authors have, however, identified a conceptual basis against which other contributions to the debate can be considered. Of particular importance is the role of the consumer surplus (or its marketing context, value in use). We shall return to Bowman and Ambrosini's argument in the context of developing a value strategy in the following chapter.

Given that value attributes, delivered in context and relatively better than by competitors, create competitive advantage, some examples are used to add emphasis.

Time and information as elements of value

Stalk and Webber (1993) describe how Japanese companies that had previously sought competition through economies of scale, lower costs, and higher quality began to compete on 'time'. 'Time-to-market' became an important value driver during the late 1980s and the 1990s. The concept was embraced quickly by Western companies as it brought a powerful agent of change:

> By looking through the lens of time, managers and workers could identify their organisations' main sequences, critical processes and horizontal linkages, the elements that define the way a company does business.

In other words, the internal component of the organisation's value proposition.

Just as importantly, the concept offers the opportunity to question what, when, where and how value can best be produced. However, as the authors recount, there emerged severe problems. In order to maintain momentum, companies were increasing financial and human resources in order to produce an expanding variety of products. Despite the apparent increase in 'value' delivered to the customer and despite the revenues generated, there was very little profitability, except in one company – Daiichi.

Daiichi developed 'a powerful information and service system, a feedback loop of customer knowledge'. In addition to the 'time' value the company added 'service' as well as 'knowledge'. Products were sold with a three-year warranty and a storage facility. Japanese homes are small with limited storage space, consequently the offer by Daiichi to store winter products in the summer and vice versa in the winter, was a welcome service feature. As products reach the end of their warranty period the company offers to send a technician to check the product for potential problems prior to the expiry of the warranty. The Daiichi technicians observe and record, on an online central customer database, details of *all* product types (and their ages) owned by the customer. Very soon after the visit the customer receives a letter detailing the 'health' of the particular item inspected, followed by an invitation to visit the nearest Daiichi store to inspect the new 'whatever model' which would be an ideal replacement for the ageing model in the customer's home. Some 70 per cent of Daiichi's sales are repeat sales, which compares well with the industry average of 20 per cent.

Daiichi is offering not just the latest fad value characteristic, which is offered by all of its competitors, but has added convenience, security and reliability in a complementary value proposition. Daiichi realised far sooner than its competitors that 'time' on its own is misleading, and that there are accompanying aspects of value that complement time to provide a competitive value proposition.

The consumption chain

Differentiation has been an acknowledged component of competitive advantage for some time. While many companies focus on products or services, MacMillan and McGrath (1997) argue that the customer life cycle, or the consumption chain is a means by which: '. . . they can uncover opportunities to position their offerings in ways that they, and their competitors, would never have thought possible'. Using a process they have labelled 'mapping the consumption chain', they capture the customer's total experience with a product or service. Such a process identifies numerous ways in which value can be added to a product or service. The mapping process to identify the consumption chain comprises a series of questions aimed at establishing aspects of behaviour that occur:

- How do people become aware of their need for a product or service?
- How do consumers find a specific offering?
- How do consumers make final selections?
- How do customers order and purchase a product or service?
- How is the selected product or service delivered?
- What happens when the product or service is delivered?
- How is the product installed?
- What is the customer really using the product for?
- How is the product or service paid for?
- How is the product stored?
- How is the product moved around?
- What do customers need help with when they select a product?
- What about returns or exchanges?
- How is the product serviced?

An omission is a question concerning disposal or recycling of the product, which is becoming an important consideration. Essentially the authors are applying Kipling's 'six loyal serving men' to an audit of customer product selection and use behaviour. Their argument is reinforced with numerous examples. The mapping process is an ideal method for identifying 'value adding' opportunities, but another benefit, not identified as such, is the opportunity it offers to review the value creation processes and consider alternative delivery methods. Clearly these may not be 'in-house' and the analysis there-fore encourages the use of external suppliers who may add even greater value to the product-service, either through extended differentiation or by cost reductions. This is the very essence of value chain strategy and management.

Customer value models are benefit and cost based

Anderson and Narus (1998) adopt a similar approach. They argue that very few suppliers in business markets are able to answer questions concerning what value actually is, how it may be measured and what the suppliers' prod-ucts (or services) are actually worth to customers. They comment:

> Customers – especially those whose costs are driven by what they purchase – increasingly look to purchasing as a way to increase profits and therefore pressure suppliers to reduce prices. To persuade customers to focus on total costs rather than simply on acquisition price, a supplier must have an accurate understanding of what it is customers value, and would value.

The authors suggest that the successful suppliers in business markets are suc-cessful because they have developed *customer value models*, which are data-driven representations of the worth, in monetary terms, of what the supplier is doing, or could do, for its customers. Customer value models are based on assessments of the costs and benefits of a given market offering in a particu-lar customer application. *Value* is defined by Anderson and Narus:

> Value in business markets is the worth in monetary terms of the technical, economic, service, and social benefits a customer company receives in exchange for the price it pays for a market offering.

Value is expressed in monetary terms. Benefits are net benefits; any costs incurred by the customer in obtaining the desired benefits, except for the pur-chase price, are included. Value is what the customer gets in exchange for the price they pay. Anderson and Narus add an important perspective concern-ing a market offer. A market offer has two '... elemental characteristics: its value and its price. Thus raising or lowering the price of a market offering does not change the value such an offering provides to a customer'. And, finally, value takes place within a competitive environment; even if no com-petitive alternative exists the customer always has the option of 'making' the product rather than 'buying' it. This proposition can be summarised as an equation:

$$(\text{Value}_s - \text{Price}_s) > (\text{Value}_a - \text{Price}_a)$$

Value_s and Price_s are the value and price of the supplier's market offer, and Value_a and Price_a are the value and price of the next best alternative. The dif-ference between value and price equals the customer's incentive to purchase. In other words, the equation conveys the fact that the customer's incentive to purchase a supplier's offer must exceed its incentive to pursue the next best alternative. This is, in effect, a practical application of the consumer surplus discussed by Bowman and Ambrosini. We shall return to this topic in the next chapter and consider its relevance in a strategy context.

Anderson and Narus are offering a structured approach to 'value in use' pricing, or life cycle costing. They consider the activities involved in generating a comprehensive list of value elements which are: '. . . anything that affects the costs and benefits of the offering in the customer's business. These elements may be technical, economic, service or social in nature and will vary in their tangibility'. The authors consider both tangible and intangible aspects of value, commenting on the difficulties that exist in ascertaining the value impact of benefits such as design services. They also discuss the problems associated with establishing monetary values to many of the elements, such as social factors like 'peace of mind'. Depending upon the nature of 'peace of mind' it is possible to consider the monetary outcome if it does not exist. For example, peace of mind may be available from an alternative because it eliminates pollution or some other problem. Not to choose that particular alternative may result in prosecution for pollution offences – the legal costs and potential fine do have monetary values!

Anderson and Narus are aware of the need to match value delivered with costs. They identify what they label as *value drains*; services that cost the supplier more to provide than they are worth to the customers receiving them and that offer no competitive advantage. They also identify two important advantages of the approach. Given the understanding of their customers' businesses, customer value models enable an organisation to be specific concerning its value proposition and from this position of advantage another follows: customer relationships are strengthened. Possibly the most important benefit comes from the fact that understanding value in business markets and translating this into delivered value, gives suppliers the means to receive an equitable return on their efforts and resources.

Service is an integral component of value to the customer

> Logistics have become central to product strategy because, it is increasingly clear, products are not just things-with-features. They are things-with-features *bundled with services*. (Fuller *et al*: 1993)

Fuller *et al* make this point establishing that companies do not create value for customers and sustainable advantages for themselves merely by offering varieties of tangible goods. They offer the goods in distinct ways, presuming that consumers value convenience, reliability and support. The authors maintain that this comprises a complex relationship, one that it is necessary to manage as an entity.

Fuller and his colleagues offer an approach to the use of logistics to reinforce manufacturing, in adding specific value characteristics to the value proposition. They identify an initial problem, one which is common across a number of industries and to companies within those industries: the problem of 'averaging'. Averaging grows out of complexity. Products flow through consolidated channels at an 'average' speed and are charged at 'average' cost. Consequently, customers needing specialised products quickly but unpredictably tend to be underserviced, while customers for more commodity-like products are overcharged. The problem has further complications. Unless logistics costs are accurately identified and applied, there is a temptation for both supplier and customer to work on gross margin and not contribution or operating margin to make decisions. The consequence of this approach is that the 'averaging' results in customers defecting. A detailed understanding of customer service expectations (the characteristics of added value) and knowledge of the processes *and* their costs can result in different strategy decisions and operating methods. The authors' proposal is to identify LDBs (logistically distinct businesses). Each LDB demonstrates specific logistics requirements: order processing, order assembly and despatch, sourcing and vendor management, inventory management, order delivery and order rectification and redeliveries. The approach is essentially identifying how logistics processes should be aligned to meet the service expectations of a range of customer companies. The LDBs are derived from a study of the value criteria that form the basis for *customer value models*.

Identifying value characteristics and developing a customer value model are essential steps in satisfying a target customer (or customers). However, simply identifying the components of the customer value model is not the complete task. The product and service characteristics must be produced and delivered, and these tasks raise questions concerning capacities and capabilities.

Capacities are essentially volume and time concerns. Can sufficient product (given specification details) be manufactured and delivered to meet customer schedule requirements? Does this require the involvement of one or more production and logistics units? Does the distribution of the market suggest concentrated or dispersed operations? If operations are to be dispersed, are there sufficient facilities available to meet the volume and time expectations at the required product specification?

Capabilities are the means by which product specifications may be met by relevant R and D strategies, the management (or coordination) of economies of specialisation, and integration (the economies of scale and scope) to ensure product volume and specification goals are met at target costs. Similar questions are asked. Can the product-service characteristics be met using the capabilities of one unit, or are other (possibly) specialist units required? Do the service support requirements differ such that they provide the basis for segmenting the customer base? These and many more detailed questions will be raised during the decision making concerning value production and delivery options. The process is complete when the positioning, strategy and organisation structure decisions are combined. Figure 2.1 illustrates the overall value identification, creation, production and delivery process, while Figure 2.2 identifies some of the product and service characteristics that comprise the customer value model.

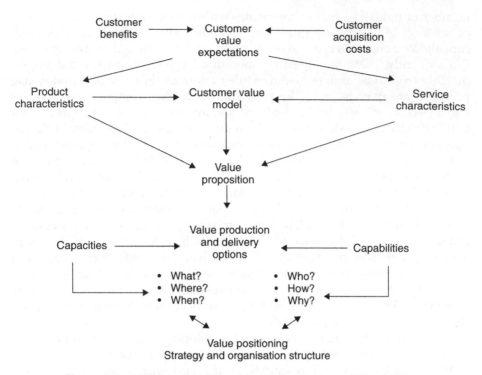

Figure 2.1 Value expectations identify market based alternatives

Product characteristics (tangible):
- Quality
- Choice
- Acquisition costs
- Ease of installation (time and costs)
- Maintenance costs and downtime
- Operating costs
- Disposal costs
- Warranty period and coverage

Product-service characteristics (intangible):
- Advice and support (before, during and after sale)
- Ordering convenience (Net, phone, and so on)
- Availability: convenience (spatial and time)
- Warranty delivery (time, service facilities, replacements)
- Financial services (ownership/transaction options)
- Design/aesthetics (appearance)
- Delivery reliability and frequency
- Product availability and availability consistency
- Response flexibility (order size, ordering process and so on)

Figure 2.2 Components of a customer value model

SUMMARY

The interpretation of 'value' and of 'value-in-use' has become an essential feature of beginning to understand customer motivation and to become a customer-centric or market led organisation.

Carothers *et al* (1989) gave a perceptive view of the paradigm that should be adopted for companies determined to succeed in the 21st century:

> The creation of value as an organising principle and as a measuring rod for efficiency can be utilised by management at every level of the organisation and at every stage of operation . . . Those firms that do not provide value, by inability, inattention, or choice, will be selectively eliminated by the customer at the point of purchase. The implications are clear. The organisation's objective in the 21st century will be to become increasingly valued by the user of their products or services, and this principle holds for producers of both industrial and consumer goods.

REFERENCES ●

Anderson, J. C. and J. A. Narus (1998), 'Business marketing: understanding what customers value', *Harvard Business Review*, November/December.

Band, W. (1991), *Creating Value for Customers: Designing and Implementing a Total Corporate Strategy*, Wiley and Sons, Toronto.

Bowman, C. and V. Ambrosini (2000), 'Value creation versus value capture: towards a coherent definition of value in strategy', *British Journal of Management*, Vol. 11, March.

Carothers, G. H. (Jr), R. D. Sanders and K. E. Kirby (1989), 'Management leadership in the New Economic Age', *Survey of Business*, Summer.

Fuller, J. B., J. O'Conor and R. Rawlinson (1993), 'Tailored logistics: The next advantage', *Harvard Business Review*, May/June.

MacMillan, I. C. and R. G. McGrath (1997), 'Discovering new points of differentiation', *Harvard Business Review*, July/August.

Stalk, G. Jr and A. M. Webber (1993), 'Japan's dark side of time', *Harvard Business Review*, July/August.

Webster, F. E. (1994), *Market Driven Management*, Wiley and Sons, New York.

chapter

3

Value as a Business Concept

LEARNING OUTCOMES

The student will be able to:

- understand the current view of the value concept and its implications for strategy decisions;
- research customer value issues using the value-in-use approach;
- explain the business concept of differentiation and cost management using customer value perception analysis.

INTRODUCTION: REVISITING BASIC CONCEPTS

Before developing a strategic perspective of value it is necessary to revisit one or two of the issues raised earlier. Bowman and Ambrosini (2000) offer a resource based theory approach to determining value and reviewed the literature to answer three questions: what is value, how is it created and who captures it? They distinguished between *use value*, value that is assessed by customers, and *exchange value*, which is the price of the product realised at the time and point of sale. Bowman and Ambrosini contend that labour performances differentiate profit achievements between firms and that value capture is determined by the perceived power relationships between buyers and sellers.

This is an interesting and helpful perspective. The introduction of the notion that *use value* is: '. . . the specific qualities of the product perceived by customers in relation to their needs', identifies the strategic implications of value creation. Thus the styling of products, their safety, performance and reliability are characteristics of use value. The authors suggest that use value is perception based, and introduce the concept of *consumer surplus*, that is the difference between the customer's valuation of the product and the price paid or the price the customer is prepared to pay is:

Price + Consumer surplus

Bowman and Ambrosini quote Bach *et al* (1987) and Whitehead (1996) as using the price plus consumer surplus equation to be the colloquial 'value for money'. Bowman and Ambrosini do not pursue the argument to suggest that use value or value-in-use (the marketing application) may be expanded by persuasion and the use of past experience with this and similar products. The economist argues that the consumer surplus is equivalent to the difference between a *reservation price* (the highest price the consumer is prepared to pay), and the actual market price. Johansson (1991) suggests that consumer surplus '. . . expresses in observable monetary units an observable gain in utility'. The role of marketing therefore is to identify the value-in-use utility gains and present these to the customer, thereby using persuasion to reinforce the perceptions the consumer may already hold.

Exchange value is defined by Bowman and Ambrosini as: '. . . the amount paid by the buyer to the producer for the perceived use value'. Exchange value is realised when a sale is made and this occurs when: 'customers [take the] view that a product confers more consumer surplus than other feasible alternatives'. Thus the authors argue that firms create exchange value and through the sale of products exchange value is realised. It follows that the production process creates use value and subsequently realises exchange value. The amount of exchange value is known only at the time of sale. In other words the authors are suggesting that the organisation '. . . will not know what the newly created use value is worth until it is exchanged'. This presents problems for any organisation and clearly a counter argument is that within acceptable ranges of probability the exchange value realised *will* be that forecast by customer research and through negotiation with resource providers. The basis of Bowman and Ambrosini's argument concerning the creation of the value and then exchange value is that resources such as raw materials are homogenous and '. . . new use value creation derives from the actions of people in the organisation working on and with procured use values'.

Profit is made if the amount of exchange value realised on sale exceeds the sum of the prices of the inputted resources. The authors then argue that profit can only be attributed to the actions of organisational members, as it is their labour *alone* which has the capacity to create new use values, which are the source of the realised exchange value. It is, the authors argue, the inputs of heterogenous and entrepreneurial labour that are ultimately responsible for performance differences between organisations, not material or capital inputs. Hence we might conclude that it is *managerial expertise* in identifying, producing, communicating, delivering and maintaining value that creates competitive advantage by expanding the perception of the customers' consumer surplus.

However this does not satisfactorily explain the organisation's perspective of value. The economist offers us the *producer surplus* to explain profitability. Johansson (*op cit*) uses the welfare economics concept of the excess of revenue over total variable cost (quasi-rent) to identify short term profit. It is agreed that quasi-rent is a 'rent' on fixed factors of production that may not persist over a long period of time, since all factors are variable in the long run. The producer surplus may be increased by reducing costs in the short run or increasing the perceived consumer surplus (through marketing activities), both resulting in increased profitability either by increasing operating margin or by expanding volume and market share. An alternative is to increase the price of the product to identifiable customers who are prepared to accept a higher price for additional benefits. The welfare economists' argument is essentially an aggregate view and does not extend into segmented markets comfortably. Furthermore, if value is to be defined in a strategic context it should be capable of measurement and comparison; these issues are considered subsequently.

Both concepts can be illustrated. Figure 3.1 identifies the consumer surplus which, together with price combines to deliver customer value-in-use. The strategy implications here are for an organisation to develop strong customer links and to work with customers in developing products that are 'customised' to meet customer needs more specifically than those of competitors using communications programs that identify benefits available rather than non-specific claims. Specific life cycle productivity performance and service support packages are also relevant. The vendor organisation should aim to ensure that his target market is satisfied with the use value delivered and

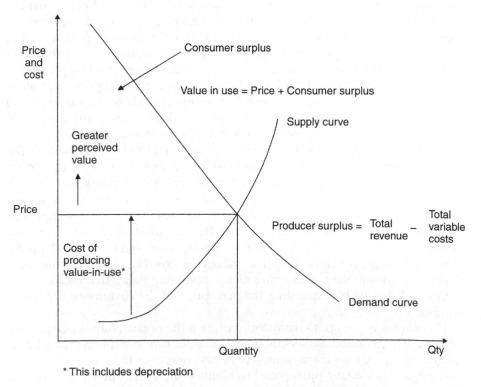

Figure 3.1   Consumer and producer surplus

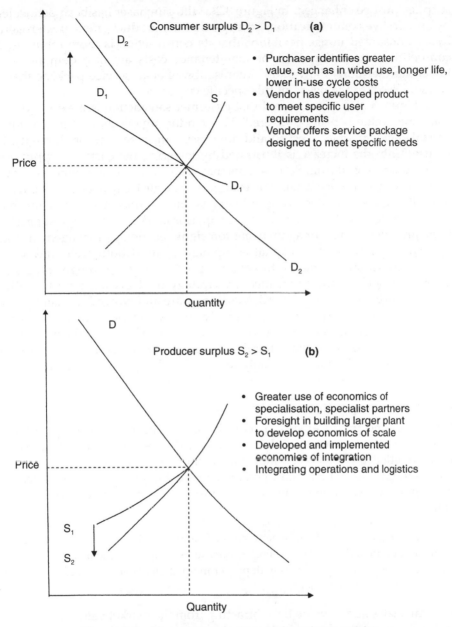

Figure 3.2 Managing consumer and producer surplus

structure the production, logistics and service organisation to meet the price acceptable to the customer and ensure an adequate return to the stakeholders: employees, suppliers, shareholders and distributor organisations. We will expand these topics later in this chapter.

In Figure 3.2, strategy options are identified and optional solutions suggested. To ensure greater customer satisfaction (to opt for D₂) the consumer surplus must be enhanced. In Figure 3.2(a) the purchaser has been persuaded by an effective communications strategy that the product offers greater value by demonstrated in-use flexibility, that its construction is more robust than competitive alternatives and/or maintenance costs are also demonstrably lower. Furthermore, the vendor organisation offers a service package that is 'personalised' to the needs of this specific customer.

In Figure 3.2(b) it is assumed that customer satisfaction is maximised and consumer value is being delivered. The vendor organisation, if it is to meet its stakeholders' objectives, should now focus on increasing productivity. In Figure 3.2(b) the increase is illustrated by lowering the costs of supply (the total variable costs) from S_1 to S_2. This may be achieved in a number of ways, none of which are exclusive. For example, specialist partners may be used; the automotive manufacturing industry is an example. A larger plant may have been designed and built because superior market knowledge suggested large growth potential or again using foresight, technology management configured a combination of capital equipment to meet both scale and scope economies. Another strategy to enhance productivity is through integrated operations such as the coproductivity strategy of IKEA whereby the IKEA supplier, IKEA itself, and the IKEA customer are all involved in manufacturing and logistics activities. Alternatively, packaging design may consider downstream activities within the distribution network such as the innovation shown by Marks & Spencer floral packaging which ensures fresh flowers throughout distribution and is only removed at the 'point of consumption'.

Practical perspectives

Consumer and producer surplus both have complications in an operational, practical context. Economists have accepted the need to demonstrate value in a quantitative, preferably, monetary context. Furthermore, any measures used should ideally be based upon available data. Kay (1993) introduces the concept of added value as 'the key measure of corporate success' and defines it thus:

> Added value is the difference between the (comprehensively accounted) value of a firm's output and the (comprehensively accounted) cost of the firm's inputs. In this specific sense, adding value is both proper motivation of corporate activity and the measure of its achievement.

Kay calculates added value by subtracting from the market value of an organisation's output the cost of its inputs:

Revenues
less (wages and salaries, materials, capital costs)
equals
Added value

He suggests that added value is a measure of the loss which would result to national income and to the international economy if the organisation ceased to exist: 'Adding value, in this sense, is the central purpose of business activity. A commercial organisation which adds no value – whose output is worth no more than the value of its inputs in alternative uses – has no long-term rationale for its existence.'

Added value in this context includes depreciation of capital assets and also provides for a 'reasonable' return on invested capital. Calculated this way, added value is *less than* operating profit, the difference between the value of the output and the value of materials and labour inputs and capital costs. It also differs from the net output of the firm: the difference between the value of its sales and material costs (not labour or capital costs). Kay's measure of competitive advantage is the ratio of added value to the organisation's gross or net output:

$$Competitive\ advantage = \frac{Revenues - (Wages + Salaries + Materials + Capital\ costs)}{Wages + Salaries + Materials + Capital\ costs}$$

These are viewed as comparisons of added value to either gross or net output. Kay's added value has similarity with the concept of a producer's surplus and has the additional benefit of being able to be calculated from accounting data. However, it should be said that inaccuracies are very likely if direct comparisons between organisations are made on a one-off basis. Local accounting practices differ and accounting statements therefore are not strictly comparable due to differing procedures and practices. But longitudinal comparisons are worthwhile, particularly over periods of three to five years when input/output and added value/output ratios may be compared.

Kay's model may be illustrated and Figure 3.3 depicts two possible outcomes, one (Figure 3.3(a)) showing a successful organisation making a positive added value (in Kay's terms, it must be remembered that added value > operating profit because it includes a return on capital therefore it *may not* be profitable). In Figure 3.3(b) the organisation represented has difficulties; wages and salaries and capital costs are greater than revenues. Figure 3.4 suggests the added value structure of a value chain. At the raw materials (primary production) stage materials costs are a low proportion of total input costs, but as value is added by successive processes materials costs become significantly more important, as do the capital costs of inventory financing.

Kay gives us a very useful approach to identifying the quantitative and qualitative characteristics of the production, logistics and service aspects of value production and will be discussed in further detail in Chapter 8. However, a more structured approach is required to measure consumer surplus in both quantitative and qualitative terms. Kim and Mauborgne (1997) offer help here. The authors are offering a value based perspective for planning strategic growth. The process involves identifying customer expectations *and* perceptions, that is the consumer surplus. They contend:

> Companies that follow the logic of value innovation free up their resources to identify and deliver completely new sources of value. Ironically, value innovators do not set out to build advantages over the competition, but they end up achieving the greatest competitive advantages.

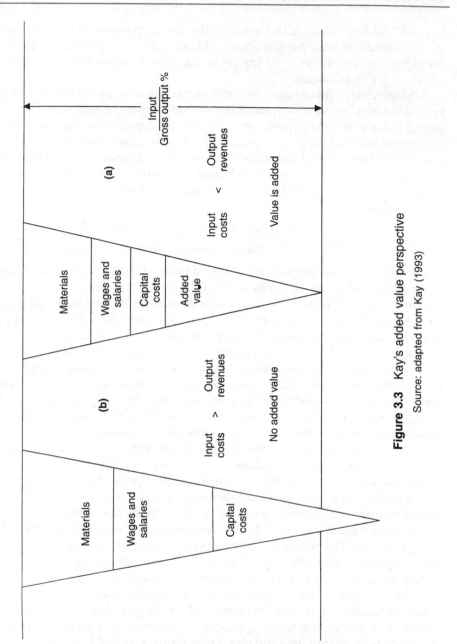

Figure 3.3 Kay's added value perspective

Source: adapted from Kay (1993)

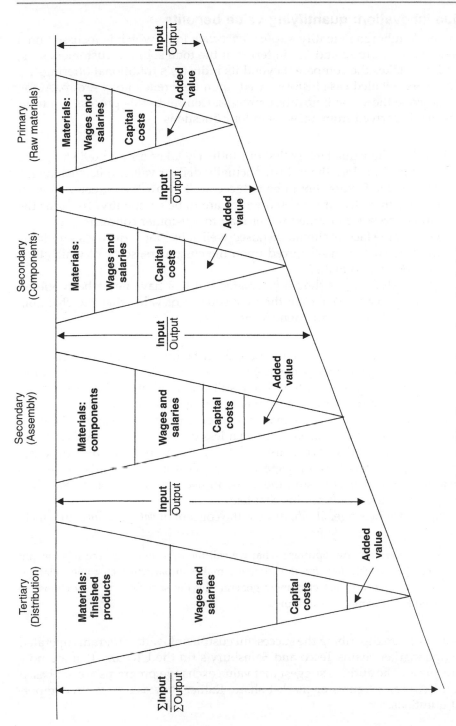

Figure 3.4 Stages in the value added chain

Source: adapted from Kay (1993)

Value innovation: quantifying value benefits

Kim and Mauborgne identify a *value innovation* logic which is focussed on a target customer group and '... in terms of the total solution customers seek, even if that takes the company beyond its industry's traditional offerings'.

In a very detailed case history based upon the French hotel group, Accor, they describe the value innovation process. Central to this process is a *value curve* that is derived from answers to four questions:

- Which of the value factors that our industry takes for granted should be eliminated, or does the industry actually deliver value to its customers?
- Which value factors should be reduced well below the industry's standard? Are there features offered which are to be competitive as far as the competitors are concerned rather than for customer concern?
- Which value factors should be raised well above the industry's standard? Are there compromises forced upon the customers, some of which they may not wish to make?
- Which value factors should be created but that have never been offered by the industry? What are the new sources of value that the changing customer dynamics are identifying?

In their case study Kim and Mauborgne describe the research undertaken by Accor to identify customer perceptions of the relative importance of features, or elements of service, of a hotel. The result is a 'plot' of the features ranked by the target customers to identify what they need most and what they can do without. Thus the result is that at a specific price the customer is given much more of what they need and much less of what they are willing to do without. It follows that Accor are qualifying the features of the consumer surplus and ensuring that for a specific target customer group the price plus consumer value is maximising the value-in-use for the customer. We shall return to this model later in this chapter.

Grant and Schlesinger (1995) discuss the concept of *value exchange* in which:

> ... companies can now optimise what we call the *value exchange*: the relationship between the *financial investment* a company makes in particular customer relationships and the *return* that customers generate by the specific way they choose to respond to the company's offering.

The authors are describing the successful customer loyalty programs operated by supermarket chains Tesco and Sainsbury's (in the UK) and that are now widespread. The authors suggest that value exchange programs are not based upon last year's figures or market share. Rather they ask three very important questions:

- What percentage of target customers is currently sold to? What percentage could this be?

- What is the 'current customer' purchasing pattern? What would be the impact on revenues if their average expenditures were across the entire range or increased by a specific percentage?
- What is the average life span of an 'average' customer? What would be the financial implications for the company if the life span could be extended?

These three 'drivers' clearly have an impact on profitability. The company should focus on the products and services that will increase each driver. Grant and Schlesinger's proposition, the *value exchange model*, offers a means by which the consumer value-in-use may be expanded, customer satisfaction increased and with it customer loyalty. Similarly, given that the customer expectations are known, it follows that the 'costs of production, logistics and service' may be identified. Given potential volumes the value exchange opportunity may be calculated. The authors make the valid observation that: '. . . customers no longer pay [for] or receive benefits they don't value . . .'.

To be effective the organisation needs to combine knowledge management (its use of its specific knowledge of customers, suppliers, employees, and so on), technology management (developing database systems and production and logistics systems to ensure the economies of integration are optimised), and relationship management (specific supplier relationships, customer loyalty relationships and employee expectations) to produce a relevant business system.

This typically implies the rethinking of *positioning strategy*, investment management, operational processes and organisational alignment. Clearly the company needs to know who its customers are, how they buy, how they perceive the company and what expectations they have of this and similar offers. Hence a positioning gap is identified and the tasks and activities necessary to fill it and to reposition the company within its target market can be evaluated. Figure 3.5 uses the consumer surplus and producer surplus concepts to illustrate this proposition. Given more accurate and detailed knowledge of the consumer the value production and delivery processes can be made more cost effective. *Investment management processes* follow once the broad positioning strategy and core exchange value attributes have been identified. At this juncture it becomes necessary to identify processes and costs associated with the broad positioning and core exchange value attributes. Increasingly it is becoming the practice to extend this process beyond the internal capabilities and capacities of the organisation, and to utilise the 'core capabilities and capacities' of other organisations. Such practices may thus expand the customer value-in-use and decrease costs of production, logistics and service and thereby increase the producer surplus. This activity leads towards firming up the *operational processes*. So far we have outlined a strategy based on the specifics of *what, how, who, where and when*, from which the operational processes are formulated. This stage identifies how the individual processes are engineered to make the value delivery effective. *Organisational alignment* considers the problems of changing the attitudes and behaviour patterns of

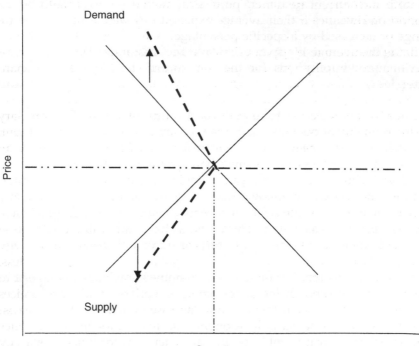

Figure 3.5 Enhancing realised margins by rethinking the positioning strategy

the organisation and staff. Not only may the organisation need to consider the attitudes and behaviour of its own staff, but also those of external organisations that have become part of the value exchange process. Sears found employee consultation and motivation an essential component of their strategy to return to being a successful and profitable organisation, and the Italian textile industry pursued a similar policy when faced with intense competition which required a conglomerate approach to manufacturing using the specialist skills across the industry.

VALUE STRATEGY DECISIONS: STRATEGIC EFFECTIVENESS AND OPERATIONAL EFFICIENCY

Profitability, productivity and value based strategy decisions

Skinner (1986), and Porter (1996) some ten years later, address the productivity/profitability dilemma. Skinner's comments were concerned with the problem that: 'The very way managers define productivity improvement and the tools they use to achieve it push their goal further out of reach'. Skinner argues that the pursuit of productivity to restore competitive positioning does more harm than it gives help. He focusses on the fact that simply applying efforts to reducing labour costs will not necessarily give the results required because typically labour costs account for a small proportion of total costs;

furthermore such efforts are damaging to staff morale and eventually result in alienation. Skinner also argues that innovation suffers: the preoccupation with cost performance shifts management focus towards cost reductions rather than product and/or process innovation. More importantly an exclusive focus on productivity ignores other ways to compete, ways that use manufacturing as a strategic resource. Quality, reliability, flexibility, short lead times, attention to service detail, rapid time-to-market and effective implementation of economies of specialisation and integration are the primary sources of competitive response in a dynamically competitive environment. And finally, Skinner contends that the productivity emphasis: '. . . fails to provide or support a coherent manufacturing strategy'.

A manufacturing strategy is becoming essential if an effective value strategy is to be developed and implemented. Skinner's perspective is probably dated inasmuch as it does not give sufficient emphasis to the potential competitive response available from strategic partnering. It also predates the view that 'production', logistics and service integrate into an operations strategy and structure which is required in an era of global activities. Nevertheless, Skinner's manufacturing strategy components of what to make and what to buy, capacity levels to be provided, the number and location of plants, choices of equipment and process technology production and inventory systems, cost management systems, information systems, workforce management policies and organisational structure are all relevant when considering value strategy and its management.

Porter (1996) continues this argument:

> . . . the quest for productivity, quality and speed has spawned a remarkable number of management tools and techniques and bit by bit, almost imperceptibly (these) management tools have taken the place of strategy. As managers push to improve on all fronts, they move farther away from viable competitive positions.

And follows this with:

> A company can outperform rivals only if it can establish a difference that it can preserve. It must deliver greater value to customers or create comparable value at lower cost or do both. The arithmetic of superior profitability then follows: delivering greater value allows a company to charge higher average unit prices; greater efficiency results in lower average unit costs.

Or, by delivering greater identifiable value-in-use to the customer, the exchange value realised (the price) will be such that both producer surplus and therefore added value will be greater.

Porter follows Skinner's argument by suggesting that operational effectiveness (that is, the quest for productivity) is insufficient for long-term success:

> . . . (competitive strategy) . . . is about being different . . . the essence of strategy is in the activities – choosing to perform activities differently or to perform different activities to rivals.

It follows that a value based strategy is one which identifies customer expectations and addresses them with innovative responses, thereby creating a strong customer/supplier relationship. It also requires a similar approach to supplier relationships. An innovative response is also one that will require creative approaches to process technology; in other words, the overall management of technology. Neither of these can be successful without a strong knowledge management base.

Effective value strategy expands corporate competitiveness

Furthermore, an effective value strategy approach takes an organisation beyond its own boundaries. It involves identifying the core competencies necessary to compete and to produce and deliver customer value expectations and to *coordinate* the value production process. Examples of value creativity through value production and coordination are expanding rapidly. The well known examples, such as Dell and Nike, have established models that are being implemented by a number of industries through a value chain approach. Recognition of the fact that not all of the necessary capabilities and/or capacities are internally available leads the progressive business towards identifying where in the value chain its resources are most effectively applied. Examples were given in Chapter 1 of how companies identify opportunities and structure value production and coordination to meet customer value expectations.

Porter's *productivity frontier* (the sum of all practices at any given time that enable an organisation to meet specific value/cost requirements) is a useful approach if we wish to identify specific value based opportunities and to make effective responses. Porter's productivity frontier is shown as Figure 3.6 and its usefulness can be extended by identifying value segments (that is, combinations of non-price/price value combinations). Figure 3.7 offers a range of 'value positions' and emphasises an earlier comment concerning the need to be precise concerning customer segments and the specific value response that eventuates. In some respects this is supported by Mathur and Kenyon (1998) whose research suggests evidence of over-differentiation and differentiation directed towards competitive response rather than as a specific customer response.

Other authors such as Grant and Schlesinger have identified the need for the organisation to review and if necessary modify its processes (and structures) to meet a changing marketplace. Figure 3.8 identifies some of the reasons for doing so. It acknowledges that customer expectations differ (and also that competitors may be active within specific value based segments of interest to the company). As a result both marketing and operations structures will differ depending upon which segment is targeted. This identifies the necessity to consider addressing opportunities from a partnership base, because some of the organisational requirements do not exist within the organisation. Furthermore, as markets become integrated, the view of Slywotzky and Morrison (1997) is that value activities are sequential and many structural elements have significance throughout the value chain

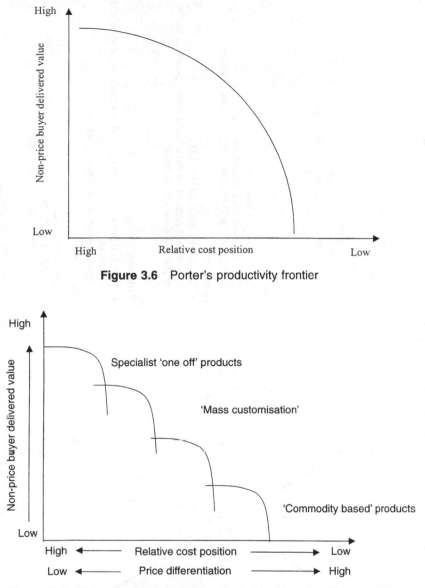

Figure 3.6 Porter's productivity frontier

Figure 3.7 Using the productivity frontier to identify value strategy options

process. Consequently organisation structure issues should be considered from both upstream and downstream perspectives.

A CONCEPTUAL APPROACH TO A VALUE STRATEGY MODEL

Value has two perspectives; value-in-use (the consumers' view of value) and exchange value (the value producers' perspective). They are not exclusive

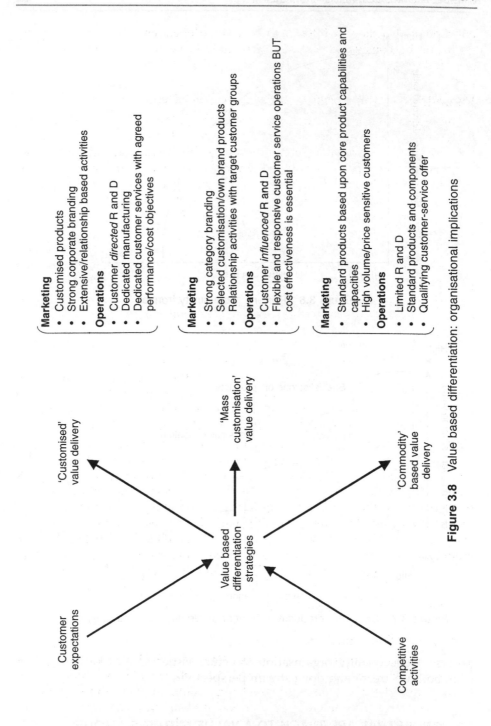

Marketing
- Customised products
- Strong corporate branding
- Extensive/relationship based activities

Operations
- Customer *directed* R and D
- Dedicated manufacturing
- Dedicated customer services with agreed performance/cost objectives

Marketing
- Strong category branding
- Selected customisation/own brand products
- Relationship activities with target customer groups

Operations
- Customer *influenced* R and D
- Flexible and responsive customer service operations BUT cost effectiveness is essential

Marketing
- Standard products based upon core product capabilities and capacities
- High volume/price sensitive customers

Operations
- Limited R and D
- Standard products and components
- Qualifying customer-service offer

'Customised' value delivery

'Mass customisation' value delivery

'Commodity' based value delivery

Customer expectations

Value based differentiation strategies

Competitive activities

Figure 3.8 Value based differentiation: organisational implications

concepts, rather they are interrelated and interdependent. Value-in-use cannot occur, or be considered as an option, unless the resources and processes required to produce the value are made available.

Value-in-use: the consumer perspective of value

Value-in-use (or use value) is the perceived value that is available to the customer/consumer when considering a purchase. At this point in time the use value is a subjective assessment of the benefits available (the consumer surplus) and the price negotiated with the vendor of the price/service. Exchange value is the price actually paid to the vendor for the perceived use value created and is realised when a sale takes place. The vendor has previously undertaken an analysis of value-in-use when evaluating the available market and the responses that the organisation can make.

Value strategy decisions are based upon an understanding of the decision processes involved. Value-in-use decisions are a considered view based upon perceptions of what benefits are available, how they will influence the recipient, when they are available, whom they are available from, why the benefits differ from alternatives. Exchange value decisions (the production of use value) require the cost effective choice and application of resources.

The models discussed earlier, while having similarities, also have comparative strengths and weaknesses. They are featured in Figure 3.9. The economists' model identifies both consumer and producer interests in value production and consumption. If we assume value-in-use *and* price to be the consumer choice criteria, we approach a commercially acceptable definition of value-in-use. Similarly with an assumption that total variable costs include depreciation, the producers' surplus approximates for a measure of profit.

Kay's model is much more about measuring corporate performance and it will be recalled that Kay's measure of competitive advantage is the ratio of added value to gross or net output. There is an implicit assumption here that the response to the consumer is appropriate and accepted by the customer. Indeed it suggests that the competitor with the highest 'competitive advantage' has made the response more successfully than have competitors. Kay's model has the advantages of using accounting data to calculate 'added value' *and* also offers an opportunity to consider value chain options (see Figure 3.4). However, the lack of a detailed customer value-in-use consideration leaves the model lacking in the detail required for value strategy decisions.

'Manufacturing' value-in-use

The *value exchange* approach suggested by Grant and Schlesinger (*op cit*) offers an opportunity to develop a model in which both customer's 'value-in-use' interests and the development of 'exchange value' may be considered and, where necessary, explored for trade-off potential among customers, suppliers and (if appropriate) a distributor network. The value exchange model identifies use value (or value-in-use) components as product value delivered, product support services value, the product transaction/ownership process and price. Exchange value components are positioning, investment management, operational processes and organisational alignment.

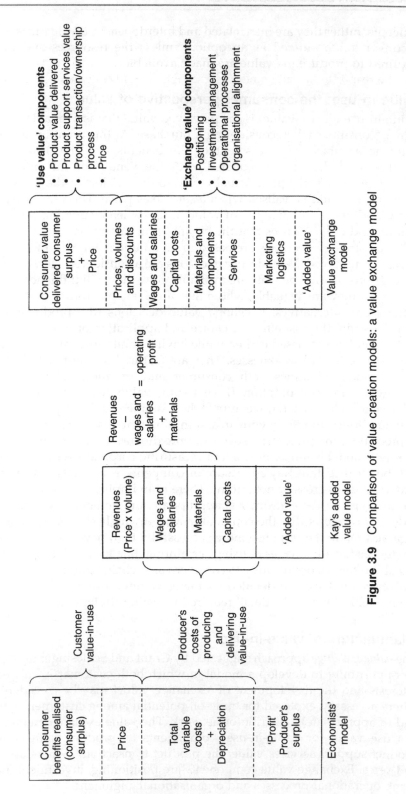

Figure 3.9 Comparison of value creation models: a value exchange model

In Figure 3.10 these components are expanded and value strategy responses are added. Each of these will be dealt with in detail in subsequent chapters; at this juncture it is important to identify the basic components and the basis of the response. It will be noticed that Figure 3.10 suggests that a trade-off of one or more components may occur. This is possible in the structure of new business-to-business, business-to-consumer organisational relationships: the 'prosumer' concept (customer involvement in design and production) and that of 'coproductivity' whereby production and distribution processes can be carried out downstream (by customers rather than suppliers) in exchange for price or other benefit considerations. IKEA, the furniture/homewares/home improvement company, is an example of how this concept can be made to work successfully. Essentially the value strategy response comprises: identifying value expectations (within the target customer group), identifying the competencies and resources required, the alternative delivery processes, structures and capital considerations; creating the value; delivering the value, and servicing the value. The primary considerations are identified in Figure 3.11 and will be explored in later chapters.

However, before options and costings can be considered, a structure or framework within which to organise an approach to value strategy and management is necessary and this is also featured as Figure 3.11. There are two primary activities: *value positioning and competitive advantage strategy* and *value production and coordination*.

Value positioning and competitive advantage: strategy facilitators

A value positioning and competitive advantage strategy is a management activity, which ensures that strategic effectiveness and *sustainable competitive advantage* are both achieved. By applying knowledge management, technology management and relationship management to identify (and explore) opportunities, structures, production and delivery options and partnership management possibilities, an effective value positioning and strategy will be derived. Each of these critically important management areas will be the subject of individual chapters, but here a brief introduction to each is essential.

Knowledge management has been variously defined but the following is a synthesis of the many definitions located:

> The organisational capability which identifies, locates (creates or acquires), transfers, converts and distributes knowledge into competitive advantage

For example, knowledge management influences strategy through R and D investment, and the application of experience based knowledge to become a learning organisation.

Knowledge management has a number of facets. The commercial context emphasises market, customer and competitor 'knowledge'. Our interest is concerned with managing knowledge as a resource. We are looking at knowledge in the same context as we do financial, human and other resources. We question how we use the knowledge base within an organisation to make

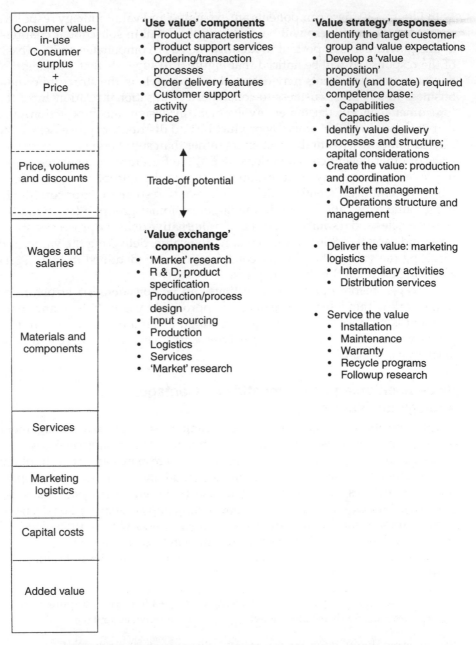

Figure 3.10   A conceptual approach to a value exchange model

more effective decisions and what additional knowledge (qualitative and quantitative) is required to increase competitive advantage. In other words the focus is on developing a *knowledge strategy*.

Relationship management also shares similar longevity. A working definition is proposed:

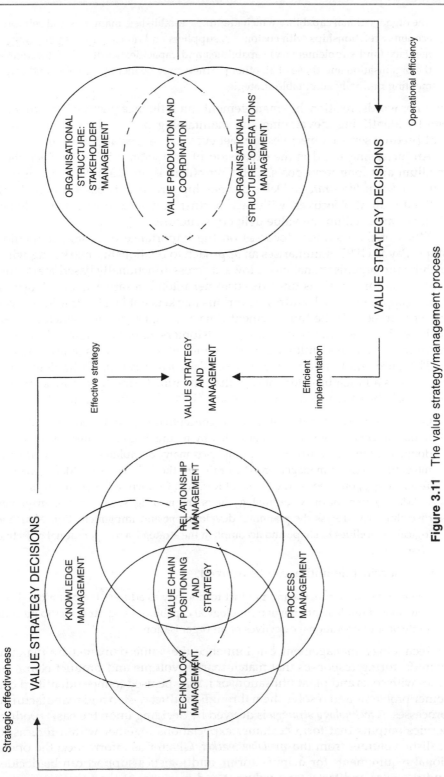

Figure 3.11 The value strategy/management process

The organisational capability which identifies, establishes, maintains and reinforces economic relationships with customers, suppliers and other partners with complementary (and supplementary) capabilities and capacities so that the objectives of the organisation and those of all other partners may be met by agreeing and implementing mutually acceptable strategies

In other words, relationship management can influence positioning and strategy by identifying, developing and maintaining partnerships which ensure that product service objectives to meet customer expectations are met.

An increasing trend is the expansion of partnership bases to meet short, medium and long term goals. Dell Computers is an example of a company with a *relationship strategy*; Dell's partnership structure is based upon clearly defined mutual objectives, with each partner very clear about their role and their rewards within the value delivery structure.

Much of the literature focusses on the importance of customer relationships. Payne (1995) summarises an approach to relationship marketing which includes an organisational move towards cross-functionally based marketing, with a shift of emphasis towards customer retention rather than acquisition, and an approach which addresses various markets not just the traditional customer market. It is the third element ('market' management) which interests us here. Payne identifies six markets: customers, suppliers, referral markets, recruitment markets, influence markets and internal markets (employees).

The third 'underlying force' is *technology management*. Technology management is a much broader concept than manufacturing/operations strategy but clearly has a close connection. Noori (1990) identifies a difficulty:

> Our prime reason for the difficulty in conceptualising and comprehending the notion of technology management is that by nature, it is cross-functional and predominantly problem driven. It encompasses many disciplines and is based on an integrative style of management. According to the Task Force on Management of Technology sponsored by the National Research Council (a US organisation):
>
> "Management of (new) technology links engineering, science and management disciplines to address the planning, development and implementation of technological capabilities to shape and accomplish the strategic and operational objectives of an organisation."

A more succinct definition can be derived:

> The integration of process and product technology to address the planning, development and implementation of technological capabilities and capacities to meet the strategic and operational objectives of an organisation

Technology management can influence the value delivered by planning manufacturing responses that match market volume and product characteristics with costs and plant utilisation; or it may be used to meet identified customer problems and resolve them through product design and manufacturing processes. A *technology strategy* is derived by deciding upon the basic product-service outputs that form customer expectations together with a forecast of realistic volumes from the *available market*. Given this information the operational requirements for manufacturing and logistics support can be decided and the roles and tasks (and volumes and margins) of the value production and delivery system members agreed. Noori's comments concerning cross-functional issues are significant here and become more so when cross-organisational factors and considerations are dealt with. A technology strategy has a number of components. It identifies the scope and characteristics of the combined 'technology package', that is, of all the partners, the inter-relationships that may exist between manufacturing and information technology, innovation trends in process and product technology, the direction(s) of technology transfer, the interface between R and D and strategic management, and consideration of the economics of integration.

Turning to *process management*, a feature shared by a large number of organisations is the way they consider each business process as a discreet function. Departments operate in isolation, unaware of the impact of their performance on that of others. Performance measurements used vary and often result in conflicting goals. Within the supply chain, trading partners can (and do) operate in strategic and operational isolation. Effort is duplicated and systems cannot interact: the outcome is competition not cooperation.

To be effective, organisations need to work together to identify core processes across the demand and supply chains. They must then explore the implications of locating these core processes within specialist, partnership organisations.

Generic core processes of the value chain include design and development, 'production', 'procurement', 'marketing' and 'service'. Logistics is the support process that provides the infrastructure vital to manage the 'stocks and flows' of products, materials and components and information throughout the value chain. Each core process in the demand chain comprises numerous sub-processes, the importance of which varies across industries. Often similar sectors of industry differ in their sub-process infrastructure. Where they do not differ is in the integration of core and sub-processes with the shared goal of maximising strategic effectiveness and operating efficiencies.

Value production and coordination: managing value creation and delivery

The activity of value production and coordination has two component activities. *Stakeholder management* extends the approach of Payne (*op cit*) and identifies markets and the market management methods necessary to implement the value strategy. 'Market' management considers not only customers but takes a broader stakeholder perspective (discussed earlier) and seeks to optimise satisfaction within the range of important stakeholder markets. For example, the response of Italian textile manufacturers to increasingly discerning customers was to specialise, and hence customer satisfaction was used to segment the production response by the industry from a range of specialist suppliers. The 'return' requirement of the investment market is another market management consideration. A response to customer value expectations that cannot be sustained unless shareholder returns are reduced is a position that is itself not sustainable.

Operations management comprises a number of activities. 'Production' often includes sourcing and procurement, the selection of manufacturing techniques and processes, capacity requirements planning and management, and the management of system flexibility. 'Logistics' considers order management (techniques and processes), customer communications, delivery management and investment options. The involvement of intermediaries becomes an important issue in this context. 'Service' includes the increasing range of activities undertaken throughout the transaction processes. These include working with customers to develop customised product specifications prior to a sale; organising financial facilities during a sale, and the installation and regular maintenance of equipment after the sale has been made. *Operational efficiency* is essential if competitive advantage characteristics are to be made sustainable and financially viable.

SUMMARY

This chapter has reviewed the conceptual arguments that may be incorporated in developing a value exchange model. The purpose has been to combine the views of the economists with those of more recent contributors. The model developed will be revisited later, when an operational value chain planning model will be developed.

REFERENCES ●

Bach, C., R. Flanagan, J. Howels, F. Levy and A. Lima (1987), *Microeconomics*, 11th edition, Prentice-Hall, Englewood Cliffs.

Bowman, C. and V. Ambrosini (2000), 'Value creation versus value capture: towards a coherent definition of value in strategy', *British Journal of Management*, Vol. 11.

Grant, A. W. H. and L. A. Schlesinger (1995), 'Realise your customers' full potential', *Harvard Business Review*, September/October.

Johansson, P. O. (1991), *An Introduction to Modern Welfare Economics*, Cambridge University Press, Cambridge.

Kay, J. (1993), *Foundation of Corporate Success*, Oxford University Press, Oxford.

Kim, W. Chan and R. Mauborgne (1997), 'Value innovation: the strategic logic of high growth', *Harvard Business Review*, January/February.

Mathur, S. S. and A. Kenyon (1988), *Creating Value: Shaping Tomorrow's Business*, Butterworth-Heinemann, Oxford.

Noori, H. (1990), *Managing the Dynamics of New Technology: Issues in Manufacturing Management*, Prentice-Hall, Englewood Cliffs.

Payne, A. (ed.) (1995), *Advances in Relationship Marketing*, Kogan Page, London.

Porter, M. (1996), 'What is strategy?', *Harvard Business Review*, November/December.

Skinner, W. (1986), 'The productivity paradox', *Harvard Business Review*, July/August.

Slywotzky, A. J. and D. J. Morrison (1997), *The Profit Zone*, Wiley, New York.

Whitehead, G. (1996), *Economics*, 15th edition, Butterworth-Heinemann, Oxford.

chapter 4

Value Based Organisations: the Growth of Flexible Response and Virtual Organisations

LEARNING OUTCOMES

The student will be able to:

- understand the changes in the business environment and be able to assess their implications for a range of industries and businesses;
- understand the concept and structure of the virtual organisation;
- show awareness of the implications of the business environment on this form of organisation structure.

INTRODUCTION

In the early chapters the role of the expectations of customers and their impact on strategy decisions were discussed in depth. The view that 'market turbulence' has resulted in fundamental changes in consumer and business markets was supported by Glazer (1991), Pine (1993), Ashkenas *et al* (1995) and Day (1999). We saw there that change was occurring due to fundamental influences: instability, low predictability, uncertainty, increased demand for quality, 'fashion' and service, were the underlying characteristics of changes in demand.

In addition there were also changes in structural factors to understand. These were identified as a shift in power towards the buyer, highly competitive saturated markets, shortening product life cycles with little predictability, high rates of technological change, smaller and less predictable customer orders in terms of order volumes and ordering frequency, and an expanding number of distribution channel alternatives.

Such changes led Ashkenas and colleagues (*op cit*) to compare the critical factors that have influenced organisational success in the recent past with those currently required and likely to be required in the future. To recapitulate, these were:

Old success factors	*New success factors*
● Size	● Speed
● Role clarity	● Flexibility
● Specialisation	● Integration
● Control	● Innovation

If the new structures are to be made effective then a fifth factor is necessary – coordination. Day (*op cit*) identified five transitions that he considers will have or have had disruptive effects. These were seen as:

● more supply, less differentiation;
● more global, less local;
● more competition, more collaboration;
● more relating, less transacting;
● more sense-and-respond, less make and sell.

Ashkenas *et al*'s new success factors, with the addition of coordination, are able to respond effectively to these 'transitions'. Sutton (1998) reviews contemporary thinking in strategy in his concluding chapter. He comments:

> The markets do not reward mediocrity, they reward excellence, and no firm can excel if it uses only the same answers as are available to every other firm. If it is to be excellent, a firm must discover better answers than other firms, or it must discover good answers before the other firms find them.

He proposes eight elements of strategic response focus, flexibility and future development. To these he adds concentration, customers' cooperation, competition and continuity; coordination is an element that should be included. The dynamic environment which greets the 21st century will require business to review its strategic perspectives and operating responses. Not that it is difficult to find alternatives. The difficulty, as identified by Sutton, is finding a response which offers sustainable competitive advantage.

Virtual approaches to competitive organisation structures

Typical of the organisational options available is the virtual organisation. Sutton (*op cit*) suggests the extensive use of outsourcing has led to the development of the *virtual firm*: '... in which coordination and possibly design become the core competency of the firm which contracts out all other opera-tions'. He too refers to the extent to which outsourcing obtains in motor vehicle manufacturing where erstwhile makers have become assemblers and systems integrators. He draws attention to computer manufacturing and airline operations who outsource 'virtually' all of their operations. He identi-fies an important issue: the coordinator, the brand owner, will be seen as the supplier and as such retain moral and legal responsibility for meeting cus-tomer expectations regardless of where, when, how and who manufactures the product or service. Virtual companies retain real responsibilities and must ensure their response and coordination are fully effective.

Malone (1998) has proposed a radical change likely in the way in which businesses organise themselves to deliver value. He recalls the development of Linux (the rudimentary version of the UNIX operating system). Torvalos, the software's developer, made the system available on the Internet and encouraged other programmers to use it, test it and modify it. The author recalls that within three years Linux had turned into one of the best versions of UNIX ever created. He continues by suggesting the anecdote as being an example of the power of a new technology fundamentally to change the way work is conducted. Furthermore he suggests it as a model for a new kind of business organisation, that in turn could develop the basis for a new kind of economy.

He proposes the basic unit of such an economy as the individual not the corporation. Tasks are not assigned and controlled through a stable chain of management but are carried out by independent, electronically connected freelancers: '. . . e-lancers – (who) join together into fluid and temporary net-works to produce and sell goods and services. When the job is done . . . the network dissolves, and its members become independent agents again, circulating through the economy, seeking the next assignment'. The *e-lance economy* is a reality. Virtual companies do exist and are expanding, as evi-denced by outsourcing, teleworking and the encouragement of intrapreneur-ship within large organisations. The author comments: 'All these trends point to the devolution of large, permanent corporations into flexible, temporary networks of individuals'. He traces the development of industrial organisa-tion and reaches conclusions similar to those reached by Pine (*op cit*) and Ashkenas *et al* (*op cit*). Technology, initially through developments in com-munications technology, facilitated the growth of large, centrally controlled, widely dispersed business organisations. Continued development has enabled business to go full circle, back to small businesses, but with a major difference – they can participate within the operations of the large organisa-tions at both an economic and physical distance.

Economic theory, through transaction cost analysis, offers an explanation of the trend towards this structure. An analysis of transaction costs discloses a range of costs of running the 'economic institutions' (in this discussion, the firm), and that they will seek to minimise (within certain constraints) these costs. In essence the works of Coase (1937) and of Williamson (1985) suggest that when it is cost efficient to conduct transactions internally, within the context of a corporate organisation, firms do so and as a result organisations grow larger. But when it is less expensive (more cost efficient) to conduct them externally with specialist independents, organisations remain small or even contract. Clearly there are a number of issues to be considered here, but typically these relate to some form of specificity that may be considered in economic/financial terms. Assessment of transaction costs now involves an intimate knowledge of the economies of specialisation, integration and coordination, these replacing the traditional economies of scale, scope and location.

Malone also uses the Italian textile industry as an example of the shift from the large integrated organisation (which in this instance was failing) into eight separate specialist businesses. The role of the electronic market for the Prato group serves as a clearing house for information about projected factory utilisation and forecast requirements, thus permitting capacity to be traded as a commodity. It is interesting to note that many larger industries (in terms of revenues and capital investment) have only recently arrived at such 'exchanges'. The author also discusses his findings from a 'futures study' of the automobile manufacturing industry. The study conducted in 1997, aimed at identifying the different ways business might be organised in the 21st century, was greeted by comments suggesting that (at that time) the industry was in some ways already moving towards such a model. As we have seen this has occurred. The author concludes from his study that:

> A shift to an e-lance economy would bring about fundamental changes in virtually every business function, not just in product design. Supply chains would become ad hoc structures, assembled to fit the needs of a particular project and disassembled when the project ended. Manufacturing capacity would be bought and sold in an open market, and independent, specialised manufacturing concerns would undertake small batch orders for a variety of brokers, design shops and even consumers. Marketing would be performed in some cases by brokers, in other cases by small companies that would own brands and certify the quality of the merchandise sold under them. In still other cases, the ability of consumers to share product information on the Internet would render marketing obsolete.

and:

> ... in an e-lance economy the role of the traditional business manager changes dramatically and sometimes disappears completely. The work of the temporary company is coordinated by the individuals who compose it with little or no centralised direction or control.

and:

> One of the primary roles for the large companies that remain in the future may be to establish rules, standards, and cultures for network organisations operating partly within and partly outside their own boundaries.

A conclusion that may be drawn from this is that we are beginning to see a significantly different approach to business organisation. There is evidence to suggest that a number of firms are reappraising the ways in which market opportunities are evaluated and undertaken. It would appear that many are achieving success by dissecting the processes involved in creating customer satisfaction and questioning where these may be undertaken such that the value that is added is maximised. Companies such as Dell and Nike (and perhaps in the not too distant future Ford) are working with a minimum of capital investment in assets they consider to be better managed by specialist manufacturing and service companies. This also raises a question concerning the aspect of value that companies such as Dell and Nike seek to address. For example, Nike is targeting a lifestyle led market, clearly influenced by fashion and as such has structured its organisation around design and brand management and marketing. Dell has identified a market segment that 'values' specification, response and convenience. Both companies have moved away from the traditional business model of vertically owned assets towards the 'virtual organisation' in which their investment is in their core competencies, assets and processes.

It can be argued that while a different approach to business organisation is apparent, it has its roots within industrial development. Pine's description of the moves towards mass customisation contains the basis for this assertion.

WHERE WE CAME FROM

Pine (1993) suggests that Britain was, during the period of the Industrial Revolution (the 19th century), the world's leading manufacturer and predominant exporter of goods. And that:

> Much of its success was based on its basic research, its ability to invent, and its unparalleled technological leadership.

Britain's position was eventually challenged by the US, a process described as the *American System of Manufactures*. Among the many factors identified the following were prominent:

- core production techniques used to develop a knowledge base for expanding into a capital based production system;
- a systematic process that depended upon the combination of highly skilled workers, automated machinery, and a new way of moving materials and goods through the factory;
- large, continuing gains in productivity and quality, due to workforce participation;
- high levels of both skill and education in the workforce;
- continual, incremental technological innovations;
- a high level of cooperation among national competitors, which helped the rapid diffusion of process innovation;

- a high degree of reliance on subcontractors for innovations and production skills;
- a strong education system;
- a unique and relatively homogenous culture;
- limitation rather than invention.

Pine observes that Britain never quite caught on to this new way of manufacturing, and eventually lost its dominance over world production and trade and that:

> The America of the nineteenth century became the world's premier manufacturer thanks to its highly skilled and educated workers, quality goods, low costs, rapid innovations and technological leadership.

SOME CONSTRUCTS

Viewed some 200 years later it could be argued that the success of the Industrial Revolution in Britain, and the subsequent successful challenge from the USA, were based upon an implicit understanding of knowledge, technology and relationship management and how they could be interrelated to create additional value for the stakeholder. What we might consider to be topics exclusive to the 1990s appear to have been management tools for some considerable time. Of particular interest are the ways in which they can be linked through their interdependencies. It can be argued that this is what the Industrial Revolution, and all that has occurred subsequently, is about.

Pine has identified some interesting and related issues. Mass production has a goal shared by both business and consumers and raises an interesting interface between technology management and relationship management. Consumers accepted standard products, which facilitated market expansion and reduction of prices through economies of scale. The restricted capabilities of manufacturers to produce differentiated products at similar prices to those of mass produced goods further encouraged the emphasis on demand from homogeneous markets. This relationship interface became institutionalised in a stable market environment. Pine points towards an inherent logic. He argues that profit is essential if companies are to remain in business. Profitability is a function of volume and margin; margins are increased if costs are kept as low as possible. Homogeneous markets are volume markets, hence an increase in volume decreases cost still further and, typically, as they are elastic, price reductions can (at least for some time) increase volume and revenues. Further cost reductions can result in price levels at which niche market customers will succumb. Those niche markets that remain are left to fringe manufacturers. The homogeneous product manufacturers apply technology (automated processes) which increase fixed costs but lower unit costs; pricing is used to expand volume still further. Product life cycles are long, and maintained that way, so as to ensure that costs can be amortised over the large volumes produced and sold. Internally the organisation operates a tightly controlled production system that uses incentives to achieve volume targets. Externally distributors accept (prefer) few product changes and customer satisfaction is realised through a combination of acceptable levels of quality and service at low prices.

Mass customisation: segmentation based on selected aggregate value characteristics

Mass customisation was a response to changing customer circumstances and expectations. Consumer disposable incomes increased, thereby increasing their spectrum of choice; these included variety and an immediacy in demand satisfaction. Through the application of 'new technology' (computer based design and manufacturing) together with new approaches to management, industry created an alternative paradigm. Here the objective is to 'deliver' affordable products and services with sufficient variety and customisation such that '. . . nearly everyone finds exactly what they want'. This differs markedly from the proposition offered by mass production, in which '. . . nearly every one can afford them'. Pine offers a logic for mass customisation. Unstable demand for specific products results in market fragmentation; product variety becomes an essential feature of customer satisfaction. Homogeneous markets become heterogeneous. Niches become important. Manufacturers undertake specific niches with a view to meeting specified and feasible customer requirements, typically through post-production methods. This is not profitable and production systems change. Initially the requirements were for shorter production runs accompanied by expensive loss of production time and 'set-ups'. However, niche customers accept premium prices that compensate manufacturers. Experience eventually enables production costs to be reduced and product variety is achieved at the same, or even lower, costs. Varying consumer demand requires a rapid time-to-market response with shorter product development cycles, which in turn result in shorter product life cycles. Demand fragments but individual producers find stability in their operations with selected niche segments.

Identifying important management interfaces

Figure 4.1 identifies further development of the management interfaces that contribute to the success of mass customisation. By inference there is stronger integration and coordination. Knowledge/relationship management has been influenced by the integration of thinking and doing, resulting in stronger external and internal alliances and thereby developing the notion of *coproductivity* (whereby suppliers and customers agree to share the production and logistics tasks for some benefit, such as price). The IKEA philosophy is an example of a series of external alliances established to achieve an increase in stakeholder value. Agreements between company, management and employees whereby 'multi-skilling' is adopted into work practices are internal

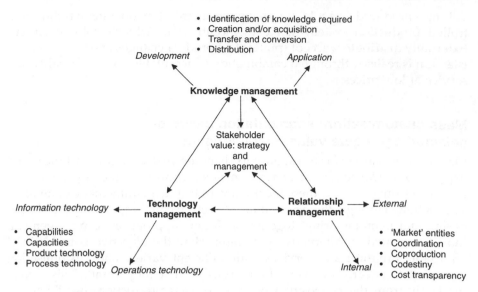

Figure 4.1 The components of stakeholder value production

alliances. These can be seen in the 'discount' airline operators such as 'easyjet', 'go' and 'Buzz'. Coproductivity can only be developed if *codestiny* is strong. Codestiny is a shared perspective of (and of the means for achieving) growth. It follows an agreed strategy and agreed implementation roles and should be reinforced if the codestiny is to be sustained.

Knowledge/technology management is influenced by the application of knowledge (typically manufacturing technology) towards two somewhat conflicting objectives: offering variety and low costs. *Economies of integration* address this issue by combining the economies of scale with the economies of scope. The development of computer aided design and manufacturing (CADCAM) has been responsible for developing flexibility and low costs in manufacturing and logistics activities. Similar motivation, that is differentiation and cost management, has directed technology/relationship management developments. Success in both is dependent upon cooperation between the organisation and its suppliers, and management and employees. Changes in production and logistics methods are not unusual; hence there is a large input from relationship management necessary.

Figure 4.2 illustrates that there are important relationships between knowledge management, technology management and relationship management. Essentially knowledge management structures or organises knowledge to create competitive advantage and has both a development role (in which the organisation identifies what it knows and, more importantly what it doesn't know) and an application role (in which knowledge is structured to obtain effectiveness and efficiency). Clearly this is not an isolated activity and, if effectiveness and efficiency are to be developed into sustainable competitive

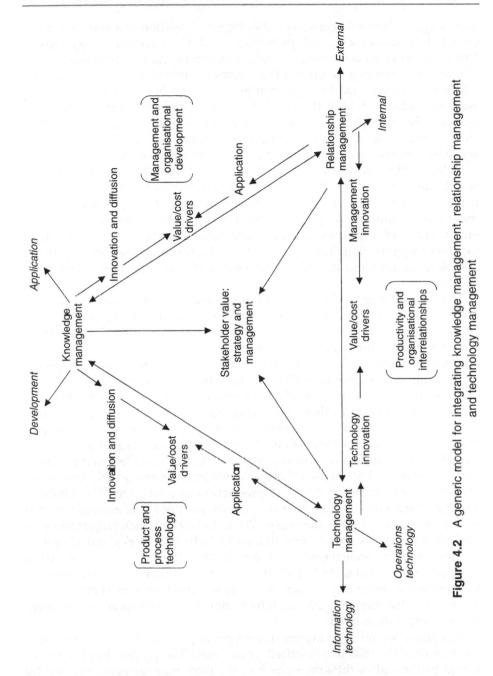

Figure 4.2 A generic model for integrating knowledge management, relationship management and technology management

advantage, a 'dialogue' between technology and relationship management is essential. Similarly for technology management. The 'new technology' (Noori: 1990) comprises a customised, or exclusive, combination of information and operations technology to ensure the relevant capabilities and capacities for addressing specific market opportunities. Again, this cannot be achieved without 'dialogue' with both knowledge management and relationship management. Knowledge management identifies new technologies, and relationship management is a required input if production *and* distribution methods are to be effective and efficient in terms of strategic and operational decisions.

Relationship management prescribes the organisation structure within which the firm operates. Payne's (1995) description of the 'market' environment in which a firm operates determines the role of relationship management that extends the scope of relationship marketing into one in which a broad range of processes can be coordinated. Relationship management includes 'coproduction' (the 'transfer' of production processes both upstream and downstream) and in which 'managed' codestiny becomes essential for success.

That knowledge, technology and relationship management were, and remain, important can be deduced from a quotation from Piore and Sabel (1984) concerning flexible specialisation, which they consider to be a '. . . strategy of permanent innovation: accommodation to ceaseless change, rather than an effort to control it. This strategy is based on flexible multi-use equipment (technology management); skilled workers (knowledge management); and the creation, through politics of an industrial community that restricts the forms of competition to those favouring innovation (relationship management). For these reasons the spread of flexible specialisation amounts to a revival of craft forms of production.' (Comments in brackets are the authors'). Sabel (1988) describes how flexible specialisation was first identified in central and northwestern Italy in the 1970s and 1980s and was responsible for the creation of areas of focussed skills and production methods. The 'Third Italy' is a string of industrial districts that are political and/or social associations that exist to service an entire community. 'The associations which range from productive associations and labour unions to industrial parks and collective service centres, provide the essential services that allow each firm to specialise in a portion of the value chain and often provide additional economies of scale that allow the community to compete with mass producers, most often by collecting and disseminating crucial information to the industrial community.' (Pine, quoting Best: 1990)

Essentially we are tracking the development process of stakeholder value creation over the past two hundred or so years. The process has been reinforced by innovative thinking in each of the three management areas *and* by their integration at their interfaces. Using Pine's analysis we have identified the progression that has occurred from the early days of the American System through to the mass production philosophy of the early 20th century (and which continues to be significant for some economies) and the development of mass customisation.

MORE RECENT EVENTS

There has been considerable social, economic and technological change in recent years such that old structures have been challenged, concepts revisited and revised. New concepts such as smokeless factories, screwdriver assembly plants and corporations without tangible assets have become realities.

The segmentation of markets in the 1970s and 1980s was followed by fragmentation during the 1990s. It was fragmentation that required a flexible response if customer expectations were to be met. There have been two responses. One has been an increase in alliances and partnerships and the other has been from manufacturing technology, which offers the ability to meet customer expectations for variety without the accompanying increases in product cost.

These arguments suggest alternative organisational structures with which to take full advantage of the marketplace opportunities that should develop. Davidow and Malone (1992) suggest:

The complex product-markets of the twenty first century will demand the ability to deliver, quickly and globally a high variety of customised products. These products will be differentiated not only by form and function, but also by the services provided with the product, including the ability for the customer to be involved in the design of the product . . . a manufacturing company will not be an isolated facility in production, but rather a node in the complex network of suppliers, customers, engineering and other 'service' functions.

. . . profound changes are expected for the company's distribution system and its internal organisation as they evolve to become more customer driven and customer managed. On the upstream side of the firm, supplier networks will have to be integrated with those of customers often to the point where the customer will share its equipment, designs, trade secrets and confidences with those suppliers. Obviously, suppliers will become very dependent upon their downstream customers; but by the same token customers will be equally trapped by their suppliers. In the end, unlike its contemporary predecessors, the virtual corporation will appear less a discrete enterprise and more an ever-varying cluster of common activities in the midst of a vast fabric of relationships.

The challenge posed by this business revolution argues that corporations that expect to remain competitive must achieve mastery of both information and relationships.

Byrne and Brandt (1992) identified the characteristics of the 'new corporate model':

Today's joint ventures and strategic alliances may be an early glimpse of the business organisation of the future: the Virtual Corporation. It's a temporary network of companies that come together quickly to exploit fast-changing opportunities. In a Virtual Corporation, companies can share costs, skills, and access to global markets, with each partner contributing what it is best at . . . the key attributes of such an organisation (include): EXCELLENCE . . . each partner brings its core competence to the effort . . . TECHNOLOGY . . . informational networks . . . partnerships based on electronic contracts . . . to speed the linkups . . . OPPORTUNISM . . . partnerships will be less permanent, less formal and more opportunistic . . . to meet a specific market opportunity . . . TRUST . . . these relationships make companies far more reliant on each other and require far more trust than ever before . . . NO BORDERS . . . this new corporate model redefines the traditional boundaries of the company. More cooperation among competitors, suppliers, and customers makes it harder to determine where one company ends and another begins.

In other words an integrated and coordinated approach towards knowledge, technology and relationship management is becoming essential. Indeed Byrne and Brandt are suggesting that one of the key success factors for all businesses is the ability to identify one's own core competencies, decide where in the value chain these are to be most cost effectively deployed, and to complement these with partnership opportunities. Figure 4.3 suggests how the tasks of integration and coordination may be approached. In this hypothetical example (but which has been developed from discussions with companies in the 'instrumentation for process monitoring' industry) the basic elements of knowledge, technology and relationship management have been identified. However, to reinforce their impact the identification of the interface areas has been undertaken, which when addressed make the entire value creation system more effective (a strategic concern) and efficient (an operational concern). There is another important consideration to be put. Given that both market expectations and market responses are changing frequently, the interface areas offer the opportunity to form alliances which are more responsive, more rapidly. If managed responsibly (and responsively) they can help avoid the high levels of investment which often occur in vertically integrated organisations. They can also encourage ongoing customer focussed R and D throughout the value chain because of the interdependencies that develop. Furthermore as product applications and end-user profiles shift, the structure of the value offer can be adjusted by agreeing to changes in the tasks of the value chain members, or changing the structure of the value chain.

WHERE WE MAY BE HEADING

There can be very little doubt the world is becoming a very different place. However, it is worthwhile to pause and ask some questions concerning both the rate and direction of change, but perhaps more importantly, to question the building blocks for the launch pad. The proliferation of 'e-commerce solutions' may be leading business towards 'mass s-e-duction' rather than towards mass customisation (Pine's case). It would be more sensible to consider e-commerce as a facilitator – or a means by which we can add flexibility, reduce operating times, increase accuracy, relevance and control to, our business – rather than be the 'e-nd' in itself.

To do so requires an organisation to identify the relevant components of the knowledge management, technology management, and relationship man-

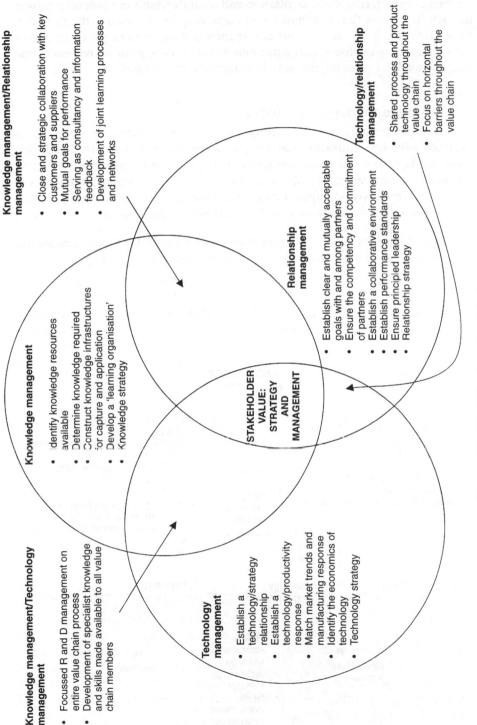

Knowledge management/Relationship management

- Close and strategic collaboration with key customers and suppliers
- Mutual goals for performance
- Serving as consultancy and information feedback
- Development of joint learning processes and networks

Technology/relationship management

- Shared process and product technology throughout the value chain
- Focus on horizontal barriers throughout the value chain

Knowledge management

- Identify knowledge resources available
- Determine knowledge required
- Construct knowledge infrastructures for capture and application
- Develop a 'learning organisation'
- Knowledge strategy

Relationship management

- Establish clear and mutually acceptable goals with and among partners
- Ensure the competency and commitment of partners
- Establish a collaborative environment
- Establish performance standards
- Ensure principled leadership
- Relationship strategy

STAKEHOLDER VALUE: STRATEGY AND MANAGEMENT

Knowledge management/Technology management

- Focussed R and D management on entire value chain process
- Development of specialist knowledge and skills made available to all value chain members

Technology management

- Establish a technology/strategy relationship
- Establish a technology/productivity response
- Match market trends and manufacturing response
- Identify the economics of technology
- Technology strategy

Figure 4.3 Identifying important interface areas

agement characteristics of the 'market' and to understand the potential power in each. It follows that a different emphasis may be required if the model is to operate across all sectors, and dominance may need to be given to one of the components to ensure that a dominant competitive position results. Some examples follow of using the new management facilitators.

A knowledge management focus

For example, a pharmaceutical company, a computer software company or perhaps a defence contractor may need to be *knowledge management* led. If this were so then it would place emphasis on knowledge management and this emphasis in turn would result in technology and relationship management strategies which would support its overall strategic direction. See Figure 4.4.

The role of *knowledge management* is increasingly significant:

> Knowledge is neither data nor information, though it is related to both, and the differences between these terms are often a matter of degree.

and:

> Most people have an intuitive sense that knowledge is broader, deeper and richer than data or information . . . What we offer is a working definition of knowledge,

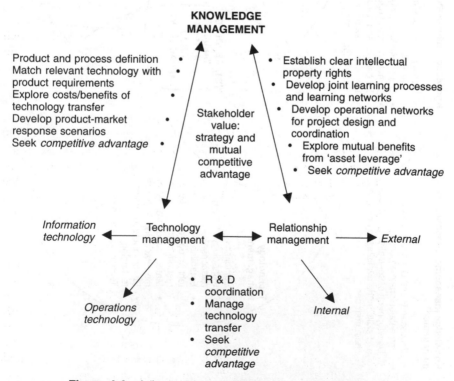

Figure 4.4 A 'knowledge management' led organisation

a pragmatic description that helps us communicate what we mean when we talk about knowledge in organisations. Our definition expresses the characteristics that make knowledge valuable and the characteristics – often the same ones – that make it difficult to manage well.

and:

> Knowledge is a fluid mix of experience, values, contextual information and expert insight that provides a framework for evaluating and incorporating new experiences and information. It originates and is applied in the minds of knowers. In organisations, it often becomes embedded not only in documents or repositories but also in organisational routines, processes, practices and norms.
>
> (Davenport and Prusak: 1998)

The authors discuss differences between data and information: 'Data becomes information when its creator adds meaning. We transform data into information by adding value in various ways.' But knowledge must be managed if a functional purpose is to be realised. One suggestion for this task comes from Hansen *et al* (1999) with:

> A company's knowledge management strategy should reflect its competitive strategy: how it creates value for customers, how that value supports an economic model, and how the company's people deliver on value and the economics.

The authors have identified two approaches. The first is *codification*, in which knowledge is encoded and structured prior to storage in databases and being made available. By contrast *personalisation* ties information to individuals who provide creative, analytically rigorous advice on high level strategic problems by channeling individual expertise. The authors express the view that executives must be able to articulate why customers buy one company's products rather than those of its competitors. What value do customers expect from the company? How does knowledge that resides in the company add value for customers? Without answers to these questions management should not attempt to choose a knowledge management strategy. Other questions are also asked concerning products and problem solving methods. Standardised, mature products typically dictate a codified approach while customised, innovative products are better serviced by a personalised approach. The type of knowledge used is also important. Explicit knowledge (market data, competitor profiles, customer characteristics and so on) can be codified. Tacit knowledge (scientific expertise, operational know-how, and industry experience and business judgement) requires a person-to-person approach. An example of codification is given by the authors. An Ernst and Young consultant was preparing a bid for the installation of an enterprise resource planning system. He had experience in some aspects of the project but none in the specific area in which he was working. Because Ernst and Young maintained extensive records and documentation pertaining to previous projects he was able to search the electronic knowledge management repository for relevant knowledge. Considerable savings in both time and cost resulted. An example of personalisation involves another consulting organisation. Bain were advising on a strategy problem for a large UK financial institution. The assignment required geographic and product-line expertise, a broad understanding of the industry, and a large amount of creative thinking. In this example the consultant used the collective knowledge of the organisation by checking Bain's 'people finder' database to identify partners with relevant expertise. Meetings and videoconferences provided an ongoing team effort to provide a project recommendation. The interface aspects identified by both of these examples concern the use of technology (information technology) to connect people with reusable codified knowledge (codification) or to facilitate building networks of individuals with a range of expertise. The other interface aspect is between knowledge and relationship management; clearly in both examples the internal cohesiveness developed by concern for 'intra' relationship management is an essential input. Creativity is an important feature of knowledge management. Deeble (1999) provides an interesting example. In an article on 'The Fourth Room', a creativity consulting company, Deeble describes an organisation that works with its clients to create networks of 'creativity'. The client companies (which include American Express Europe, Safeway, MFI, Prudential, 3I, and Abbey National) subscribe to a series of workshops which consider a range of topics thought to be of importance to each of them. Recent topics ranged from the threat of the Internet to traditional companies to ways of opening the mind to creativity and Reiki healing. The workshop series also includes 'evenings with successful creative entrepreneurs'.

Effective knowledge management can also be used to ensure efficient time response to customer expectations. Pine (*op cit*) cites as examples the 'quick response' time based strategies of a number of organisations. The Peerless Saw Company, Levi Strauss and The Limited are companies that have reengineered their processes based upon knowledge management processes (notably information and telecommunications technologies) to accelerate time. Each organisation along the value chain is linking together through these technologies so that the entire chain knows what is selling at the end-user level and therefore what to produce and distribute at each level in the chain.

Technology management: economies of integration

A manufacturer of computer components for hardware assembly is likely to be concerned with cost effective process technology and hence be *technology management led*. In a similar context technology leadership may be dominant in automotive assembly companies where product technology and R and D are essential strategic features. See Figure 4.5.

The new technologies use computer based techniques to manufacture (within a predetermined envelope of variety) a range of products without cost penalties for manufacturing any one part versus another; '. . . yielding a manufacturing system that can quickly respond to changes in demand'. (Pine: *op cit*). The principle of computer-integrated manufacturing links 'islands of automation' *into a single, integrated* system that is fast, responsive, flexible and

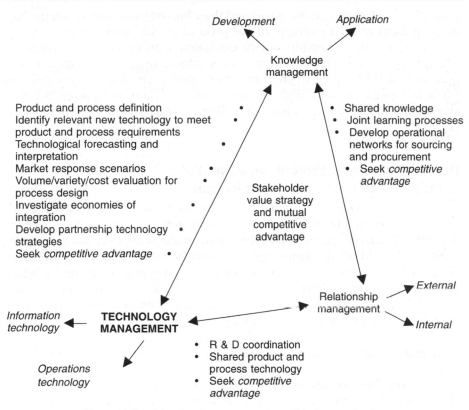

Figure 4.5 A 'technology management' led organisation

relatively low cost. Noori (1990) defines this as *economies of integration* result-ing in a situation in which unit costs decrease as output increases because the volume of the *entire* operation is increased. Furthermore, the integration of new manufacturing technology and information technology brings the customer into the design process. Toffler (1980) identified the *prosumer* as pro-ducer and consumer defining *and* producing the product in concert. Nike offers customers the facility to design their own shoes via the Nike website (see Chapter 1). The automotive industry is also close to offering this facility. It has, of course, been available for some time; but TIME was a problem – the delivery time period was some weeks! The initiative now pursued aims to offer delivery in days not weeks. Hobsbawm (2000) also comments on the increasing trend towards 'prosumerism' by extending the concept into the future. He suggests that eventually end-user involvement will go beyond the current situations in which they play an active role in manufacturers' pro-duction processes, helping reduce the costs of manufacturing staff and costs by specifying design features online and building their own, bespoke, product. Hobsbawm further suggests that the current relationship between consumers and manufacturers in which the consumer is designing the next generation of products and services will continue to expand. He gives the example of Netscape who have released their browser source code on the Net, inviting users to collaborate in virtual product development teams. The rise in employee share ownership and the explosion of online investing will create a new wave of owner-worker-consumers which, suggests Hobsbawm, will blur the distinction between companies, customers and employees still further. Hobsbawm has clearly identified an important technology/relationship management interface, one that is likely to increase in significance very rapidly.

Relationship management: an essential component of the virtual organisation

Relationship management leadership is important for both consumer goods manufacturers and distributors. For manufacturers, relationship management is a critical concern, particularly when their markets are dominated by powerful retailers. Much the same argument may be made from the distributors' point of view. There are one or two brands in any product category which dominate consumer selection processes; not to stock one of these brands may result in not being included in a consumer's selection of stores to visit when contemplating purchases. Relationship management is also important in service product companies, particularly financial services where the superior management of customer relationships may result in further sales. See Figure 4.6.

However there are less obvious examples that demonstrate how relationship management interfaces with technology and knowledge management. Dell Computers is an excellent example of the benefits offered by relationship management. At start-up Dell could not afford to create every piece of the value chain but the company did question why it should want to do so. They concluded that *leveraging* the investments of others would be their best option. Magretta (1998) gives chip manufacture as an example. At the time of its inception the chip industry was very competitive, investment was high and profitability low. Dell concluded that if, as a company, it was to be profitable and earn higher returns, capital should be allocated to activities that add value for customers, not into activities that need to be done. Michael Dell argues that this model has allowed the company to leverage its relationships with both suppliers and customers to such an extent that the companies are *virtually integrated*. The role played by Dell Computers is one of coordinating activities such that they are able to create the most value for customers. Dell (quoted by Magretta) suggests there to be benefits beyond those of leveraging partners' assets: 'You actually get to have a relationship with the customer. And that creates valuable information that, in turn, allows us to leverage our relationships with both suppliers and customers. Couple that information with technology, and you have the infrastructure to revolutionize the fundamental business models of major global companies.'

Relationship management has been used in a number of strategic situations. Nanda and Williamson (1995) describe one such situation. Philips, the Netherlands based electronics company identified its US$1.5 billion domestic

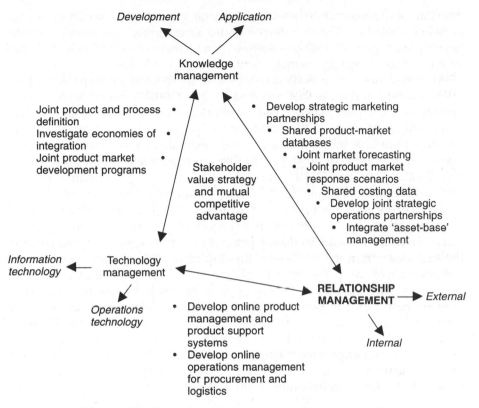

Figure 4.6 A 'relationship management' led organisation

appliance division as not essential to its future. Its performance had been poor and an outright sale of the division would not have realised anywhere near the value of its assets. To rectify its problems required considerable cash investment, and being a non-core activity the appliances division was usually last in line for this. Whirlpool Corporation was looking to expand beyond its US base and a strong European position had attraction. Furthermore the industry was becoming global and this offered cost advantages from sourcing, manufacturing and marketing across an international market. However, Whirlpool was hesitant. A joint venture was an ideal solution; Whirlpool agreed a purchase price, and assumed a 53 per cent ownership with an agreement to purchase the remaining 47 per cent within three years. It gave Whirlpool an opportunity to learn about the reality of operating the appliance division and to implement improvement plans before assuming complete ownership. Whirlpool also benefited from Philips' continued involvement in the business; the accumulated knowledge was available for consultation and many of Philips' technology based infrastructure systems were utilised. The sale was eventually completed for a further payment. The benefit for Philips was the opportunity to demonstrate to Whirlpool the 'value' of the appliance division, and eventually to realise a sum far greater than would otherwise have been obtained. The case demonstrates an integrated perspective of relationship management with technology management (production and control systems) and knowledge management.

An interesting (proposed) development in the relationship/technology management interface is that reported by Tait (2000). General Motors, Ford and Daimler-Chrysler plan to create the world's largest electronic marketplace and could involve tens of thousands of suppliers. Their combined purchases are more than $200 billion a year and their extended supply chains are worth hundreds of billions of dollars each. The announcement follows some three months after Ford and GM announced links with large Net system providers to create AutoXchange and TradeXchange. Both have been energetic in their attempts to encourage suppliers and dealers to join. They have also attempted to induce other large manufacturers to become involved. Suppliers expressed reservations such as an increased pressure on prices, the independence of the exchanges from the carmakers, the duplication of software costs and the implications of using the 'wrong' exchange and thereby annoying GM, or vice versa. The announced exchange is a response by the manufacturers who suggest it as a response to suppliers' reservations concerning separate exchanges. To reassure suppliers, the manufacturers stressed the intended independence of the proposed exchange and that it would probably be floated on the stock exchange once it had established a successful operating record. Initially the three manufacturers will have equal equity shares and Commerce One and Oracle will collaborate on the technology.

SOME DIRECTIVES FOR THE FUTURE: THE VIRTUAL ORGANISATION

In a comment made after the Rover/BMW decision, MacRae (2000), argued: 'From the point of view of the whole country, the global shift to design and marketing is good news'. McRae referred to a remark made by Jacques Nasser, the head of Ford, who late in 1999 suggested that Ford might in the future outsource all of its manufacturing. He reasoned that this is not because Ford was bad at manufacturing but because its particular skills are located at other parts of the value chain, such as design and marketing. Manufacturing has become a 'commodity'. While there is nothing here that other organisations have not already contemplated McRae does rightly comment: '. . . there is a seismic change taking place in the way our economy is organised'. He contrasted the Rover/BMW outcome with the result of the flotation of Lastminute.com and compared the views held of the value (or economic utility) that both contribute. The motor vehicle offers the traditional tangible view of value with form, time and place utilities, each contributing part of the value/utility offer. The value offer made by Lastminute.com is to make the industries it services run more efficiently by increasing capacity utilisation:

Any revenues from the last few airline seats are almost pure profit. All the talk on the lines of 'new economy good, old economy bad' misses the crucial point that the most important aspect of the new economy is the way it is [improving] and will improve the efficiency of the old.

Prahalad and Ramaswamy (2000) develop the notion of experience as a component of economic value. They comment: 'Customers are stepping out of their traditional roles to become co-creators as well as consumers of value'. They argue that not only do consumers play an active role in creating and competing for value, they are becoming a source of competence for organisations: '. . . competence now is a function of the collective knowledge available to the whole system – an enhanced network of traditional suppliers, manufacturers, partners, investors and customers'. Prahalad and Ramaswamy recommend management to identify and understand 'three instrumental realities' if they are to engage customers in active, explicit and ongoing dialogue: to mobilise communities of customers; to manage customer diversity; and to work with customers to create personalised rather than just customised products. The authors offer examples of Internet companies and 'thinking products' such as Amazon.com and Philips electronics with Pronto, who use information technology to structure personalised or profiled products that use current purchasing and consumption patterns to provide the product format for future uses.

Given the apparent continuity in the development of industry's organisational response to its environment, what are the directives for the future? Figure 4.2 provided a model based on the developments seen by Pine and others. Figure 4.7 extends this to identify emerging characteristics of virtual organisations. The thesis presented by this model is that no structural changes are likely to occur. There may be changes of emphasis but the concepts upon which the model is based, in other words the developments in knowledge management, technology management and relationship management, form the bases for organisational response. It assumes the current trends of focussing upon core competencies, and outsourcing processes better performed by specialists because of capability and/or capacity advantages, will continue.

Knowledge management continues to experience rapid development. To capitalise on this current growth, organisations should adopt a 'make or buy' approach towards investment in knowledge resources. The basic criteria to be used by any organisation for any investment in resources are: what are the aspects of knowledge that will make decision making more effective, and what are the most cost effective means of acquiring them? To do this requires an audit of the 'decision making/knowledge available' relationship within an organisation (and here the term 'organisation' is used to include the whole value production/delivery system). Such an audit will assist in developing clear requirements for qualitative and quantitative knowledge inputs. An audit should establish stocks and flows of knowledge in order that a knowledge based infrastructure can be built. Given that an organisation can establish what it is it knows, and what it is it should know, the next step is to build a 'learning organisation' based upon the identified requirements.

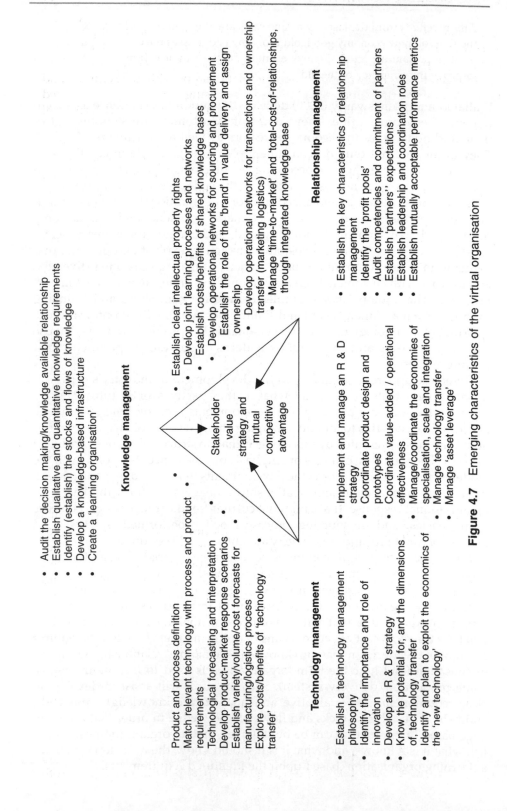

Knowledge management

- Audit the decision making/knowledge available relationship
- Establish qualitative and quantitative knowledge requirements
- Identify (establish) the stocks and flows of knowledge
- Develop a knowledge-based infrastructure
- Create a 'learning organisation'

- Establish clear intellectual property rights
- Develop joint learning processes and networks
- Establish costs/benefits of shared knowledge bases
- Develop operational networks for sourcing and procurement
- Establish the role of the 'brand' in value delivery and assign ownership
- Develop operational networks for transactions and ownership transfer (marketing logistics)
- Manage 'time-to-market' and 'total-cost-of-relationships', through integrated knowledge base

Relationship management

- Establish the key characteristics of relationship management
- Identify the 'profit pools'
- Audit competencies and commitment of partners
- Establish 'partners'' expectations
- Establish leadership and coordination roles
- Establish mutually acceptable performance metrics

Stakeholder value strategy and mutual competitive advantage

Product and process definition
Match relevant technology with process and product requirements
Technological forecasting and interpretation
Develop product-market response scenarios
Establish variety/volume/cost forecasts for manufacturing/logistics process
Explore costs/benefits of 'technology transfer'

- Implement and manage an R & D strategy
- Coordinate product design and prototypes
- Coordinate value-added / operational effectiveness
- Manage/coordinate the economies of specialisation, scale and integration
- Manage technology transfer
- Manage 'asset leverage'

Technology management

- Establish a technology management philosophy
- Identify the importance and role of innovation
- Develop an R & D strategy
- Know the potential for, and the dimensions of, technology transfer
- Identify and plan to exploit the economics of the 'new technology'

Figure 4.7 Emerging characteristics of the virtual organisation

Technology management has become more embracing in its application. Accordingly it requires a technology management philosophy. To be effective, technology management should identify the most cost effective role that can be achieved through developing ongoing relationships with marketing, R and D and manufacturing/operations management using the notion of 'leveraged assets'. Michael Dell has been widely quoted for his conviction about minimal ownership of assets and maximising the utilisation of suppliers' dedicated capabilities and capacities. This is the first step in developing an R and D strategy that will take its direction towards favouring product or process technology, the role of customers and of suppliers in the R and D process derived from the technology management philosophy. The economies of integration are important in this respect. Noori (1990) commented: 'The challenge is to devise an "organisational structure" to match the flexibility and complexity of the new technology, a structure that meshes all the necessary technical and non-technical elements and blends the functional expertise as needed . . .'

Profit share is more important than market share: identifying profit pools

Relationship management requires management to adopt the view that collaboration, not conflict, or necessarily competition, is an essential feature of the 'new economy'. As suggested by Figure 4.8 on p. 84, there are a number of issues contributing towards success. The first is to understand the key characteristics of relationships within an industry, market or market segment. A useful method for achieving this is to identify the *profit pools* within the value creation system and then to explore the characteristics of the 'actors and the processes' involved. Gadiesh and Gilbert (1998) offer a model based upon the notion that: 'Successful companies understand that profit share is more important than market share'. A profit pool is defined as the total profits earned in an industry at all points along the industry's value chain. The pool may be 'deeper' in some segments of the value chain than in others and variations may be due to customer, product and distribution channel differences, or perhaps there may be geographical reasons. Often the pattern of profit concentration differs markedly from revenue concentration. Gadiesh and Gilbert use the US automotive industry to demonstrate the variations of revenue and profit distribution, and to provide an approach to mapping profit pools:

- *Define the pool:* determine which value chain activities influence the organisations' ability to generate profits, now and in the future.
- *Determine the size of the pool:* develop a baseline estimate of the *cumulative* profits generated by all profit pool activities.
- *Reconcile the estimates:* compare the outputs of steps one and two and reconcile where necessary.

The authors recommend that the model be used to identify profit trends and to create an awareness of the implications of future structural shifts. The profit pool approach does explain why a number of the large automotive manufacturers are questioning their long term viability as just manufacturers and are researching the feasibility of involvement elsewhere in the value production system. However in the virtual organisation the strategic implications are more significant. Profit pools can be used to identify structural options and to question them in terms of optimal stakeholder value delivery. Additionally we can identify trends, establish scenarios and identify where relationship strategies and structures need to be changed and identify the financial implications of each of the options.

Profitability and the management interface areas

The interrelationship aspects of the three management areas will demand close integration and coordination. For *knowledge/technology management* the importance of product characteristics for competitive advantage *and* cost effective/efficient structures offering flexibility, will require close attention, specifically the detail of matching technology with both product *and* process requirements. The emphasis on using knowledge based systems (or expert systems) to replicate decisions made by management at both strategic and operational levels can be expected to expand. Slack *et al* (1998) identify a number of decision areas currently addressed. These include capacity planning, facility location and layout, aggregate planning, product design, production and logistics scheduling, quality management, inventory control and maintenance. Qualitative applications of knowledge management applications are being applied to strategic concerns. The author is currently conducting a research program looking at financial data (financial ratios) and their knowledge inputs. The study is working with senior executives who use financial ratios for planning and control purposes and is aimed at identifying the role of corporate knowledge (either codified or personalised) in setting financial objectives and in evaluating results. To date the findings suggest that it is more the personalised knowledge that is brought into decision making and control evaluation. However these are particularly important in the appraisal of investment alternatives where experience (personalised knowledge) is used to set hurdle rates for evaluating the return on technology investment.

The *technology/relationship management* interrelationship offers opportunities for partnerships to explore shared activities in R and D as well as in manufacturing and logistics. The remark of the Ford CEO, suggesting the company could consider outsourcing manufacturing entirely, is an indication of the lengths to which large organisations are prepared to go in establishing partnership led organisations. It is also an indication of the degree to which trust and the exchange of commercial confidence is being extended. Dell Computers is a working example of the direction virtual organisations can be expected to go. Technology/relationship management can improve profitability, productivity and cash flow if product specification and operations processes are managed as a partnership. It is interesting to conjecture over the cage pallet issue of the 1970s in which Asda attempted to pioneer a manufacturing/logistics concept that offered very significant cost benefits (to Asda).

It may well have had a very different outcome if it had been introduced recently. Developments such as EFTPOS and EDI were approached with caution, but more recently JIT, QR and linked inventory management systems have been accepted with more enthusiasm.

Relationship/knowledge management has been influenced by developments in information technology and database management facilities. The thaw in the once strained manufacturer/distributor relationships has resulted in an increase in trust and in confidence exchanges, as have the changes in attitudes concerning collaboration, rather than hostile competitiveness, among competitors. The result of these developments is leading to joint ventures in manufacturing and marketing as well as in sourcing and procurement. The use of specialists in specific processes is expanding due to the rapid changes occurring in the marketplace (such as fragmentation) and the need for detailed understanding of customer expectations and trends. Customer retention programs are dependent on the strength of the relationship/knowledge management interrelationship for success. It is arguable that benefits drive customer loyalty but there is an equally strong argument to suggest that it is the 'knowledge base' held on each customer that ensures the accuracy of the response to the customer, which is the key factor. Given the reported expansion of Web based home shopping, the opportunities for more detailed customer knowledge and more accurate and timely response by suppliers can be expected. These developments will extend the number of marketing logistics options required to deliver 'customer value'. The impact of companies such as Lastminute.com can be expected to initiate major changes in customer expectations for value delivery and as a consequence bring out significant changes in channel structures and logistics services. The role of the 'brand' is also open to question. If the product-service is purchased via a Net based company offering value that conventional 'bricks and mortar' suppliers cannot (or are unwilling) to provide, the intangible service features of the Net company will supersede the tangible characteristics of the brand and may well dilute any established brand loyalty.

SUMMARY

The recent rapid development of knowledge management and learning organisations; of technology management and the economics of integration and of relationship management through alliances and partnerships, may lead to many organisations overlooking the basic analysis of requirements for success. While the contemporary argument suggests that the life span of most structures will be constrained by the opportunity, it remains a responsibility of management to ensure that a rigorous approach to identifying and evaluating virtual structures (any structures for that matter) is followed. Increasingly technology is making communication within alliances faster and more accurate, truncating both time and distance. Markets and their management are undergoing significant changes. What is certain is that for virtual structures to be successful a change in the approach and attitudes towards busi-

Characteristics	Traditional organisation	'Virtual' organisation
• Structure	• Hierarchical	• Networks
• Scope	• Internal/closed	• External/open
• Resource focus	• Capital	• Knowledge, relationship, technology management
• State	• Static, stable	• Dynamic, changing
• HRM	• Management	• Specialists
• Direction	• Management directives	• Empowerment/intrapreneurship
• Basis of action	• Control	• Empowerment
• Motivation	• Meet Corporate management directives	• Achieve team goals
• Learning	• Specific skills	• Broader competencies
• Compensation	• Position/seniority	• Achievement
• Relationships	• Competitive	• Cooperative/collaborative
• Information communications among partners	• 'Need to know' basis	• Open and transparent

Figure 4.8   Traditional business structures versus 'virtual' organisation structures

Source: Adapted from Tapscott, D. and A. Caston (1993), *Paradigm Shift*, McGraw-Hill, New York

ness structure is necessary. Figure 4.8 identifies and compares the important differences between the characteristics of traditional organisations and emerging virtual organisations such as Dell and Nike.

REFERENCES •

Ashkenas, R., D. Ulrich, J. Todd and S. Kerr (1995), *The Boundaryless Organisation*, Jossey-Bass, San Francisco.

Best, M. (1990), *The New Competition: Institutions of Industrial Restructuring*, Harvard University Press, Boston.

Byrne, G. and W. Brandt (1992), in Davidow, W. A. and M. S. Malone (eds), *The Virtual Corporation*, Harper Collins, New York.

Coase, H. R. (1937), 'The nature of the firm', *Economica* vol. 4.

Davenport, T. and L. Prusak (1988), *Working Knowledge*, Harvard Business School Press, Boston.

Davidow, W. A. and M. S. Malone (eds) (1992), *The Virtual Corporation*, Harper Collins, New York.

Day, G. (1999), *The Market Driven Organisation*, The Free Press, New York.

Deeble, S. (1999), 'Fourth Room opens doors of perception', *The Financial Times*, 31 December.

Gadiesh, O. and J. L. Gilbert (1998), 'How to map your industry's profit pool', *Harvard Business Review*, May/June.

Glazer, R. (1991), 'Marketing in an information-intensive environment: strategic implications of knowledge as an asset', *Journal of Marketing*, October.

Hansen, M. T., N. Nohria and T. Tierney (1999), 'What's your strategy for managing knowledge?' *Harvard Business Review*, March/April.

Hobsbawm, A. (2000), 'We're all prosumers now', *The Financial Times*, 26/27 February.

MacRae, H. (2000), *The Guardian*, 18 May.

Magretta, J. (1998), 'The power of virtual integration: an interview with Dell Computers' Michael Dell', *Harvard Business Review*, March/April.

Malone, T. M. (1998), 'The dawn of the e-lance economy', *Harvard Business Review*, September/October.

Nanda, A. and P. J. Williamson (1995), 'Use joint ventures to ease the pain of restructuring', *Harvard Business Review*, November/December.

Noori, H. (1990), *Managing the Dynamics of New Technology*, Prentice-Hall, Englewood Cliffs.

Payne, A. (ed.) (1995), *Advances in Relationship Marketing*, Kogan Page, London.

Pine III, B. J. (1993), *Mass Customisation*, Harvard Business School Press, Boston.

Piore, M. and C. F. Sabel (1984), *The Second Industrial Divide: Possibilities for Prosperity*, Basic Books, New York.

Prahalad, C. K. and V. Ramaswamy (2000), 'Co-opting customer competence', *Harvard Business Review*, January/February.

Sabel, C. F. (1989), 'Flexible specialisation and the re-emergence of regional economics', in Hirst, P. and J. Zeitlin (eds), *Reversing Industrial Decline? Industrial Policy in Britain and Her Competitors*, Oxford, Berg Publishers.

Slack, N., S. Chambers, C. Harland, A. Harrison and R. Johnston (1998), *Operations Management*, Second edition, Financial Times/Pitman Publishing, London.

Sutton, C. (1998), *Strategic Concepts*, Macmillan Business, Basingstoke.

Tait, N. (2000), 'Car giants plan joint electronic trade exchange', *The Financial Times*, 26/27 February.

Toffler, A. (1980), *The Third Wave*, Morrow, New York.

Williamson, O. E. (1985), *The Economic Institutions of Capitalism: Firms, Markets, Relationship Contracting*, Macmillan, Basingstoke.

chapter 5

Supply Chains and Value Chains: Definitions, Characteristics, Differences and Directions

LEARNING OUTCOMES

The student will be able to:

- discuss the differences between the supply chain and the demand chain;
- identify the requirements for the design of a value chain structure.

INTRODUCTION

It could be argued that consumer change has resulted in responses from business that have in turn resulted in faster product development, increasingly flexible manufacturing systems, global sourcing and manufacturing, R and D collaboration and a range of changes to the processes and practice of management. Alternatively we might argue that the application of technology to production and distribution has expanded the possible number of options available to the consumer. Either way, and despite the benefits (actual or imagined) to consumers, the unprecedented number and variety of products competing in markets ranging from apparel and durables to power tools and computers continue to increase. It raises the question: is the supply chain a relevant concept for the 21st century?

Fisher *et al* (1994) comment on the problems created for manufacturers and distributors who end up with excess inventories that are marked down to be sold (possibly sold below cost) and who lose potential sales because of the lack of space to carry current inventories. The authors suggest the problem is exacerbated by poor forecasting and suggest further that a spate of production-scheduling systems has made the situation far worse. Quick response programmes, such as just-in-time and manufacturing resource planning (MRP) inventory systems have but a small impact on a supply chain that is full.

The importance and the benefits of identifying demand chain characteristics

For Fisher and his co-authors the problem is one which can be rectified by incorporating demand uncertainty into their production-planning processes. Add to this the accelerating rate of new product introductions and the uncertainty increases further. They suggest an irony about recent (at that time) developments, but which continues to have validity. Given the improved quantity and quality of information on consumer purchasing habits, and the benefits of flexible manufacturing systems (that is, reduced costs of small quantity production) companies are now able to manufacture a wider variety of products with the objective of providing customers with exactly what they want. Even traditional industries have introduced a notion of 'fashion' into their ranges. But there are problems that most companies fail to address. Frequent introductions of new products bring with them side effects. They reduce the average life span of products, which introduces the problem of uncertainty in demand forecasting and increases the costs of inventory holding as the obsolescent products become difficult to sell in competition with replacement, new products. Furthermore, to the inventory and storage costs must be added the cost of lost sales due to the lack of both space and working capital necessary if they are to be held to meet customers' (changing) demand. Fisher *et al* also suggest problems from proliferation. As product groups expand demand is divided over an increasing number of stock keeping units (SKUs) thus making product sales difficult if not impossible to predict.

Fisher and his co-authors suggest *accurate response* as a solution. In effect they claim that *quick response* is an orientation that inevitably leads to the problems identified. They use the Sport Obermeyer Company as an example. Sport Obermeyer is a 'fashion skiwear' business and in its market demand is 'heavily dependent upon a variety of factors that are difficult to predict – weather, fashion trends, the economy and the peak of the retail selling season is only two months long'. Using *accurate response* the company has been able to eliminate almost entirely the cost of producing skiwear that customers do not want and of not producing skiwear they do want.

Sport Obermeyer's products are newly designed each year to include changes in style, fabric and colour. Until the mid-1980s the design-and-sales cycle followed: design the product, make samples, show samples to retailers in March, place production orders with suppliers in March and April after receiving retail orders, receive goods in September and October and ship to retail outlets. This approach had worked well for more than 30 years but problems occurred in the mid-1980s. Volume increases met with manufacturing constraints during the peak production periods. This was 'resolved' by booking production well ahead, in November – a year before goods were likely to be sold – and based on speculation as to what retailers would order! Pressures on costs forced the company to develop a complex and extended supply chain, thereby supporting the increased variety requirements and decreasing costs but at greatly increased lead times. A new product group – children's' fashion skiwear – was met by demands from retailers for early delivery to meet the 'back-to-school' season.

Sport Obermeyer undertook a variety of quick response initiatives to relieve the problem imposed by retailer demands for shortened lead times. One step was to invest in computer systems, the other was to anticipate material requirements, and to preposition them to be able to commence manufacture as soon as orders were received. A third step was to use airfreight to expedite deliveries from the manufacturing partners in the Far East. They also persuaded some of the important large retailers to place their orders early, thereby providing the company with early information on the likely popularity of colours, styles, and so on. Despite these initiatives the problems of stockouts and markdowns persisted.

It will be recalled (Chapter 3) that Skinner (*op cit*) and Porter (*op cit*) identified problems such as those reported by Fisher *et al* and suggested that they narrow the focus of management such that productivity, decisions dominate strategic concern for identifying and delivering customer value. In this regard supply chain managers, who respond to customer and consumer demand for ever increasing productivity, miss opportunities to identify and create specific customer/consumer value and, therefore, the opportunity to be proactive and develop value strategies which deliver sustainable competitive advantage.

Sport Obermeyer's solution was found in an *accurate response* model. The model is a complex computerised mathematical model which creates an optimal production schedule which fills non-reactive capacity with styles for which demand forecasts are most likely to be accurate. This then releases reactive capacity to make as many of the unpredictable styles as possible. What Sport Obermeyer realised was that the capacity used to make ski products changes in character as the season progresses. Early in the season, when there are no orders, capacity is non-reactive and production decisions are based solely on predictions rather than a reaction to market demand. As orders are received, the information they contain enables the capacity to become reactive.

This example illustrates the problems that can occur within structured supply chains. What the case study does not identify is the extent to which either the target customers' expectations change during the 'season' or the alternative possibility that there are different customer types served. One group may be 'innovators' or 'fashion trend setters', the other group may have price/quality motives in that they seek quality in preference to leading-edge fashion and consequently are prepared to purchase later in the season safe in the knowledge (based upon experience) that markdowns will occur. Clearly in both situations the value expectations identified are better met by different value creation/delivery strategies. The former may well be prepared to pay a premium for customised products as with the Levi or Nike approach. The other customer group may be attracted by even lower prices that may be possible by identifying alternative distribution channels.

The supply chain: advantages and disadvantages

The Sport Obermeyer example identifies the shift that has occurred within distribution management from a discipline that was (and continues to be for many organisations) concerned primarily with:

> The process of planning, implementing and controlling the efficient, cost-effective flow and storage of raw materials, in-process inventory, finished goods, and related information flow from point of origin to point-of-consumption for the purpose of conforming to customer requirements.   (Council of Logistics Management)

Supply chain management first appeared in the literature in the mid-1980s but as Cooper *et al* (1997) suggest it is based upon fundamental assumptions emanating from managing inter-organisational operations (which can be traced back to channels research in the 1960s); systems integration research in the 1960s, and more recently on information management and inventory control information. Supply chain management has been defined by members of 'The International Centre for Competitive Excellence' in 1994 as:

> Supply chain management is the integration of business processes from end-user through original suppliers that provide products, services and information and add value for customers.

Cooper *et al* suggest the scope of the supply chain can be defined in terms of the number of firms involved within the supply chain and the activities and functions involved. Initially the scope of the supply chain was across firms but now includes internal integration within organisations before expansion to other firms. Important from the point of view of this discussion is the direction in which supply chain planning and coordination 'travels'. Initially the view held was that it covered the flow of goods from supplier through manufacturing and distribution to the end user (Keith and Webber: 1982). Stevens (1989) expanded this scope both upstream and downstream to include sources of supply and points of consumption. The number of functions and activities included in supply chain management varies. Common points of agreement include information systems and 'planning and control', with other views taking in marketing functions (including product design and development) and customer service functions.

The objectives of supply chain management have also received various treatment. The suggestions include productivity based objectives such as to 'lower the total amount of resources required to provide the necessary level of customer service to a specific segment' (Houlihan: 1985; Jones and Riley: 1985). Stevens (*op cit*) refers to synchronising the requirements of the customer with the flow of materials from suppliers. Cooper *et al* (1997) suggest objectives of inventory investment reduction within the supply chain, increasing customer service and building competitive advantage for the supply chain, while Lalonde (1997) includes the objective of adding value. Again the inference to be drawn concerning the purpose or *raison d'être* of supply chain management is one of a support function that moves towards the end-user customer.

Cooper *et al* conclude that '. . . confusion exists in terms of what supply chain management actually is. Nevertheless, some commonalities do seem to exist . . .'. These, they suggest, are that supply chain management:

- evolves through several states of increasing intra- and inter-organisational integration and coordination. In its broadest sense it spans the entire chain from initial sourcing to end-user customer;
- involves independent organisations, thus the management of intra- and inter-organisational relationships is an essential feature;
- includes bidirectional flows of 'products' and information and the management of these activities;
- seeks to fulfil the goals of providing high customer value with an appropriate use of resources, and to build competitive chain advantages.

Once again the inference that may be drawn is that supply chain management is a support function. It is essentially operational and reinforces strategy implementation.

Supply chain processes, components and structure

Cooper *et al* continue by developing a conceptual framework for supply chain management. The basis of the structure is three components: business processes, management components and supply chain structure.

Supply chain management processes are based upon a definition of business processes: '. . . a structured and measured set of activities designed to produce a specific output for a particular customer or market'. To this Cooper *et al* add: 'A process is a specific ordering of work activities across time and place, with a beginning, an end, and clearly identified inputs and outputs, a structure for action'. This is particularly useful for both supply chain *and* value chain analysis and will be returned to in subsequent chapters. The authors remind us that supply chain (and for that matter, value chain) processes invariably cross intra- and inter-organisational boundaries. In their search for consensus concerning supply chain processes they suggest those identified by the International Centre for Competitive Excellence: customer relationship management, demand management, order fulfilment, manufacturing flow management, procurement, product development and commercialisation. This comprehensive list emphasises the increasingly strategic role of the supply chain. For example, customer relationship management is described as 'identifying key customer targets and then developing and implementing programs with key customers'. This does suggest a prescriptive and proactive role but because the 'programs' are not identified it is difficult to comment beyond the suggestion of an attempt to integrate supply chain management with strategic direction.

Supply chain management components have a common theme amongst authors and Cooper *et al* identify these across all business processes and supply chain members. The authors' synthesis of these suggests ten components, the first six being: planning and control, work structure, organisation structure, product flow, facility structure, information flow facility structure (all seen as tangible and measurable in terms of direct influence and impact on change within the supply chain). The remaining four are: management methods, power and leadership structure, risk and reward structure, and culture and attitude (suggested to be intangible, difficult to assess but nevertheless influential factors). These components are suggested to span '. . . the range of management decision making within a firm'. They are essentially operational components, typically used to implement strategy. Product structure issues are concerned with coordination across the supply chain and the product portfolio. The inference is the concern for supplier capabilities and capacities and suggests a strategic interest.

Supply chain structure is described in terms of concern for complexity, number of suppliers (and availability of specific suppliers). There is an inferred importance of the amount of value that suppliers will contribute, but the precise nature of how structure should be developed remains vague, for example: 'The closeness of the relationship at different points in the supply chain *will differ*. More partnership characteristics *will probably* be exhibited with key suppliers or customers. Critical components *may* need closer management further up the channel to avoid shutting down production lines' (italics are the author's). The proposals here are more of a partial checklist which omits a vital point made by Sutton (1998) that as business expands the 'virtual concept' coordination becomes an essential strategic characteristic and objective and accordingly responsibilities require clear definition, understanding and acceptance throughout.

Waller (1998) reviews the role of supply chain management as business 'globalises'. He discusses 'customer driven' logistics as an increasingly accepted concept: '. . . as businesses begin to understand that their future existence depends upon the loyalty of the end users of their products'.

The answer, suggests Waller, is for organisations to ensure that every business activity along the 'total supply chain' is geared toward customer satisfaction. He adds that a flexible manufacturing response is an essential feature. Waller claims that 'visibility and control of the end-to-end supply chain provides manufacturers with a mechanism for ensuring customer satisfaction and capturing customer needs'. But does it? Waller continues by claiming that 'For retailers, it has been their focus on the supply chain back into suppliers that has provided the mechanism for value chain visibility and control as a formula for generating effective end-delivered cost and consumer satisfaction'. He cites Marks and Spencer as having 'long been regarded as leaders in this'.

Events at Marks and Spencer in 1999 suggest this is not so. Similarly another 'market dominant', Sainsbury's (the UK former market leader in food retailing) found it too was confronted with customer dissatisfaction! The reality, it appears, is that supply chain structure priorities were more focussed on logistics and operational productivity than customer satisfaction. In the 'heady' days of the mid-1990s retailers were expanding as a response to customers' expectation of availability and convenience. During this period an annual report from Sainsbury's published the impact on overall profitability of its increased logistics productivity. This suggests the dominant focus of many (not all) supply chain streams is supply (downstream) oriented. Waller assumes a 'consumer steady state' and structures manufacturing and supply operations to meet customer satisfaction. The problems that Marks and Spencer, and to a degree Sainsbury's, have experienced are not because they mismanaged the *operational effectiveness* of the business but rather because they missed the shift in customer expectations and did not respond (have not responded) strategically. In other words they failed to monitor their customers' value expectations and respond with a relevant *value strategy*.

Thus it could be argued that the supply chain has outlived its usefulness. Waller suggests modifications that may increase productivity through cost trade-offs. These include outsourcing and the whole issue of core competencies, shared product development and, for retailers, the formation of regional buying alliances to support their international aspirations.

At this juncture it appears that a rethinking of *what* it is we are attempting to achieve and *how*, by *whom*, *when* and *where*, and clearly *why*, is essential.

THE VALUE CHAIN PERSPECTIVE

O'Sullivan and Geringer (1993) remind us of the purpose of value chain analysis. Given that the organisation has limited access to resources, value chain analysis has, as its primary objective, the purpose of ensuring that the resources of the enterprise work in a coordinated way such that full advantage may be taken of market based opportunities. It follows that the analysis should identify the optimal configuration of both the macro- and micro-business systems that will maximise value expectations. Thus the conceptual concerns of the supply chain and the value chain begin to converge.

It follows that to take full advantage of the current resources available, three activities are involved. First the value expectations of the end user (customer) must be established; then the resources and structures required should be identified; and finally the value delivery systems required to deliver the expected value must be structured. This may introduce alternative structures that include inputs from other organisations within the macro-business systems.

The value chain: early perspectives and characteristics

Porter (1985) proposed the value chain as a means by which business actions that transform inputs could be identified (in other words, value chain stages).

Furthermore, he proposed that stages in the value chain be explored for inter-relationships and common characteristics. This could (he argued) lead to opportunities for cost reduction and differentiation. A more detailed view of the value chain and its efficacy is that its purpose at either level (macro- or micro-business systems) is to:

1. identify the business actions (stages) which transform inputs;
2. identify relationships (commonalities and interdependences) between stages for both systems. Within the organisation the micro-system is used to identify meaningful differentiation characteristics which are unique, or exclusive, to the organisation;
3. identify costs and cost profiles within the organisation together with cost advantages that do or could exist;
4. choose the business's competitive positioning:
    ● market segments
    ● customer applications/end uses
    ● technologies;
5. identify alternative value chain delivery structures (that is, interrelationships internally and between business units within the industry delivery structure – the macro-business system).

Brown (1997) pursues a conventional approach to the value chain but does add emphasis to the need for an industry perspective:

> The value chain is a tool to disaggregate a business into strategically relevant activities. This enables identification of the source of competitive advantage by performing these activities more cheaply or better than its competitors. Its value chain is part of a larger stream of strategic activities carried out by other members of the channel – suppliers, distributors and customers.

He introduces two additional perspectives to the value chain: the emphasis on links or relationships between activities in the value chain; and, the firm's competitive scope as a source of competitive advantage. Links and relationships between buyers, suppliers and intermediaries can lower cost or enhance differentiation. Competitive scope may concern the range of products or customer types (segment scope); the regional coverage (geographic scope); its integration (vertical scope); or its activities across a range of related industries (industry scope).

The changes in, and convergence of, information and communications technologies are identified as significant issues by Brown. He illustrates changes in value chain structures in newspaper production, video entertainment and 'branchless' banking: 'The emerging value chains in these examples promise to restructure those industries and redistribute value among different components and players in the value chain'.

The impact of these changes will be very significant, with irrevocable shifts in retailing and distribution, the elimination of intermediaries, shifts in market share and moves towards mass customisation. Each of these views of the value chain starts with the organisation and its industry, onto which customer interests are grafted. While they now include the role of outsourcing to achieve effective value delivery it could be argued that the value chain concept would be more effective if in fact it is created around customer value expectations.

The value chain: a strategic management perspective

Scott (1998) takes a strategic management view. He uses the value chain concept to identify the tasks necessary to deliver a product or service to the market. His approach is to combine segmentation and value chain analysis and he suggests a number of questions:

- In which areas of the value chain does the firm have to be outstanding to succeed in each customer segment?
- What skills or competencies are necessary to deliver an outstanding result in those areas of the value chain?
- Are they the same for each segment or do they differ radically?

He argues:

> All firms, whether industrial or services have a value chain, each part requires a strategy to ensure that it drives value creation for the firm overall. For a piece of the value chain to have a strategy means that the individual managing is clear about what capabilities the firm requires to deliver effective market impact.

It follows that the firm may not have the relevant competencies to match opportunities. Two questions follow:

1. Is the structure of the organisation relevant and are its managers competent?
2. Can the firm compete effectively by forming a partnership/alliance with other firm(s)?

The core elements of Scott's value chain fall into seven areas:

1. operations strategy;
2. marketing, sales and service strategy;
3. innovation strategy;
4. financial strategy;
5. human resource strategy;
6. information technology strategy;
7. lobbying position with government.

Coordination across the value chain is essential and Scott identifies the fact that traditionally this did not occur. The relationship between a company's value chain and its SBUs (strategic business units) is discussed. He suggests that certain parts of the value chain are likely to be common to all its SBUs. These include human resources, information technology and large parts of its financial and selling functions. It could be argued that the information requirements of individual SBUs might differ and require specific services. It could also be argued that in a market/customer focussed business (and most make this claim) the core elements of the business should be capable of developing specific service inputs to ensure competitive advantage.

'Customer-centric' thinking

Slywotzky and Morrison (1997) discuss the value chain in the context of 'customer-centric' thinking. They suggest that the traditional value chain begins with the company's core competencies and its assets and then moves to other inputs and raw materials, to a product offering, through marketing channels and finally to the customer. In customer-centric thinking the modern value chain reverses the approach. The customer becomes the first link and everything else follows: '. . . everything else is driven by the customer'. Managers should think of:

1. their customers' needs and priorities;
2. what channels can satisfy those needs and priorities;
3. the service and products best suited to flow through those channels;
4. the inputs and raw materials required to create the products and services;
5. the assets and core competencies essential to the inputs and raw materials.

And:

> The value of any product or service is the result of its ability to meet a customer's priorities. Customer priorities are simply the things that are so important to customers that they will pay a premium for them or, when they can't get them, they will switch suppliers.

Slywotzky and Morrison are suggesting that value opportunities are distinguished by understanding customers' priorities and monitoring priorities for change. They give examples. Nicolas Hayek (Swatch) understood that a growing segment of consumers would buy watches based upon taste, emotion and fashion rather than on prestige. Jack Welch (General Electric) identified customers who saw less value in the product and more in services and financing.

This suggests a broad perspective of value, well beyond direct benefits and one that encompasses the nuances of basic criteria. Basic value criteria are broad characteristics like security, performance, aesthetics, convenience, economy and reliability. However, at the next level these may be seen to be wide-ranging criteria.

The approach suggested by these authors would change the traditional value chain such that it takes on a customer-driven perspective. Slywotzky and Morrison go further:

> In the old economic order, the focus was on the immediate customer. Today, business no longer has the luxury of thinking about just the immediate customer. To find and keep customers, our perspective has to be radically expanded. In a value migration world, our vision must include two, three, or even four customers along the value chain. So, for example, a component supplier must understand the economic motivations of the manufacturer who buys the components, the distributor who takes the manufacturer's products to sell, and the end use consumer.

Value creation: a strategy/structure model

The organisation's value chain becomes merged with those of other value chain members. An important feature is the role of information management that provides a coordinating activity. Other authors have made contributions. Of particular interest is that of Normann and Ramirez (1993) who suggest:

> Strategy is the art of creating value . . . the way a company defines its business and links together with the only two resources that really matter in today's economy: knowledge and relationships on an organisation's competencies and customers.

They see the value chain as an analytical tool that facilitates strategy: '. . . strategy is primarily the art of positioning a company in the right place on the value chain – the right business, the right products and market segments, the right value-adding activities'.

They go on to add:

> Their focus of strategic analysis is not the company or even the industry, but the value creating system itself, within which different economic actors – suppliers, business partners, allies, customers – work together to co-produce value. Their key strategic task is the reconfiguration of roles and relationships among this constellation of actors in order to mobilise the creation of value in new forms and by new players . . . their underlying strategic goal is to create an ever improving fit between competencies and customers . . .

The value chain has an expanded role. It becomes an integral component in the strategy process: '. . . the evaluation of the company's core competence and its fit in the overall creation of value'. The questions to be asked are:

- What is the combination of value drivers required by the target customer group?
- What are the implications for differentiation decisions?
- What are the implications for costs: do economies of scale or scope exist?
- Are there opportunities for trade-offs to occur between the value creation system partners?

Normann and Ramirez also offer an example of the application of fresh thinking. They use IKEA as an example of a company that epitomises the new logic of value:

> . . . any product or service is really the result of a complicated set of activities: myriad economic transactions and institutional arrangements among suppliers and customers, employees and managers, teams of technical and organisational specialists . . . what we usually think of as prospects or services are really frozen activities, concrete manifestations of the relationships among actors in a value creating system.

The IKEA example is interesting because the company has:

> systematically redefined the roles, relationships and organisational practices in the furniture business. The result is an integrated business system that invents value by matching the various capabilities of participants more efficiently and effectively than was ever the case in the past.

This approach has been extended into the relationship between IKEA and its customers. Customer relationships are based upon the customers' acceptance of a new view of the division of labour in which the customers 'agree' to undertake key tasks traditionally done by manufacturers and retailers – the assembly and delivery of products to customer homes. The value delivered to the customer is a well designed, quality 'manufactured' product priced anywhere from 25 per cent to 50 per cent below competitor offers.

This notion is further developed by Vollman and Cordon (1999) who explain the derivation of demand management in a logistics context as:

> Essentially, a company has a 'pipeline' of capacity which is filled in the short-run with customer orders, and in the long-run with forecasts of demand. The point is that order entry consumes the forecast, and demand management explicitly integrates both of these processes.

They suggest a more current view to be one that includes a band of knowledge, and expand this argument to suggest that in a manufacturing context 'knowledge' is an understanding of precise requirements.

Normann and Ramirez (1993) suggest that value is created, not in sequential chains, but in constellations: 'The role of business is to involve customers in creating value, taking advantage of the expertise, skills and knowledge possessed by each member of the value creation system'. As value creating systems become complex and varied so do the component transaction relationships needed to produce and deliver the value offer. A company's principal task becomes the reconfiguration of its relationships and business systems. However it should not overlook the production, logistics and service activities in value production. For example, automobiles and consumer durable products are a complex of each of these.

Normann and Ramirez were predicting the growth of the virtual organisation in which the 'company's principal task becomes the configuration of its relationships and business systems'. However, for this to be managed effectively both upstream and downstream relationships are involved, and the task becomes one of identifying specific partners for specific processes; the coproductivity concept becomes multi-directional. Slywotzky and Morrison's comment concerning the importance of considering value migration assumes even greater significance. There are important issues such as conformity, consistency and continuity of the value offer to be managed. Not only do these have to meet the customers' expectations but they become part of the 'brand'. Thus the company should be mindful of the fact that for the end-user customer the product is an entity and the 'brand owner' is responsible for coordinating conformity, consistency and continuity of all aspects of product performance and support service.

It has been suggested that many arguments about creating value are only about customer satisfaction and assume profit may be taken for granted. However, companies need to think about their comparative advantages in the value chain even before they start thinking about how to reconfigure it for their customers. If they do not, they are not making strategy; they are simply engaging in business process re-engineering.

The value chain comprises the supply chain *and* the demand chain

Beech (1998) argues for an integration of the supply and demand chains:

> The challenge can only be met by developing a holistic strategic framework that leverages the generation and understanding of demand effectiveness with supply efficiency. First, organisations must bring a multi-enterprise view to their supply chains. They need to be capable of working cooperatively with other organisations in the chain rather than seeking to outdo them. Secondly they must recognise the distinct supply and demand processes that must be integrated in order to gain the greatest value.

He suggests three key elements:

● the core processes of the supply and demand chains, viewed from a broad cross-enterprise vantage point rather as discrete functions;
● the integrating processes that create the links between the supply and demand chains;
● the supporting infrastructure that makes such integration possible.

Beech makes an important contribution to the construction and operation of value chains and this will be considered in a later chapter.

Bornheim *et al* (2001), in considering the impact of information communication technology on the development of value chains, discuss the decline of traditional hierarchies and the growth of digital value chains:

What we are starting to see is that different elements of new value chains display different economics, skill sets, and so on, forcing them to think and subsequently organise along new organisational boundaries. And contrary to the old hierarchies, supplementing their organisations with networks of, for example, suppliers to offer a better or cheaper product, the new value chains do not start with existing organisations and their capabilities, but rather with market opportunities. On the basis of these opportunities, products and services are designed and the necessary web of value providers is assembled.

CURRENT PERSPECTIVES

The application of the value chain approach has largely been through Internet based networks and relationship developments through partnership. Activity has been frenetic (early 2000s) and outcomes far from clear.

The automotive industry

One of the largest developments has been in the automotive industry where both General Motors and Ford moved quickly to create Internet based exchanges to manage their procurement activities. Tait (2000) reported the GM and Ford developments, identifying the anticipated benefits: 'Beyond crude dollar savings there would be a better information flow and more low-level supplier involvement in product development . . . other car makers would be persuaded to join the exchanges . . .'. Tait also identified potential problems. Large suppliers have either established their own networks (or are considering doing so). But there are general concerns regarding price concessions that may be expected, the fact that the *trade exchanges* plan to take a 'percentage' of all deals transacted through their systems, the problem that being involved with TradeXchange may preclude them from any business with AutoXchange.

The two 'exchanges' have different approaches. Ford stresses that AutoXchange will be an 'open architecture' network in which ideas and product design can take place. It will also offer suppliers 'private portals' so that they can retain some sense of their own procurement networks. AutoXchange may become an independent e-commerce business within an independent board and management within a year of it being established. TradeXchange will require all suppliers to join. Its primary goal is to lower the costs of all participants. Tait reports the comments of an Oracle executive who suggests that if too many exchanges are established efficiencies will be reduced.

Burt *et al* (2000) report on the expansion of the trade exchange e-commerce activities of both North American and European motor vehicle manufacturers. They also reports on 'expert views' concerning distribution developments. Sales have shown rapid growth, such that both Ford and GM have established their own online retail outlets '. . . which could eventually bypass traditional dealers, regulatory reform permitting'. They suggest that procurement consolidation through Internet exchanges and product consolidation through mergers and acquisitions are not unrelated. They see them as strategies that are ultimately defensive: 'Most are girding themselves for an eventual market contraction, hoping that Internet schemes and product innovation will offset falling sales. Cash-rich companies are also contemplating deals that will fill gaps in their product and geographic portfolio'.

These comments from Burt *et al* suggest the reasons why the value chain is different from the supply chain. It is a strategic concept in that it can identify trends and opportunities as well as identifying and suggesting virtual solutions. The supply chain, by contrast, typically works within a shorter timespace. Given the 'M and A' activities in the automobile manufacturing industry there is an obvious requirement for flexibility; the trade exchange approach offers this. The fact too that surplus capacity exists on a global basis makes the Ford CEO's statement that the company could ultimately outsource manufacturing more than a possibility. Given a value chain approach Ford would still own the brand and be seen by customers *as the brand*; this is the point made by Sutton (*op cit*).

Both vehicle design and parts services are clearly seen as outsourcing possibilities in the value chain approach. Burt *et al* report on a Ford initiative to create a London-based 'design centre' for product design. They make the point that since product platforms are becoming important in the industry (common chassis and shared engines and transmission units), it follows that design is playing an increasingly important role in competition for sales.

Burt *et al* report on developments in relationship management and technology management in component supplies. *Supplier parks* are the logistics solution to filling the gap between final assembly and component manufacturing. These satellite operations have resulted in suppliers taking more responsibility for more of the component assembly, delivering entire systems at the time required by manufacturers. They suggest that 'just-in-time' has now become 'just-in-sequence'. In the drive to reduce inventory levels (and therefore costs), parts and assemblies are delivered to the 'line' just at the point in time they need to be installed. There are both advantages and disadvantages. Manufacturers relieve themselves of inventory costs (and the infrastructure costs, such as storage). Component suppliers obtain long-term contracts and often become partners in other projects, product development being an obvious area.

Some suppliers (such as Valeo, the French components manufacturer) are critical of supplier parks. They argue that they work well in predictable and stable manufacturing situations. They also argue that 'commonality' of components and systems means they manufacture for several different customers, hence they prefer to supply from a central or large existing plant where they have economies of scale. Burt *et al* cite Garel Rhys (a motor industry specialist) who suggests the trend towards supplier parks offers manufacturers the benefits of outsourcing, but control is retained, as is a physical link, with suppliers. Suppliers may well be concerned and are clearly faced with a dilemma as the large manufacturers rationalise supplier bases *and* move into partnerships through mergers and acquisitions.

As the system evolves it becomes clear that the benefits are differential. It is suggested that large components with customised design often see benefits from shared locations. By contrast, 'commodity' items can be delivered in volume, quickly, to respond to unexpected demand increases.

The value objectives expressed by a wide range of brands and product applications are being addressed by strategic alliances. Often these extend to geographical coverage. One such example is the objectives announced by VW and Daimler/Chrysler in which both companies took 34 per cent of their target companies. The VW/Scania alliance offers VW a larger presence in commercial vehicle markets by expanding its product range. Mitsubishi gives Daimler/Chrysler key access to small car platforms and engine technology and, importantly, access to Asian sales potential where Daimler/Chrysler has a target of increasing sales from four per cent to 25 per cent of total revenues (Burt: 2000). Another important point made by Burt is the growing attraction of alliances in preference to acquisition. This offers considerable benefits for a relatively small equity stake. The onerous tasks of marking bids is avoided by the company which '. . . still gets a boardroom voice and the promise of joint purchasing and distribution savings in the future'.

FMCG service products and consumer durables applications

An interesting market segmentation application of the Internet has been introduced by Glynwed, the manufacturer of Aga cookers. The company is converting its website into a lifestyle portal. The aim is to offer a single sales channel for products appealing to people who own (or aspire to own) an Aga or Rayburn cooker. 'Glynwed's vision is of a portal where green-wellied web surfers would be able to order fine wines, check out the latest four wheel drive, or book a holiday in Tuscany' (Burt *et al*). Glynwed estimates that three-quarters of households with web access have an income in excess of $60,000 a year, and this fits well with the profile of Aga buyers. The company plans to launch a website targeted at customers and dealers in the £500 million commercial food service business. The objective is both to promote sales but also to help customers contain the excess spending of operations branch managers.

Heller (2000) offers an insightful view of the changing perspective of brand value. Heller uses the problems of a number of major companies to develop an argument concerning consumer attitudes towards both brands and value. He cites the large decreases in capitalisation of both Coca-Cola and Gillette together with the decreases in popularity of retail brands such as Marks and Spencer, Somerfield and Arcadia.

Heller suggests that e-commerce activities by competitors have made a significant impact, certainly on the retailers. The high gearing of many 'bricks-and-mortar' retailers can make a ten per cent shift loss in volume a loss crisis. But it is consumer perceptions that are, possibly, more significant. Heller argues that consumer commitment to one brand (an 'Eighties/Nineties' phenomenon) has fragmented; meanwhile consumer power has increased and this is reflected by consumer perceptions of value. He argues that a company such as Marks and Spencer 'alienated its middle-class shoppers with falling quality'. The basis of Heller's argument is that these companies are failing to monitor changes in customer expectations (and their responses to competitive alternatives), or even worse, they are assuming that they can manipulate the quality/cost relationship without the customer noticing! Marks and Spencer found to their cost that this could not be done. Heller cites research (which confirms similar research elsewhere) that '. . . shows conclusively that customers desert even the strongest brand if prices rise above the perceived value . . . you can't afford to lose support anywhere in a climate of rapidly proliferating alternatives'. Heller also raises another important issue: the relationships between the organisation and its 'markets': 'Employees, for example, are the visible face of the brand. The suppliers are its prime agents of quality – squeeze their prices or unceremoniously dump them and, as M&S has found, there is trouble in store. Nor can you ignore the opinion-formers, who can rapidly undermine any image'. Heller also suggests the Internet (and e-commerce and e-tailers) has had an impact on identifying alternatives for consumers and that 'word-of-mouse' and 'share-of-mind' backed by huge marketing expenditure has significant impact. But as yet this, he argues, is *theory* because it cannot be fully tested as the Internet marketplace is still immature. What is now available, as the Glynwed example suggests, is a means of targeting relevant customer groups more cost-efficiently, using Internet facilities.

The attraction of Internet based procurement is strong in retailing. Kingfisher, a UK retail international conglomerate with 2700 stores in 13 countries and 115,000 plus employees and major brands, has felt margin and share price pressures. Kingfisher is using knowledge technology and relationship management to establish a global supply base with three elements to its strategy. Collective buying (of common products) across the group's outlets has led to cost savings *and* increased scale when dealing with manufacturers. Direct sourcing, particularly for own brand products, has resulted in starting savings; and a more towards own brand development has had an impact on margins (Burt *et al*).

IMPLICATIONS: A VALUE STRATEGY

The foregoing examples suggest important and significant changes may make strategy decision making more effective. Day (1999) advocates 'the market driven organisation' with its essentially customer focussed business philosophy. He develops an argument in which he suggests that customer value is delivered more effectively by assuming that the value delivery processes are '. . . more like loops of interacting processes. Instead of a value chain, a linear process, we have a value cycle, which is a self-reinforcing process . . . Instead of viewing the process as a chain that delivers value *to* customers, the market-driven firm views the process as an interaction *with* customers'. It is difficult to criticise this view, because it is what successful businesses have done for many years. A point that can be made is that as the value cycle is a philosophical approach to developing value based strategies, the value chain approach is a means by which value based strategies are implemented.

There are a number of long established examples of value chain operations delivering customer value! The example of the Prato district in Italy is an example of a value production and coordination response to markets that became increasingly flexible. The textile industry in Prato fragmented into a number of 'specialist shops': 'To combine them into a flexible production system and to reduce their independence on large firms, it was necessary to coordinate their separate skills in autonomous federations – federations that attended to the currents of fashion. Such coordination became, as of the late 1950s, the function of the *impannatore* (Piore and Sabel: 1984). These authors recall that the *impannatore* was a descendant of the medieval merchant and early-modern *Verleger* (putter-outers). The *impannatore* became '. . . a designer, responsible for shaping and responding to fashion, as well as for organising production'. Clearly what we are considering is resurrecting an approach to business based upon identifying customer value expectations, responding with a value proposition, producing/creating the value, communicating and delivering the value and servicing the value. The following chapter identifies the characteristics of a viable value chain strategy and this example is explored in detail in Chapter 12.

SUMMARY

At this point it is suggested that value chain management has superseded supply chain management. At best supply chain management served the functions of facilitator and as a means of differentiating a product offer by adding generic or specific elements of service. By contrast value chain management is broader. It is customer-centric, often working with customers to identify problems – then solutions. Hence it assumes the role of innovator, integrator and operations (production, logistics and service) coordinator. Value chain management majors on codestiny, coproductivity and prosumerism to ensure optimal value is delivered to stakeholders.

REFERENCES ●

Beech, J. (1998), 'The supply-demand nexus' in Gattorna, J. (ed.), *Strategic Supply Chain Alignment*, Gower Press, Aldershot.

Bornheim, S. P., J. Weppler and O. Ohlen (2001), *e-roadmapping digital strategising for the new economy*, Palgrave, Basingstoke.

Brown, L. (1997), *Competitive Marketing Strategy*, Nelson, Melbourne.

Burt, M., J. Harvey, R. Guthrie, A. Voyle, R. Islam and N. Tait (2000), 'Carmakers take two routes to global growth', *The Financial Times*, 26/27 February.

Cooper, M. C., D. M. Lambert and J. D. Pugh (1997), 'Supply chain management: more than a new name for logistics', *The International Journal of Logistics Management*, Vol. 8, No. 1.

Day, G. (1999), *The Market Driven Organisation*, The Free Press, New York.

Fisher, M. L., J. H. Hammond, W. R. Obermeyer and A. Raman (1994), 'Making supply meet demand in an uncertain world', *Harvard Business Review*, May/June.

Heller, R. (2000), 'Man of the people', *Business Review Weekly*, 15 September.

Houlihan, J. B. (1985), 'International supply chain management', *International Journal of Physical Distribution and Materials Management*, Vol. 15, No. 1.

Jones, T. C. and D. W. Riley (1985), 'Using inventory for competitive advantage through supply chain management', *International Journal of Physical Distribution and Materials Management*, Vol. 15, No. 5.

Keith, O. R. and M. D. Webber (1982), 'Supply chain management: logistics catches up with strategy', *Outlook*, cit. Christopher, M. (1992), *Logistics: The Strategic Issues*, Chapman and Hall, London.

Lalonde, B. J. (1997), 'Supply chain management: myth or reality?' *Supply Chain Management Review*, Spring, Vol. 1, Issue 1.

Norman, R. and R. Ramirez (1993), 'From value chain to value constellation: designing interactive strategy', *Harvard Business Review*, July/August.

O'Sullivan, L. and J. M. Geringer (1993), 'Harnessing the power of your value chain', *Long Range Planning*, Vol. 26, No. 2.

Piore, M. and C. F. Sabel (1984), *The Second Industrial Divide: Possibilities for Prosperity*, Basic Books, New York.

Porter, M. E. (1985), *Competitive Advantage*, The Free Press, New York.

Scott, M. C. (1998), *Value Drivers*, Wiley, Chichester.

Slywotsky, A. J., D. J. Morrison and R. Andelman (1997), *The Profit Zone*, Wiley, Chichester.

Stevens, G. C. (1989), 'Integration of the supply chain', *International Journal of Physical Distribution and Logistics Management*, Vol. 19, No. 8.

Sutton, C. (1998), *Strategic Concepts*, Macmillan Business, Basingstoke.

Tait, N. (2000), 'Car giants plan joint electronic trade exchange', *The Financial Times*, 26/27 February (with contributions from Burt and Voyle).

Vollman, T. and C. Cordon (1999), 'Building a smarter demand chain', in *Mastering Information Management (Part 4, The Smarter Supply Chain)*, Financial Times, 22 February.

Waller, A. (1998), 'The globalisation of business: the role of supply chain management', *Management Focus*, Issue 11, Cranfield School of Management.

6

Value Based Organisations: the Value Chain Approach

The student will be able to:

- differentiate between alternative perspectives of value – the customer and the organisational views;
- discuss the importance of value-in-use as a concept for effective planning;
- understand the development of value chain theory and its application to strategic analysis.

INTRODUCTION

A successful value based strategy is one that enhances *value-in-use* characteristics of the product or service offered in its value proposition. There is also the essential requirement of meeting organisational objectives and typically these are quantitative and qualitative.

Earlier chapters introduced the concepts of value-in-use, consumer and producer surpluses. It will be recalled that they are linked by the price mechanism:

Value-in-use   = Consumer surplus + *Price*
Producer surplus = Total revenue   – Total variable cost
                   (*Price* × volume)

The value chain approach provides an organisation the opportunity to evaluate a number of options that either increase value-in-use (by 'enhancing' the attributes of the consumer surplus), increasing the producer surplus (by optimising operations costs), or perhaps achieving changes in both.

Value-in-use is the end-user or *consumer value* delivered in response to identified opportunities. It represents a package of benefits comprising the quantitative attribute, price, and qualitative features that often are specific to the customer or customer segment. Clearly there are aspects of qualitative features that may be quantified. These metrics are introduced to measure relative market performance, and as internal organisational performance measures. The point to be made is that they differentiate the product or service for the customer/end-user and enhance the consumer surplus. For business-to-business markets the benefits do contain a quantitative element. For example, the reduction of service intervals, the extended period of a warranty, a replacement 'vehicle' during maintenance, and field technical advice are all elements of value that may be quantified. Customer value is then the 'balance' between customer benefits realised and the customer's costs of acquiring the benefits. A positive balance suggests the consumer/customer is obtaining value from a transaction. If customer benefits > customer acquisition costs then by definition we are delivering value to our customers. Figure 6.1 illustrates the process by which the organisation attempts to increase the value in use for customers by differentiating its product-service benefits, thereby making the product more desirable *at the same price*. This may be achieved by *enhancing* the benefits or by *decreasing* the customer's acquisition costs. The suggested benefit improvements (see Figure 6.1) have two purposes: they offer additional value to the original value proposition and differentiate the product such that 'exclusivity' is established and customer loyalty increased. Using the value chain approach enables more options to be considered, both in the number of ways that the product/service may be differentiated and in the cost-effectiveness of alternative strategies.

Value opportunities: identifying options

Organisational value is the value realised from the producer surplus. Within the context of value chain operations organisational value is very different to that of the individual organisation. Clearly the concern is for profitability, productivity and cash flow performance but the difference is that individual performance is linked with the overall performance of the value production and delivery system. Each member or partner depends upon others within the organisation to maximise organisational value. Often the choice is simple. Without the value chain and its requirements of cooperation and coordination no organisational value can be created. The Du Pont control model may be readily applied to value chain performance. Figure 6.2 reflects the basic elements of organisational value (profitability, productivity, investment management and shareholder value management) and has served as a fundamental tool for planning and control for numerous organisations. Given the coordination aspect of the value chain the model offers a useful vehicle for exploring value chain combinations.

The essence of a successful value chain strategy is the maximisation of both customer and organisational value and it assumes that value chain member participation is predicated on the basis that participation ensures the indi-

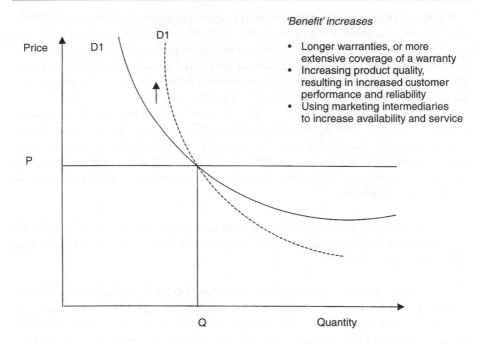

Figure 6.1 Enhancing customer value-in-use by increasing the customer benefits-in-use or decreasing customer costs

'Profit'		**Sales**		**Assets**		**'Profit'**
Sales	x	**Assets**	x	**Equity**	=	**Equity**
Margin management		Asset base management		Financial management		Risk/return management
[PROFITABILITY]		[PRODUCTIVITY]		[INVESTMENT MANAGEMENT]		[SHAREHOLDER VALUE MANAGEMENT]

Figure 6.2 The Du Pont planning and control model

vidual organisation greater returns than those available if there is no participation. The 'philosophy' is simple; without the cooperation of other members
no end-user satisfaction or value can occur and, therefore, nor can revenues
and profits. It may be extended by considering the benefits accruing through
membership of a larger organisation, one from which a share of a much larger
activity will be greater than the returns available from individual activities.

Clearly markets can be expanded. Simply through participation and cooperation (within the value chain) *available markets* are by definition larger and
subsequently *penetrated markets* are also larger. If the elements of the Du Pont
model are examined on this basis some obvious assumptions can be made
about the options available to maximise revenues, profitability, productivity
and shareholder value.

It follows that *sales* can be expanded because markets hitherto unavailable may become available due to partnership activities within the value chain. For example, Glynwed (Aga and Rayburn cooking equipment) referred to in the previous chapter found expectations of product characteristics to be similar among their customers; a website now offers Glynwed customers access to a selected range of wines, holidays and so forth.

Within the 'sales less costs' or the *profitability* component considerable opportunity exists for profit enhancement. Structured partnerships enable fixed costs to be shared and variable costs to be reduced. The growth of business-to-business exchanges is accelerating. Burt *et al* (2000) report on the rapid growth of industry sponsored exchanges in the automotive, airline, chemicals and textiles industries:

> All round the world competitor companies are joining forces to harness the net's transparency and accessibility to cut procurement costs, reduce inventories and broaden supply networks.

Cooperation and coordination not only increase operating efficiencies but also offer scope for such combinations to exert 'monopoly' power in 'low margin' markets. Burt *et al* cite a Price Waterhouse Cooper survey that reported industry investment in business-to-business Net exchange applications exceeds that in business-to-consumer. A very large attraction is the effect on time saving through value chain coordination. Sainsbury's (a large UK food retailer) found that sourcing cheese over the Internet reduced to just four hours a process that once took several weeks. A Morgan Stanley report (cited by Islam) suggests the key benefit lies in integrating procurement with demand forecasting, and exchanging information that may reduce excess inventory holding. The report suggests a US$2700 per motor car saving for the European car industry. Islam identifies potential regulatory problems. The US Department of Justice has shown interest in exchanges in which competitors cooperate on components or supplies for resale purposes.

Manufacturing and marketing costs are also being reduced as are service costs. By focussing on R and D and brand development (development and marketing processes within the value chain), a large number of cost items can be reduced. In manufacturing many fixed costs of production assets and logistics are shared or avoided; hence, Ford's announcement suggesting the possibility of outsourcing vehicle production and focussing on its competencies of design and development and marketing.

Asset management, *productivity*, can also be improved. From the previous paragraph it follows both fixed assets and working capital may be reduced by value chain participation. Nike, Dell and Coca-Cola (and an increasing number of other organisations) have given examples of the notion of asset leverage. Similar examples exist for working capital investment and management. The focus on the demand chain as opposed to the supply chain has resulted in more accurate forecasting of volume and time requirements; thus it follows that the value chain has offered a new perspective to postponement and speculation. Bucklin (1966), with his postponement and speculation theory, drew attention to what were primarily product form and inventory issues, but service products and accounts receivable are becoming important considerations in this context.

Equity and debt management, *investment management*, can also show enhanced performance. The value chain will, if managed strategically, optimise the amount and the location of capital in the value chain thereby ensuring an optional ROI to investors. This follows if organisations such as Dell and Nike manage demand and capacities within the value chain. Optimal utilisation will occur ensuring investment levels in fixed assets and working capital *throughout* the value chain.

The cash flow imperative

Cash flow management is not considered directly by the Du Pont approach but it can be derived by considering profit, depreciation and changes in working capital, fixed capital and investment funding. An easier way of examining cash flow issues from a value chain perspective is to consider how cash flow patterns differ throughout value chain alternatives. Clearly a value chain option that results in excessive benefits and problems (that is, cash flow surpluses and deficits) across the value chain members will be unacceptable.

Figure 6.3 identifies the principal cash flow entities and some considerations that need to be made. *Cash flow from earnings* is a conventional measure of cash flow. From the value chain perspective the alternative value chain configurations should be considered and obvious concerns are the dollar value, the margins occurring in the value chain options (in other words, levels, number of payments and percentages) and timing (that is, seasonal issues and buyer/supplier influences) and timing of cash returns. Depreciation is a difficult issue, being an 'accounting measure'. Certainly it is influenced by the type and location of assets. For example, asset specific industries (such as computer hardware manufacturing) are likely to have considerably larger asset values (and therefore depreciation) than 'low technology' industries such as furniture manufacturing. The 'age profile' should be addressed similarly for the same reasons. Clearly the larger the value chain (levels and participants at each level) and the number of value chain options the more important it is to estimate depreciation values. The increase in 'asset leverage' that has accompanied business model designs such as those favoured by Dell and Nike probably makes this less of an issue. By focussing production into specialist areas within the value chain to benefit from capabilities the impact on capacity is likely to result in high utilisation rates and, therefore, a more effective use of assets and improved cost recovery.

To adjust cash flow from earnings to *cash flow from operations* changes in working capital requirements should be considered. A number of factors influence the value. Inventories are required as work-in-progress, for finished goods (which is influenced by operations strategy, that is JIT versus servicing orders from inventory) and inventory for 'service' purposes such as 'sale or return' marketing strategy options. Receivables are items such as distributor/end-user credit allowed. Of direct concern is the level of accounts receiv-

- Profit after tax (NOPAT)   ←—   - 'Value-in-use' (pricing)
                                                     - Volume
                                                     - Margins (percentages)
                      +   - Timing

- Depreciation   ←—   - Asset type and location
                                                     - Assets age profile
                      =   - Number of chain members

Cashflow from earnings

                      ±
- Working capital requirement   ←—
  (current)
                                                     - Inventories:
                                                       - work in progress
                                                       - finished goods
                                                       - 'service'
                                                     - Receivables:
                                                       - direct
                                                       - indirect
                                                     - Payables:
                                                       - supplier power
                                                       - distributor power
                                                     - 'Negative' working capital

                      =
Cash flow from operations
                      ±
- Fixed asset requirements   ←—   - Manufacturing
  (current and future requirements)   - Logistics
                                                     - Infrastructure systems
                      ±   - Methods

- Working capital requirements   ←—   - Operational development
  (future)   - Market development
                      ±
- Equity funds   ←—
                                                     - 'Shareholder value'
                                                     - Risk/return
                                                     - Investment opportunity
                                                     - Interest rates (organisational)

                      ±
- Funds from long term debt   ←—
                                                     - 'Shareholder value'
                                                     - Risk/return
                                                     - Investment opportunity
                                                     - Interest rates
                      =   - Taxation
Strategic cashflow (Free cashflow)

Figure 6.3 Cash flow management in the value chain

able that is necessary to maintain an existing level of business. However if the overall business is expanding credit allowed may have an important role in business development. How much credit, for how long and to whom become value chain considerations. Payables, trade creditors, are an important concern for value chain structures. The 'supplier power' issue is important because in a value chain suppliers/distributors/customers are stakeholders and cash flows should be optimised to ensure that at no point does there occur an unnecessary need to borrow short-term funds to address cash flow problems. Similarly excess levels of cash are wasteful and changes should be made to ensure an overall optimal cash flow situation. Negative working capital should be a value chain objective rather than the objective of each member. In recent years a number of large organisations have been working towards 'zero working capital' and supplier/distributor relationships are a dominant concern. However, an effective and efficient value chain (that is, strategically and operationally workable) should attempt to structure cash flows to meet customer service expectations and meet the overall performance objectives of the value chain system.

Strategic cash flow (free cash flow) considers the impact of fixed asset and working capital requirements for future development purposes. *Fixed asset requirements* include capital investments in manufacturing, logistics and infrastructure systems. Clearly this has major implications for all stakeholders and the options have significant outcome for all value chain participants. Not only is a review of the structure of operations (manufacturing, logistics and service activities) required but so too is a review of the method of funding. In a value chain it is not surprising to see participants preferring to convert fixed costs into variable costs by outsourcing operations processes, but clearly somewhere within the value chain these processes must take place. There are numerous considerations, many being product-market specific, but issues such as demand and technology life cycle characteristics, structure of supply and consumption markets and growth prospects are important in any situation. Working capital concerns are similar to those discussed above. *Operational development* refers to process or organisational changes that may be required within the value delivery system, while *market development* issues include the inventory and credit requirements of new 'markets'.

Equity fund concerns include contraction as well as expansion of the shareholders' investment. Given the recent attention to shareholder value by many large corporations and the number of 'buy back' instances it becomes important to consider the individual company needs as well as those of optimal financing for the value chain. *Shareholder value* management is a complete topic on its own. Here we should be aware that involvement in the value chain adds another dimension to the equity/debt issues for individual organisations. Some of the concerns of an ongoing and shared nature also include the risk/return profile of the individual organisations comprising the value chain and the extent to which these are modified by participating within the value chain. A similar perspective exists concerning debt decisions, clearly they are closely related and both are influenced by the asset structure requirements of the overall value chain. One concern that can complicate the decision process, particularly for global value delivery systems, are taxation laws in individual countries of the operation.

As regards the *producer surplus* concept, a number of options are presented in Figure 6.4. The value offered may be enhanced by decreasing costs (both fixed and variable costs) and moving from S1 to S2. An underlying theme exists: by identifying core competencies that are required currently (and in the future) the 'cost' decreases (producer surplus) may be planned and implemented during the design and development stages of a product or service. In this way the value chain can be structured to use partner organisations as an integral part of the value proposition.

It will be recalled from Chapter 5 the value chain approach is clearly customer focussed. It identifies market opportunities (using market segmentation techniques) and assembles a value production and delivery process to meet the expectations of a target customer market. It differs from the supply chain in a number of aspects. Figure 6.5 illustrates these simple but important differences. The supply chain is a facilitator. It is a competitive necessity in as much as without efficient supply chain management the logistics of resources management cannot be optimised. Efficient supply chain manage-

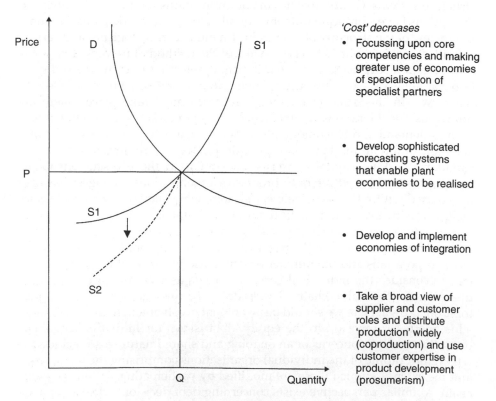

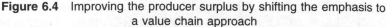

Figure 6.4   Improving the producer surplus by shifting the emphasis to a value chain approach

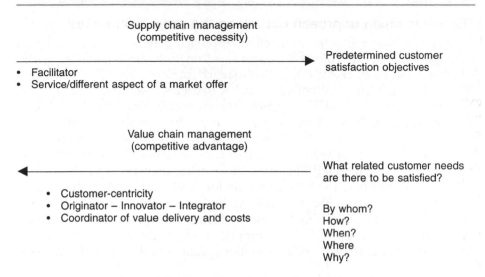

Figure 6.5   The value chain *vs* the supply chain

ment ensures that resources stocks and flows are managed such that prede-termined customer satisfaction objectives are met.

The value chain offers opportunities for creative marketing and operations decisions

By contrast with the supply chain, the value chain is a structure that is able to identify customer expectations *as well as* operate a production and delivery system to deliver customer value. It is customer-centric but differs from the supply chain in a creative, innovative sense. The creativity extends across and along the value chain with the objective of coordinating the value production and delivery processes. Often the processes are 'moved' from traditional owners and completed elsewhere in the value chain. The terms coproductivity and prosumer are commonplace. The value chain approach is similar to that taken by the virtual organisation: the dominant characteristics are planning, control and coordination. This is essential because typically opportunities and resource requirements cannot be met within the organisation structure of one company and a process of identifying workable part-nerships begins. The value chain that results meets the expectations of all stakeholders. End-user customers 'buy' the value offered (through the value proposition), while reseller and manufacturing and logistics stakeholders' objectives are met in terms of their own profitability, productivity and cash flow objectives. The principle of value chain strategy, structure and operations is that all stakeholders benefit from involvement: either they cannot compete as independent units, because they do not command the competencies (or resources), *or* membership changes the 'shape and size' of the offer such that their individual gains are increased from cooperating within the value chain structure.

The value chain approach optimises the potential market

A primary advantage of the value chain approach may be explored using an analysis of the market volume available to a firm. In Figure 6.6 the process by which a potential market is researched to reach *potential market demand* is illustrated. It is necessary that before a market becomes 'realisable' a number of questions should be asked concerning the characteristics of that market. A market will be influenced by the *interest* a product creates, the disposable *income* of prospective purchasers and the *availability* (location, volume, convenience and so on) of the product. Given these issues can be resolved the *available market* is defined. The available market may be expanded by an organisation unable to meet the demands for availability due to low volume capacity problems or perhaps marketing logistics if it uses partners' capacities and capabilities to overcome these problems. *Constraints* may be imposed by overseas governments and may comprise restrictions based upon currency shortages, labour/employment problems and often material contents.

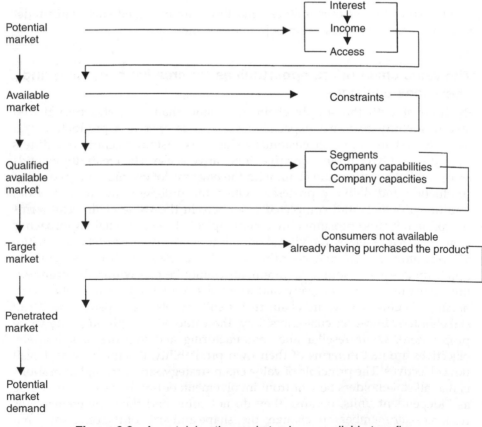

Figure 6.6   Ascertaining the market volume available to a firm

Again the value chain approach offers solutions through local manufacturing and licensing agreements. The *qualified available market* may, therefore, be expanded, but so too can the *target market* by building on the loyalty of the organisations of the value chain partners and by them developing specialisation processes within the value creation and production processes. It follows that the *penetrated market* can be both maintained and expanded as customer expectations *and* interests are developed around the aggregated core competencies of the value chain partners.

Given *potential market demand* a business plan may be developed. Figure 6.7 suggests how the market forecast can be used to make both capacity and capability decisions. Given potential market demand we consider issues such as product-market developments that are forecast over the planning time period. An essential concern is the impact that overall industry activity (in R and D and marketing expenditure) may be having on the market's characteristics and consumer/end-user behaviour trends.

A *market forecast of demand* will take into account expected competitive marketing strategies and changes in segmentation and positioning that may be expected (or indeed are currently observed). A more detailed look at market demand by examining existing and developing customer preferences will identify current and potential opportunities. A *value chain forecast* follows. Influences to be considered include a review of current and potential competitors together with a review of the value strategies currently active. Forecasts need projections; it follows that changing segments and positioning responses may have major implications for the structure of competitive value chains, as do changes in current and potential opportunities. These can prove to be particularly important because the value chain aggregate capacity and its capabilities are able to address a wider range of opportunities than the single integrated firm. Not only is it more flexible but its response time (time-to-market) is shorter. *Value chain market potential* may be assessed by comparisons between the R and D, investment and marketing activities of major competitors and the responses possible from the value chain combination. When capital (fixed and working capital) considerations are added, together with the non-financial considerations of cooperation, coordination and commitment a *capacity planning profile* for the value chain becomes possible. Before specific response decisions can be made the socio-economics of response options should be considered. 'Social' issues are the organisational developments expected throughout the value chain. For example, recent moves (2000) by major UK brewers to sell their brewing interests and focus on leisure markets is an indication of a 'social' or organisational change as well as an economic reality. The developments in technology management that place more emphasis on the economics of specialisation and integration are also important to the effective and efficient operation of the value chain. The result of this process is a business plan detailing *competitive response decisions*. Initially these are options that are subsequently qualified by reviewing and agreeing structure, product/price characteristics and capacity flexibility requirements.

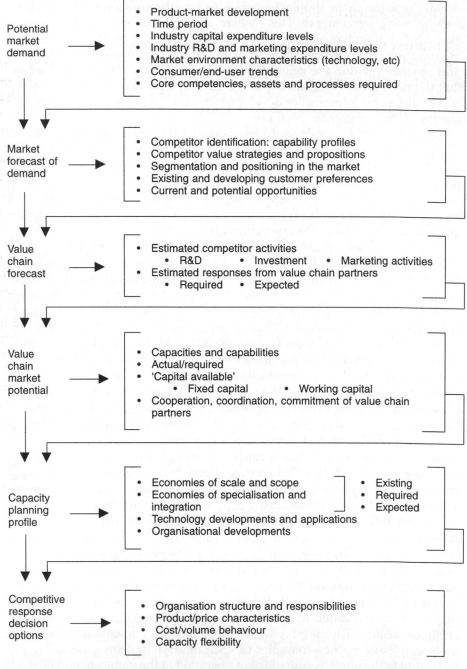

Potential market demand
- Product-market development
- Time period
- Industry capital expenditure levels
- Industry R&D and marketing expenditure levels
- Market environment characteristics (technology, etc)
- Consumer/end-user trends
- Core competencies, assets and processes required

Market forecast of demand
- Competitor identification: capability profiles
- Competitor value strategies and propositions
- Segmentation and positioning in the market
- Existing and developing customer preferences
- Current and potential opportunities

Value chain forecast
- Estimated competitor activities
  - R&D   • Investment   • Marketing activities
- Estimated responses from value chain partners
  - Required   • Expected

Value chain market potential
- Capacities and capabilities
- Actual/required
- 'Capital available'
  - Fixed capital   • Working capital
- Cooperation, coordination, commitment of value chain partners

Capacity planning profile
- Economies of scale and scope
- Economies of specialisation and integration
- Technology developments and applications
- Organisational developments

  - Existing
  - Required
  - Expected

Competitive response decision options
- Organisation structure and responsibilities
- Product/price characteristics
- Cost/volume behaviour
- Capacity flexibility

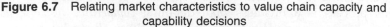

Figure 6.7   Relating market characteristics to value chain capacity and capability decisions

ORGANISATIONAL ISSUES

A market or customer focus is becoming essential

Slywotzky (1996) and others suggest significant changes are occurring in management's emphasis on the perception of what customers are and on achieving customer satisfaction. See Figure 6.8. Their argument contends that managerial emphasis *was* product focussed and centred on the productivity of the tangible asset base. This they suggest has shifted. The product focus has been replaced by the importance of customer relevance and the productivity of the intangible asset base has taken priority over tangible asset base performance. The arguments behind these assertions are based upon observed behaviour. Customer relevance has become important because of the improved accuracy, currency and availability of customer information; the facility to monitor customer purchases and preferences and to use these to create more relevant responses is a primary reason why a customer or market focus has replaced the importance of product. The concepts of value-in-use (customer perceived benefits or value satisfaction) together with life cycle costing (the research into aggregate customer costs over the life span of use of products) has enabled customer specific pricing to become a reality. The 'market' orientation proposed by Abell (1980) and subsequently reflected in the writing of Webster (1994), Day (1990) and others has influenced a shift towards a *market-product* strategy rather than a product-market strategy, which for many firms has brought about major change in strategy and structure perspectives. The overall shift has been towards specific target customer groups with emphasis on relevant and effective means of segmentation. The

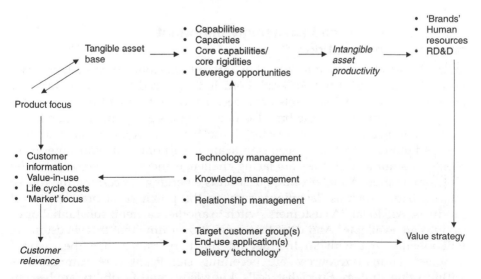

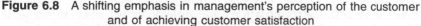

Figure 6.8 A shifting emphasis in management's perception of the customer and of achieving customer satisfaction

end-use(s) to which a customer puts products is (are) also an important change; rather than suggest to the customer they change their processes to gain maximum benefit from products and services, it is the supplier who changes the product specification to meet end-user needs. The 'thinking' or *learning organisation* realises the importance of this and addresses the issue during the product development stage. Finally 'delivery technologies' are becoming important components of the value strategy. Delivery technologies can be expanded to include the ordering, transaction and delivery processes that comprise the activity of managing the 'physical' aspects of customer satisfaction.

A *market product strategy* emphasis may be found in Ansoff's (1968) original product-market strategy model. It will be recalled that Ansoff identified market development as an optional strategic direction and the inference to be drawn is that corporate capabilities are such that market development offers a lower risk option for growth than that offered by product development. A market-product strategy is one in which a basic product platform exists and completion of the product is postponed until the last moment in order to meet more closely specific customer specifications. The Dell model is an example of a market-product strategy. The Dell value chain is structured such that commitment to the final product specification is postponed in order to meet individual customer orders rapidly, thereby creating an exclusive value proposition.

Given this approach, which is essentially the mass customisation strategy discussed earlier, Dell and others adopting the model are in effect using a product formula that offers flexibility and that facilitates a target market strategy that is aimed at meeting specific expectations on an end-user preference basis. Clearly there are cost benefits if the value delivery processes can be managed effectively.

Intangible assets: an increasingly important strategic consideration

Intangible asset productivity is just as interesting. Companies such as Nike, Dell, The Gap, and it would seem, Ford have realised how important their investments in intangible assets have become to the future of their organisations. The importance of the brand is becoming a significant strategic factor as the Internet assumes increasing importance in commercial activities. Branded products that have been significant in corporate and consumer reckoning for a number of years are facing challenge and confrontation from the 'dot.com' brands. An interesting question is emerging concerning the role of intermediaries such as 'lastminute.com' in the purchase of branded travel products. Will loyal BA customers switch to another carrier if substantial price savings are available? And does this suggest over time that travel customers will identify first with an Internet intermediary rather than the carrier/ supplier? Human resources are becoming significant core competencies within value strategy. Specialist skills, knowledge and flexibility are becoming critical to both the formulation and implementation of customer focussed strategy. The recent (1999/2000) problems of Marks and Spencer have been influenced by lack of staff and staff 'attitudes' towards customers. The role of research design and development (RD&D) is becoming well identified as is its importance. The 'high-tech' companies have proven the importance of ongoing investment in RD&D. For some (Dell for example) it is their core competency – to the exclusion of other processes!

Value strategy has become an important feature of the corporate strategy process. As we have seen management philosophy is changing. Three influences have been significant: knowledge management, technology management and relationship management. They have not acted independently but rather have had joint influences on the organisation's ability to meet the changes in the business environment.

Organisation structures are undergoing change alongside the changes in managerial philosophy. Figure 6.9 illustrates this change. Any strategy requires an organisation strategy within which strategy may be evolved, evaluated and decided upon. It also requires an efficient implementation facility. Figure 6.9 suggests fundamental changes. Effective value strategy requires the emphasis on cost reduction and administrative efficiency to be replaced by one which focusses on value creation for customers using innovation in the design, production, marketing, delivery and servicing components of value. Organisation strategy should emphasise empowerment of employees in order to meet customer expectations for product relevance and service. This differs markedly from the production focus or emphasis all too frequently seen

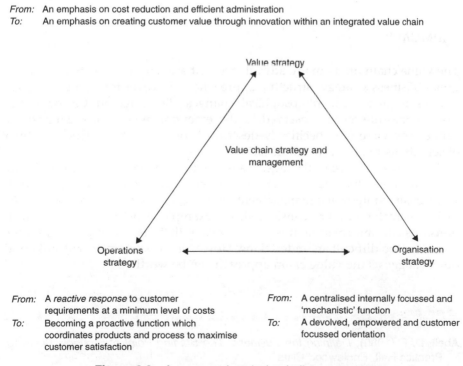

From: An emphasis on cost reduction and efficient administration
To: An emphasis on creating customer value through innovation within an integrated value chain

Value strategy

Value chain strategy and management

Operations strategy

Organisation strategy

From: A *reactive response* to customer requirements at a minimum level of costs
To: Becoming a proactive function which coordinates products and process to maximise customer satisfaction

From: A centralised internally focussed and 'mechanistic' function
To: A devolved, empowered and customer focussed orientation

Figure 6.9 An approach to 'value led' management

Characteristics	Traditional organisation	Virtual organisation
• Structure	• Hierarchical	• Networks
• Scope	• Internal/closed	• External/open
• Resource focus	• Capital	• Knowledge, relationship, technology management
• State	• Static, stable management	• Dynamic, changing
• HRM		• Specialists
• Direction and basis of action	• Management directives	• Empowerment/intrapreneurship
• Motivation	• Control	• Empowerment
	• Meet corporate management directives	• Achieve team goals
• Learning	• Specific skills	• Broader competencies
• Compensation	• Position/seniority	• Achievement
• Relationships	• Competitive	• Cooperative/collaborative
• Information communications among partners	• 'Need to know' basis	• Open and transparent

Figure 6.10   A review of organisation structure differences

Source: Adapted from Tapscott and Caston (1993)

within many organisations. Operations strategy should become proactive rather than be reactive. In many respects we have the growth of supply chain management and operations management techniques sharing the responsibility for this. Just-in-time, quick response, materials requirement planning, and so on are essentially cost reduction activities applied to processes which may be more effective if customer satisfaction maximisation were the primary objective.

SUMMARY

The value chain offers many advantages that are not available from conventional business strategy/structure approaches. However for it to be effective it does require some philosophical changes. Tapscott and Caston (1993) discuss the differences observed in the emerging modes of organisations. While they were not specifically descriptive of value chain structures their observations require few modifications.

A review of Figure 6.10 suggests a quite different set of characteristics are necessary for value chain structures. The changes required are necessary if value chain strategy *and* management are to be successful. When some of the major characteristics are considered, for example structure, resources, relationships and information, it is not surprising that many companies find the transition too difficult an undertaking. However, the success of Dell, Nike and others suggests the value chain approach can be worthwhile.

REFERENCES ••••••••••••••••••••••••••••••••••••

Abell, D. F. (1980), *Defining the Business: The Starting Point of Strategic Planning*, Prentice-Hall, Englewood Cliffs.

Ansoff, I. G. (1968), *Corporate Strategy,* McGraw Hill, New York.

Bucklin, L. P. (1966), *A Theory of Distribution Channel Structure*, University of California, Berkeley.

Burt, M., J. Harvey, R. Guthrie, A. Voyle, R. Islam and N. Tait (2000), (untitled), *Financial Times*, 26/27 February.

Day, G. (1990), *Market Driven Strategy*, Free Press, New York.

Slywotsky, A. J. (1996), *Valve Migration*, Free Press, New York.

Tapscott, D. and Caston, A. (1993), *Paradigm Shift*, McGraw Hill, New York.

Webster, F. (1994). *Market Driven Management,* Wiley, New York.

7

Strategic and Operational Characteristics and Components

INTRODUCTION

Previous chapters have explored the development of value as a strategic concept. There has been an emphasis on the emerging difference between supply chain management and value chain management. It has been argued that value chain strategy and management has the *expansion* of customer satisfaction as its primary objective as opposed to the optimisation of supply chain costs while meeting specified customer objectives. Figure 7.1 illustrates this essential difference. Value chain management is a proactive approach to customer satisfaction while supply chain management is a cost-efficient response to existing customer objectives. Glynwed (an example given in

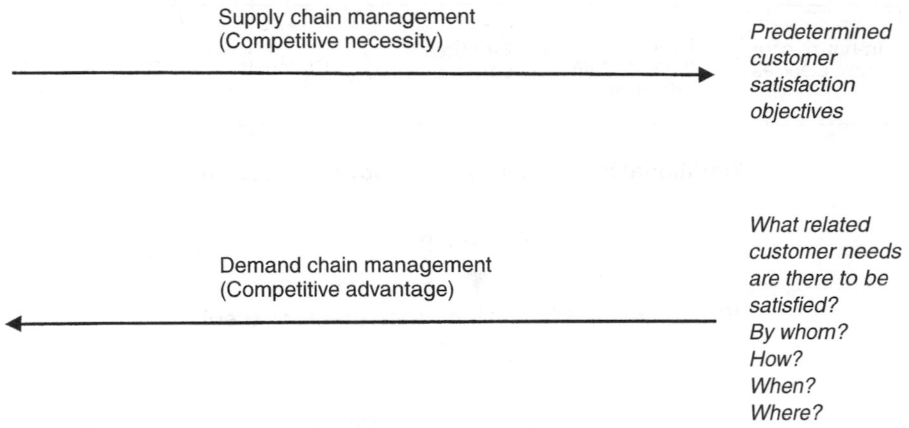

Supply chain management
(Competitive necessity)

Predetermined customer satisfaction objectives

Demand chain management
(Competitive advantage)

What related customer needs are there to be satisfied? By whom? How? When? Where?

Figure 7.1   The value chain: a combination of supply chain
and demand chain management

Chapter 6) identified the fact that their customers had many more 'product' aspirations other than the Aga and Rayburn ranges. Consequently Glynwed established a web based information source that identifies 'product' ideas and sources; as a consequence Glynwed plays an important role in the expansion of a response to the customer value satisfaction needs of an expanded customer base.

There are other examples of value chain strategy and management. Brown (1997), using the newspaper, video entertainment and banking industries as examples suggests:

> The emerging value chains in these examples promise to restructure these industries and redistribute value among different components and players in the value chain.

Brown also suggests, using Porter's (1985) view on competitive advantage, that. 'The way in which [a business] manages its value chain will affect its cost structure and the differential benefits offered to its customers, and thereby its competitive advantage'. This latter comment is of less interest than the first. The restructuring and redistribution of value issues are central to value chain analysis, strategy and management.

Other examples are available. Lai (2000) presented Hewlett Packard's view of the shift or transition from the traditional product focussed business design towards a customer focussed design. Figure 7.2 illustrates the HP philosophy that is clearly based upon the concept of value chain management in which customer needs rather than corporate core competencies are given primary focus. In this example the realisation that flexibility is essential is very clear. It suggests that the paths trodden by Dell, Nike and others are applicable to both products and services.

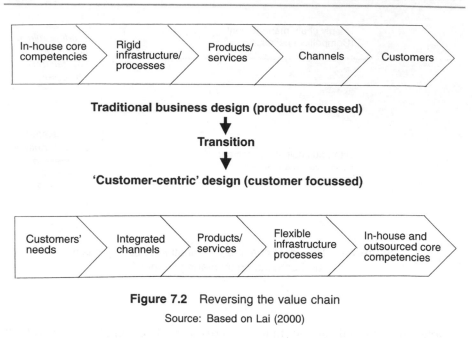

Figure 7.2   Reversing the value chain

Source: Based on Lai (2000)

A GENERIC APPROACH

The value chain approach is not new. Anterasian and Phillips (1988) proposed a generic model which has three base elements. See Figure 7.3:

- *Choose the value*; a process of customer and customer needs identification
- *Provide the value*; in which the product/service response is developed and the marketing strategy activities of distribution, service and pricing are also developed
- *Communicate the value*; completes the value chain processes by implementing the marketing strategy with a strong emphasis on customer communications

While this is helpful, it has some omissions, possibly the most significant being the value delivery process in which service is given an expanded role. In a value chain context *service* should include the physical distribution aspects of value delivery, such as availability (time and location), frequency and reliability of this aspect of the service. Figure 7.4 expands the original marketing based value chain proposed by Anterasian and Phillips.

More recently Day (1990) proposed a value cycle comprising value identification, value creation, value communication, value delivery and value maintenance (service). Day's approach is represented as Figure 7.5. Day argues that value creation is an ongoing process and is central to a market (or customer) focus that is becoming evident within successful organisations. In Day's

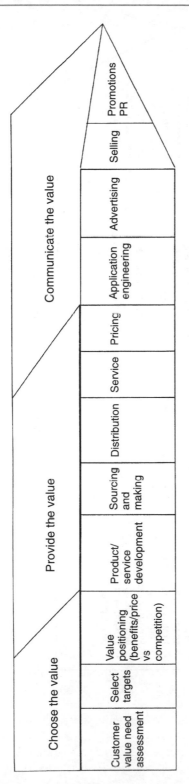

Figure 7.3 The marketing value chain

Source: Anterasian and Phillips (1988), [reproduced with permission]

Notes
Value = Benefit – Price
Benefit = Attribute(s) desirable to customer (in customer's eyes)
Price = Total costs to customer (as perceived by customer)
Superior perceived value = Customer believes buying/using the product or service gives a net value superior (more positive) than alternatives' value

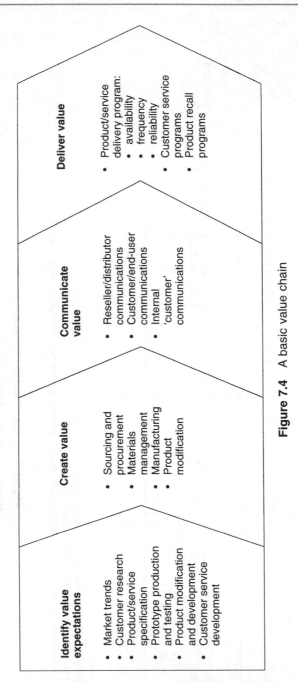

Identify value expectations

- Market trends
- Customer research
- Product/service specification
- Prototype production and testing
- Product modification and development
- Customer service development

Create value

- Sourcing and procurement
- Materials management
- Manufacturing
- Product modification

Communicate value

- Reseller/distributor communications
- Customer/end-user communications
- Internal 'customer' communications

Deliver value

- Product/service delivery program:
  - availability
  - frequency
  - reliability
- Customer service programs
- Product recall programs

Figure 7.4 A basic value chain

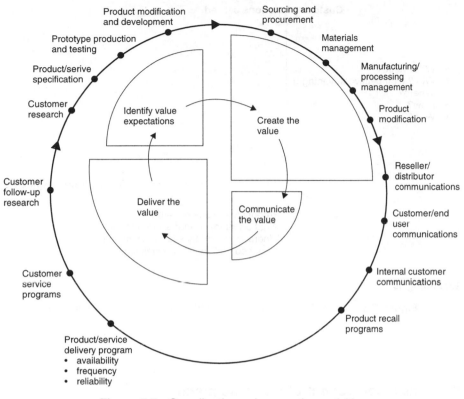

Figure 7.5 Coordinating value creation activities

Source: Developed from Day (1990)

model the circularity of value chain strategy is knowledge based: as customer satisfaction is built by the process so the customer database generates a knowledge base facilitating product-service modifications and potentially additional 'value based opportunities'.

Brown (*op cit*) makes another significant contribution to the value chain argument by introducing research by the PA Consulting Group, Sydney; Edwards (1995) suggests a process (or activity) management perspective to the restructuring of value chains. This is very helpful because it goes further in the disaggregation of the *existing* value chain structure of the firm and/or the industry in which it participates. Brown's argument, based upon the PA Consulting Group's work, is strongly influenced by the Porter perspective on competitive advantage *within* an existing product-market structure. Slywotzky and Morrison (1997), Normann and Ramirez (1993), Webster (1994), Mathur and Kenyon (1998), O'Sullivan and Geringer (1993), Scott (1998) and Vollman and Cordon (1999) all consider value opportunities and satisfaction to be *outwith* the existing product-market structure as well as within the existing scope.

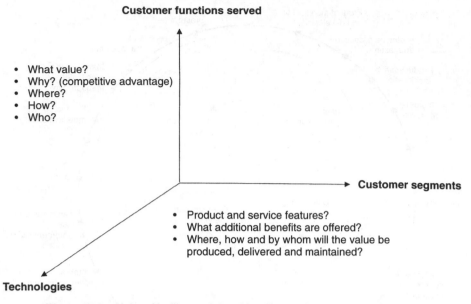

Customer functions served

- What value?
- Why? (competitive advantage)
- Where?
- How?
- Who?

Customer segments

- Product and service features?
- What additional benefits are offered?
- Where, how and by whom will the value be produced, delivered and maintained?

Technologies

Figure 7.6   Using Abell's model to identify a value strategy direction

Value as a component of strategic planning

Abell's (1980) strategy model is useful in this context. See Figure 7.6. Abell's model offers a simple but very effective approach for determining strategic direction. By identifying the three basic characteristics of strategy decision options – customer groups, customer/end-user product applications and 'technology' – Abell has provided an ideal model for value chain strategy and structure decisions. Figure 7.6 has interpreted 'technology' as delivery technology and applies product technology to customer applications decisions. The value chain approach enables an organisation to move out of its 'market cell' in any of three directions without necessarily having the core competencies required within the business. Given an opportunity exists and is financially viable a business structure may be formulated using the approaches of Hewlett Packard (Figure 7.2), Nike, Dell, or Coca Cola to name but a few.

Brown uses an example from Hamel and Prahalad who report on how the Japanese television manufacturing industry used Porter's 'low cost differentiation' concept as a means of establishing initial competitive advantage. This was subsequently modified to be based on 'quality and reliability'. Brown (*op cit*) reports that further investment is being made to enable 'mass customisation' to provide 'exclusive value' to smaller, specific customer segments. Using Abell's model we can argue that this customer opportunity could only be addressed given the developments in both product and process technologies.

A GENERIC VALUE CHAIN

Industry, organisation or both

Value chain analysis extends across industries and organisations and it is useful to consider both when value strategy is being evaluated. An industry perspective identifies opportunities for market expansion either by identifying new product opportunities for existing customer markets, the possibility of extending the market coverage to new customer groups, or expanding delivery options by applying technology developments in production and logistics as they become available and relevant. Value chain analysis also identifies sectors of the value chain that are underserviced or which offer opportunities for improving value added contributions to participants by directing companies towards sectors of the value chain to which their competencies could be applied effectively. This can result in increased profitability *and* competitive advantage.

The organisation perspective of the value chain is one which identifies not only where to compete but how. Burt (2000) reports on interviews with the CEOs of Ford and General Motors, whose views differ. Ford has pursued an aggressive acquisition program while General Motors have sought to build strategic alliances. Burt suggests that Ford, through its acquisition strategy can position its offers, rapidly and without the prior agreement of partners. The General Motors approach offers shared risk and lower investment values. Ford has aggressively acquired major industry brands and clearly sees its future in design and development and in marketing.

Figure 7.7 illustrates the generic value chain, equally appropriate for industry and organisational analysis. The diagram identifies the processes required to translate customer and stakeholder expectations into delivered value; ownership of the processes need not be the province of one organisation. As earlier chapters have implied, there is a growing view that a virtual approach to value production and delivery is increasingly acceptable and often is strategically more effective.

The processes may not relate with specific activities exclusively but rather occur across a series of activities. In Figure 7.8 value creation occurs across the entire range of activities. Clearly this makes allocation of roles and tasks very difficult but it does open up the potential for inputs to the processes from external sources easier to accept conceptually, if difficult to manage. It is here that value chain strategy and management has much to offer – it broadens management's planning perspective to consider external involvement in the value chain.

The roles and tasks of each process are indicated in Figure 7.9. These are very general, and specific applications of the model are likely to produce more detailed roles and tasks. Again the role of outsourcing becomes apparent; many of the tasks are likely to be specialist in their nature and may only be available from 'third party' suppliers because of high capital requirements or specialist human resources skills. Dell (1999) suggests that the high quality production requirements of computer hardware systems require high quality

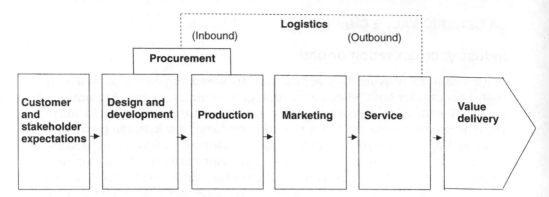

Figure 7.7 A generic value chain

suppliers (in Dell's case Sony) and to manufacture the components 'in house' would require a large capital investment that would prevent investing in marketing and R and D and customer value delivery systems.

Another reason for considering the partnership option is that competitive intensity may be reducing margins and an alternative is for value chain members to specialise in selected areas of the value chain processes. This presumably is the rationale behind the Ford statement (Chapter 6) suggesting that the company may, in the near future, focus on development and design and marketing, leaving production to outsourced specialists. Such a strategy may be accompanied by unacceptable levels of risk for some; as a result, partial ownership in the form of a limited equity holding may offset this risk. Either way, through alliances (asset leverage) or partial equity ownership, there is a requirement for effective (strategic) and efficient (operational) planning, coordination and control throughout the value chain. This is suggested in Figure 7.9.

Value chain strategy and management suggests a shift in the emphasis previously given to the supply chain. In Figure 7.10 a current view of supply chain management is offered. This perspective includes production and service management and adds communications management (through EDI, scanning applications and so on) to logistics management. Effective and efficient supply chain management results from the integration of these activities and is the combination of supply chain coordination, supply chain operations and service delivery. 'Service' in this context is concerned with adding value to an existing 'product' through availability, delivery frequency, reliability and flexibility.

Strategic operations management (value chain strategy and management) requires a more comprehensive approach. Figure 7.11 supplements the supply chain management processes with the remaining value chain processes and suggests two main activities: supply chain management and demand chain management. Demand chain management includes those processes which identify, create and service the value process thereby ensuring effective value delivery. Demand chain management is the proactive element of value

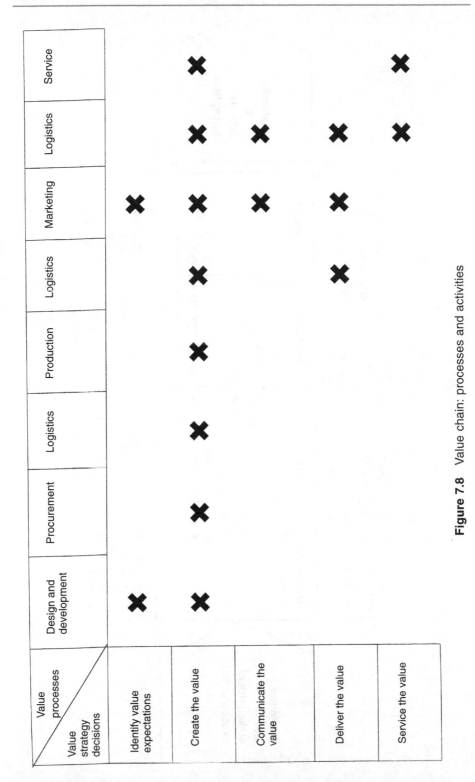

Figure 7.8 Value chain: processes and activities

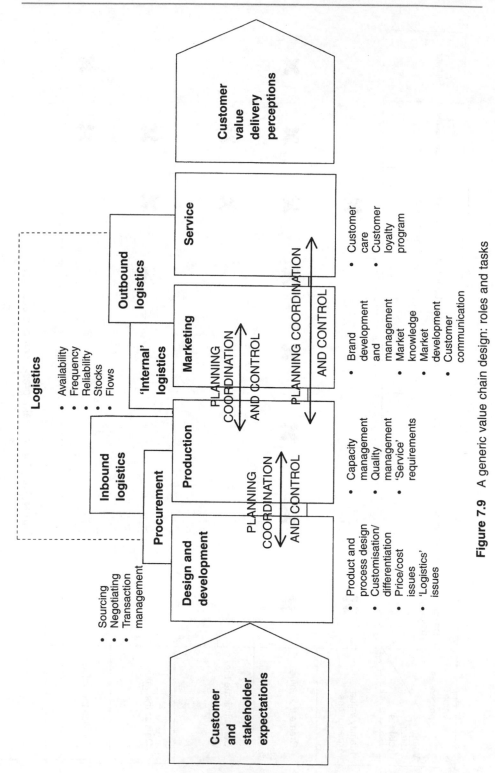

Figure 7.9 A generic value chain design: roles and tasks

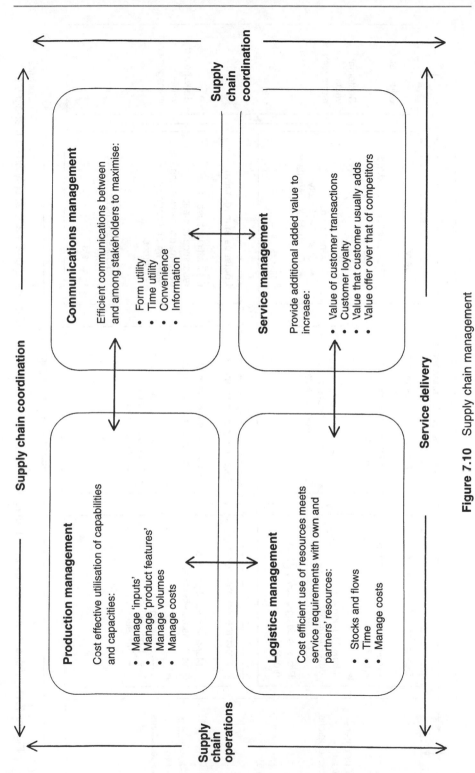

Figure 7.10 Supply chain management

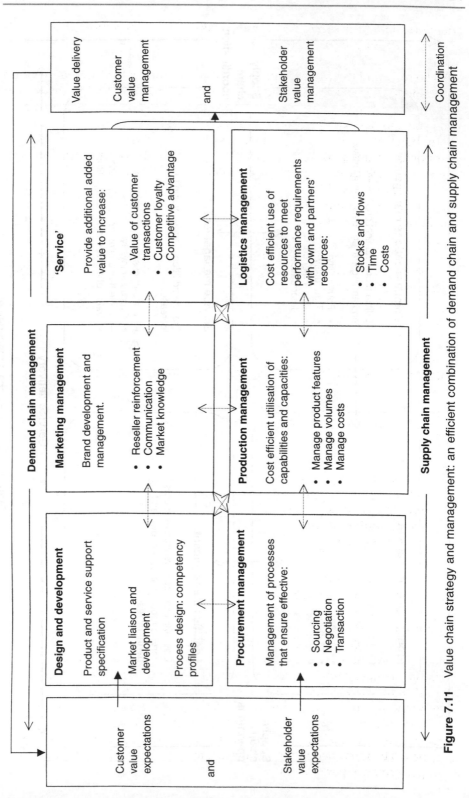

Figure 7.11 Value chain strategy and management: an efficient combination of demand chain and supply chain management

delivery. It identifies the customer and stakeholder expectations (suggested in Figure 7.1); supply chain management is the response to customer and stakeholder expectations.

The roles and tasks of each process within the models illustrated by Figures 7.10 and 7.11 are specified. The role of logistics management deserves some additional comment. Effective value chains are those in which the customer and stakeholder expectations are met within the three parameters identified in both diagrams. Unless there is an efficient flow of 'product and information', supported by adequate inventories (this includes both locations and levels), at times specified by customers and value chain intermediaries (in other words, frequencies and reliabilities), at optimal costs it is unlikely that either customer or stakeholder value will result. It follows that logistics management has an important role in ensuring the efficiencies of stocks and flows and the accuracy of timing and of budgeted costs, and without this the value chain will not be able to meet either customer or stakeholder objectives. For this reason it is suggested that 'logistics' assumes an important role in value creation, *bridging* procurement, production, marketing and service processes. This view is illustrated as Figure 7.12 which summarises the generic view of the value chain.

KEY ISSUES AND QUESTIONS FOR VALUE CHAIN DECISIONS

Thus far we have identified the strategy and structure model of the value chain. Effective decisions require information inputs and for this purpose a value chain audit model is proposed. Its main areas of enquiry are:

- the concept of the 'served market';
- revenues, profits, productivity and cash flow;
- processes and activities;
- configuration of core competencies;
- awareness and adaptability to change: flexibility.

The concept of the 'served market'. Abell's approach to marketing strategy is a starting point. With a clear view of the characteristics of the market, customer expectations and the 'drivers' of the market, a perspective concerning market opportunities within the value chain can be reached.

Revenues, profits, productivity and cash flow. It is important to identify the what, where, how, when (and why) patterns of these important financial criteria. Gadiesh and Gilbert (1998) (see Chapter 4) use the concept of 'profit pools' to develop strategy. They argue that many companies '. . . chart strategy without a full understanding of the sources and distribution of profits in their industry'. Plotting the revenue, profits (and therefore cost profiles) productivity and cash flow characteristics of alternative value chains enables options to be identified in the knowledge and understanding of critical financial performance parameters.

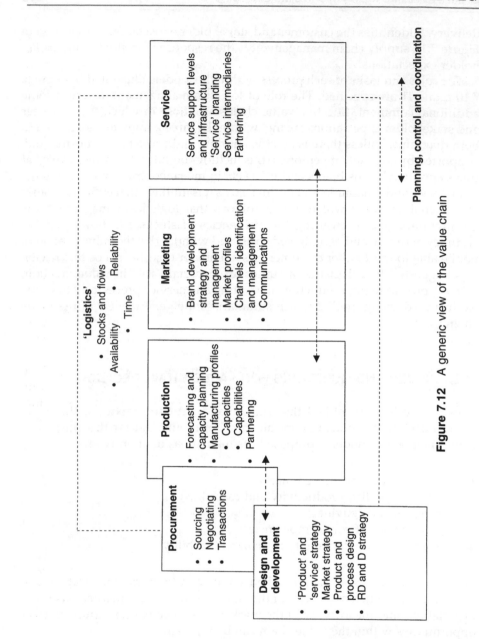

Figure 7.12 A generic view of the value chain

Processes and activities. Porter's (1985) original view of the value chain was that it examines all activities a business performs by disaggregating functions into discrete but interrelated activities. This allows understanding of both how value is generated and the behaviour of costs. Process management and business process re-engineering have had mixed reception but nevertheless have offered a means by which the 'value and cost drivers' of a business can be identified. McHugh *et al* (1995) develop the original concept and their work offers an holistic approach which is '. . . market and opportunity driven, and customer focussed'. Whereas business process re-engineering focusses on core business processes, McHugh *et al* are promoting an 'holistic business system' that extends the original concept such that it becomes more consumer oriented, possibly to the extent that the customer becomes a prosumer. It follows that an industry perspective of the value chain is helpful in identifying basic processes and activities (Brown: *op cit*) but that the specific processes and activities required to meet mass customisation and selective exclusivity opportunities are becoming essential. McHugh *et al*'s notion of a BreakPoint process innovation, '. . . a new level of process innovation – as measured by the value set of cost, quality, lead time, delivery reliability and product functionality – that provides a significant and positive market impact', is an essential feature of value chain analysis. Figure 7.13 suggests these may have far reaching implications for both industry and the organisation.

Configuration of core competencies. The contribution of Hamel and Pralahad in this area is well documented. Within the context of the value chain audit Hamel's 'three tests' to judge if a capability is a core competency are relevant:

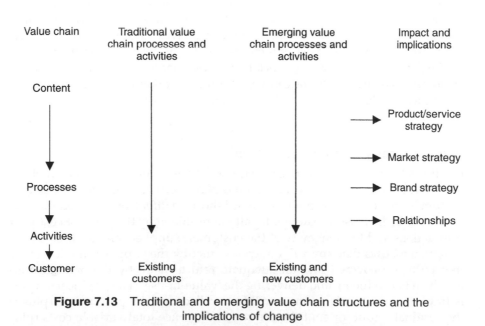

Figure 7.13 Traditional and emerging value chain structures and the implications of change

- Does it make a disproportionate contribution to customer value?
- Does it offer the opportunity to build competitive distinction?
- Is it applicable in other businesses, locations or products?

These criteria apply to tangible and intangible assets (in other words, fixed assets such as plant and equipment *and* R and D, brands, human resources and so on) and are applicable throughout the value chain. Of particular interest in the value chain context is the recognition (and response) by customers to core competencies, their distribution of 'ownership' within the value chain and trends in their influence. This latter issue suggests the notion of core rigidities (see Leonard-Barton: 1992); these are core competencies which become core rigidities due to the dynamics of product and process technology. This topic will be discussed in detail in a subsequent chapter.

Awareness, adaptability to change: flexibility. Change is inevitable and the strategic audit should monitor changes occurring in technology and organisational theory. Both may have significance to value chain structure, particularly in value production and delivery. Change has implications for strategy and operations decisions because of the impact that it may have for investment and subsequent return on investment.

ADDING VALUE IN THE VALUE CHAIN

Adding value from both the customer and stakeholder perspectives was introduced in Chapter 3. Two concepts were introduced, the consumer surplus and the producer surplus. Both will be revisited briefly here to introduce a discussion on the value added by processes within the value chain. Value in the context of business markets is the worth in monetary terms of the technical (product or process improvements or advantages), economic (cost reductions), service (possibly cost reductions due to the supplier conducting part of the 'production' task) and social (lifestyle, status, and so on) benefits a customer receives for the price they pay for a market offer. This value (the consumer surplus) together with price comprise *value-in-use.*

Value strategy is customer based

It follows that value chain strategy should be based around an overall objective that seeks to increase the actual (and perceived) value-in-use, such that a customer considers the benefits to exceed those on offer from competitors. The result will be increased customer loyalty determined by the value of customer transactions and the longevity of the customer/supplier relationship.

It also follows that any value response met by the supplier should ensure that costs are covered and an adequate return made by the organisations involved in producing and delivering the 'value-in-use'. The producer surplus is important in this decision. It will be recalled that the producer surplus is the residual 'profit' or contribution remaining once total variable costs (plus an allowance for capital consumption) are deducted from total revenues. It is therefore important that the producer (producers) utilise the available economies of operations (that is scale, specialisation and integration), the cost benefits that accrue from cumulative experience, and identify, evaluate and utilise partnership structures available from alliances with suppliers, customers and even competitors. By ensuring that all options are explored the value chain structure then becomes the most *cost-effective* strategy available.

Gadiesh and Gilbert's (*op cit*) proposal that mapping the industry profit pool should be considered as a preliminary activity in strategy decisions can be extended. Figure 7.14 proposes an additional step. For each process in the value chain the investment requirements are identified and performance expectations determined at levels that will ensure an adequate return for all process owners in the value chain. In addition to financial expectations, marketing investment and performance metrics should be clearly determined and agreed. It is clear that unless a minimum level of marketing performance (market share volume and volume/share growth rate) is achieved it is unlikely that the desired financial performance will result. By the same token the analysis should consider the impact of high market share and growth rate levels. It is not necessarily the case that maximum market share (or growth rate) results in maximum financial performance. Often a strategy to maximise market share results in suboptimal performance. Examples of suboptimal performance may be excessive credit allowed resulting in high levels of bad debts. Low inventory turn rates resulting from availability levels that are unnecessary and resulting in obsolescence and subsequent markdowns provide another example; unnecessary product availability can result in punitive cost increases.

The value chain approach can minimise or share the risk involved. Clearly there are costs in the form of coordination and communication, but these are offset by the improved flexibility of 'leaner' operations.

THE VALUE CHAIN: ORGANISATIONAL PROFILE CHARACTERISTICS: AN EMPHASIS ON VALUE FOR THE CUSTOMER AND THE SHAREHOLDER

The impact of the availability of information and its concurrent decrease in cost has encouraged many organisations to reconsider what it is they actually deliver to customers, how it is produced and what it costs. It forces a self-evaluation process by which they start with a blank piece of paper and question the entire value process. The increasing number of 'boundary-less companies' or 'virtual organisations' may soon be joined by Ford which, it has been rumoured, may soon outsource its manufacturing.

The value chain as a concept has been with us for some time. Traditionally it started with a view of the assets and core competencies of an organisation and then moved towards inputs and other raw materials, to the delivery mechanisms and finally to the customer. Thus it began with assets and competencies (skilled staff, specialist equipment, supplies and services) then

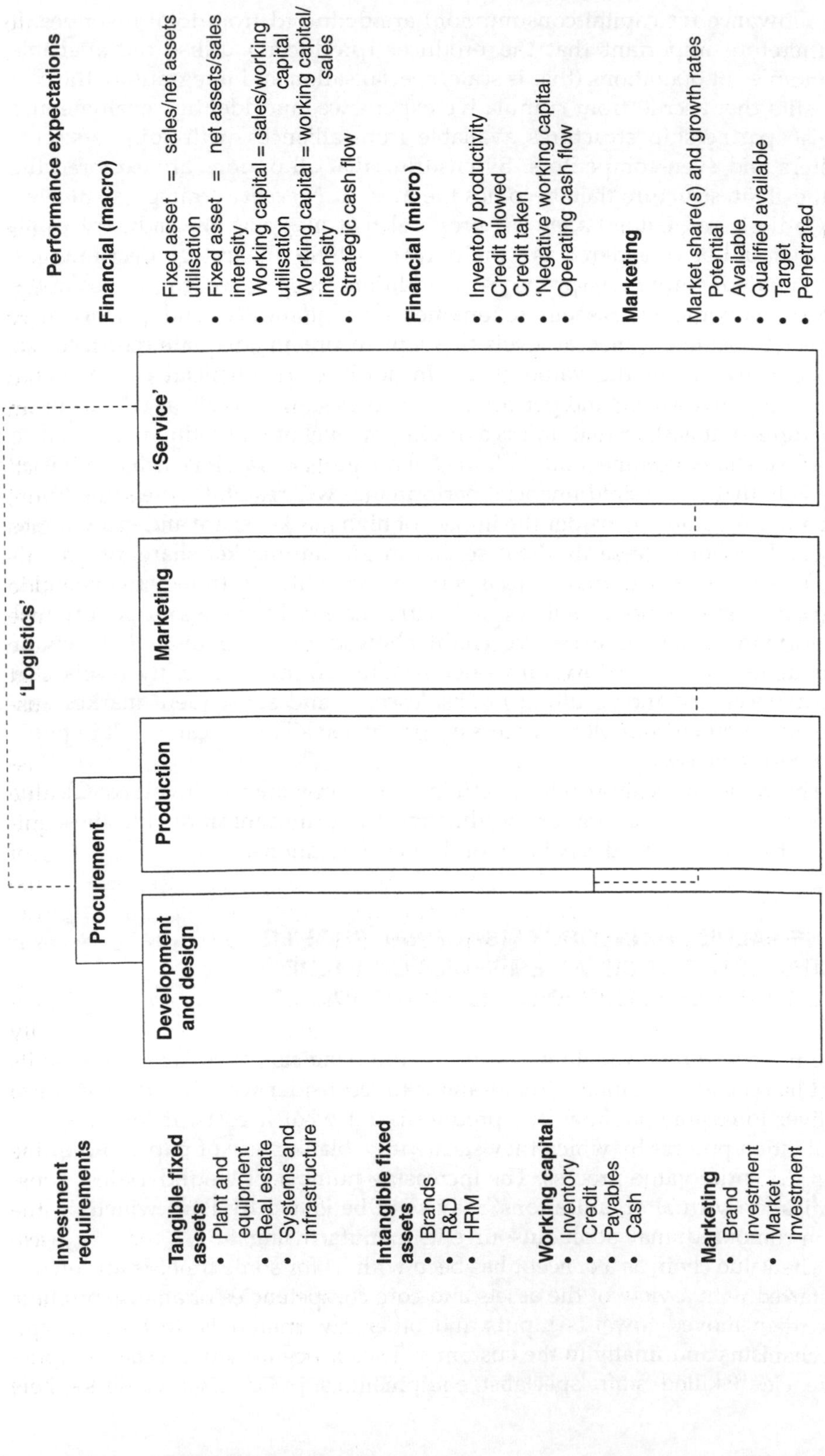

Figure 7.14 Value chain: investment requirements and performance expectations

Investment requirements

Tangible fixed assets
- Plant and equipment
- Real estate
- Systems and infrastructure

Intangible fixed assets
- Brands
- R&D
- HRM

Working capital
- Inventory
- Credit
- Payables
- Cash

Marketing
- Brand investment
- Market investment

'Logistics'

Procurement

| Development and design | Production | Marketing | 'Service' |

Performance expectations

Financial (macro)
- Fixed asset = sales/net assets utilisation
- Fixed asset = net assets/sales intensity
- Working capital = sales/working utilisation capital
- Working capital = working capital/ intensity sales
- Strategic cash flow

Financial (micro)
- Inventory productivity
- Credit allowed
- Credit taken
- 'Negative' working capital
- Operating cash flow

Marketing

Market share(s) and growth rates
- Potential
- Available
- Qualified available
- Target
- Penetrated

found a way to make the assets into a product or service that fits a template that is important to a customer.

Value chains as customer led structures: essential components

The current approach reverses the process. See Figure 7.15. Thinking begins with customer problems, needs and priorities (the value drivers) and identifies options through which these may be met. It reverses traditional thinking. Managers should identify customer needs, the most relevant delivery methods suited to satisfy these customer needs, the inputs required to create product-services, and then what assets and core competencies are required to compete successfully. It follows that a comprehensive understanding of an organisation's value chain characteristics is essential.

During any 'purchase' situation certain aspects or attributes of a 'product' represent *customer value*. Value attributes enhance a customer's situation, resolve problems, or offer solutions. They are the all important *value drivers* (the additional features that customers will pay additional premia to obtain – or, if they are not available will switch suppliers or brands). Examples include time-to-market, innovative product and/or service solutions, service response times, and 'customisation', as well as the more typical responses that include quality and so forth. Typically they are combined into a *value proposition* that has particular relevance for a particular customer: they appeal to the customer's value criteria. But customers have costs.

Customer acquisition costs are incurred when considering a purchase. Customers maximise value when they select the option for which customer value criteria exceed customer acquisition costs. Both the value criteria and acquisition costs are influenced by external features, such as the 'significance' of the expenditure, the strength of the vendor's brand (reputation), the customer's life cycle/style characteristics and their purchasing expectations (the benefits to be delivered). They can, perhaps should, include opportunity costs, as these are often significant in choice situations.

Any organisation, if it is to be successful, should have a set of *core competencies* or possess the *key success factors* necessary to compete successfully in its 'market(s)'. Typically these relate to its competencies (described by its capabilities and its capacities); its cost structures (economic characteristics) and the 'technology' it has available.

Customer value expectations together with the key success factors combine to produce a *value proposition* that identifies *what* is to be delivered to the customer and by *what means*. In other words the value proposition identifies the benefits and costs for the customer and the internal activities (or processes) necessary to produce the benefits (value).

No organisation should consider entering a contractual arrangement unless its own value expectations can be met (that is, corporate value). These typically relate to profitability, productivity, cash flow (and a number of qualitative features) and typically includes the utilisation of tangible and intangible

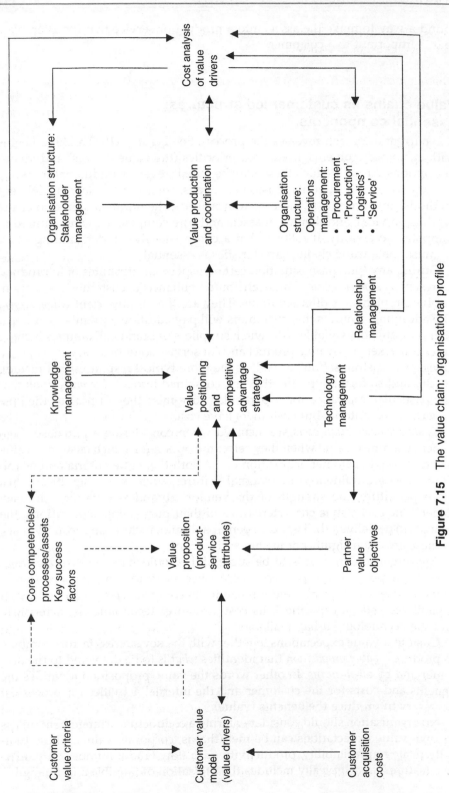

Figure 7.15 The value chain: organisational profile

assets; equipment, staff, etc target response times; reputation for innovation, and development of 'knowledge'.

From this *a value positioning and competitive advantage strategy* is derived which simply states what the organisation sees as the scope of its business, in other words what product-services it will offer, how these will be 'promoted' to its customers and how the services will be delivered. There are three component influences. These are knowledgement management, relationship management and technology management. The context will vary by organisation but in a generic context can be considered to be as follows:

Knowledgement management has already been suggested as 'the organisational capability which identifies, locates (creates or acquires), transfers and converts knowledge into competitive advantage'. In other words, what is the organisation's knowledge strategy? How does it perceive its research as a contribution to its competitive advantage? What are the capabilities of its information systems? What is the role of knowledge, and can the organisation become a 'learning organisation'? Does knowledge exist outwith the organisation? How can this knowledge be accessed?

Relationship management is concerned with what is required by the organisation to identify, establish, maintain and reinforce relationships with customers, suppliers and other partners with *complementary* capabilities and capacities so that the objectives of the organisation *and* of its partners may be met. In other words, how should an organisation work successfully with *all* of its partners to ensure mutual success?

Technology management is the integration of process and product to meet the value objectives of the organisation (as expressed in its value proposition).

The value, positioning and competitive advantage strategy now requires to be implemented. *Value production and coordination* has three influences.

The first influence is an *organisational structure* to cope with '*market management*'. Organisations have a number of 'markets'. These are customers, 'distributors', referral organisation, suppliers; an internal market; 'influencers', and 'investors'. Each requires a strategy for managing the interface between the organisation and the 'market' component.

The second influence is an *organisational structure* to specify *operations management* issues concerning the management of the three aspects of 'production', 'logistics' and 'service'.

Production management is the process by which value is 'manufactured'. It is a process during which decisions concerning what, where, how and when, production processes occur; it identifies options for in-house activities and outsourcing (that is, 'who' is responsible for 'what' processes).

Logistics management considers both material and non-material (service) flows throughout the value chain and its component organisations. The value-added concept here refers to enhancing the perceived value of the product-service to the customer. Economists consider value in terms of utility created and this they suggest has the dimensions of form, possession, time and place. The logistics function was initially concerned with time and place utilities but increasingly the role is being expanded as information sciences influence the concepts of postponement and speculation in the value chain.

Service management in turn has three aspects: pretransaction, transaction and post transaction. Precisely where emphasis is placed depends much upon the nature of the opportunity identified *and* the competitive advantage sought. Information systems connecting internal and external activities and suppliers become a major concern, particularly in the coordination of outsourced activities and services. The production of service products is becoming an important aspect of the 'new economy', and the involvement of the customer in product specification places emphasis on 'pretransaction' in service management. This emphasis is becoming commonplace in manufacturing as Internet applications are developed.

The third influence on value production and coordination is that of core competencies (key success factors), which are essential if an organisation is to compete successfully in its industry or market sector. Value drivers are specific to end-user customers. Value drivers are '. . . the things that are important to customers' (Slywotzky and Morrison: 1997). They reflect customer priorities such that they will pay a premium for them or switch suppliers. Value drivers reinforce competitive advantage BUT meeting value drivers has cost implications for the business. It follows that value chain organisations need to identify the relationships between customer satisfaction (what creates customer satisfaction) and the cost incurred.

VALUE CHAIN: DECISIONS AND PROCESSES

The organisation and profile characteristics establish the need to identify the decisions required in the value chain and the processes that are necessary to make them effective and efficient, in other words the strategic and operational features of the value chain.

Value chain processes

Figure 7.16 identifies the decisions that are typically required within the value chain processes. *Design and development* decisions respond to customer (and reseller) value criteria and acquisition costs. It will be recalled that 'value-in-use' is an aggregate of user benefits together with price. User benefits include those attributes making positive contributions to value-in-use, either through enhancing an existing product (or service) produced by the customer or by reducing the customer's costs during the production process. Hence value-in-use profiles, and the value proposition based upon these are an essential outcome of this process.

Production decisions also reflect initial customer expectations. Decisions are based upon market volume, location, quality and specific market customer determinants (such as choice, availability, and so on). An important concern here is the identification of specific production processes. What specifically is manufactured, by whom, where, when, how and why (the rationale of the decision)?

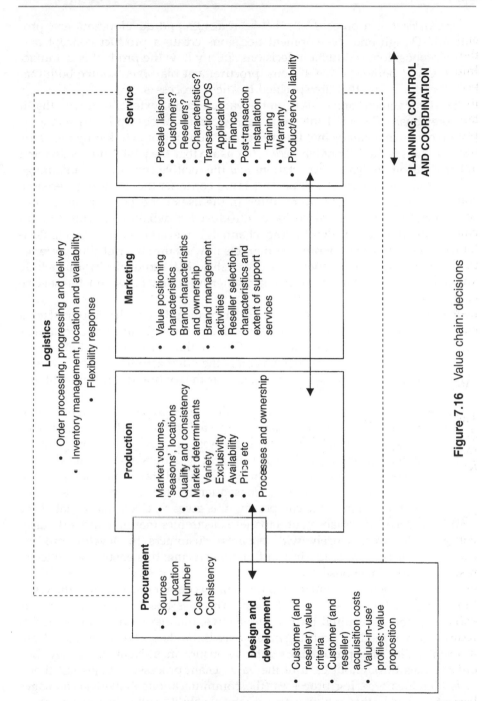

Figure 7.16 Value chain: decisions

Procurement as a process 'sits' between design and development and production. Design and development decisions create a product concept and value proposition; production decisions specify how the product is manufactured. Given both sets of decisions, procurement may then source both materials and services that are specified by these processes.

The involvement of *marketing* in the value chain is extensive. Given that it has previously identified the value characteristics of customer expectations, the involvement extends into the critical decision area of positioning the value offer in the 'market'. Concern here is to ensure that the positioning statement reflects customers' value expectations *and* the relative competitive advantage the product possesses. An important issue concerns the branding decision. Increasingly partnerships are resulting in the use of specialist organisations. The Internet and e-commerce have introduced a debate concerning brand loyalty and the 'power' that Internet channels can exert over purchasing decisions. The issue for many product-markets now assuming critical importance concerns brand identification and ownership. Marketing decisions include reseller selection criteria in terms of reseller roles and tasks and the service support required.

Other *marketing* activities are basic. They include the development of a knowledge base and disseminating knowledge throughout reseller channels (where appropriate) and to end-users. Clearly this is the information aspect of a communication activity; persuasion is the other activity. Probably one of the most important activities for marketing is that of brand development and management.

An essential feature of *service* in the value chain concept is to ensure that the design and development decisions reflected in the production and marketing decisions (and subsequently, processes) are delivered. For example, Caterpillar (construction equipment) designers understand the need for a response system that can cope with the extremes of distance and isolation that are imposed upon their products. Consequently, they incorporate a 'wear' indicator in the design of the component; this gives an electronic signal of the imminent need for replacement. Japanese electronics manufacturers (Hitachi for example) work closely with business customers to develop product specifications prior to tendering and manufacturing: this ensures an efficient 'time-to-market' response.

The role of *logistics* within the value chain becomes crucial. Given the value chain is proactive (it seeks market opportunities and 'designs' a response structure) and is required to be cost-effective, there are a number of critical decisions to be made concerning inventories throughout the value chain. Consequently a logistics process is essential to ensure an efficient and timely flow of materials throughout each of the value chain processes. 'Logistics' therefore identifies ordering processes (the communications activities), manages inventory levels throughout and designs flexibility into the procurement/ production/reseller/end user interfaces. Processes and decisions result in activities. Within the value chain there are some activities that are common to most. In Figure 7.17 a range of these commonplace (or generic) activities are identified. *Logistics* activities are therefore directed towards managing the

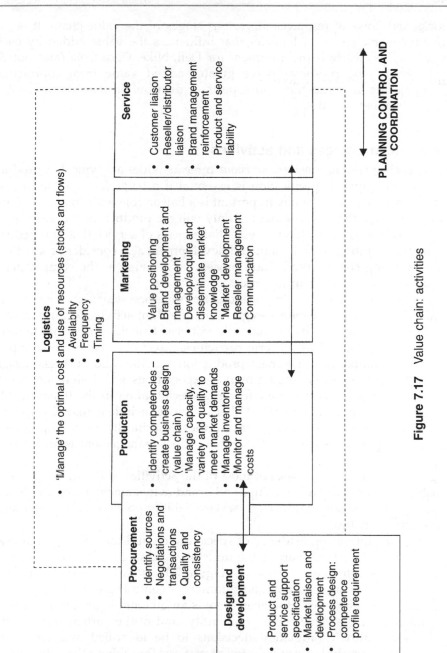

Figure 7.17 Value chain: activities

stocks and flows of resources at various stages of the value chain. It is the effective management of logistics that influences the value added by each process. This clearly is the argument for Dell, Nike, Coca Cola (and potentially Ford) who presumably see greater added value from contractual arrangements in production and aspects of distribution than that available from integrated facilities.

Value chain process and activities

To meet *design and development decisions* three activities are typical. A product and service support specification is essential if a tangible response to customers is to be made. Equally important is a liaison role with customers (and often resellers); this ensures that not only will the product meet customer 'in use' expectations but so too will essential aspects of service that may reduce customer operating costs. Design and development also consider production, by identifying specific production process issues such as the competencies required in the manufacturing process.

Competencies and their implications for a *business design* are reflected in *production* activities. Business design is an important activity because from it evolves a structure which designates the pattern of facilities necessary to meet market expectations. This concerns capacities, capabilities *and* ownership patterns. An example of value chain production activities and business design that was a response to changing market expectations and design and development activities was the move towards specialisation in the Italian textile industry (Piore and Sabel: 1984). Other activities include a shared responsibility with logistics to manage inventories, specifically work-in-progress, through techniques such as MRP and JIT. Cost management is an integral activity.

Liaison comprises the basis of most of the activities of the *service* process. Customer and reseller relationships and brand management are clearly based upon effective liaison. Product and service liability policies are implemented by service activities.

Given the increasing tendency of specialisation and the 'virtual' organisation of the value chain, part of the decision making concerns the extent of ownership of value chain processes. Figure 7.18 is based upon discussions with a number of organisations and summarises control/coordination profiles of value chain processes. However, there is an inherent logic. Clearly it is in the interests of the value chain as an entity (and of the participants specifically) for control/coordination decisions to be identified and resourced because these are the basis of investment patterns throughout the value chain. This is the role of strategic operations management. But they are also related to the need for an effective market based response by the brand controller. For example, if Ford eventually outsources its manufacturing, retaining design and development and marketing, this will be based not only on competency criteria but also the need to have a strong influence in areas of importance to the end-user customer. Thus creative designs and strong brand management are key success factors which require strong management, whereas closely

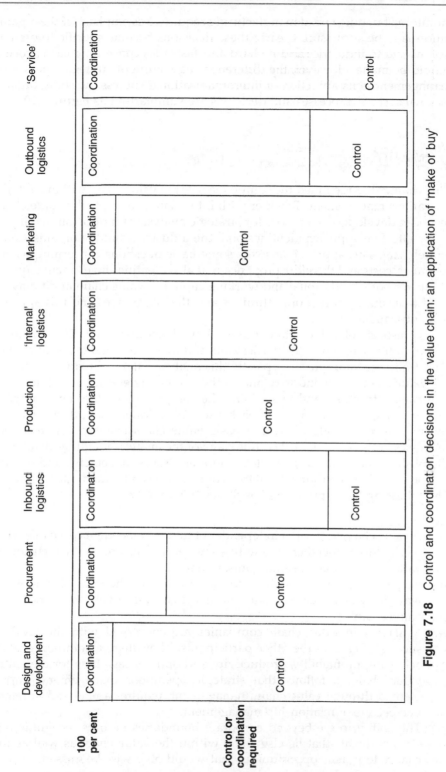

Figure 7.18 Control and coordination decisions in the value chain: an application of 'make or buy'

monitored but outsourced manufacturing requires less emphasis if the organisation is to be successful. Clearly these decisions become specific to organisations and to industries and no hard and fast rules concerning each process should be made. However, the differentiating feature of strategic operations management is its approach to interorganisational success, not only organisational success. Processes and decisions are summarised as Figure 7.19.

SUMMARY

This chapter has identified the components of the value chain within strategic operations management. Together with interrelated concepts the value chain has been developed as a model for strategic analysis and decision making.

An effective approach identifies both the industry's and the organisation's value chain. This approach answers some basic questions concerning where revenues, costs and therefore profit occur. It also identifies investment requirements for both fixed capital and working capital. A value chain audit may be used to evaluate market opportunities and the alternatives and this appears in a subsequent chapter.

Two aspects of value chain strategy have been discussed. The organisational profile determines the participants and their roles (and expectations) in (and from) the value chain. Typically this analysis offers a broad structure of the value chain of the industry and of the competing entities. It will identify alternative structures and in so doing the competitive profiles and competitive advantage characteristics of each alternative. Value chain decisions concerning processes follow. Given a basic value chain in which the essential processes have been established this stage of the analysis identifies detail and establishes (and evaluates) alternative models. Issues that emerge and require to be resolved are investment, control, coordination and 'brand' identification. The following list of principles concludes this chapter:

- A value chain is: 'a set of independent but interdependent companies that work closely together to identify, create, deliver and service customer value expectations . . . an organisational form'.
- Each participant has a stake in the success of the others: '. . . they look for ways in which resources can be utilised cost-effectively throughout the value chain'.
- Managers in value chain companies are concerned with the level of success of each of the other participants. They share a common goal of achieving profitability, productivity and optimal cash flow for the entire value chain. It follows that strategic operations management, implemented through value chain management, requires a new and different perspective of relationship management.
- The ability to see beyond corporate boundaries permits recognition of serious threats that lie elsewhere within the value chain as well as the chance to pursue opportunities that would otherwise be missed.

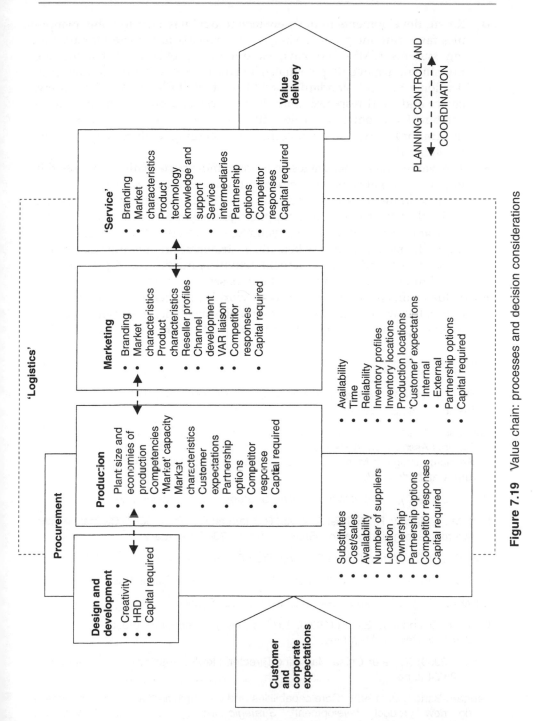

Figure 7.19 Value chain: processes and decision considerations

- Recent developments in the 'new technology' have led to many companies favouring integration. Many have invested in flexible manufacturing systems (FMS) and have experienced problems in making the investment achieve its potential. The culture and practices of long production runs and standardisation do not fit the emphasis on variety, choice and short response times. However, many other companies have combined economies of scale with those of scope (the economies of integration) very successfully in the emerging culture of *technology management*.
- The value chain encourages expertise and specialisation and all this implies for organisation structure and *relationship management*.
- Because knowledge is shared, the value chain participants understand each other, their customers, suppliers and competitors. *Knowledge management* ensures competitive advantage.
- Value chains can secure the benefits of strategic and operating economies by sharing R and D, procurement activities, manufacturing technology, distribution facilities and market databases.
- Value chains have 'the best of both worlds'; the coordination and scale associated with large companies and the flexibility, creativity and low overhead structures typically found in small companies.

REFERENCES ●

Abell, D. F. (1980), *Defining the Business: The Starting Point of Strategic Planning*, Prentice-Hall, Englewood Cliffs.

Anterasian, C. and L. W. Phillips (1988), *Discontinuities, Value Delivery, and the Salwe-Returns Association: A Re-examination of the 'Share-Causes-Profits" Controversy*, Research Program Monograph, Report No. 88-109, The Marketing Science Institute, Cambridge, MA.

Brown, L. (1997), *Competitive Marketing Strategy*, Nelson, Melbourne.

Burt, M., J. Harvey, R. Guthrie, A. Voyle, R. Islam and N. Tait (2000), 'Carmakers take two routes to global growth', *Financial Times*, 26/27 February.

Day, G. (1990), *Market Driven Strategy*, Free Press, New York.

Dell, M. (with C. Fredman) (1999), *Direct from Dell*, Harper Collins Business, London.

Edwards, R. (1995), Report, PA Consulting Group, Sydney.

Gadiesh, O. and J. L. Gilbert (1998), 'How to map your industry's profit pool', *Harvard Business Review*, May/June.

Lai, A. (2000) (Greater China Marketing Director, Hewlett Packard), Comment made on 23/24 June.

Leonard-Barton, D. (1992), 'Core capabilities and core rigidities: a paradox in managing new product development', *Strategic Management Journal*, Vol. 13, No. 2.

Mathur, S. S. and A. Kenyon (1998), *Creating Value: Shaping Tomorrow's Business*, Butterworth-Heinemann, Oxford.

McHugh, P., G. Merli and G. Wheeler III (1995), *Beyond Business Process Reengineering*, Wiley, Chichester.

Normann, R. and R. Ramirez (1994), *Designing Interactive Strategy: From Value Chain to Value Constellation*, Wiley, New York.

O'Sullivan, L. and J. M. Geringer (1993), 'Harnessing the power of your value chain', *Long Range Planning*, Vol. 26, No. 2.

Piore, M. J. and C. F. Sabel (1984), *The Second Industrial Divide*, Basic Books, New York.

Porter, M. (1985), *Competitive Strategy*, The Free Press, New York.

Scott, M. (1998), *Value Drivers*, Wiley, Chichester.

Slywotzky, A. J. and D. J. Morrison (1997), *The Profit Zone*, Wiley, New York.

Vollman, T. E. and C. Cordon (1998), 'Building successful customer-supplier alliances', *Long Range Planning*, Vol. 31, No. 5.

Webster, F. (1994), *Market Driven Management*, Wiley, New York.

chapter 8

Corporate Value, Performance Management, Coordination and Control: Issues and Options

LEARNING OUTCOMES

The student will be able to:

- understand the role of stakeholders and stakeholder objectives in the value chain;
- apply the 'balanced scorecard' concept to value chain planning decisions;
- apply the balanced scorecard and strategy mapping to exploring and evaluating value chain alternatives.

INTRODUCTION

Previous chapters have identified the components of strategic operations management. Chapter 7 presented a generic value chain in which the organisation was 'profiled' to identify the activities involved in delivering value together with the expectations of member organisations. Value chain decisions and processes necessary to make the value chain an effective means through which strategic operations management objectives may be met were added to the discussion.

Performance management in an individual company 'controlling' the entire value production process is difficult. The difficulties compound themselves within a value chain structure. Consequently there is a requirement for a performance management model capable of coordination, as well as control and performance measurement. Coordination and control within the value chain are critical roles. McHugh *et al* (1995) identified 'the role of the virtual company integrator' in their work on *Beyond Business Process Reengineering*. An integrator is '. . . often a visionary who sees how putting pieces together will create a better core business process'. The concern is to ensure the defined business moves along, arbitrates disputes, manages contracts with customers and monitors performance. Integrator roles differ and the authors identified two types. One role concerns start-up situations, where the role is to identify participants and to define a structure which best meets the value expectations of the target customer group. The other role is one in which the complete network has been defined and the integrator role is more involved with customer and contract relations. For both roles there is a communications management task: the integrator receives market feedback and communicates this feedback across the value chain structure. The integrator sets, monitors and evaluates performance measures. Performance measures concern 'not only the economic achievements . . . but also the humanistic goals set (by the value chain)'.

The 'value chain integrator' has responsibility for:

- creating and coordinating a multi-enterprise organisation;
- collecting, analysing, structuring and disseminating knowledge from and to stakeholders rapidly and efficiently;
- ensuring empowerment is effective at critical decision making points;
- developing and/or managing concurrent operations – simultaneous process management using a value chain approach;
- responding to the demands of customisation and mass customisation;
- creating and coordinating organisation structures that identify and respond to 'global' challenges and opportunities in a planned manner;
- maximising the value of the enterprise by identifying, linking and coordinating core competencies from a range of value chain participants.

This role predicates the requirements of a performance management system capable of reflecting composite performance across the value chain and which reflects the interests of the principal stakeholders. The structure of value chains implies that different approaches may be required and, therefore, that performance management becomes customised.

THE STAKEHOLDER APPROACH

Interorganisational systems – interrelated objectives

The notion of interrelated systems is not new. Koch (1994) refers to the role of information technology and its ability to span corporate boundaries, necessitating a review of interorganisational structures and relationships. Well before the IT revolution, thought was being given to the *functional* aspects of distribution versus the view that considers distribution as an activity performed by a number of *institutions*. Intermediaries are seen as system functionaries, their designations are incidental: '. . . what is critical is the system design through which functions can best be performed' (Dommermuth and Andersen: 1969). The impact of information systems extends beyond distribution channels (as suggested by Short and Venkatraman: 1992), and now has an impact across entire operational processes. Thus their comment concerning the impact of information systems: '. . . [they can] redefine market boundaries, alter the fundamental rules and basis of competition, redefine business scope, and provide a new set of competitive weapons', is particularly relevant. Add to this: 'Just as importantly, they change the emphasis in interorganisational relations from *separation* to *unification*' (Stern *et al* 1996), and the contention that interorganisational functions and processes are becoming increasingly integrated leads to a significant role for strategic operations management.

The growth of 'virtual organisations' has added emphasis to the need for a strategic operations perspective. Oates (1998) discusses outsourcing in the context of virtual organisations. He refers to a contribution by Moran (in a *Daily Telegraph* supplement on outsourcing, 28 May 1997) to the effect that outsourcing was no longer seen as: '. . . a way to reduce costs, it is now perceived as a route to improve business performance and competitive strength'. Oates also refers to a survey by Andersen Consulting, aimed at finding out what 350 executives expected their companies to look like in 2010. Comments regarding outsourcing suggest cost reduction remaining as a prime motivating force, but six other reasons were offered:

- to improve overall business performance;
- to sharpen business focus;
- for accessing external skills;
- for improving quality and efficiency of the outsourced process;
- to achieve competitive advantage;
- to create new revenue sources.

These benefits are realisable through strategic operations management: 'Rather than owning assets, companies look to outsource functions to achieve a high level of flexibility in providing services. There is a shift in focus to communication and linkages between the various outsourced functions and distributed assets' (Beech: 1998). It extends its interest and influence into developing and managing networks of logically related assets (the virtual organisation). The owners of the processes clearly have their own objectives. As stakeholders in a virtual enterprise their interests merge with their responsibilities.

Stakeholder expectations remain important in the virtual organisation

Stakeholders and their interests are described in Figure 8.1. There are a number of principal stakeholders. *Shareholders* have expectations for capital

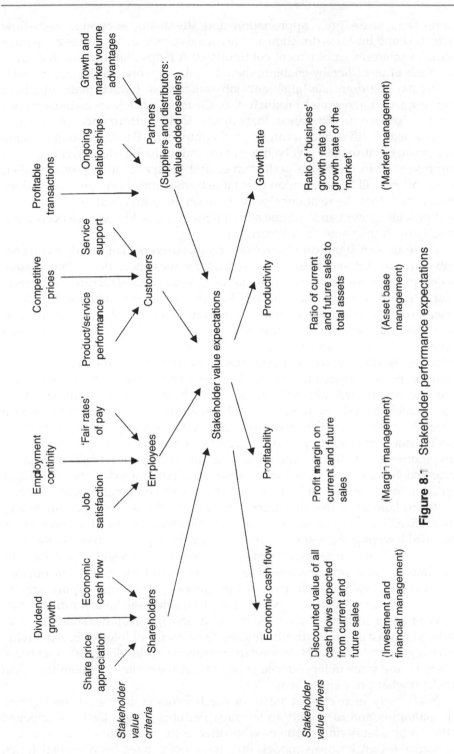

Figure 8.1 Stakeholder performance expectations

gains from share price appreciation and dividends, economic cash flow reflects sound business direction and financial decisions. *Employees* have three primary interests: employment continuity (this helps plan their own future); fair rates of pay (thereby enabling them to balance work and leisure interests – and pay the domestic bills); and job satisfaction, (which maintains their commitment, interest and productivity). *Customer* value expectations are for product/service performance that meets their performance/price/value expectations, with service as an integral component. *Partner organisations* are important because their involvement in the value chain is dependent upon an improvement in their own performance and prospects; it follows that their expectations will be based upon profitable transactions from the relationships established, that the relationships become ongoing and mutually beneficial, and provide growth and volume advantages that would not have been available outwith the value chain structure.

There are four significant 'stakeholder value drivers' that together will contribute to meeting and satisfying stakeholder value expectations. They present no surprises. *Cash flow* is an essential of any business structure. Long term cost-effective economic cash flow is key to the success of the value chain. Figure 6.3 (Chapter 6) identified the components of operational and strategic cash flow, and reflection on these will demonstrate the importance of developing a value chain structure that considers the *influences* as well as the total. Introducing discounted cash flow (DCF) procedures to the cash flow calculation permits an evaluation of alternative value chain structures and the implications of these alternatives for value chain partners. Examples of the importance of such evaluations can be seen in the ongoing changes in a number of industries. Ford sees the use of Net technologies as offering benefits in using customer responses to decrease production schedule time, lower inventories and reduce markdowns. The impact on cash flows is to increase profit contribution, lower working capital requirements (and interest changes on inventory holding) and lower the fixed asset requirements necessary currently to hold excessive inventories. Ultimately the technology will reduce many fixed asset requirements thereby not only lowering the demand for cash but also lowering the cost of capital as risk perceptions of investors fall.

Profitability is also essential. Strategic operations management should have profitability as a primary objective. An increase in margins is an obvious incentive for value chain partnership development. The opportunity to expand volumes *and* lower operating expenses through collaborative activities has, again, obvious attractions. However, the opportunities should be considered against apparent disadvantages. The benefits of Internet based buying exchanges can be a *tenfold decrease* in transaction costs, BUT participants are likely to lose some independence of action and the choice of whom they deal with, at what price and when!

Productivity increases accrue from the benefits of increased throughput, specialisation and the ability to leverage partners' assets. Dell has achieved success by identifying partners who offer both capabilities and capacities that fit the Dell business model. But the benefits have been mutual (often collective) as the benefits of scheduling a known (and guaranteed) volume contribute to lower operating costs. Another benefit of value chain membership concerns investment in fixed and current assets. Partnership should result in eliminating much of the inevitable guesswork concerning capacity provision and, furthermore, permits currency in the investment decision.

Value chain stakeholder expectations concerning *growth rate* are for growth which is consistent, predictable and exceeds that likely to occur if the 'partner' remains independent. These expectations can be expected to materialise provided that the value chain integrator pursues a market based strategy (see earlier chapters), interpreting and responding to customer expectations (and changes to these) and identifying additional market led opportunities with existing and new customers.

Clearly planning strategic operations management performance is an activity requiring perception, innovation and persuasive coordination. Any performance management model must be capable of identifying alternative solutions to meeting market based objectives, evaluating alternative structures and influences on 'corporate performance' and then managing (through coordination) an integrated value chain. Not easy, but nor is it impossible.

This topic is pursued by Kalmbach and Roussel (1999) of Andersen Consulting who use the practice's data to show that only 51 per cent of alliances use formal performance measures, and: '. . . of those that do, just 20 per cent . . . believe the measures to be sufficient. All told, barely 10 per cent of alliances have meaningful measures of performance'.

The authors identify the fact that problems exist. Many resources and deliverables have no attached market price: partners are forced to value intangibles such as knowledge, managerial advice, market positioning and so on, to create a 'picture of performance'. They suggest that many benefits accumulate outwith the alliance, with the benefits then applied to other projects. Alliance performance is hard to measure because partners may not make all of the information about the value of the alliance available. Kalmbach and Roussel suggest a final problem: there are no established accounting models that could present (impose) a 'standard' view on performance assessment. They contend that: 'Despite the difficulties, alliance performance can and must be measured . . . performance measurement is a critical tool for managing any entity; it would be dangerous to presume that alliance performance is an exception'. They continue by describing three possible models: a 'balanced scoreboard', a 'dollar defence' and 'accounting for surplus value'.

Performance measurement for virtual organisations

The *balanced scoreboard* is ideal for alliances. The nature of alliances – multifaceted and fluid – makes it important to monitor performance from a variety of perspectives. The authors cite the example of an energy company that established 10 to 15 performance measures for each alliance. The number was large enough to incorporate the alliances' interests and limited enough to ensure that management would allocate time to monitor (and act upon) the measures. The measures provided a balanced combination of perspectives encompassing financial and strategic measures over the short and longer terms and measures that monitor processes and end results. One measure in common was *customer satisfaction*.

The authors describe three specific techniques under the *balanced scorecard* technique:

- *Measure the effect on share price.* Andersen have worked with academics to develop the Partnership Value Assessment, a statistical tool that investigates the impact of pre and post alliance activities on the partners' share prices and subsequently aggregates the effects along a number of dimensions to analyse the value creating effect of various industry factors and alliance features.
- *Elevate a few measures.* Two or three performance measures are identified as 'red flags' that quickly indicate when there are critical problems. They become focal points for alliance members. The authors cite SEMATECH (a semiconductor alliance) that has focussed on member firm return on investment and individual project performance.
- *Link to individual incentives.* The authors argue that performance measures gain much more attention when linked directly to reward systems. They suggest that devising appropriate rewards for alliance performance generally is a straightforward task and for optimal effectiveness, companies should ensure that at least a few senior managers are evaluated on the basis of the full balanced scoreboard of between 10 and 15 measures.

The balanced scorecard is of particular interest to value chain management and will be returned to later in this chapter.

A *dollar defence* is: '. . . an indisputable, stable source of financial value that allows the alliance to pursue strategic benefits without living under the constant threat of venture dissolution'. It also sends strong messages to financial markets that the alliance continues to create significant value.

Surplus value is value generated by alliances but typically recognised by only one partner. It is the 'halo' effect a small partner gains from association with a larger partner. It is argued that the alliance is an endorsement of the small company and raises investor enthusiasm, business contacts and overall market opportunities.

The authors conclude: '. . . alliances present real challenges in measuring performance . . . different corporate interest, work in short time frames and deal with non-financial benefits and surplus value. Difficult as it may be, however, it is simply not possible to have consistent success in alliances without overcoming these issues'.

USING ADDED VALUE AS A PERFORMANCE MEASURE

It will be remembered that Kay (1993) uses added value to measure corporate success. Kay's measure of competitive advantage is the ratio of added value to the organisation's gross or net output:

$$\frac{\text{Competitive}}{\text{advantage}} = \frac{\text{Revenues} - (\text{Wages} + \text{Salaries} + \text{Materials} + \text{Capital costs})}{(\text{Wages} + \text{Salaries} + \text{Materials} + \text{Capital costs})}$$

Kay uses the model to explore corporate strategy issues on the basis that:

> Corporate success derives from a competitive advantage which is based on distinctive capabilities, which is most often derived from the unique character of a firm's relationships with its suppliers, customers, or employees and which is precisely identified and applied to relevant markets.

He asks:

> Did it make sense for Benetton . . . to move into retailing, and was it right to decide to franchise most of its shops to individual franchises? . . . What segment of the motor car market was most appropriate for BMW?

He questions the measurement of success and performance, suggesting size, a firm's sales, its market share, and its value on the stock market as options typically used together with a 'rate of return': this can be measured as return on equity, on investment or on sales. Other measures commonly used include growth, productivity, and increased earnings per share or the price earnings ratio. Kay argues that while these measures are aspects of successful performance the *key measure of corporate performance is added value,* in other words the difference between the (comprehensively accounted) value of a firm's output and the (comprehensively accounted) cost of the firm's inputs.

Business relationships are crucial and Kay argues that the added value statement is not simply a means of looking at financial consequences. It describes the set of relationships that constitute the firm. In the *virtual organisation model* its role can be extended beyond *relationship management* to include both *knowledge management* and *technology management.* The flexibility of the model enables any options to be considered. In particular a model of the industry, or the sector, that explores these components from the perspective of alternative formats can result in identifying the preferable location of the firm within the industry or sector value chain. The analysis, suggests Kay, is based upon ' . . . a careful appreciation of the strengths of the firm and the economic environment it faces'. Kay uses the added value model to explore the added value perspectives of stages in the value chain. Primary (extraction) industries have materials and capital costs as dominant inputs. Secondary organisations (for example, those engaged in consumer durable manufacturing) are suggested to have a predominance of materials and wages and salaries as input costs. Tertiary businesses are typically dominated by materials costs, some labour costs, and depending upon management's view of infrastructure ownership (typically retail outlets and distribution networks) capital inputs may, or may not, be significant.

The scope of strategic operations management within the context of the *new economy* and the *virtual organisation* is of particular interest. As many organisations question their future structure and begin to review competencies within the context of the virtual operations model there is a vital need for the organisation to map the input/output profiles of its value chain partners and to engage at a point where its strengths and weaknesses can be matched with opportunities and threats such that stakeholder value (that is, the value accruing to shareholders, customers, suppliers, employees and the community) is optimised.

Kay's model, modified a little to explore the concept within the context of strategic operations management is illustrated as Figure 8.2 which considers the role of strategic operations management in exploring factors that influence effective responses. For example, a number of questions should be raised concerning the procurement and/or manufacture of *materials and components*. The ownership structure of materials or component manufacturing may be concentrated, in which case the ability to differentiate a product by incorporating an outsourced component will be limited. Marketing, by maintaining an ongoing 'dialogue' with customers, is in a position to identify the costs and benefits of outsourcing or insourcing the item and the impact on added value. From this analysis it follows that alternatives may be sought and evaluated.

A similar argument may be made with regard to *wages and salaries*. Here the concern is that *knowledge* (management expertise and specialist labour skills) may not be available 'in house'. The reality is that with a virtual organisation it is of no consequence because the virtual organisation structure encourages the leverage of both management expertise and specialist labour. The concept of the *economics of integration* is one that utilises *knowledge management* to identify the precise combination of *technology* that will provide competitive advantage. *Relationship management* expertise is essential to coordinate the extensive cooperation and coproductivity among value organisation partnerships. Distance is no longer a constraint. The example given by Li and Fung, who act for major brand owners from their Hong Kong base providing a range of service processes for their global principals, is one of an increasing number of such partnerships. Li and Fung provide an extensive range of processes, from developing product prototypes from their principal's specifications to managing the logistics of delivering specific consignments to designated locations throughout the world. Meanwhile the brand owner continues with what they are particularly good at – managing the marketing of their brand portfolio. But the basic issue is one of understanding the marketplace, of understanding customer expectations and deriving specifications of the product and service that will deliver the customer value specifications.

THE BALANCED SCORECARD

Another contribution towards measuring comprehensive performance is the *balanced scorecard*. Kaplan and Norton (1993) contend: 'Executives also understand that traditional financial accounting measures like return-on-investment and earnings per share can give misleading signals for continuous improve-

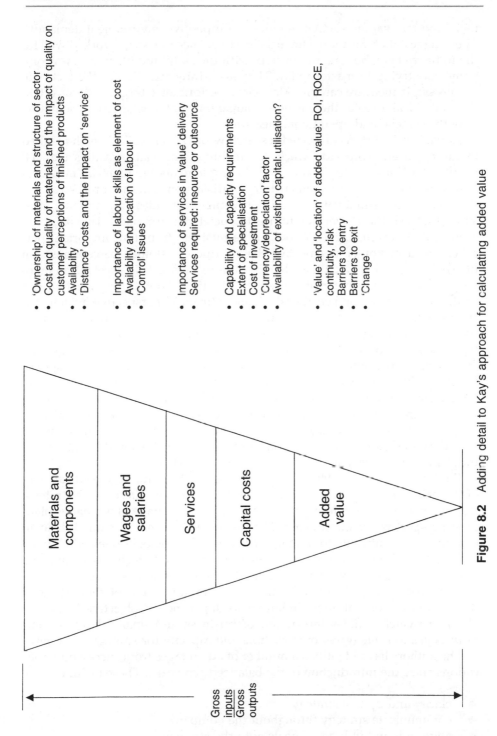

- 'Ownership' of materials and structure of sector
- Cost and quality of materials and the impact of quality on customer perceptions of finished products
- Availability
- 'Distance' costs and the impact on 'service'

- Importance of labour skills as element of cost
- Availability and location of labour
- 'Control' issues

- Importance of services in 'value' delivery
- Services required: insource or outsource

- Capability and capacity requirements
- Extent of specialisation
- Cost of investment
- 'Currency/depreciation' factor
- Availability of existing capital: utilisation?

- 'Value' and 'location' of added value: ROI, ROCE, continuity, risk
- Barriers to entry
- Barriers to exit
- 'Change'

Materials and components

Wages and salaries

Services

Capital costs

Added value

Gross inputs
Gross outputs

Figure 8.2 Adding detail to Kay's approach for calculating added value

ment and innovation – activities today's competitive environment demands'. They suggest that traditional financial performance measures worked well for the industrial era, but are 'out of step' with the skills and competencies companies are trying to master today. They also draw attention to the fact that: '. . . no single measure can provide a clear performance target or focus attention on critical areas of the business. Managers want a balanced presentation of both financial and operational measures'.

Kaplan and Norton conducted research with 12 companies which resulted in the balanced scorecard, which: '. . . includes financial measures that tell results of actions already taken. And it complements the financial measures with operational measures on customer satisfaction, internal processes, and the organisation's innovation and improvement activities – operational measures that are the drivers of future financial performance'. The balanced scorecard allows managers to look at the business from four important perspectives: a customer perspective (based upon customer perceptions); an internal perspective (detailing what the organisation should excel at); an innovation and learning perspective (which identifies how an organisation can continue to improve and create value); and a financial perspective (which considers stakeholders' value expectations). They report on experiences of user companies and suggest two major benefits: a composite report which brings together hitherto 'disparate elements of a company's competitive agenda', and performance information on customer orientation, corporate response times, quality team work and management, product launch activities, and long term directions. These are examples of the aggregate of knowledge management provided by the balanced scorecard. Subsequent experiences suggest additional advantages: 'The real benefit comes from making the scorecard the cornerstone of the way you run the business. It should be the core of the management system, not the measurement system'.

Kaplan and Norton (1996) also pursue the strategic management capacity of the balanced scorecard. See Figure 8.3. They claim its success as a strategic management system, offering management the advantage of a broader planning perspective by introducing four processes: '. . . that, separately and in combination, contribute to linking long-term strategic objectives with short-term actions'. These processes are *translating the vision* (which helps managers build a consensus around the organisation's vision and strategy); *communicating and linking* (facilitates managers' communication of their strategy throughout the organisation, linking it to departmental objectives); *business planning* (which enables integration of business and financial plans); and *feedback and learning* (gives organisations the capacity for strategic learning).

The authors have identified a number of advantages from successful applications since the introduction of the balanced scorecard. These include:

- clarify and update strategy;
- communicate strategy throughout the company;
- align unit and individual goals with the strategy;
- link strategic objectives to long-term targets and annual budgets;
- validate cause-and-effect relationships;

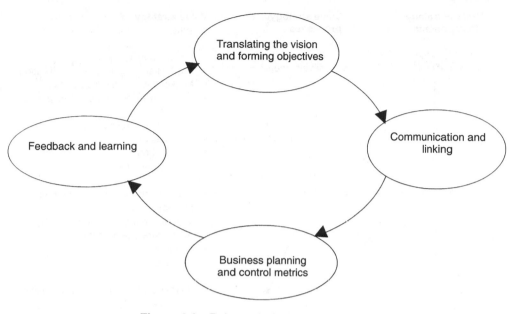

Figure 8.3   Balanced scorecard processes

- identify and align strategic initiatives;
- conduct performance reviews to learn about and improve strategy.

The scorecard is easily modified for use in strategic operations management. Kaplan and Norton have reported its successful application within a number of organisations. However, strategic operations management considers performance planning and measurement across a *number* of organisations. This requirement suggests the need for modifications to accommodate a stakeholder approach.

DEVELOPING A STRATEGIC OPERATIONS MANAGEMENT PERFORMANCE PLANNING COORDINATION AND CONTROL MODEL

The balanced scorecard offers strategic operations management a valuable model for planning and control. It does require some changes, the most important being its modification to accommodate the value chain structure that strategic operations management creates.

Value creation and delivery is a complex process. Figure 8.4 considers the extent of the value strategy response. Strategic operations can be disaggregated into *processes* (design and development, production and so on, together with the support processes of procurement and logistics) and from processes

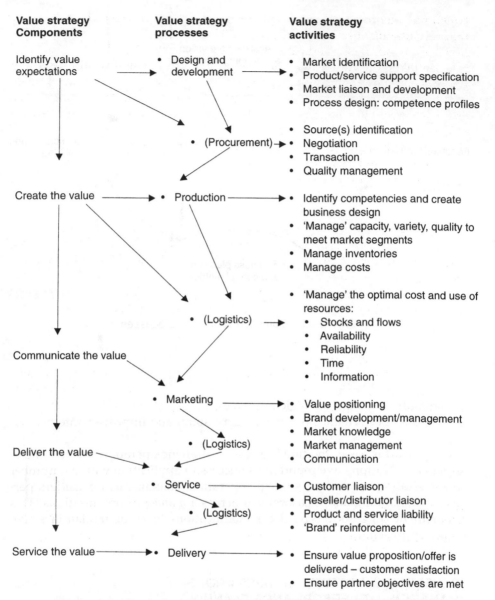

Value strategy Components	Value strategy processes	Value strategy activities
Identify value expectations	• Design and development	• Market identification • Product/service support specification • Market liaison and development • Process design: competence profiles
	• (Procurement)	• Source(s) identification • Negotiation • Transaction • Quality management
Create the value	• Production	• Identify competencies and create business design • 'Manage' capacity, variety, quality to meet market segments • Manage inventories • Manage costs
Communicate the value	• (Logistics)	• 'Manage' the optimal cost and use of resources: • Stocks and flows • Availability • Reliability • Time • Information
Deliver the value	• Marketing	• Value positioning • Brand development/management • Market knowledge • Market management • Communication
	• (Logistics)	
	• Service	• Customer liaison • Reseller/distributor liaison • Product and service liability • 'Brand' reinforcement
	• (Logistics)	
Service the value	• Delivery	• Ensure value proposition/offer is delivered – customer satisfaction • Ensure partner objectives are met

Figure 8.4   Strategic operations: planning value creation and delivery

specific *activities* are derived. The direction of strategic operations management is towards using specialists in a value chain context and it follows that entire processes, certainly activities, may be outsourced to specialist organisations. Planning, coordination and control become inter-organisational rather than have an intra-organisation focus. The critical issue for strategic operations management is to ensure that the value chain both delivers customer satisfaction *and* meets the objectives of the value chain participants. Oates

(1998) has identified an important concern for strategic operations decisions that rely on outsourcing arrangements: 'However, outsourcing – like delegation – does not mean abdicating total responsibility. The day-to-day worry may be taken off your hands, but the ultimate responsibility still rests with the outsourcing organisation. At the end of the day, a company's customers will not want to know who specifically is to blame for a failed delivery . . . The customer will simply reassess its opinion of the provider, regardless of who actually caused the foul up'. The point Oates makes is simply that unless the value delivery process is value production and coordination based, and is structured around the expectations and objectives of all stakeholders, suboptimal performance can be expected.

Modifying the scorecard

Clearly the first modification is to make stakeholder objectives *and* linking performance a major feature. Figure 8.5 illustrates this change and also expands the *perspectives* of the scorecard model by adding an *external* perspective. The purpose of the additional perspective is to ensure that competitive responses are identified, monitored and met with due consideration and actions.

A number of questions are posed in Figure 8.5 for each perspective. Each question is significant in that the answer prescribes the direction of the value creation processes and the coordination and control functions the scorecard will be expected to monitor. The *financial perspective* considers the financial objectives of the value chain participants. Essentially the performance considerations are focussed on measures of 'return on investment' and the risk of exposure of the investment. It follows that value added resellers (VARs) would prefer a structure that minimises inventory holding and, at the same time, maximises their use of suppliers' working capital. The amount of added value created, and where, within the value chain is an important issue as the 'distribution' may not match the 'investment' by individual value chain partners. Consequently there may be concern over the 'equity' of its distribution. The *internal perspective* has as its primary concern the relevance of the value chain structure (that is, partnerships and processes) to meeting customer satisfaction. The linkage with the financial perspective will ensure cost-effectiveness. The *customer perspective* is clearly focussed on achieving customer satisfaction. Its linkages with the internal and innovation and learning perspectives ensure a relevant structure of response processes and that these are monitored and acted upon. *Innovation and learning* are concerned with monitoring customer satisfaction, competitive responses and the efficacy of internal structures in meeting participant and customer value expectations and, further, that any changes that occur can be met. The *external perspective* completes the linkage. In almost any industry or market structure there are a number of ways in which customer value can be (and is) delivered. An external perspective monitors these alternatives with regard to the extent that customer value delivery differs (as do the responses from customers) and the structures and delivery costs of competitive alternatives. The central role of *strategic stakeholder objectives* is to ensure optimal performance is achieved: that

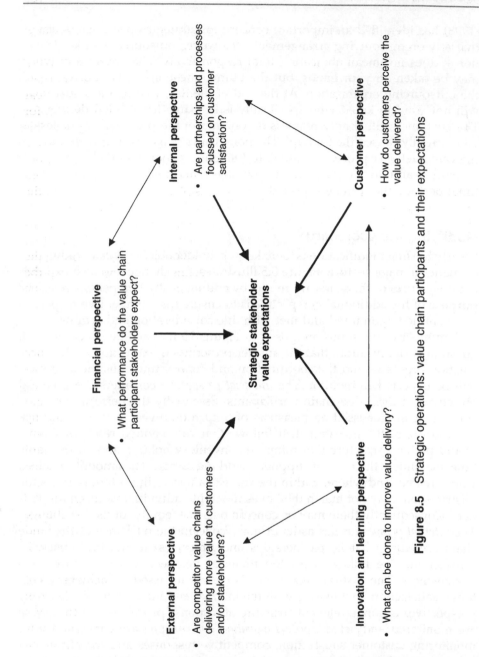

Figure 8.5   Strategic operations: value chain participants and their expectations

the customer receives the value expected and that value chain participants' objectives continue to be met.

Stakeholder value expectations should reflect the components identified in Figure 8.1. This is particularly important in business-to-business markets where typically value expectations are financially oriented and have clear implications for customer value expectations. It is safe to assume that if, for example, VAR expectations are satisfied VARs will choose to maintain this state by ensuring that end-user satisfaction is maintained. Assuming the value chain integrator is aware that tangible, premium and latent growth components are critical for the success of the value chain organisation and that consequently these must be reflected in the business plan for the value chain, the 'value' of the value chain as an enterprise can only increase. This concern is reflected in Figure 8.6 where the process moves further by raising questions concerning activities and relationships within the value chain and in eliciting the answers begins to formulate a series of potential metrics. For example the *internal perspective* asks whether partners are meeting their objectives, and the *customer perspective* is seeking to establish customer perceptions of the value offer and 'checking' these against their (the customers') loyalty and transaction responses. The relationship link is concerned to ensure that both customer and partnership satisfaction occur.

Figure 8.6 moves the analysis towards identifying specific performance characteristics. The innovation and learning perspective performance characteristics are suggested to be based upon achieving market leadership characteristics, technology management achievement and research, design and development. Customer loyalty is measured by achieving and maintaining preferred supplier status and the length of time over which that status is maintained. Customer profitability reflects satisfaction through a regular series of transactions and service costs at or below budgeted levels. Customer satisfaction is also measured by positive responses to perceptions of product and support services together with a willingness to become involved with value chain participants in joint development activities. The strength of the linkage performance is indicated by the extent to which joint activities in product and process development and technology management indicate positive growth of added value over time.

The overall benefits to the value chain will be indicated in the growth of enterprise value characteristics. For example, the growth of *tangible value* can be measured by capacity utilisation and output from asset leverage arrangements. *Premium value* growth may be assessed using the Partnership Value Assessment model to monitor partner share prices (market value) on an ongoing basis. *Latent value* can be measured by increasing efficiencies in 'production and distribution systems' and returns generated on brand investment decisions through brand leverage.

The balanced scorecard as a scenario evaluation model

Consider the hypothetical problem identified in Figure 8.7. Declining return on capital employed (ROCE) performance is responsible for the decline in added value and in 'market value' (share prices) of the value chain members

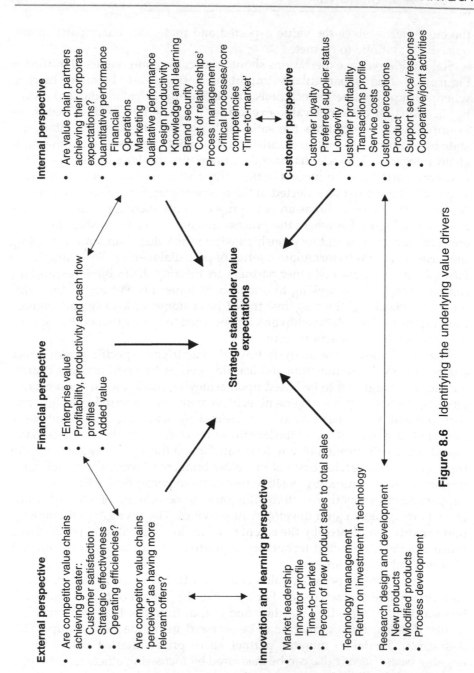

External perspective

- Are competitor value chains achieving greater:
  - Customer satisfaction
  - Strategic effectiveness
  - Operating efficiencies?
- Are competitor value chains 'perceived' as having more relevant offers?

Financial perspective

- 'Enterprise value'
- Profitability, productivity and cash flow profiles
- Added value

Internal perspective

- Are value chain partners achieving their corporate expectations?
- Quantitative performance
  - Financial
  - Operations
  - Marketing
- Qualitative performance
  - Design productivity
  - Knowledge and learning
  - Brand security
  - 'Cost of relationships'
- Process management
  - Critical processes/core competencies
  - 'Time-to-market'

Customer perspective

- Customer loyalty
- Preferred supplier status
- Longevity
- Customer profitability
  - Transactions profile
  - Service costs
- Customer perceptions
  - Product
  - Support service/response
  - Cooperative/joint activities

Innovation and learning perspective

- Market leadership
  - Innovator profile
  - Time-to-market
  - Percent of new product sales to total sales
- Technology management
  - Return on investment in technology
- Research design and development
  - New products
  - Modified products
  - Process development

Strategic stakeholder value expectations

Figure 8.6 Identifying the underlying value drivers

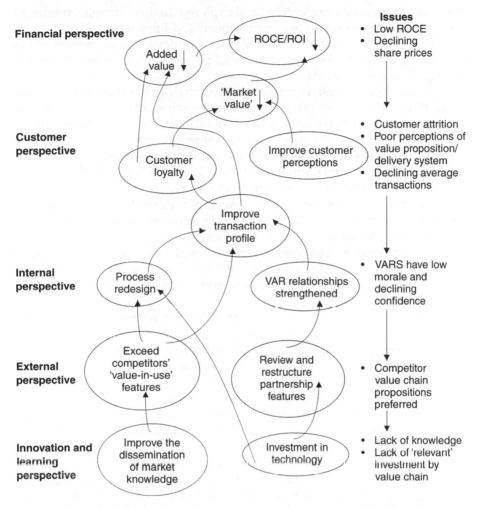

Figure 8.7   Using the balanced scorecard approach to identify and respond to strategic operations issues

and, therefore, in enterprise value. Research indicates that customer loyalty is low, as are customer perceptions. Customer transactions are declining. The morale of VARs is poor and is influencing their performance. There appears to be a strong customer preference for competitor value offers. A conclusion has been reached concerning the lack of knowledge and knowledge management throughout the value chain. Recent investment has largely been irrelevant.

The scorecard would lead to these conclusions because of poor performance reported by key indicators. The linkages would appear after some investigation. The scorecard also offers a means of responding to the problems. Because of the interrelated characteristics across the perspectives, and the cause and effect relationships within and across each of the perspectives, potential solutions can be identified and explored. In this example investment enables process redesign to be commissioned and improvements in partnership structures (with suppliers and VARs) is undertaken; improvements in customer transactions follow and financial performance may be returned to the original intended levels.

The scorecard, through its 'cause and effect' facility has the potential to ask 'what if?' questions when pursuing alternative value chain structures. Figure 8.8 considers an hypothetical situation in which *financial perspectives* expectations are for an increase in enterprise value by increasing added value (through an increase in revenues and a reduction in operating costs). At the same time working capital throughout the value chain is to be reduced as are tangible assets. It is intended to increase the aggregate investment in intangible assets (brand values and R and D). Actions required to meet the financial perspective objectives would include an investment in brand positioning together with an increase in sales volumes. A reduction in tangible assets could be achieved by reducing inventories and customer credit. A major reduction in tangible assets would be realised if, as suggested, low volume product groups were outsourced. This would also have an impact on operating costs.

A principle of the balanced scorecard is to review the linkages between 'perspectives'. As Figure 8.8 demonstrates these are *numerous* in the case of this hypothetical scenario. The changes required in the *customer perspective* objectives could include actions that will result in increasing customer loyalty and customer 'visits' ('visits' may be interpreted as orders or perhaps 'visits' to websites), together with an increase in either the number or value of transactions, or the average value of each order received. A planned reduction in service waiting time may also be considered. Actions necessary to meet customer perspective objectives could include work on product improvement and the introduction of electronic order processing and progressing through Net technology. Service enhancement could be achieved by improving product availability and a planned reduction in service response time for key customers.

The *internal perspective* responses (expressed as objectives) would follow. Again linkages are important. Likely changes would include a review of processes and activities, followed by changes required by the decisions to outsource low volume product manufacturing, to increase service responses and customer transactions (either numbers or average value). New product development may be considered as this would generate interest and have an impact on customer loyalty and customer visit frequencies. An important change would occur if VAR relationships were reviewed and restructured to obtain more involvement from them in service activities. Actions required include NPD programs that offer more 'functional' and useable products and a review of customer service organisation.

Two components of the *external perspective* would require attention. If customer responses are to improve, then 'value-in-use' delivered by the value chain's value proposition should be seen to be greater than competitive offers (this could be reflected in a new product development policy to make

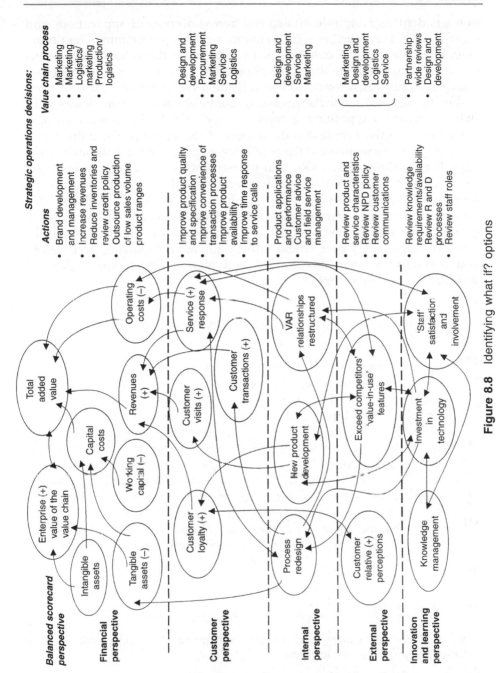

Figure 8.8 Identifying what if? options

products demonstrably more functional across a range of applications and easier to use). This together with a communications programme identifying noticeable differences in customer benefits between the value chain consortium and its competitors, should be planned to have an impact on customer loyalty. Actions which would follow include a comparative review of competitor product and service offers and of communications effectiveness with respect to reinforcing positive perceptions. A review of *innovation and learning perspectives* objectives concludes the review of the scenario. The influence of 'knowledge' as a resource and the possibility of increasing this through structural changes (links with VARs) and investment in 'knowledge technology' would appear necessary. The involvement of staff in creating knowledge would be required as would their involvement in enhancing the service response. Actions necessary to make these changes occur would be a review of knowledge requirements, availability and means by which gaps may be filled. The technology base would also be reviewed following decisions to change product functionality. Kaplan and Norton (2000) offer a detailed approach to strategy mapping.

SUMMARY

Working with value chains requires that a stakeholder perspective be taken. This, in turn, requires the acceptance of shared objectives, joint planning and shared outcomes. The added value model was reintroduced to propose a means by which both inputs and outputs may be identified, quantified and 'located'. The balanced scorecard was proposed as the primary vehicle for this cross-organisation, cross-process task. Of particular interest is the application of the scorecard to stakeholder performance planning and measurement.

The scorecard model was modified for use as a scenario planning model in which improvements in stakeholder performance expectations may be identified. Its cross-perspective facility, together with its cause and effect analysis that enable 'what ifs?' to be asked concerning alternative strategies and structures, make it an ideal model for strategic operations management planning and control.

REFERENCES •

Beech, J. (1998), 'The supply-demand nexus', in Gattorna, J. L. (ed.) *Strategic Supply Chain Alignment*, Gower, Aldershot.

Dommermuth, W. P. and R. C. Andersen (1969), 'Distribution systems: firms, functions and efficiencies,' *MSU Business Topics*, Vol. 17, No. 2 (Spring).

Kalmbach, Jr, C. and C. Roussel (1999), 'Dispelling the myths of alliances', *Outlook*, June.

Kaplan, R. S. and D. P. Norton (1993), 'Putting the balanced scorecard to work', *Harvard Business Review*, September/October.

Kaplan, R. S. and D. P. Norton (1996), 'Using the balanced scorecard as a strategic management system', *Harvard Business Review*, January/February.

Kaplan, R. S. and D. P. Norton (2000), 'Having trouble with your strategy? Then map it,' *Harvard Business Review*, September/October.

Kay, J. (1993), *Foundations of Corporate Success*, Oxford University Press, New York.

Koch, C. (ed.) (1994), 'The power of interorganisational systems', *Indications*, Vol. 11, No. 1.

McHugh, P. G., G. Merli and W. Wheeler III (1995), *Beyond Business Process Reengineering*, Wiley, Chichester.

Oates, D. (1998), *Outsourcing and the Virtual Organisation*, Century Business Books, London.

Short, J. E. and N. Venkatraman (1992), 'Beyond business process redesign: redefining Baxter's business network', *Sloan Management Review*, Fall.

Stern, L. W., A. I. El-Ansery and A. T. Coughlan (1996), *Marketing Channels*, Prentice Hall, Englewood Cliffs.

chapter 9

Managing Customer Value and the Value Proposition

LEARNING OUTCOMES

The student will be able to:

- conduct research into customer value preferences and purchasing decisions;
- construct a customer value model and identify the important value drivers;
- formulate a value proposition.

INTRODUCTION

Achieving customer satisfaction requires success in a number of aspects of supplier/customer relationships. By far the most important is to understand the underlying reasons why customers select both products and suppliers. The business-to-business customer/supplier relationship is usually founded upon a commercial logic relating to efficiencies in either input processes or outputs. The business-to-consumer relationship is often less rational; many purchases are made for emotional reasons, or replacement because of 'psychological wear and tear'. In both situations some structure can be applied and a model developed.

Tracking customer 'decision and use behaviour'

Another important element is an understanding of the purchaser's use of the product. MacMillan and McGrath (1997) suggest that competitive advantage may be realised if the *consumption chain* is identified. The authors claim that 'a company has the opportunity to differentiate itself at every point where it comes into contact with its customers – from the moment customers realise they need a product or service to the time when they no longer want it and decide to dispose of it'.

MacMillan and McGrath's consumption chain has an interesting and worthwhile application for strategic operations management decisions, particularly their implementation through the value chain. The technique identified, 'all the steps through which customers pass from the time they first become aware of your product to the time when they finally have to dispose of it or discontinue using it', describes the customer life cycle typically used in life cycle costing. The process considers a number of questions: awareness, availability, choice, purchasing procedures followed, product delivery and installation, financing payment, storage, mobility, end-user uses, applications service, returns or exchanges, maintenance and disposal issues. Each of these activities creates cost for customers and, as such, needs to be considered when the customer is making a purchase decision. Customer acquisition and life cycle costs must be deducted from the benefits delivered by the product or service to derive a measure of total delivered value.

Managing information in the value chain increases customer value satisfaction

The information provided by consumption chain mapping can be directly applied to value chain decisions. Two examples will illustrate the benefit of such an analysis. Ordering procedures are being revolutionised with Net technology and, in the future, these may be automated as wireless technology is applied to both business-to-business and business-to-consumer markets, making reordering an automatic response to levels of use and inventory holding. The American Hospital Supply application to inventory management of customer installations of computers has been widely adopted over the years. The recent wireless technology developments are forecast to replace this technology with even more intelligent replenishment systems. Value chain intermediaries are currently developing intelligent technology that will link consumers' refrigerators with home delivery services that will relieve consumers of yet another chore.

Remote diagnostics are used by Tandem Computers and Caterpillar Construction equipment for identifing product component malfunctioning. This advance notice of failure allows early dispatch of replacement parts (thereby reducing field inventories and the alerting of technical staff (increased utilisation of human resources), both of which reduce costs for customers and the value chain.

The authors explore 'customers' experience' as a means to gaining insight into the customer by: '. . . appreciating the context within which each step of the consumption chain unfolds'. A series of simple questions: What? Where? Who? When? How? are used to identify opportunities for additional directions in which the product-service may be offered. The question: Why? (omitted by MacMillan and McGrath) should be included as this may identify two important strategic questions: Why this product-service? And why this particular value delivery alternative and not another? Not only can

'Kipling's six serving men' identify additional options for differentiation; they can also be used to reinforce the existing value offer.

Both the consumption chain and an analysis of customer experience are useful approaches when using the *customer value model* and they can also be helpful in exploring value chain configuration options. The knowledge that specific expectations are critical in a customer's choice set may require particular competencies that are not 'in-house' and therefore must be co-opted.

A CUSTOMER VALUE MODEL

There are a number of important influences on a customer's purchasing decision. Figure 9.1 identifies a number of concerns that are important to both customers and suppliers.

Identifying 'rigidities' in the buying process

The previous section reviewed the *consumption chain* and discussed its application to both value chain design and as an influence on customer purchasing decision making. A detailed analysis of the consumption chain will also

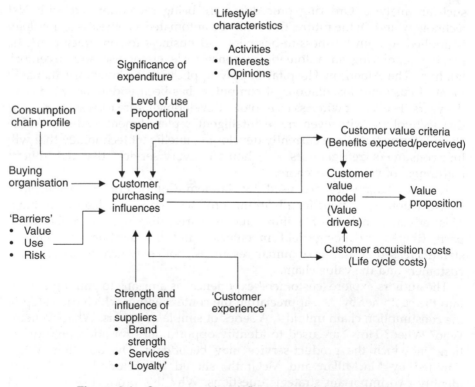

Figure 9.1 Customer value: influences and delivered value

identify *rigidities* in the consumer decision process and an in-depth analysis of these will reveal reasons and potential optional solutions. An example of a *rigidity* is given in MacMillan and McGrath's hypothetical example of petrol (gas) purchasing in which personal security is identified as a possible influence in the choice between a remote and poorly illuminated outlet and one offering the assurance of safety. Similarly, in the business-to-business context, security may be considered as important and issues such as 24-hour service availability may be a significant factor in the selection process. MacMillan and McGrath's example 'solves' the problem by offering pump attendants a mobile phone service (offered through a partnership arrangement) as well as the adoption of additional lighting. In the business-to-business example, the security may be added by a partner organisation specialising in quick response service on a 24-hour basis with a regional/national network.

Current purchasing and product use experiences facilitate value delivery system design

The *customer experience* can be applied to purchasing and product-service usage experiences. Both are particularly useful in designing value delivery systems. Product-service use may require (for some customers) an installation or assembly service. IKEA promote an assembly service in their stores, which is offered by a partner organisation. Similar, but often more specialised services, are offered in home improvement (or DIY) outlets, where plumbing, electrical and joinery services are available. Experiences vary during the specification, search and evaluation stages of a purchase decision. For large capital equipment purchases, suppliers typically work alongside customers to 'design and develop' a product-service that is capable of delivering specific value. Pine (1993) discusses the development of 'mass customisation', the use of technology to offer customers: '. . . exactly what they want – when, where and how they want it . . .'. Customisation (and mass customisation) are both candidates for partnership arrangements. Increasingly the application of knowledge management to supplier/customer situations provides an opportunity for an organisation to identify differentiation attributes that partner organisations can contribute (through well managed relationships) and using partners' assets (an aspect of technology management) – the value chain approach.

The role of supplier influence

The *strength and influence of suppliers* can also be responsible for directing purchasing decision making. Three influences are present. Clearly brand strength is important but recent developments in communication and distribution processes through Net technology have raised the issue concerning whose brand? It is likely that brand leverage will be increasingly influenced by service response and service flexibility, thus Internet intermediaries' brands can be expected to be as strong as the producer brands. The second feature, service, follows. Manufacturing technology is now following the trend set by information technology: it is becoming less expensive but at the same time offering greater capability to control quality of output, variety and customisation. Therefore, the service augmentation around conventional product offers becomes increasingly important. Moreover, in terms of costs of response, it is usually 'less' expensive to use service features to augment or differentiate the value offer. Loyalty is also a strong influence and loyalty programs are becoming essential features in marketing activities. The adage of 'it costs much less to keep a customer than it does to attract a new customer' is well ingrained in corporate philosophy. Not only do financial incentives promote and influence loyalty but 'convenience' in ordering and transaction processes, together with information technology based linkages, are commonplace in business-to-business transactions.

Identifying the 'risk barriers'

Purchasing activities are often required to overcome *barriers* and these may be practically based or influenced, or be psychological in their nature. For example, a *value barrier* is a product's lack of performance relative to price when compared with substitute products. Assael (1995) suggests manufacturers can overcome the value barrier in two ways. The first uses technology to reduce the price. The second is to communicate value attributes (to potential consumers) that they have not been made aware of or have not identified for themselves. Assael is suggesting the use of process technology to reduce costs and then price but product technology may have the effect of reducing in-use costs. This leads to the notion of *usage barriers*. Usage barriers occur when a product or service is not compatible with consumers' current practices. This may be due to system incompatibility such as computer systems being unable to 'connect' or it may be caused by user doubt concerning the efficacy, quality or security of the 'innovation'. Problems concerning credit and security have inhibited Internet sales in consumer markets. Assael advocates the use of change agents as opinion leaders who use their credibility to convince potential users that their concerns are unnecessary. *Risk barriers* represent '. . . consumers' physical, economic performance or social risk of adopting a social innovation'. Assael identifies consumer product risk barriers but business-to-business risk barriers can be financially catastrophic. The risk in this context concerns such considerations as capital equipment investment, new product introduction timing and product modification programmes. Risk barriers can be financial, the business-to-business consideration, or 'social/psychological', typical in fashion apparel markets. Solutions to risk barrier problems are often similar to usage barrier problems, in other words, the use of opinion leadership to introduce the product (or concept) and establish credibility.

Understanding customer 'buying organisations'

The structure of the customer's *buying organisation* and its decision making process is an important factor to consider. It is usual to consider organisational issues in business-to-business markets, where typically a purchasing decision may require agreement across a number of relevant interests. The more complex the purchase, the more expensive in terms of a capital budget or perhaps as a proportion of input costs, the more involved the organisation members become. In these situations, it becomes essential to identify both the 'customers' and their value criteria, together with their perspectives of customer acquisition (or life cycle) costs. Clearly in a business-to-business transaction, the customer value model becomes complex. Value criteria may be extensive, ranging from the convenience of ordering the product, to quality consistency and spare parts available. Acquisition costs may comprise technical support (during specification and installation), operating and maintenance costs and so forth. Not only may these be extensive, but they may well be expressed across an organisation – even across a number of organisations as Internet based buying exchanges expand. However, a moment's reflection will identify many similar consumer product purchasing decisions. These may extend well beyond durable products and be used for consumable products, particularly when differing lifestyles have to be considered.

Lifestyle: activities, interests and opinions – an important influence

Lifestyle characteristics are clearly important. The preceding example identifies one aspect of lifestyle that has in important influence on purchasing decisions. What may appear to be uncomplicated decisions concerning, for example, breakfast cereals are influenced by attitudes towards health, by time availability and often fashion or fad. The lifestyle inventory variables first proposed by Plummer (1974) remain valid. A number of approaches to identifying and measuring lifestyle variables have appeared since Plummer's original contribution. An issue for the value chain approach is to identify how value may be enhanced by an inter-organisational approach through value-adding partnerships. Partnership contributions will include both product and service infrastructure contributions. The lifestyle concept is applicable to business-to-business (B2B) markets where activities, interests and opinions are equally relevant. For example, Plummer listed under *activities* 'community', and many B2B companies make explicit their activities within the community to express social responsibility. Retailers offer 'computers for schools' programmes and many manufacturers offer educational scholarships. Both are approaches that can and do influence customer purchasing decisions. *Interests* for B2B firms have similar application, for example under this heading 'achievements' are applicable to both B2B and business-to-consumer (B2C) market situations. The B2B organisation publicises awards given for 'excellence' from government (services to export), industry (quality and service) and from influential customers. These are clearly used by their customers in reaching purchasing decisions. Finally, *opinions* are clearly important. Commercial organisations can, and do, express opinions on social issues, the future and often on business itself. Once again these expressions of opinions are important for customers who may express similar views or who may share the views, even if they do not make them explicit.

Expenditure size and importance is a significant influence

The *significance of expenditure* is an important influence for B2B and B2C customers alike. Capital equipment procurement decisions may take considerable time not only because of the dollar value of the purchase but because of inter-related functions and activities as well as the life cycle span of the purchase. This factor has similar concerns for consumables. An input that accounts for a significant proportion of total input costs will be constantly reviewed in terms of cost, quality and supplier service to ensure that all aspects of value are met. One consideration often overlooked by suppliers is the level of use of its products within an organisation. The fact that some equipment (and perhaps some components) has complexities not fully understood by the customer's workforce is often overlooked and the need to provide training, advice or at least detailed information is neglected. Again this can have implications for the purchasing company for whom a training package which will recover costs and may improve workplace safety is important. The value chain approach offers a means by which a specialist partner may be a cost-efficient contributor.

Customer purchasing influence can be seen (Figure 9.1) to have an important role in the customer's development of a value model. These result in the customer identifying benefits that are expected and the customer eventually taking a view on the extent to which they have (or have not been) delivered. It also results in the customer identifying the costs, the total costs, of alternative sources of supply or solutions to specific problems. A detailed view of both customer benefits and acquisition, or life cycle costs is offered in Figure 9.2.

COMPONENTS OF CUSTOMER VALUE

Quantifying the customer value model

The notion of a customer value model is not new. Heskett *et al* (1997) propose a *customer value equation* which in addition to customer benefits and acquisition costs also includes process quality and price. The model is described by:

$$\text{Value} = \frac{\text{Results produced for the customer} + \text{Process quality}}{\text{Price to the customer} + \text{Costs of acquiring the product}}$$

In their model *results produced for the customer* are based upon results, not products or services that produce results. *Process quality* has been described by Parasuraman *et al* (1988) as:

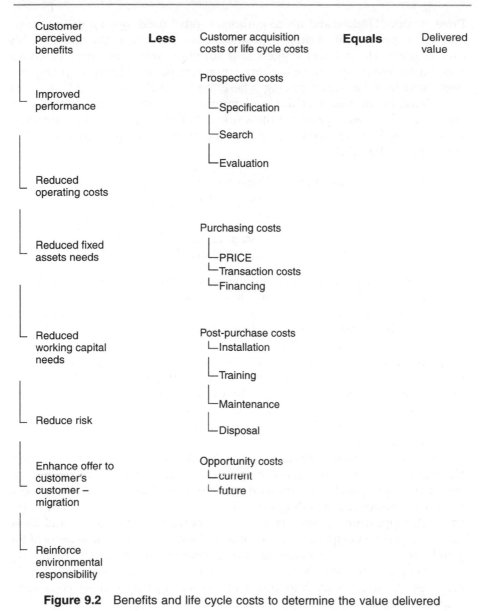

Figure 9.2   Benefits and life cycle costs to determine the value delivered

- dependability (did value provider do what was promised?);
- responsiveness (was value provided in a 'timely' manner?);
- authority (did provider elicit feeling of confidence during the delivery process?);
- empathy (was a customer view taken?);
- tangible evidence (was evidence left that the value was delivered?).

Price, observe Heskett and his co-authors, is often used by both the customer and the supplier, but clearly acquisition costs may be high, and possibly exceed price. The authors suggest that suppliers who can lower customer acquisition costs may be able to charge premium prices. This relationship has been used in value based pricing where the life cycle costs of products are considered as an aspect of the total purchase (in other words, acquisition costs) and these with price are the value actually delivered. This argument was presented earlier (see Chapter 3) in the discussion of consumer surplus. It will be recalled that:

$$\text{Value in use} = \text{Consumer surplus} + \text{price}$$
$$\begin{bmatrix} \text{Positive benefits} \\ + \\ \text{Reductions in} \\ \text{acquisition costs} \end{bmatrix}$$

Reductions in acquisition costs may be realised by considering how design and development may be directed towards technical concerns (improved quality, reduced maintenance costs), economic aspects (volume discounts through scale operations), service (free installation, staff training) and social factors (pollution reduction). Some or all of these features may have such a large impact on customers' costs that as Slywotsky (2000) suggests they will be prepared to pay an extra premium to obtain them or to switch suppliers. While marketing principles suggest that costs should not be used to determine prices, cost efficiencies may be used to influence prices. Thus the producer surplus may be used (together with the consumer surplus) to increase value-in-use.

Two important issues are suggested in the life cycle costs depicted in Figure 9.2. Customer acquisition costs (life cycle costs) can influence the transaction decision at pre-purchase, purchase and post-purchase stages, the precise pattern of influence depending very much upon the customer as well as the product. Opportunity costs are also an important consideration and these have both a time perspective and may be influenced by specific aspects of the purchasing process. The increasing use of partners' assets and the preference for leasing as opposed to purchasing fixed assets when ownership is the only option, suggests the importance of considering opportunity costs as an acquisition cost.

Qualitative components in the customer value model

It is essential that customer value criteria are 'qualified'. In Figure 9.3 typical 'generic' customer value criteria are identified. For example, *security* in the context of customer value may be expressed as a need for comprehensive warranty coverage, thus offering the customer the 'peace of mind' that no unexpected costs or loss of production will occur during the warranty period. Often this facility is used in consumer markets to increase competitive advantage – the automobile market is an example. *Performance* is often reflected in

Customer value criteria	Customer value component	Customer value perceptions
Security	Warranty Parts availability	• Response to claims • Service parts for emergencies
Performance	Productivity	• Plant utilisation • Decrease in number of reworked products • Decreased R & D expenditure • Increased competitive advantage
Aesthetics	Customisation Style/design	• Enhanced workplace image – 'modern' appearance – PR benefit
Convenience	Order management system	• Ease of ordering, rapid response. Order progressing information readily available
Economy	Price levels maintained	• Price consistency ensures margins maintained and competitive position held
Reliability	Delivery and product-service availability consistent	• Inventory holding can be maintained at financially viable levels • Customer's customer service delivery

Figure 9.3 Customer value criteria and value perceptions

productivity as reflected by plant utilisation, reworking or other quality measures. *Aesthetics* is usually considered to be a consumer marketing concern but increasingly style/design in important in B2B markets. For example, delivery vehicles that are new, carrying the company logo and always clean, reflect a positive image to both customers and potential customers – even to 'publics' that are unlikely ever to be customers! Customer costs can be reduced by considering aspects of *convenience* across a number of processes; ordering and inventory management are typical areas. Competitive pricing or price maintenance is an obvious *economy* measure. Best (1997) uses the Lexus case study to demonstrate how 'economy value' was delivered: customer specified improvements were incorporated in a redesigned vehicle while price was maintained. *Reliability* is important in B2B markets. End-user expectations of availability of drugs are an essential feature of value in pharmaceutical markets. Reliability may be an expensive element of value delivery when life span and storage of products are tightly specified.

Reducing customer acquisition costs enhances customer value

Customer acquisition costs are important value delivery issues for customers. Figure 9.4 also uses generic examples. For many B2B technical industries *specification* of component products represents a major element of cost. Increasingly this is becoming a joint venture between suppliers and major customers. The *search* process (the identification of suppliers and products) is often combined with specification in order to achieve continuity as well as cost efficiencies and to save time. The fact that manufacturing technology is widely available on a global basis adds a number of decision variables hitherto unavailable and which may lower costs or increase quality across a range of products and processes. The capital/labour substitution decision is often used to ensure access to dedicated labour which when trained becomes skilled in specific tasks. Given knowledge of the skills inventory and potential cost profile, products are designed with the manufacturing process in mind. Often this process is facilitated by an experienced intermediary. Magretta (1998) describes how Li and Fung has developed 'dispersed manufacturing' and a value chain that allows its customers to delegate many of

Customer acquisition costs	Customer value component	Customer value perceptions
Specification	Advice/assistance with product/service design	• Time-to-market reduced • R & D expenditures more effective
Search	Performance data, costs, delivery information available	• Procurement cycles (and costs) are lowered
Transactions	Ordering process	• Online processes for speed and accuracy
	Financing	• Capital preserved for expanding core competencies
Installation	Supplier undertakes to ensure rapid installation and to train staff	• Reduces staff requirements • Equipment operating efficiently – sooner • Staff operational sooner
Operations	Staff training Low operating costs	• Less waste/higher quality • Higher operating margins – more competitive prices
Maintenance	Maintenance programmes Simplified maintenance	• Lower fixed costs of service personnel • Less downtime
Disposal	Remove and dispose of 'old' equipment	• Reduces operating costs • Social responsibility

Figure 9.4　Customer acquisition costs and value perceptions

the essential but lower-value-added tasks which Li and Fung manage. *Transactions* processes are currently undergoing considerable change.

The development of buying exchanges has transformed buying/selling processes as well as relationships. Considerable cost savings have been achieved and many large industries have restructured their procurement processes by combining them with those of their competitors. Net technology has enhanced quality and reliability with considerable cost saving. *Installation* (particularly of capital equipment) may be 'designed' into capital equipment projects, as can *maintenance* and *operations* factors. The benefits of value chain operations are such that provided end users' operating profiles are identified at the design stage (and factors such as location, customers' customers and so on are identified) both capital products and consumer durables can be customised to meet, more specifically, user needs and situation. Obvious features include the extended service intervals now commonplace in the automobile market and remote diagnostics used by Tandem Computers and Caterpillar (discussed earlier). The increased acceptance of social responsibilities for environmental conservation has led to legislation and to companies introducing additional processes into the value chain. Ford purchased an automotive recycling activity in the USA and European manufacturing is beginning to design both products and processes around EU recycling mandates.

The customer value model has many aspects to be considered and therefore just as many opportunities for these to be incorporated into value chain processes, thus becoming elements of competitive advantage. In subsequent chapters the linkages between the customer value model, core competencies (key success factors) and value drivers will be explored and developed into a potential for sustainable competitive advantage.

The product-service-attribute value matrix

A useful approach that may be used by suppliers to identify their own benefit/cost situations is proposed in Figure 9.5. Commercial market research often identifies situations in which many of the features assumed necessary and offered on consumer durables (even fmcg products) are found to be unnecessary, as they are not used. This results in 'over-engineered' products and components and unnecessary costs. Figure 9.5 illustrates a simple matrix approach which first identifies attributes seen by consumers as desirable and those actually used by customers. These are then compared on a market price basis with the objective of making a price/attitude offer that meets the target customers' expectations. The value chain implications of this analysis follow. Given an uncompetitive positioning, such as that suggested by 'A', alternatives should be sought to ensure that the offer at 'B' can be made. This may involve outsourcing an in-house process or subprocess, but the analysis indicates the need for a disaggregated, but coordinated approach to value delivery to be made. The model may also be used to identify alternative segments. For example, there may be a significant market segment in a 'high

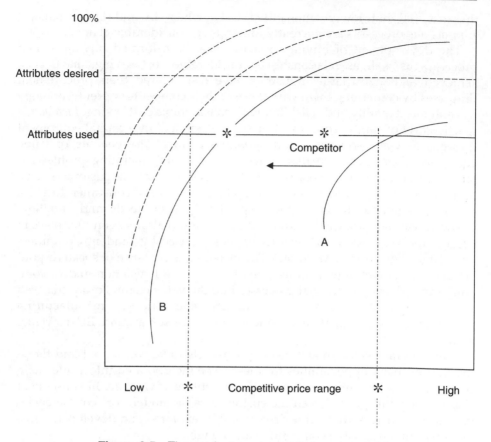

Figure 9.5   The product-service-attribute value matrix

price/high attribute' sector and the value chain format for this segment differs significantly from that required to service the 'popular' segment. A moment's thought directed towards consumer durable products would identify with these options. The broken lines suggest positions that should be investigated. Clearly a low price/sufficient attribute option has immediate appeal, but the infrastructure necessary to maintain both supply and service with any reliability may not cost much less than that for higher priced options *and*, depending upon the product type, credibility may be an issue.

THE VALUE DELIVERY GAP

Managing customer value delivery

Heskett *et al* use the customer value equation to identify and quantify customer needs. They suggest that, based on their research, this leads to a service objective that ensures '. . . a substantial overlap between customer needs and the capabilities of the organisation itself'. Such an objective could prove difficult for the organisation, as a 'substantial overlap' does imply excessive use of resources. Customer value delivery in the context of the value chain implies the optimal use of resources; any other strategy would result in problems within the value chain in terms of returns and resource contributions. Figure 9.6 develops the Heskett service delivery model. The objective of the model is to ensure that rather than achieve an overlap the situation is reached where customer value expectations = customer perceptions of delivered value. The customer value model identifies for the customer a range of value characteristics (customer value criteria and customer acquisition costs, see Figures 9.3 and 9.4). The supplier perspective, customer value management, is the resultant corporate value model in which the objective is to meet a situation where customer expectations and perceptions are congruent and costs are optimal. Measurement of customer expectations and perceptions (customer satisfaction) is managed through a customer satisfaction index, an ongoing measurement of needs and the efficacy of the value delivery management processes in meeting them. Delivery is achieved through the management of the delivery options available to the value chain 'integrator' whose role it is to ensure effective value delivery through the systems available. The overlap in Figure 9.6 should be minimised by the process of matching expectations and perceptions through a process of optimisation: customer value expectations are met by coordinating the resources available. Some examples may help.

Customised products and services are attributes that both customers and suppliers are currently identifying as 'ideals' to be achieved. The degree of customisation, once identified, becomes the objective the strategic operations management activity will seek to deliver by managing value chain processes to ensure this objective is met. Similarly product availability, managed through intermediaries, offers customers lower inventory holding costs and storage costs but the same reliability of delivery. The task of the value chain is to meet these value expectations at affordable costs, having first evaluated their role in developing a strong position for the customer *and* that this also strengthens the position of the value chain with the customer. The advantage a value chain approach offers is the number of options available to meet customer value expectations and, therefore, to optimise process costs. Figures 9.7 and 9.8 illustrate the undesirable situations of under and over achieving value delivery.

Continuous monitoring of customer satisfaction will identify whether the objectives are being met, or if under or over achieving is occurring. Under achievement raises questions concerning the precise needs of the customer, indeed it also suggests that the customer (or customer group) / value chain fit is strategically wrong; at best it suggests a need to review core competencies for their currency. Over achievement of customer satisfaction is a waste of value chain resources and also signals a lack of understanding of customers' operations and, possibly, implies a lack of concern and ability. Figure 9.9 is the ideal to be realised.

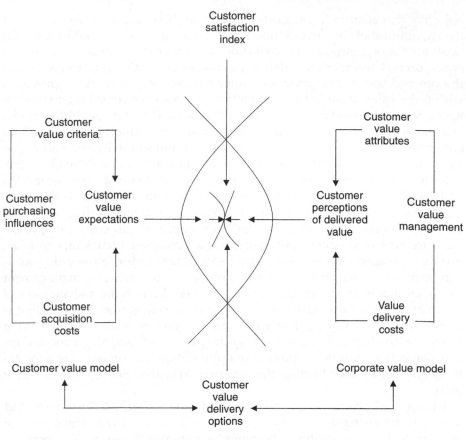

Figure 9.6   Managing customer value delivery

Closing the 'value delivery gap'

Clearly some structure in identifying and delivering value expectations is necessary. Figure 9.10 suggests a four style approach. In *exploration*, a customer's business is 'dissected' and the main processes that produce value are identified and understood, and the value it produces is also identified. *Translation* attempts to identify customer performance in terms of optimal performance and issues, areas and so on related to value delivery. *Interpretation* attempts to understand reasons for the performance achievements. It is probably more important to understand why optimal performance is achieved than why under or over achievement occurs. Consistent optimal performance may help the value chain to make changes to become more efficient in value delivery. Finally there is *implementation*, given that changes may be necessary, objectives and strategies are to be revised and agreed and communicated to customers. Once everything is in place monitoring the modified value chain continues to ensure that customer and 'corporate' expectations are met.

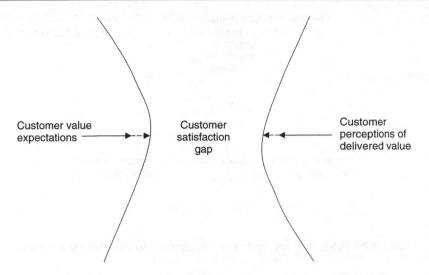

Customer value expectations → Customer satisfaction gap ← Customer perceptions of delivered value

Figure 9.7   Value delivery: under achieving – wrong customer satisfaction attributes or wrong customer?

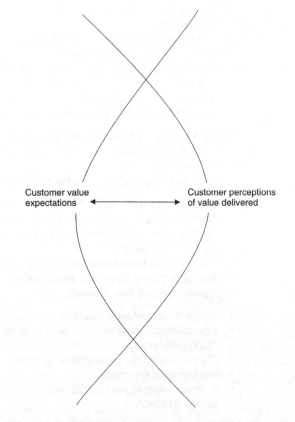

Customer value expectations ← → Customer perceptions of value delivered

Figure 9.8   Value delivery: over achieving and incurring excess costs

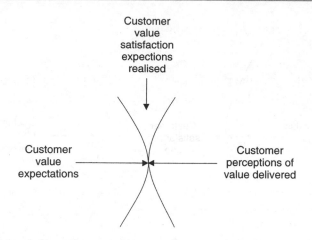

Figure 9.9 Value delivery: optimising customer and supplier expectations

Value delivery style	Identifying and closing the value gap
• Exploration	• Understand customers' business and 'needs' – the main process • Identify value characteristics that the customer is currently producing that could be supplied • Identify value production trends in the market/market segment • Measure the gap between customer perceptions of value delivered and value expected currently

• Translation	• Establish the features of value delivery
	  • Under achieving
	  • Over achieving
	  • Optimising customer and supplier expectations

• Interpretation	• Establish reasons for performance achievements • Review value delivery organisation and cost structures • Identify alternative delivery structures, their costs and coordination issues • Consider the implications of change on customer satisfaction and corporate expectations • Agree changes with partners
• Implementation	• Agree new/revised value delivery objectives • Communicate objectives to both customers and value chain partnership • Monitor customer perceptions of value • Monitor delivery costs • Monitor value chain partner 'returns' performances: realised/expected

Figure 9.10 Value delivery: managing for customer satisfaction

POSITIONING: THE VALUE PROPOSITION

Positioning is the strategic decision making, the analytical, conceptual and creative processes that lead to the positioning statement. The positioning statement, . . . the value proposition, puts the concept into words and performs two critically important functions:

1. It becomes the selling proposition to potential customers, the reason they should do business with the company, rather than its competitors.
2. It communicates to the whole organisation a sense of specific purpose and direction, coordinating their efforts toward the overarching common purpose of creating a satisfied customer.

(Webster: 1994)

Webster provides three reasons for this proposition. First is its focus on customer value and that it relates positioning to the value-delivery concept of strategy. Second, it goes beyond the limited notion that positioning is based solely on communication; and thirdly, it is aimed not just at customers but at the entire value producing organisation or system – at the value chain. It is in fact the basis for the value chain strategy and structure.

Components of the value proposition

Within the context of strategic operations management the value proposition has three important components. These are identified in Figure 9.11. Clearly the value proposition must identify for the target customer how *customer expectations* are to be met. It should be an explicit statement of customer value attributes (both value criteria, and how acquisition costs are minimised for the customer). This will include both product or service characteristics *and* service-support features. Customer expectations typically reflect availability concerns. These are not only concerns for service levels but include location and the range of intermediaries, or VARs, that offer the product-service. Information has two aspects: one concerns the scope of availability and includes pricing and other product-service features, the other is information concerning product-service application and end-user details concerning optimal use of the product-service and the available support infrastructure.

Webster contends that positioning and the development of the value proposition must be based on an assessment of the product offering and of the firm's distinctive competencies *relative to competitors*. Hence the value proposition should make clear its *relative competitive positioning*. In doing so it should communicate to the target customer the distinctive competency portfolio of the value chain participants, demonstrating that it extends its collective skills and resources beyond the current dimensions of competitive necessity into creating competitive advantage which, in turn, offers customers an opportunity to do likewise.

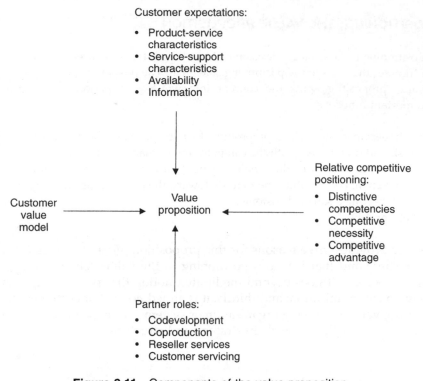

Figure 9.11 Components of the value proposition

A vital component of the value proposition is the role it performs in identifying the *roles and tasks of partner organisations*. Here the issue is one of communication to both partners and customers. If these are made explicit it serves to create credibility for the value chain in the eyes of the customers and increases their confidence in dealing with the organisation. Four aspects should be considered. Codevelopment indicates an agreement within the value chain structure that an ongoing commitment to improving the product-service offer and value production and delivery processes exists, and that this is prosecuted for the benefits of both customers and partners. Coproduction seeks to identify where the 'production' process is most effectively conducted. The IKEA example used by Normann and Ramierez (1993) is widely published and is an excellent example of dispersed production across distributed assets to the benefit of all stakeholders.

A 'total-value' approach: the FQVP hypothesis

An interesting, and valuable, contribution to deriving the value proposition is made by Thakor *et al* (2000). The authors present a model, the Four Quadrant Value Propositions (FQVP) hypothesis, derived from their *Wholonics*

Model, a total-value approach, described as a means for aligning strategy and leadership.

The four quadrants comprise:

- *collaborate/capability:* focussing on developing abilities that create sustainable competitive advantage;
- *create/innovation:* focussing on innovation in products, processes and services, leading to growth and industry leadership;
- *control/efficiency:* which focusses on improving process efficiency and which will create better products at lower cost;
- *compete/market awareness:* which focusses on competitive advantage through agility, market awareness and speed of response, thereby creating productivity and shareholder value.

The authors' definition of value drivers is essentially organisation based with the value drivers taking a prominent role in defining strategy. This differs from the approach taken in this text which considers value drivers as being customer focussed (the Slywotzky and Morrison view): '. . . the things that are important to customers' and reflect customer priorities such that '. . . they will pay a premium for them or will switch suppliers'.

In the strategic operations model the FQVP concept is useful in formulating decisions on the composition of the value proposition. However some modifications are necessary. *First* is that the value proposition is customer based; it is derived from customer value expectations that determine the primary value drivers on which the value proposition is based. *Second*, the value proposition determines the core competencies, processes and assets required if the organisation is to compete successfully. And *third*, unless all partners' objectives are met (that is, financial, market and those of individual organisations) it is unlikely that either customer value or shareholder value satisfaction goals will be achieved.

CREATING A VALUE PROPOSITION: A CASE STUDY

Li and Fung have been described as Hong Kong's largest export trading company and an innovator in supply chain management development (Magretta: 1998). Li and Fung work with European and American retailers sourcing clothing and other consumer products ranging from toys and consumer electronics to luggage. In an extensive interview Magretta discusses the role of the company with Victor Fung, the chairman. Victor Fung considers the company to be '. . . part of a new breed of professionally managed, focussed enterprises that draw on Hong Kong's expertise in distribution-process technology'; these are described as a host of information intensive service functions including product development, sourcing, financing, shipping and logistics. The company has been taken through a series of developments by Victor Fung and his brother, making the transition from buying agent to supply chain manager. Magretta suggests that Li and Fung '. . . are creating a new kind of multinational, one that remains entrepreneurial despite its growing size and scope'. Within the context of a definition of strategic operations management Li and Fung have extended their business well beyond supply chain management and represent one of the few examples of companies that have combined both supply chain management and demand chain management, and are rapidly building the knowledge technology and relationship based infrastructure to become effective strategic operations management exponents.

The Li and Fung case study will be used here and in subsequent chapters to illustrate strategic operations management. In this chapter the company will be used to demonstrate how customer value and a value proposition may be derived: *core competencies* and *partner objectives* form part of this process and will be identified ahead of a comprehensive discussion of core competencies, key success factors and value drivers in the next chapter.

Managing customer value in a derived demand situation

Li and Fung operate in a derived demand led value chain. Their customers have identified their own customers' expectations and these are interpreted thus: 'For next season, this is what we're thinking about – this type of look, these colours, these quantities. Can you come up with a production programme?'

Given this situation both an end-customer value model and an inter-mediary customer value model are necessary. Figure 9.12 identifies the criteria for both components. *End-user customer value criteria* are influenced by past experiences and preferences. In apparel markets typical value criteria include brand loyalty, based upon previously experienced design, quality and price value. Retailer research suggests customers expect change and most segments expect style/design currency. The convenience aspects of location, time and availability are important as is the continuity of a style/quality/price offer upon which brand loyalty is built. Customer acquisition costs for end users vary. For many apparel shopping is part task and part 'interest' based. Most have style/quality/price profiles that form the criteria for individual specification and evaluation activities. These criteria, then, form the basis for selection, to which are added 'operating and maintenance' costs such as garment care (and costs) and design longevity.

Given the end-user customer value model, the retailer/intermediary develops, in turn, a series of value expectations. These are clearly more technical and form the basis for negotiations with suppliers – Li and Fung. The value criteria (suggested by Magretta) are both economic and technically based; they include expertise, quality, quantity and time criteria as well as cost. The retailer value criteria are influenced by a need for consistency over time to ensure continuity of product characteristics for end users. Li and Fung are particularly concerned to ensure customer acquisition costs are minimised. To make sure that specification and evaluation costs are contained the service offered by Li and Fung undertakes to locate matched suppliers for their customers. This ensures quality and volume continuity and relieves customers of the supplier search and evaluation tasks. Li and Fung also manage other func-

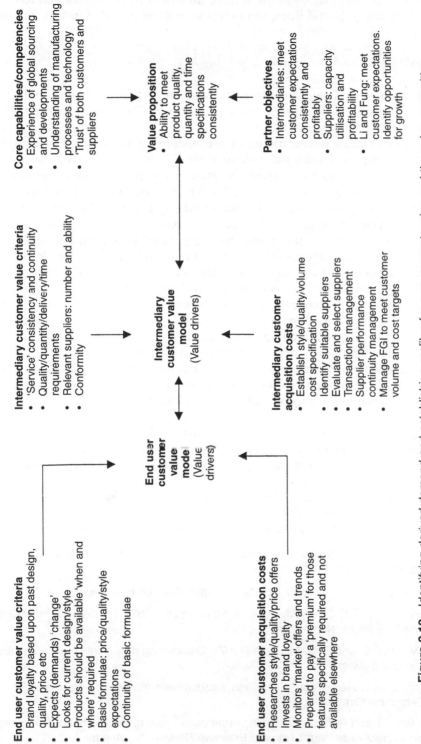

Core capabilities/competencies
- Experience of global sourcing and developments
- Understanding of manufacturing processes and technology
- 'Trust' of both customers and suppliers

Value proposition
- Ability to meet product quality, quantity and time specifications consistently

Partner objectives
- Intermediaries: meet customer expectations consistently and profitably
- Suppliers: capacity utilisation and profitability
- Li and Fung: meet customer expectations. Identify opportunities for growth

Intermediary customer value criteria
- 'Service' consistency and continuity
- Quality/quantity/delivery/time requirements
- Relevant suppliers: number and ability
- Conformity

Intermediary customer value model
(Value drivers)

Intermediary customer acquisition costs
- Establish style/quality/volume cost specification
- Identify suitable suppliers
- Evaluate and select suppliers
- Transactions management
- Supplier performance continuity management
- Manage FGI to meet customer volume and cost targets

End user customer value model
(Value drivers)

End user customer value criteria
- Brand loyalty based upon past design, quality, price etc
- Expects (demands) 'change'
- Looks for current design/style
- Products should be available 'when and where' required
- Basic formulae: price/quality/style expectations
- Continuity of basic formulae

End user customer acquisition costs
- Researches style/quality/price offers
- Invests in brand loyalty
- Monitors 'market' offers and trends
- Prepared to pay a 'premium' for those features specifically required and not available elsewhere

Figure 9.12 Identifying derived demand and establishing profiles for core competencies and the value proposition

tions such as transactions management, inventory management and reordering. A review of Li and Fung competencies will be included in Chapter 10.

SUMMARY

This chapter has considered two important, and related, concepts: managing customer value and creating a value proposition. They are closely related as the chapter demonstrates.

Customer value is determined by the customer process of matching value attributes expected with the cost of their acquisition. As demonstrated, a number of influences condition the purchasing process which eventually determines the customer value model. The process was explored by introducing an analysis of perceived benefits and acquisition or life cycle costs. The value delivered is acceptable if a 'positive' balance results from this review. Both customer value criteria and the components of acquisition costs were explored in detail and examples used to demonstrate the need for close attention, and rigour, at this stage of the value chain definition. The influence of product-service-attributes usage was considered and used to make the point that unless the customers' use of the product is understood, not only can excess costs be incurred, but value chain commitments (such as investment in fixed assets) may eventually prove incorrect.

Customer value delivery management is an important activity reflecting the expectations of customers to be identified and evaluated and then appraised in a corporate value model which would determine how customer value expectations are to be met. A process for achieving this outcome was proposed.

Finally the value proposition was discussed. The importance of the value proposition in identifying the value offered to customers, and the processes involved, are equally important to both customers and value chain partners.

REFERENCES ●

Assael, H. (1995), *Consumer Behaviour and Marketing Action*, South Western Publishing, Cincinatti.

Best, R. J. (1997), *Market-Based Management*, Prentice Hall, Englewood Clifts.

Heskett, J. L., W. E. Sasser Jr and L. A. Schlesinger (1997), *The Service Profit Chain*, The Free Press, New York.

MacMillan, I. C. and R. G. McGrath (1997), 'Discovering new points of differentiation', *Harvard Business Review*, July/August.

Magretta, J. (1998), 'Fast, global and entrepreneurial', *Harvard Business Review*, September/October.

Normann, R. and R. Ramirez (1993), 'From value chain to value constellation: designing interactive strategy', *Harvard Business Review*, July/August.

Parasuraman, A., V. A. Zeuthamil and L. Berry (1988), 'SERVQUAL: A multiple-item scale for measuring customer perceptions of service quality', *Journal of Retailing*, Spring.

Pine II, B. J. (1993), *Mass Customisation*, Harvard Business School Press, Boston, MA.

Plummer, J. T. (1974), 'The concept and application of life style segmentation', *Journal of Marketing*, Vol. 38, January.

Slywotzky, A. J. (2000), 'The age of the choiceboard', *Harvard Business Review*, January/February.

Thakor, A. V., J. De Graff and R. Quinn (2000), 'Creating sustained shareholder value and dispelling some myths', in *Mastering Strategy*, *Financial Times*/Prentice-Hall, London.

Webster, F. E. (1994), *Market-Driven Management*, Wiley, New York.

chapter 10

Core Competencies, Key Success Factors, Value/Cost Drivers and Process Management

LEARNING OUTCOMES

The student will be able to:

- differentiate between core competencies and key success factors;
- determine the competencies/capabilities needed for success in a value chain structure;
- identify distinctive competencies/capabilities from reproducible competencies/capabilities;
- distinguish between competencies and key success factors;
- understand process management as a concept and its application to value chain management;
- derive value drivers within the value chain context.

INTRODUCTION

The literature in the area of core competencies has been dominated by Hamel and Prahalad whose contributions are constantly cited. In this chapter a

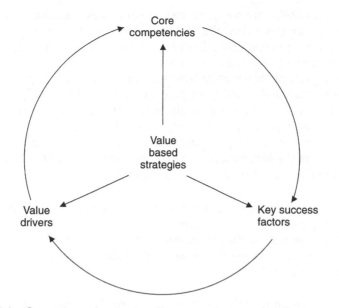

Figure 10.1   Customer value expectations: qualifications for the value chain to meet

broader approach will be taken: the purpose will be to link core competencies, key success factors and value drivers within the context of strategic operations management decisions.

The growth of inter-organisational business structures refocusses attention on core competencies. Hamel and Prahalad's work provides a basis from which to develop a model linking core competencies, key success factors and value drivers with the central focal point – customer value expectations.

An obvious place to start is to review what it is each component is seen to be. From these the need to link the three components and the importance of the linkage to value chain decisions will emerge. Figure 10.1 illustrates this objective.

CORE COMPETENCIES/CAPABILITIES

Hamel and Prahalad (1994) have defined a core competency as:

> . . . a bundle of skills and technologies that enables a company to provide a particular benefit to customers.

They suggest that competencies that are most valuable are those offering a gateway to a wide variety of potential product markets. This contention is argued by citing Sony (for whom miniaturisation has led to a wide range of personal electronic products); Hewlett-Packard (who with competencies in measurement, computing and communications have developed a key niche position); and 3M's core competencies in adhesives, substitutes and advanced materials, which have been the basis of numerous products.

An interesting perspective that may be derived from this definition is that it is an aggregate of 'skills and technologies' and as Hamel and Prahalad contend, 'represents the sum of learning across individual skill sets and individual organisational units'. And they suggest '. . . it is unlikely to reside in a single individual or within a small team'. This is a primary reason for an organisation to consider participating with other organisations, together with the fact that the dynamics of competition, technology and consumer value expectations make investment in core competencies unattractive. Hamel and Prahalad make very clear their views concerning this issue:

> In the concept of core competency there is no suggestion that a company must make everything it sells . . . although Canon has a very clear sense of its core competencies, it buys more than 75% of components that go into its copiers. What a company should seek to control are those core competencies that make the biggest contribution to customer value.

This view also identifies the clear need for core competencies to be linked with customer value generation. It also identifies the trend towards *virtual integration* in which the core competencies required to compete are identified and, rather than being developed or acquired, they are leased and aggregated to create an entity which answers the question 'What can we do that other organisations could not easily do as well?'

This is also expressed by Rumelt (1994) who argues:

- Core competencies support several businesses and products.
- Products and services are only a temporary manifestation of core competency – the latter develops more slowly and is more stable than products.
- Competency is knowledge and therefore increases with use.
- In the long run, competency, not products, will determine who succeeds in competition.

COMPETENCIES AND CAPABILITIES

Kay (2000) introduces an interesting view on the issue of competitive structure requirements in the 'new economy'. Kay discusses the concept of *economic rent* in the context of strategy. Ricardo introduced the concept in the early part of the 19th century to explain excess returns. Kay argues that the objective of a company is to increase its economic rent, rather than its profits, adding:

> A company that increases its profits but not its economic rent – as through investments or acquisitions that yield less than the cost of capital – destroys value.

Intentionally or not Kay identifies an emerging issue, that of the competitive structure of the 'new economy'. Kay's *contestable market* has the characteristics of new economy markets: '... one in which entry by new companies is relatively early and exit by failing companies is relatively quick...'. This describes the fate of many of the Internet companies of the past two years. He argues that those that only just survive will earn the industry cost of capital on the replacement value of their assets.

And:

> Economic rent is the measure of the competitive advantage that effective established companies enjoy, and competitive advantage is the only means by which companies in contestable markets can earn economic rents.

Competitive advantage is determined by capabilities, and these vary. Kay identifies two categories: *distinctive capabilities* such as institutional sanctioned items: patents, copyrights, statutory monopolies, and so on; but also feature '... powerful idiosyncratic characteristics ... built by companies in competitive markets'. These are strong brands, patterns of supplier and/or customer relationships, specialist skills, knowledge and processes. *Reproducible capabilities* can be created (or purchased or leased) by any company with reasonable management skills, skills of observation and financial resources. Both process and product technology are reproducible; the automotive industry is but one example.

Capabilities as economic rent

Rents as a basis for strategic competencies or capabilities have attracted the attention of Spender (1998). Spender's review of contributions in the area of economic rents identifies a number of views relevant to this discussion and which concur with the views expressed by Kay and extend the Ricardian concept.

Robinson (1969) provided a succinct definition of rent:

> ... the surplus earned by a factor of production over and above the minimum earnings necessary to induce it to do its work.

Robinson argued that the concept was much larger and more significant than the literature suggested (in other words, the notion of Nature's free gifts) and that the rents due to human innovation, entrepreneurship, technology or organisational characteristics are different. Such factors are not fixed in supply, and '... presuppose an expendable 'internal' or artificial source of rent rather than the fixed natural source 'external' to the enterprise'. This view may be contested. In the 'holonics'/virtual organisation, the value chain concept suggests, internal and external sources of rent are equally common. Rents/capabilities are 'leasable' and success may be attributable more to the ability of being able to *identify* a number of appropriate rent characteristics and to organise, or integrate, them into an 'exclusive/unique set' of characteristics or processes; in other words, the integrator role in the virtual organisation concept.

Certainly other views on rents suggest this mobility feature. Entrepreneurial and Pareto rents (Rumelt: 1987) would support this view. Entrepreneurial rents have been suggested as being individually or internally owned but the virtual (or holonic) organisation structure replaces this with an 'organisational' perspective. The holonic network, or the *value chain* as it is more commonly known, provides a new perspective of capabilities and of competition. Future competition is moving towards competing value chains, rather than competition between specific, individual organisations. While it is arguable that the capability/rent is attributable to *an* entrepreneur or possibly to *a number of* entrepreneurs, located at different parts of the value chain, the individual entrepreneur is dependent upon other members of the value chain if an advantage based on rent is to materialise.

The same argument may be made concerning Pareto rents, monopoloy rents due to social knowledge or individual knowledge. Penrose (1959) discussed knowledge in the context of coordination by the firm of its inputs. This is the role of the integrator in the virtual organisation. Such a view, in the context of Kay's approach, is an internal *distinctive capability*. Penrose argued that the firm was, in current parlance, a *learning organisation* and the knowledge benefits increased its capacity to expand. Again in the context of the holistic or virtual organisation model it can be argued that the knowledge and subsequent learning benefits can be shared or leveraged by the application of entrepreneurial rents.

Alchian and Demsetz's (1972) concept of 'team production' dealt with collective knowledge focussing on the resource produced by the joint activity, or from Kay's perspective '. . . patterns of supplier or customer relationships, and skills, knowledge, and routines embedded in teams'. Nelson and Winter (1982) discussed collective action and the notion of organisational routines learned from repetitive experience and embedded in the organisation's practices. An interesting aspect of their argument concerns the difficulty experienced in changing routine. This also relates to Kay's comments concerning the differences between success and survival and between the returns to each.

There is sufficient evidence from this brief diversion into the literature to support Kay's view that *capabilities* have *economic rent* as their basis. But organisational structures are changing in nature and these changes suggest a blurring of the characteristics of what is *'internal'* and what is *'external'* to the organisation, of the *organisation* as a concept, and indeed of the concept of *ownership*.

The value chain enables capabilities to be shared – particularly intangibles

Quinn (1992) emphasised the need to cultivate a core competency and suggests that manufacturing companies are becoming more and more dependent within the value chain on links consisting of services or intellectual activities. Olve *et al* (1997) suggest that the underlying driver of long term strategic performance is intellectual capital and use Stewart's (1997) definition to give the term meaning, that is 'packaged useful knowledge', and suggest it is due to this approach that a company may be valued at more than the sum of its 'hard' assets. Other approaches suggest the term 'intangible assets' and this has the advantage of including or detailing specifics seen as brand values, R and D and management development. The concern is to understand the relationship between intellectual capital and its influence on core competencies. Given Olve *et al*'s perspective it could be suggested that there is a relationship that can be derived: *intellectual capital*, packaged useful knowledge, acts as a data-bank of knowledge from which *competencies* emerge; the point is how competencies are identified ahead of their application. In other words, the business environment is becoming dynamic to the point at which competencies that are recognised may be becoming *core rigidities* (Leonard-Barton: 1992) and as seen, have limited life spans. This view introduces the notion of core competencies appearing as balance sheet items. Olve *et al* reproduce an item from the Skandia annual report (a supplement titled 'On Processes Which Create Value') and subsequently introduce a 'competency balance sheet'.

This is an interesting concept for strategic operations managers. Given the proposal that the dynamics of the business environment will lead to a situation where knowledge and core competencies will be viewed as having specific shelf lives, the onus is on the company to identify the core competencies necessary for its future. Olve *et al* extend their argument concerning a *competency balance sheet*. They argue that a traditional way of evaluating a company is to analyse its balance sheet and use the notion of gearing to explore the value of the business. A feature of the balance sheet is the ratio of shareholder equity to total assets, the financial gearing of the company. They use the usual arguments concerning the extent and influence of gearing, suggesting that if the company is overly self financed (that is, it relies too heavily on its own competencies), it will need to earn profits in excess of 'normal' levels to ensure shareholder satisfaction. Therefore, they suggest, few companies are totally self financing.

The competency/capability 'balance sheet'

The analogy for planning competency requirements uses the principles of financing for growth. The 'assets' required for success are identified as competencies, and the 'liabilities' indicate how the competencies are to be financed – who is to provide them. The authors continue with the notion that competencies have limited life expectancies and therefore suggest that the liabilities reflect a degree of competency leverage. Figure 10.2 illustrates the proposal. In this hypothetical example, a major asset is suggested to be product/service development (indicated by the 'proportion' of the 'assets' it represents). The competencies are largely 'financed' by value chain partners. The contribution made by partners is large and is complemented by externally sourced temporary competencies, required to meet specialist needs.

Hamel and Prahalad comment that: 'Preemptive investment in a core competency is not a leap into the dark . . . it is the simple desire to build world

'Assets'	'Liabilities'

• Product characteristics
  • applications
  • impact on customer delivered value
	• Externally sourced temporary
	  competencies
	  • value production
	  • value communication

• Customers
  • loyalty relationships
	• value delivery
	  • value maintenance/servicing
	   (specialist services)

• Service characteristics
  • response time
  • depth of response
	• Partnership network contributions
	  • production
	  • customer liaison
	  • value delivery

• Product/service development
  • time-to-market
  • specifics
   • customisation
   • uniqueness
	• service management

• Production management
  • flexibility
  • response times
  • costs – lean	

• Logistics management
  • infrastructure scope
  • response	

• Administration
  • order management processes
   • response
   • accuracy
   • empowered staff
	• Own competencies
	  • design and development

Figure 10.2   The competency/capability balance sheet

leadership in the provision of a key customer benefit, and the imagination to envision the many ways in which that benefit can be delivered to customers, that drives the competency-building process'. They continue by suggesting that competencies that are most valuable are those representing a gateway to a wide range of potential product markets: a core competency leader possesses the option to be a major participant in a range of end-product markets. This is a particularly important issue for strategic operations management because the options become much wider when a value chain approach is considered. Hamel and Prahalad consider this with their competency matrix. Figure 10.3 has been adapted to offer the broader approach required by strategic opera-

Product-market decisions

		Existing	New
Core competency decisions	External	What new core competencies are required (and should be 'leased') to protect and extend our franchise in current product-markets? Are they core or non-core competencies?	What new core competencies should we seek in partnership arrangements if we wish to participate (dominate) in selected new product-markets? Are they core or non-core competencies?
	Internal	What new core competencies are required (and should be investment areas for the organisation) to protect and extend our franchise in current product-markets?	What new core competencies should form part of the investment program of the organisation if we wish to participate in selected new product-markets?
	Existing	What is the opportunity to improve our position in existing product-markets by leveraging existing competencies?	Can the existing core competencies be utilised in alternative product-markets?

Figure 10.3 Core competencies and the value chain

tions management decisions. Implicit in Hamel and Prahalad's original model is the requirement that some forward thinking be undertaken to determine the direction of 'potential product markets' prior to investing in core competency leadership. Indeed the value chain approach offers an option to spread risk and in the context of Figure 10.2 this would be reflected by an even greater proportion of externally sourced temporary competencies.

The product life cycle: demand and technology cycles identify capability requirements

Clearly this is a not an easily resolved problem. One proposition that may be considered is to adapt Ansoff's perspective of the product life cycle as a means of identifying the required competencies and from this make a judgement concerning their predicted longevity, influence, possible cost and the need to own or to lease them.

Ansoff (1984) suggested the product life cycle was in fact an ongoing generic demand life cycle which over time was serviced by a sequence of alternative technologies. Figure 10.4a describes this concept. Using 'calculating assistance' as a generic product the argument is that as a product it has an 'infinite' life cycle. The technological 'ways and means' of satisfying demand

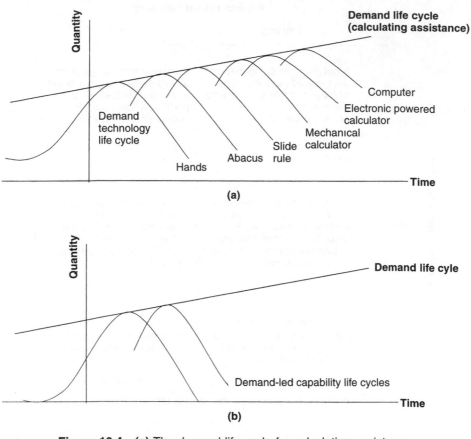

Figure 10.4 **(a)** The demand life cycle for calculating assistance
(b) The demand-led capability life cycle

clearly change over time. In Figure 10.4b a demand led competency life cycle
replaces the demand technology life cycle. The modification identifies more
closely with Ansoff's original concept because it includes competency features
other than technological expertise and these will be a combination of core and
non-core competencies. The life cycle approach identifies with the notion of
preemptive investment in a core competency and adds to the dynamics of the
decision.

From this follows the ownership decision. Given a review of the marketplace, which should identify both the importance and the life span of the competency, so the decision concerning ownership or 'leasing' the competency can
be reached. This procedure is described by Figure 10.5. Competency specificity
(importance) is compared with time and market risk. The options identified
act as a guide to the potential investment decision.

A more comprehensive approach, using Hamel and Prahalad as a basis,
and extending the arguments of Quinn, Rumelt, Stewart and Olve *et al*, is to
consider the competency base as comprising a *strategic combination* of knowl-

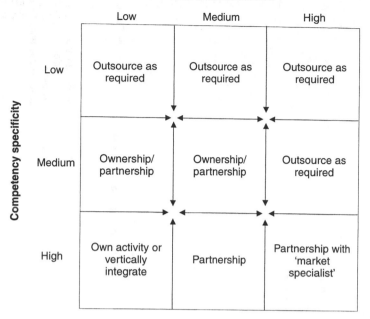

Figure 10.5 Guide to selecting partnership options in value chain decisions

edge management, technology management and relationship management. This is suggested by Figure 10.6, where important relationships between knowledge management, technology management and relationship management are indicated. Essentially, knowledge management structures and organises knowledge to create and reinforce competencies. This requires both development and application for knowledge management. Clearly effective competencies are not created in isolation and a 'dialogue' between technology management and relationship management is an essential feature of the process. Technology management ('new technology'; Noori: 1990) comprises a customised combination of information and operations technology to ensure the relevant capabilities and capacities, address specific market opportunities. A 'dialogue' between knowledge management and relationship management facilitates the acceptance of the new technology into production (an internal consideration) and distribution (an external consideration) thereby ensuring the reinforcement of the 'skills' aspect of competency. Relationship management includes 'corporation' (the 'transfer' of production processes both upstream and downstream) and in which managed 'codestiny' (a shared perspective of strategic direction) is created internally and externally.

KEY SUCCESS FACTORS

Hamel and Prahalad are very clear in their assertions defining the differences between core competencies, competitive advantage and key (critical) success

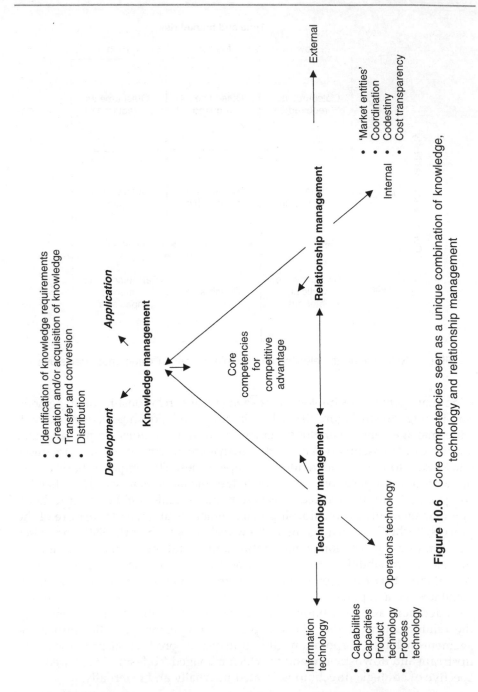

Figure 10.6 Core competencies seen as a unique combination of knowledge, technology and relationship management

factors. A core competency is 'an aptitude, a skill. A business may possess many advantages *vis-à-vis* competitors that don't rest on skills or aptitudes'. It is a source of competitive advantage because it is competitively unique and makes a contribution to customer value (or cost). Similarly, they argue, every core competency is likely to be a key (critical) success factor (KSF/CSF) but not every key success factor will be a core competency. Key success factors are characteristics or features such as plant location (close to raw materials or low cost labour) or an exclusive licence for manufacturing or importing a specific product. These, they suggest, are both key success factors and competitive advantage characteristics; but not aptitudes or skills and therefore not core competencies.

Leidecker *et al* (1984) suggest:

> Critical (key) success factors are those characteristics, conditions or variables that when properly sustained, maintained or managed, can have a significant impact on the success of a firm competing in a particular industry.

They continue by suggesting that a CSF (KSF) can be a characteristic such as a price advantage – it can also be a condition such as capital structure or advantageous customer mix; or an industrial structural characteristic such as vertical integration. They provide examples of key success factors for a number of industries:

Automotive industry

● Styling
● Strong dealer network
● Manufacturing cost control
● Ability to meet EPA (Environmental Protection Agency) standards

Semi-conductor industry

● Manufacturing process: cost efficient, innovative cumulative experience
● Capital availability
● Technological competency
● Product development

Food processing industry

● New product development
● Good distribution
● Effective advertising

Key success factors: a competitive necessity?

Hofer and Schendel (1978) had earlier applied the concept to strategic analysis. They suggest key success factors are important at three levels of analysis:

specific to the firm, to the industry and to the business environment. Analysis at each level can identify a source of potential key success factors.

Grant (1995) follows a similar line of argument. He suggests an analysis of demand (What it is that customers want?) and competition (How does the firm survive?) which identifies the relevant key success factors. See Figure 10.7 for a review of steel, fashion retailing and superstore activities.

It follows that key success factors *require* core competencies to be in place; they evolve from the marketplace (customers and competitors) but are themselves not based upon aptitudes or skills. Competitors can, and do, challenge competitive advantage positions and replicate the key success factors.

An important consideration for value chain configuration is for the strategic operations manager to identify this characteristic and furthermore, to identify also the total competency and key success factors required to build sustainable competitive advantage. Another concern is that the key success factors identified have implications for the entire organisation. The benefit the value chain approach offers is the facility to assemble both competencies and key success factors from partner organisations. Dell is an example of a combination of core competencies; Dell's design and marketing aptitudes and skills, and Sony's quality management of component manufacturing with key success factors reflecting customer response systems and optimised assembly costs.

An important issue or point to be made concerning core competencies is that alone they cannot deliver customer value delivery performance. Certainly they ensure an 'excellence' in the process but they work through key success factors which in turn define the processes required to deliver customer value. See Figure 10.8; core competencies underwrite strategy and competitive advantage in the value chain but lack the specificity to create and deliver customer value.

VALUE DRIVERS

Creating value incurs cost and for many organisations there is a decision to be made concerning the precise relationship between the value delivered to the customer (and the value generated for the organisation and other stakeholders) and the cost of creating, producing, communicating, delivering and servicing the value. The value chain has a strategic principle: the notion that to optimise value and cost it establishes partnerships (or alliances) with other organisations who offer competencies and/or assets not otherwise available.

Typically value drivers are not exclusive to a specific core competency nor to key success factors. It is more likely they influence one or some of these. If an organisation is to develop a strong competitive position it clearly needs to identify the value drivers that are important to the end-user customer and to structure a value delivery system that reflects these *and* the objectives of the other value chain participants. Slywotzky and Morrison (1997), in their 'customer-centric' approach to the value chain suggest:

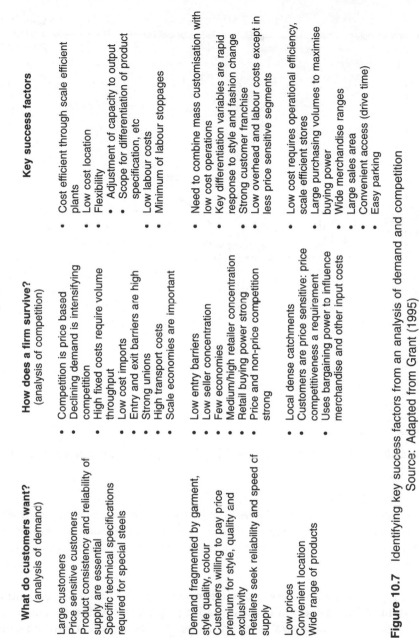

Steel

What do customers want?
(analysis of demand)

- Large customers
- Price sensitive customers
- Product consistency and reliability of supply are essential
- Specific technical specifications required for special steels

How does a firm survive?
(analysis of competition)

- Competition is price based
- Declining demand is intensifying competition
- High fixed costs require volume throughput
- Low cost imports
- Entry and exit barriers are high
- Strong unions
- High transport costs
- Scale economies are important

Key success factors

- Cost efficient through scale efficient plants
- Low cost location
- Flexibility
  - Adjustment of capacity to output
  - Scope for differentiation of product specification, etc
- Low labour costs
- Minimum of labour stoppages

Fashion retailing

What do customers want?

- Demand fragmented by garment, style quality, colour
- Customers willing to pay price premium for style, quality and exclusivity
- Retailers seek reliability and speed of supply

How does a firm survive?

- Low entry barriers
- Low seller concentration
- Few economies
- Medium/high retailer concentration
- Retail buying power strong
- Price and non-price competition strong

Key success factors

- Need to combine mass customisation with low cost operations
- Key differentiation variables are rapid response to style and fashion change
- Strong customer franchise
- Low overhead and labour costs except in less price sensitive segments

Superstore activities:
- **food**
- **home improvement**

What do customers want?

- Low prices
- Convenient location
- Wide range of products

How does a firm survive?

- Local dense catchments
- Customers are price sensitive: price competitiveness a requirement
- Uses bargaining power to influence merchandise and other input costs

Key success factors

- Low cost requires operational efficiency, scale efficient stores
- Large purchasing volumes to maximise buying power
- Wide merchandise ranges
- Large sales area
- Convenient access (drive time)
- Easy parking

Figure 10.7 Identifying key success factors from an analysis of demand and competition
Source: Adapted from Grant (1995)

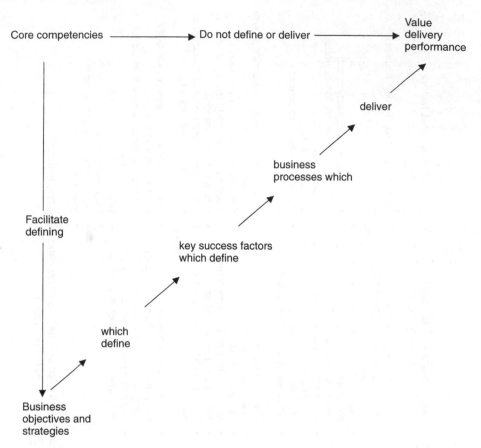

Figure 10.8 The relationship between core competencies and key success factors

The value of any product is the result of its ability to meet a customer's priorities. Customer priorities are simply the things that are so important to customers that they will pay a premium for them or, when they can't get them, they will switch supplier.

The 'things that are so important to customers' are the value drivers and the important value drivers are those adding *significant* value to customers. Within the context of the value chain, value drivers assume a twofold significance. One is clearly that of adding value for customers; the other is the ability to differentiate the value offer such that it creates competitive advantage. Four questions emerge:

● What is the combination of value drivers required by the target customer group? What is the customer group's order of priority?
● What are the implications for differentiation decisions? Are there opportunities for long term competitive advantage?

- What are the implications for cost structures?
- Are there opportunities for trade-offs to occur between value chain partners that may result in *increased* customer value (and stakeholder value) or *decreases* in the value system costs or the costs of the target customer group?

It follows that the relationship between value drivers and cost drivers is important. Scott (1998) comments:

> Since time immemorial there have been two sorts of activities in companies; those that drive value creation and those that drive unproductive cost . . .

Scott suggests that the harsh reality of globalisation and the accompanying increase in competition have forced most companies into making efficiency gains. However, the persistence of competitive pressures means that the speed of efficiency gains in production and the speed of market responsiveness necessary to compete are increasing. And:

> Cost structures are shifting dramatically year by year as new producers come on line and new technologies propel shifts in business processes. Everything is moving faster and will continue to accelerate. Today's competitive 'paradigms' will be tomorrow's old hat.

It follows that value expectations may not necessarily change, but the way in which value is created and delivered almost certainly will do so. Consequently to remain both competitive and cost effective/efficient, an ongoing surveillance of value expectations, value drivers (and cost drivers) becomes essential. And, equally importantly, the search for more effective value chain structures is an ongoing task.

CORE COMPETENCIES/CAPABILITIES, KEY SUCCESS FACTORS AND VALUE DRIVERS

There are links between core competencies, key success factors and value drivers; Figure 10.9 illustrates these. Core competencies are the underlying skills and technologies that enable an organisation to establish itself in a market sector and are essential if continuity of leadership is to be maintained. There are those competencies that are fundamental and drive the organisation and those which may be 'leased'. Olve *et al* (1997) emphasise the long term aspects of competencies and their intellectual, knowledge base. If this view is taken, their contention that the core competency base increases with use suggests that competencies are the long term investment the organisation should protect. Core competencies are also vital in value chain design. Quinn's comment concerning cross-organisational 'fit' of core competencies is important in a time of expanding relationship management.

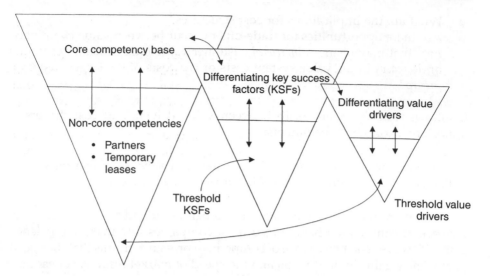

Figure 10.9   Linking competencies, key success factors and value drivers

While Hamel and Prahalad are clear in their view that core competencies and key success factors share no congruence, there is a link. If an organisation is to establish sustainable competitive advantage there need to be some linkages between the two. An organisation such as Walmart has clear skills based competencies; it has also key success factor characteristics that leverage the competencies. A key success factor has been the presence of important brands on which to demonstrate the company's skills in offering 'everyday low prices' by managing their relationship with Proctor and Gamble. The use of technology to ensure that costs are maintained at levels which ensure both companies make satisfactory profits through minimum inventory levels and just-in-time manufacturing is an example of the technology component of the competencies being brought into focus.

The suggestions of most authors are that key success factors may not be permanent. Indeed the KSFs identified for each of the industry sectors by Leidecker and by Grant contain no unique or even long term exclusives. Technology has typically eroded the lead established by KSFs and more recently new forms of business models such as virtual integration have replaced most of the remaining features. It could be argued that knowledge, technology and relationship management are emerging as core sources for key success factors and for core competencies. Furthermore this model responds to the dynamics of the marketplace.

Value drivers are customer based. They emerge from the customer's value expectations and the related acquisition costs. However, without the underlying core competencies and the KSF structure they cannot be delivered cost-effectively. It is an issue of cost-effectiveness rather than cost-efficiency because value drivers are long term, strategic concerns. This needs qualification. If, as appears likely given current developments, the virtual organisation becomes a significant business model, it follows that the business perspective of short, medium and long term must be revised. Virtual organisations are flexible organisations reflecting a structural need at a point in time. If the need changes (the value driver characteristics) then the structure of the virtual organisation will also change to accommodate customer preferences *at that time*.

Thus it is argued that while core competencies and KSFs are not one and the same, it is a valid argument to suggest that all three are linked and further, the more effective the management of the linkages the stronger the competitive positioning will become.

BUSINESS PROCESSES: A CONDUIT FOR VALUE CHAIN OPERATIONS

The notion that a business comprises a number of core processes and not a bureaucratic structure of functions is not new. Indeed the fundamental difference between organisations and processes is one that is central to the concept of strategic operations management, in other words that organisations are hierarchical and that processes are horizontal, and reflect the decision making process of the value chain structure (Bellis-Jones: 1992). It is a very useful concept, possibly a key concept for strategic operations management. Johansson *et al* (1993) plot the development of 'process management thinking', suggesting that value based performance criteria in the form of quality, cycle time, service and cost are core metrics for success. They define 'process' in a business context as:

> A process is a set of linked activities that take an input and transform it to create an output. Ideally, the transformation that occurs in the process should add value to the input and create an output that is more useful and effective to the recipient either upstream or downstream.

The authors discuss the relevance of the impact of techniques such as just-in-time, total quality management and others and conclude that they are: '. . . part of the price of admission, the mere adoption of tactical process-oriented principles – and even their successful implementation – does not bring companies to the cutting edge of international competition. While over time these various tools and techniques create vast improvements in internal effectiveness they cannot provide the means to break out from the deadlocked market competitive position – once everybody is playing the same game a position of essential parity is reached'. Porter (1996) echoes this principle.

The effects of implementing these processes and principles are that work flows more smoothly, inventories are reduced and capacity is released. The authors conclude that two responses result. A *market driven* response typically involves a manipulation of price/volume in the existing marketplace, or becomes *value chain driven* by closing or mothballing facilities, marketing the capacity of the core technology or back-sourcing – bringing back in-house the manufacture of components (or subassemblies) previously outsourced. As they further conclude: '. . . the result of all this effort is essentially marketplace parity'.

The 'price of admission' does not offer any guarantee of long term success. This, they contend, occurs when companies identify and embrace the next generation of the basis of competition. This requires the organisation to be positive and to accept new forms of differentiation that require flexibility and an acceptance of the notion of the virtual organisation.

Business process management is customer-oriented; it envisages the business as a set of customer-oriented core business processes rather than a set of organisational functions. A *core business process* is a set of linked activities that crosses function and (increasingly) organisational boundaries. Thus the needs of the marketplace drive the (virtual) organisation's capabilities.

Expanding the business process concept

Womack and Jones (1994), discussing the development of the lean enterprise, review industrial developments from a number of perspectives. They argue that the Japanese delivered an enormous benefit: '. . . the ability of big companies to focus on the needs of the value stream unimpeded by functional reforms, career paths within functions and the constant struggles between members of the value stream to gain advantage over each other'. There has been a cost: '. . . the creation of new knowledge backing the technical functions has languished'. Companies such as Toyota and Matsushita '. . . have now largely cleared the shelf of available ideas for generating fundamentally new, innovative products and processes'.

The authors propose a shift in roles of functions. Functions should assume a 'teaching' role; by systematically summarising current knowledge, they search for new knowledge and pass this to their members: '. . . who then spend time on value-creating process teams'. Functions should develop best practices or guidelines for operational use and together with worthy colleagues identify joint practice codes. Functions (the authors contend) should give way to cross-functional product-development and production teams who should select suppliers, develop products and oversee routine production activities. Traditional purchasing should prescribe principles for supplier relationships and work with suppliers to improve performance. The 'new' product-development team assumes the traditional job of purchasing or deciding quantities, quality and prices from specific suppliers related to the life of 'their' product. *Marketing* would define supplier/distributor roles and relationships with 'ideal' partners.

The traditional roles of marketing and sales, product specification, taking orders and scheduling deliveries become the task of the product development and production teams. Engineering defines best practices and searches for new capabilities and alternative materials and methods. By overcoming current problems it can apply its new knowledge to the next generation of products. Womack and Jones continue with a 'job-specification' for a new process-management function. It should define the rules for managing cross-functional (organisational) teams and the continuous flow of production. They suggest:

> While functions become 'support' for value-creating process teams every function has a deeper and more coherent knowledge base than was possible when it divided its attention between thinking and doing. Moreover, this knowledge base is more relevant to the company's long term needs because function members returning from value-creating assignments in the processes bring new questions for the function to answer.

Womack and Jones' concern is with lean enterprises but their comments apply to the value chain orientation: by and large the issues are the same: 'Most companies today do too much and do much of it poorly'. They suggest: '. . . the assembler . . . may find that it no longer needs to design or produce any of the major component systems in its product because product development (in collaboration with suppliers and distributors) and final assembly are its real skills'. Similarly: 'The component system supplier may discover it no longer needs to make the parts in its systems because design of the complete system (in collaboration with customers and its own suppliers) is its competitive advantage'.

The 'rules' for regulating behaviour in a value chain are the same as those prescribed by the authors for lean enterprise activity. There should be clear agreements on target costing, acceptable levels of process performance, the rate of continuous improvement (quality and cost considerations), consistent accounting systems to analyse costs and formulas for 'splitting pain and gain'.

Business process: a value chain perspective

Beech (1998) considers the topic of business processes from a value chain perspective. He argues for an integration of the supply and demand chains: 'The challenge can only be met by developing a holistic strategic framework that leverages the generation and understanding of demand effectiveness with supply efficiency. . . . First, organisations must bring a multi-enterprise view to their supply chains. They need to be capable of working cooperatively with other organisations in the chain rather than seeking to outdo them. Secondly they must recognise the distinct supply and demand processes that must be integrated in order to gain the greatest value.' He suggests three key elements:

- the core processes of the supply and demand chains, viewed from a broad cross-enterprise vantage point rather than as discrete functions;
- the integrating processes that create the links between the supply and demand chains;
- the supporting infrastructure that makes such integration possible.

Beech adopts a similar argument to Womack and Jones, in other words, that many businesses operate each business process as an isolated discrete function with departments operating in 'functional silos'. Beech is more focussed on the 'supply-demand nexus' and advocates the identification of: '. . . core processes across the demand and supply chain, as well as exploring the impact of each of these processes on the different functions and organisations across the various chains'. Beech proposes the core processes of the *demand chain* include product development, trade marketing, selling, value added distributors, category management and store marketing. *Supply chain* processes include the purchasing of raw materials, manufacturing, warehousing and distribution, purchasing of finished goods and store operations. Integrating processes that synchronise the supply and demand chain core processes are planning and servicing; these ensure that supply and demand do in fact integrate and offer benefits such as reduced inventory investment, improved return on assets and enhanced customer satisfaction. Figure 10.10 identifies the demand and supply processes and their linkages.

The *integrating processes* (planning and service) are detailed by Beech. *Planning processes* comprise: channel strategies, planning of manufacturing, inventory, distribution and transportation, demand planning and forecasting, and marketing and promotional planning. Beech emphasises the need for these to be an inter-organisational activity. *Service processes* include such functions as credit order management, load planning, billing and collection, dispute resolution and promotional activities. Service processes coordinate the flow of materials, information and funds between trading partners. Beech suggests an integrated model including information technology, finance, HR and administration.

The *supporting infrastructure* is being driven by IT systems. They are required to handle routine transactions but increasingly IT plays a more critical role in coordinating planning, production, purchasing, production and distribution data at an expanding number of levels and complexity.

Thinking of the business as a number of integrated core processes enables management to focus on streamlining the processes and identifying inter-organisational linkages which result in creating more value for less effort. This is very different to current activities aimed at reducing functions simply to reduce costs, often with no tangible impact on value outputs. Beech comments: 'It is the linking between enterprises that can lead to the ultimate goal of moving beyond supply chain efficiency to integrating supply with demand. The performance outcome is synchronization'.

A strategic perspective is taken by Armistead *et al* (1999). The authors identify themes 'associated' with business process management. Strategic choice and direction consider that because an organisation cannot pursue every opportunity it makes choices or trade-offs, and these determine the resource patterns of organisations and eventually the development of core competencies. These, in turn, lead to competencies that influence subsequent strategy. Strategic business process management forces companies to 'examine their form and structure', having an influence on boundaries, structure and power within organisational design. An important component of the authors' model

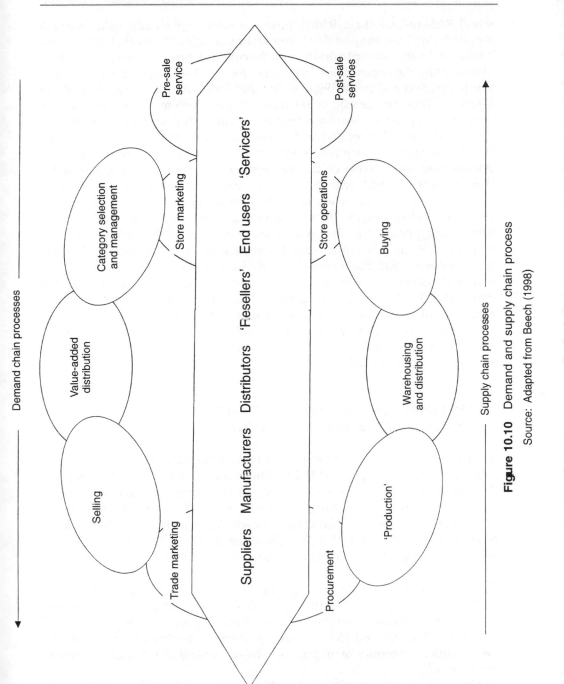

Figure 10.10 Demand and supply chain process

Source: Adapted from Beech (1998)

is the market value chain which 'links the stages which add value along a supply chain'. They suggest that *within* an organisation the market value chain is taken to be the conceptualisation of the core processes and activities which represent the the organisation in process terms: 'They capture the activities which start and end in the organisation and link with other organisations in the chain'. They further suggest the market value chain reinforces the resource based view of the organisation because it forces the identification of core processes from which core competencies and competitive advantage emerge. Performance management is another perspective of strategic business process management which 'relies on the management of resources and on a series of measurement systems', without which progress towards goals and any necessary corrective action is not possible. Organisational coordination occurs internally and externally (that is, with suppliers and customers). This is particularly 'pertinent as the boundaries of internal processes become more ill-defined'. It could be argued that it is even more important than the boundaries between value chain organisations (such as the prosumer relationship between customer and supplier). This perspective adds emphasis to the importance of relationship management. The authors also identify knowledge management as a component of their model. Organisational learning and knowledge management are enhanced by business process management; it 'provides a framework for organisational learning and can incorporate the management of knowledge'.

CORE COMPETENCIES/CAPABILITIES AND KEY SUCCESS FACTORS: LI AND FUNG CONTINUED

Li and Fung (see Chapter 9 for the first part of the 'case study') demonstrate clear competencies. Figure 10.11 identifies these and suggests the interrelationships of knowledge, technology and relationship management.

Underlying the Li and Fung business is a wealth of knowledge that has been developed over the years. This knowledge is market and 'technology' based and supplemented by the relationships built over time. Furthermore Li and Fung demonstrate expertise in managing the interfaces between each management category.

Their expertise in the knowledge management/technology management dialogue is clearly demonstrated by their understanding of the production and logistics processes required to meet quality/cost/time requirements of customers. This has led to a core competency – distributed manufacturing and logistics economics management – basic features of strategic operations management.

Knowledge management/relationship management is driven by the depth of trust developed by the company with both customers and suppliers. This interface has resulted in Li and Fung being able to identify, work with and develop entrepreneurial organisations. It has also led to the development of a 'customer-centric' organisation structure.

The technology management/relationship management interface is dominated by the management of the economics of integration (Michael Dell's asset

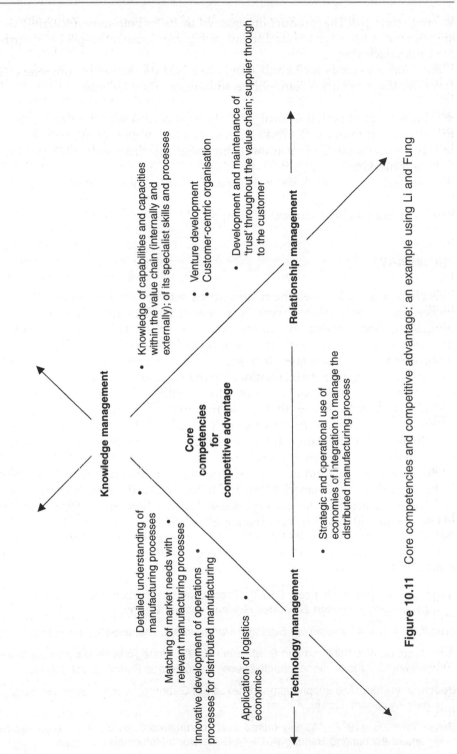

Figure 10.11 Core competencies and competitive advantage: an example using Li and Fung

leverage concept). The 'production process' includes both manufacturing and logistics and adds a behavioural (relationship management) aspect to distributed manufacturing.

Key success factors for Li and Fung are based on their core competencies and offer the company a competitive advantage. They include:

- knowledge of both the 'local' and global specialist supply infrastructure;
- strong communications links throughout the supply infrastructure;
- an understanding of customers' business objectives and strategies and their markets;
- internal, financially based performance management controls.

Value drivers will be discussed in Chapter 11.

SUMMARY

This chapter has addressed the relationships between core competencies, key success factors and value drivers. A review of the literature identifies views suggesting clear concepts and differences between core competencies and key success factors. Recent industry developments (such as the virtual organisation) blur these differences. It is suggested that knowledge management, technology management and relationship management have through the 'virtuality' concept moved both concepts closer, within distance of each other.

Value drivers are 'things that are so important to customers that they are willing to pay premium prices or switch suppliers'. Value drivers add costs and the benefit/cost relationship is one of critical importance in the structure of a response to customer expectations.

Business processes and process management are emerging as an important feature in value chain management. The focus on processes and not functions and the application of this concept *across* organisations make for successful management and competitive advantage.

REFERENCES ●

Alchian, A. A. and H. Demsetz (1972), 'Production, information costs and economic organisation', *American Economic Review*, Vol. 62, December.

Ansoff, H. I. (1984), *Implanting Strategic Management*, Prentice-Hall, New York.

Armistead, C., J-P. Pritchard and S. Machin (1999), 'Strategic business process management for organisational effectiveness', *Long Range Planning*, Vol. 32, No. 1.

Beech, J. (1998), 'The supply-demand nexus', in Gattorna, J. (ed.), *Strategic Supply Chain Alignment*, Gower, Aldershot.

Bellis-Jones, R. (1992), 'Activity-based cost management', in C. Drury (ed.), *Management Accounting Handbook*, CIMA/Butterworth-Heinemann, London.

Grant, R. (1995), *Contemporary Strategy Analysis*, Blackwell, Oxford.

Hamel, G. and C. K. Prahalad (1994), *The Core Competences of the Corporation*, Harvard Business School Press, Boston.

Hofer, C. H. and D. Schendel (1978), *Strategy Formulation: Analytical Concepts*, West Publishing, St Paul, Minnesota.

Johansson, H. J., P. McHugh, A. J. Pendlebury and W. Wheeler III (1993), *Business Process Reengineering*, Wiley, Chichester.

Kay, J. (2000), 'Strategy and the delusion of grand designs', in *Mastering Strategy, Financial Times*/Prentice-Hall, London.

Leidecker, J. K. and A. V. Bruno (1984), 'Identifying and using critical success factors', *Long Range Planning*, February.

Leonard-Barton, D. (1992), 'Core capabilities and core rigidities: a paradox in managing new product development', *Strategic Management Journal*, Vol. 13, No. 2.

Nelson, R. R. and S. G. Winter (1982), *An Evolutionary Theory of Economic Change*, Belknap Press, Cambridge, Mass.

Noori, H. (1990), *Managing the Dynamics of New Technology*, Prentice-Hall, New Jersey.

Olve, N., J. Roy and M. Wetter (1997), *Performance Drivers*, Wiley, Chichester.

Penrose, E. T. (1959), *The Theory of the Growth of the Firm*, Wadsworth, Belmont, California.

Porter, M. (1996), 'What is strategy?' *Harvard Business Review*, November/December.

Quinn, J. B. (1992), *Intelligent Enterprise*, Free Press, New York.

Robinson, J. (1969), *The Economics of Imperfect Competition*, Macmillan, London.

Rumelt, R. P. (1987), 'Theory, strategy and entrepreneurship', in Teece, D. (ed.), *The Competitive Challenge: Strategies for Industrial Innovation and Renewal*, Ballinger, Cambridge, Mass.

Rumelt, R. P. (1994), *Foreword*, in Hamel, G. and A. Heene (eds), *Competence Based Competition*, Wiley, Chichester.

Scott, M. (1998), *Value Drivers*, Wiley, Chichester.

Slywotzky, A. J. and D. Morrison with B. Andelman (1997), *The Profit Zone*, Wiley, Chichester.

Spender, J-C. (1998), 'The geographies of strategic competence: borrowing from social and educational psychology to sketch an activity and knowledge-based theory of the firm', in Chandler, A. Jr, P. Hagstrom and O. Solvell, (eds), *The Dynamic Firm: The Role of Technology, Strategy, Organisation, and Regions*, Oxford University Press, New York.

Stewart, G. B. (1997), *Intellectual Capital. The New Wealth of Nations*, Doubleday, New York.

Womack, J. P. and D. T. Jones (1994), 'From lean production to lean enterprise', *Harvard Business Review*, March/April.

chapter 11

Where Value Strategy and Value Operations Meet

LEARNING OUTCOMES

The student will be able to:

- develop a strategic operations model format for a business or collection of business partners;
- identify the value chain alternatives available to the organisation.

INTRODUCTION

The concept underlying strategic operations management has been part of a number of management practices for some time. Baldwin and Clark (1997) discuss *modularity* in the computer and automotive industries and append a direction for further reading which includes contributions commencing in 1989 and numerous applications cases from the early 1990s.

The authors define modularity as '. . . building a complex product or process from smaller subsystems that can be designed independently yet function together as a whole'. They contend that 'Many industries have long had a degree of modularity in their production processes', but suggest that '. . . a growing number of them are now poised to extend modularity to the design stage'. They also suggest that it is the computer industry that has both facilitated and benefited from modularity. Baldwin and Clark contend that modularity has enabled companies to restructure products into subsystems or modules that result in flexibility, and this results in allowing different companies to take responsibility for separate modules: '. . . confident that a reliable product will arise from their collective efforts'.

The essence of Baldwin and Clark's concept lies with product development. Strategic operations management is much more 'macro' in its approach. Its concern is with organisational development. This difference notwithstanding, there are some strong similarities and conceptually the two are close. Indeed, many of the comments made by the authors concerning benefits that have been identified are well noted. And their comments concerning the evolutionary stages of modularity compare with the views of McHugh *et al* (1995) and their 'holistic' organisation.

Strategic operations management extends beyond product and technology and considers the structure of organisations and entire industries. It is customer or market focussed, rather than being product and/or process focussed and it is likely to extend across industries and certainly within them. Baldwin and Clark propose two strategy alternatives. An organisation '. . . can compete as an architect, creating the visible information or design rules for a product made up of modules, or it can compete as a designer of modules that conform to the architecture, interfaces and test protocols of others'. Again the similarity is strong. Strategic operations management has both the integrator and value chain specialist roles. However, the integrator role is more strategic and assumes a market strategist role identifying opportunities for expansive customer satisfaction, extending well beyond specific products.

Management practices are similar. Baldwin and Clark suggest: '. . . managers will have to become much more attuned to all sorts of developments in the design of products, both inside and outside their own companies . . . Success in the marketplace will depend upon mapping much larger competitive terrain and linking one's own capabilities and options with those emerging elsewhere, possibly in companies very different from one's own'. The 'skills' required of the integrator and modularity architect are similar. Both need to be able to link technologies, financial resources and human resources. They are essentially entrepreneurial. The authors quote a comment by Stevenson, who described entrepreneurship as '. . . the pursuit of opportunity beyond the resources currently controlled'. Perhaps the quotation should now be updated to read '. . . the pursuit of opportunity virtually'.

A FRAMEWORK FOR INTEGRATING VALUE STRATEGY AND VALUE PRODUCTION

It could be argued that strategic operations management owes much to the work of Coase (1937) who, it will be recalled, provides an initial perspective of the economics of alliances and partnerships through the concept of transaction costs. The issue Coase addresses is the relationship between the cost of producing goods or services internally and purchasing them from an external supplier. In addition to 'market prices' there are transaction costs generated by the search and negotiating processes involved in finding an appropriate partner organisation, negotiating a supply agreement and the associated time based costs. Tedeschi (2000), writing in the *New York Times* (and reproduced in the *Australian Financial Review*), comments that at the time

Coase proposed this theory, transaction costs were 'prohibitively high' due to the lack of timely and accurate information and cramped and slow supply chains that fostered the preference for ownership of resources through vertical integration. Some sixty years on, within the 'new economy', rapid moving, accurate and low cost information offers 'virtual-instant' information about potential suppliers and business partners, thereby facilitating the formation of alliances at a fraction of the costs of even five or ten years ago. Coase maintained that with diminished transaction costs, more alliances would be inevitable. More recently, Tedeschi has commented that understanding transaction costs in the new economy will result in a return to the theories of Adam Smith and specialisation: 'It enables you to have more specialisation and greater production because you're more efficient . . . You'll get more small firms as a result, but large firms will also get larger, because they can concentrate on core activities and con contract out what they can't do well'.

The integrating role of strategic operations

Strategic operations management has three primary tasks in the process of integrating value strategy and value delivery. Figure 11.1 illustrates the proposal that strategic operations management is a process in which customer value opportunity is identified, value production processes are coordinated and, provided that partners' objectives can be met, customer value is delivered. Figure 11.1 also identifies the conceptual management infrastructure necessary to implement the value strategy. The value chain is a structure of networks between value producers and customers; if it is to be successful, then an understanding and an acceptance of tasks, roles, responsibilities and accountabilities is necessary. It is the role of strategic operations management to coordinate the network between and among the value chain producers and the customer. In the context of the value chain, the networks are not simply information technology based, but are relationship, knowledge and technology based. They develop from the experience of working with partner organisations, developing an understanding of the specific skills and resources each possesses and also developing trust and respect for the owners of those skills and resources. Typically, as experience and trust expand, confidence grows and with it the willingness to share knowledge, so that eventually the network develops a knowledge base that it can use to its competitive advantage. Similarly, technology management also expands and the trust enables partners to develop dependencies upon each other. Dell (1999) gave examples of how trust had developed relationships in the computer industry to the point where 'asset leverage' has become commonplace.

Establishing a value profile: customer value expectations, options and implementation

Returning to the role of the integrator or system architect in strategic operations management, it is essential that an initiative be taken in the identification of customer value expectations and the exploration of alternative delivery

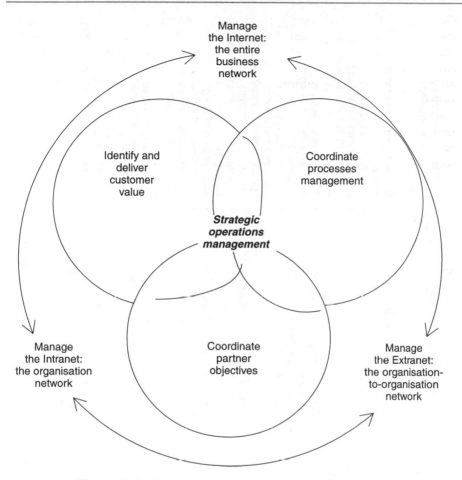

Figure 11.1 Integrating value strategy and value delivery

modes by which the value strategy can become operational. Figures 11.2a and 11.2b present an hypothetical *value profile* in which customer value expectations are identified, interpreted as value strategy options and extended into possible delivery (value production/implementation) alternatives. Both customer expectation and acquisition costs are identified and dealt with. The role of strategic operations management is to identify the value production processes required if the effective and efficient delivery of value is to be realised. The effective delivery of value is the strategic alignment of process owners. Efficient delivery only occurs if process management meets the performance expectations required by customers and value chain participants. The emphasis for success is based upon cooperation and coordination. Some examples using figures 11.2a and 11.2b will demonstrate this point.

Within the context of business-to-business markets, a clear concern by both vendor and purchaser is for profitability and productivity. It follows that this concern should be reflected in all aspects of the vendor value strategy.

Customer value attribute expectations	Value expectations	Value strategy options	Value production/ implementation
• Security	• Warranty; • After-sales service facilities • Service augmentation	• Continuity of profitability/ productivity • Minimise downtime	• Design to eliminate *product failure* • Focus R&D on *reliability* • Design around *product platforms* • *Partner* with 'national' service franchise
• Performance	• Quality • Consistency • 'Output'	• *TQM* agreements internally and externally • *Branded* components included in the value chain	• Partner with leading manufacturers to leverage reputations • Use *modular* systems to guarantee performance – use specific modular specialists
• Aesthetics	• *Functional* design • *Cosmetic* design	• Make *design* a key success factor	• Use design consultants • Partner with VARs with a reputation for design
• Convenience	• Product *flexibility* • Time saving products • Location/access • Information	• *User friendly* products and service packages to enhance *customer* profitability and productivity	• *Modular* product design • Internet/Extranet networks with customers and suppliers to enhance transparency
• Economy	• Product *availability* • Price/value attribute mix	• Product design for operating economies, maintenance *and* initial price offer • Design for reliability • Incorporate diagnostic reporting systems • Increase the product knowledge levels of internal and external staff	• *Modularisation* using standard assemblies/components • Design for low cost maintenance • Establish product development committees: designers, users, component suppliers and distributors
• Reliability	• Product • Service • Information		

Figure 11.2a Interpreting customer value expectations

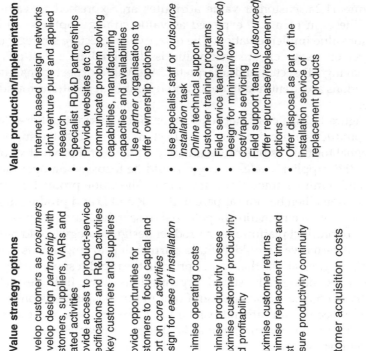

Customer acquisition costs	Value expectations	Value strategy options	Value production/implementation
• Specification	• Information and advice on product/service relevance • Assistance in developing performance criteria for NPD • Supplier competency profiles	• Develop customers as *prosumers* • Develop design *partnership* with customers, suppliers, VARs and related activities • Provide access to product-service specifications and R&D activities to key customers and suppliers	• Internet based design networks • Joint venture pure and applied research • Specialist RD&D partnerships • Provide websites etc to communicate problem solving capabilities, manufacturing capacities and availabilities • Use *partner* organisations to offer ownership options
• Search			
• Transactions and ownership transfer	• Transaction and ownership options	• Provide opportunities for customers to focus capital and effort on *core activities*	
• Installation	• Minimum time to achieve full operations	• Design for *ease of installation*	• Use specialist staff or *outsource installation* task
• Operations	• Standard inputs • Low operating costs • Operating simplicity	• Minimise operating costs	• *Online* technical support • Customer training programs • Field service teams (*outsourced*) • Design for minimum/low cost/rapid servicing
• Maintenance	• Minimise downtime for servicing • Minimise service costs	• Minimise productivity losses • Maximise customer productivity and profitability	• Field support teams (*outsourced*) • Offer repurchase/replacement options
• Disposal	• Maximise *total return on investment*	• Maximise customer returns • Minimise replacement time and cost • Ensure productivity continuity	• Offer disposal as part of the installation service of replacement products

Figure 11.2b Interpreting customer acquisition costs

In Figure 11.2a, customer value attributes are expressed as value expectations. These, in turn, are explored as value strategy options, and again as tasks for value implementation. The objective of effective strategic operations management is to ensure that value is delivered in a cost-efficient way. Thus having 'dissected and interpreted' the value expectations, the strategy implications are identified in detail and operational solutions found for value delivery.

In Figure 11.2a, a customer requirement for a warranty, after-sales services and a product-service package is, in effect, notice to potential suppliers that it is essential for the customer to maintain profitable and productive operations. Hence, the supplier's *value strategy* should be focussed on operational continuity and minimal amounts of downtime. The value production/implementation options then become apparent. Both R and D and product design could be targeted at an elimination of potential (researched) areas of product failure. The use of product platforms as a product design strategy would reinforce this option. Alternatives would include partnership arrangements with service franchise organisations that would provide the rapid response cover required.

Often technologically sound organisations have little aesthetic/design expertise. Often aesthetics are significant in purchasing decisions and should, therefore, become an integral part of the value strategy. For those organisations without the expertise, industrial design companies are an implementation solution.

For two or three of the customer value attributes, for example: performance, convenience and economy, there is a suggested solution option that appears frequently – modularisation. This repetition adds emphasis to the role of modular design (or as will be described later 'distributed manufacturing'), and suggests an early rather than later consideration of the incorporation of design joint ventures into product and service design for effective strategies and efficient production/implementation.

Customer acquisition costs (Figure 11.2b) can be reviewed using the same approach. For example, product-service specification, for which customer value expectations would include advice and assistance to differing degrees, may have a *value strategy* response that resolves these problems by involving customers or developing three-way research design and development partnerships that may be 'virtual' organisations that focus on specific design/specification problems. The value production/implementation options include a dialogue based, Internet based design network (the Fiat solution when redesigning the Punto), joint venture pure and applied research activities in which third parties, such as a specialised university research function (for example, The Centre for Laser Technology at Macquarie University) bring highly focussed research expertise to bear on a specific problem.

Transactions and ownership concerns for customers may be reduced by value chain participants. Increasingly, businesses are opting for value production strategies that show preferences for minimal investment in tangible assets, with branding, R and D, knowledge, technology and relationship management (intangible assets), receiving funding and development.

Examples of this have already been discussed and include Dell, Nike, Coca-Cola, Ford and others. The value chain response is seen in financial institutions becoming involved in 'ownership options' ranging from sale and leaseback arrangements (for example, David Jones', the Sydney department store, sale of its prime retail location in Elizabeth Street) to the development service function in which fixed costs become variable costs and capacity is purchased as required. Ownership becomes a non-issue.

'Disposal' is a downstream acquisition cost consideration. The European Union is close to recycling legislation and others will likely follow suit. The disposal of obsolete plant and equipment can be expensive (even prohibitive in some fields of activity). Consequently it is advantageous to understand customer motivation in this regard. Clearly in business-to-business sectors, the primary purpose of using plant and equipment is to maximise a return on investment. Seen in this context, it is not surprising that a number of organisations seek to maximise returns that include the consideration of disposal values of plant and equipment and others, such as Ford, take equity interests in recycling plants. Therefore, given that customer expectations for 'maximum ROI' are commonplace, value strategies should be structured to ensure the continuity of profitability and productivity. Accordingly, production/implementation options include 'buyback plans' whereby guaranteed repurchasable values form part of contractual arrangements between vendors and purchasers and typically involve partner organisations in disposing of the 'remaining productive capacity' of the product into markets where capital availability is limited. The 'ownership' of recycling facilities may also be seen as a political imperative, particularly important for global operators.

THE VALUE CHAIN: ORGANISATION PROFILE

Given a clear understanding of customer expectations and their implications for strategic operations management, they can be used for developing strategy and operations options. The models developed in Chapter 7 will be useful in identifying how the options may be evaluated.

The previous chapter suggested that the organisation's core competency base, its '. . . bundle of skills and technologies . . .' was underwritten by a strategic combination of knowledge management, technology management and relationship management. Knowledge management, it was proposed, structures and organises knowledge to create and reinforce competencies. Technology management results in a customised combination of information and operations technology to ensure relevant capabilities and capacities. Relationship management includes 'coproduction' – the transfer of production processes upstream and downstream – and creates 'codestiny' (a shared perspective of strategic direction) which is managed internally and externally. Successful value positioning and strategy also depend upon these factors, indeed, it is argued that they are essentially the same. Core competency is a

unique (or at least exclusive) combination of knowledge, technology and relationship management, while all three contribute to the competitive advantage
sought by establishing a 'unique or at least exclusive' combination of these
important management concepts.

Figure 11.3 completes the value chain organisational profile model.
Given the 'unique or exclusive' positioning and strategy, the production task
involves management and coordination of stakeholder contribution and the
physical processes of procurement, production logistics and service. *Value
drivers* influence both positioning and strategy and value production and
coordination. It will be recalled that value drivers reflect customer priorities.
They are '. . . simply the things that are so important to customers that they
will pay a premium for them or, when they can't get them, they will switch
suppliers' (Slywotzky and Morrison: 1997).

The interpretation of the value response to customer expectations is then
complete. The value proposition has four formulating influences: the customer value model, partner objectives, the ability to respond in some unique
or exclusive manner, and core competencies. For the proposition to become a
realistic offer it requires both a strategic input/positioning and strategy and
to be 'manufactured', the value production and coordination activity. The
influence of value drivers adds the 'customer-centricity' essential in a business environment in which customisation is rapidly becoming a benchmark
requirement.

THE VALUE CHAIN: PROCESSES, ACTIVITIES AND DECISIONS

McHugh *et al* (1995) discuss 'demand-driven' logistics in much the same
context as Beech (1998) and comment: 'It is the backbone of the actual day-
to-day execution of a virtual company. By forming a virtual company among
and integrating with a product's suppliers, the end customer can be more
completely serviced'. The authors also introduce the term 'co-makership'
which is used to suggest the integrated 'production and coordination' role in
the organisation profile model discussed in the previous paragraphs. They
suggest co-makership to be: 'a partnering philosophy and technique that complements the process-oriented approaches . . .'. McHugh *et al* also discuss the
approach of manufacturing companies who now regard suppliers as partners
and comment on 'supplier equity' as a core competence. They also differentiate between two quite different focuses: 'product out', which is operations
based, and 'market in', which identifies business opportunities offered by
the marketplace and translates them into products the company could make
given its processes and capabilities. This itself is insufficient and they suggest
that increasingly for success it is also necessary to '. . . have a culture that is
group oriented'. They argue that businesses that compete and win today, and
will continue to do so through the 21st century, are those with what they
describe as a venture/'market in' approach. Put more pragmatically, their
'way of doing business' is to include both suppliers and customers within the
value chain and its communications.

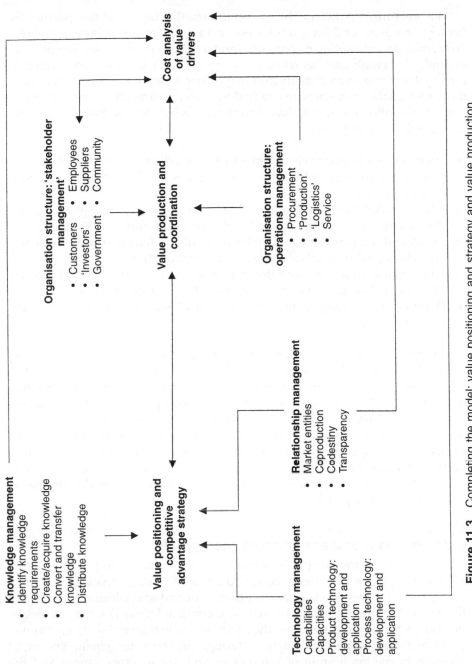

Figure 11.3 Completing the model: value positioning and strategy and value production

The venture/'market in' business adopts the Japanese perspective by taking a medium and long term view of the market and combines it with Western approaches of market analysis and a focus on innovation and product diversity. McHugh and his co-authors argue: 'Their basis of competition is quality, lead time and flexibility and they engage their partners up and down the value chain in discussions regarding these competitive aspects'. They employ the following system-based strategies, which are the essence of strategic operations management:

- vertical coordination/virtual integration of a 'logistic network' that 'integrates' the interest and activities of suppliers and customers throughout the value chain;
- the co-makership logic adopted in design and development procurement, production, marketing and service delivery, not only in operations;
- a rationalised supplier base that becomes integrated into the business and provides quality, flexibility as well as cost reduction;
- the creation of a common information system for planning and controlling the value chain and that identifies change opportunities;
- support and management processes considered for outsourcing to specialist partners.

Within the strategic operations management context, partners become integrated into a 'virtual organisation' in which their processes are modified to meet an overall 'input-transformation-output' model. Cooperation in product and service design is a 'norm', codestiny pervades procurement, production, marketing and service delivery. Communications are typically electronically managed to ensure not only that resource uses are optimal but that responses to customer changes in expectations are also rapid. The logistics function does become 'the backbone' of the actual day-to-day execution of the value chain organisation. This is illustrated in Figure 11.4, which extends the discussion commenced in Chapter 7.

Establishing a process and activities profile

Figure 11.4 illustrates the implementation of the value chain process profile. Each of the processes is identified and the role of strategic management is to identify the competencies, skills and resources and specialisations necessary for the venture/'market in' approach to be applied. Figure 11.4 suggests logistics is in a driving role, ensuring the accurate (correct quantity, timely) movement of materials and information throughout the value chain. The rapid increase in the application of Internet technology to procurement and the development of buying exchanges suggests that this process is also becoming a primary process that is common across an industry and may be incorporated into a number of competitive value chains within the industry. Within the procurement process cell in Figure 11.4, the coordination of primary, secondary and tertiary suppliers is suggested. This reflects the increasing use of POS (point of sale) data to structure the inbound supply of materials and

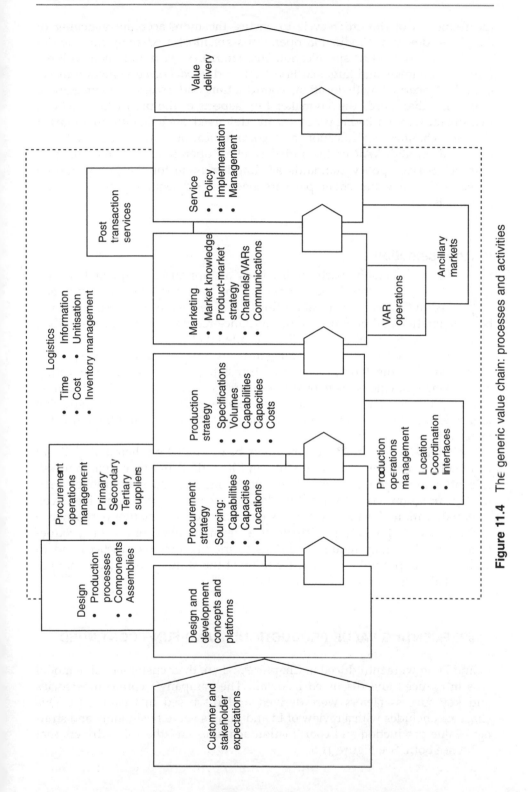

Figure 11.4 The generic value chain: processes and activities

the reduction of the order cycle to ensure the more accurate matching of supply to demand. Production operations are illustrated as *specification*, in which finished product specification characteristics are determined, volume forecasts are made and target costs determined. *Production operations management* is concerned with location, coordination and interface management issues, in other words the 'co-makership' aspects of the production process. In a similar way marketing processes are 'devolved' such that product-market strategy, channels specification and communications are determined and extended through VAR (value added reseller) operations and into ancillary markets. Service policy standards are another issue for the 'integrator' to agree with the value chain partners and are subsequently managed by specialists.

Partner selection

Selecting co-makership partners involves an appraisal of qualitative and quantitative performance characteristics. The balanced scorecard approach (discussed in Chapter 8) is ideal for this task. The balanced scorecard enables both qualitative and quantitative performance requirements to be prescribed and subsequently monitored. It will be recalled that Kaplan and Norton (1992) claim that the scorecard offers management a broader planning perspective by introducing the four processes of translating a vision, communicating and linking strategic plans to objectives throughout an organisation, business planning integration, and feedback and learning. The scorecard perspective identifies the objectives of a value production organisation and therefore, the expectations of its participants.

McHugh *et al* (*op cit*) suggest members be evaluated on their ability '. . . to meet current requirements for quality and lead time and their "willingness" to continually improve'. The authors refer to methods such as supplier certification programmes with quantifiable performance expectations. However, the qualifications for membership extend beyond quantitative performance and into a willingness to participate as a 'team-member' of a value production chain. This may require members to modify process practices and to adjust throughput volumes in order to meet the strategic objectives that the value chain has been structured to achieve.

IMPLEMENTING VALUE PRODUCTION: LI AND FUNG CONTINUED

Li and Fung were introduced in Chapter 9, where their customer value model was introduced and discussed in detail. The company's core competencies and key success factors were derived and discussed in Chapter 10. This chapter concludes with a review of Li and Fung's value positioning and strategy, value production and coordination activities and the value drivers that influence both. See Figure 11.5.

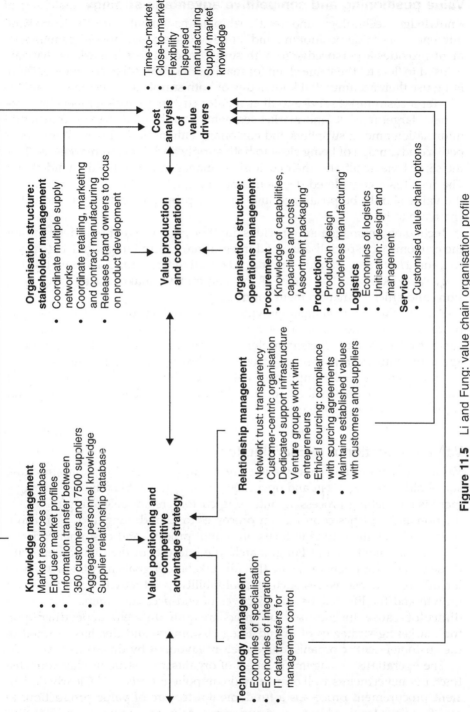

Figure 11.5 Li and Fung: value chain organisation profile

Value positioning and competitive advantage strategy

Knowledge, technology and relationship management are also important influences on value positioning and strategy decisions. Knowledge management provides a perspective to both supply and customer markets that can be used to 'locate' the value chain for maximum strategic effectiveness. Li and Fung use their accumulated knowledge of both supply and customer markets to offer a customised service to their retailer customers which meets the customers' target market (and market segment) profiles. The efficient transfer of information among suppliers and customers enhances the Li and Fung competitive advantage of being close to both supply and demand markets and, at the same time, facilitates their customers' management of the demand chain. The result is a considered decision concerning *what* value is required, *where* the value should be positioned and *who* the principal partners in the value chain are to be.

Technology management provides another perspective. By understanding the economies of specialisation and integration, Li and Fung can decide upon *how* and *when* value should be produced effectively and reinforce both the *who* and *where* decisions. The use of IT for data transfer makes for effective decisions and efficient management controls.

Relationship management provides additional input into *how* and *who* produces value and through network trust (and the support infrastructure) ensures effective and efficient implementation of decisions. Value chain management requires transparency across and throughout its operations as well as an agreement (and compliance) with an established set of values. Li and Fung assume the responsibility of ensuring the overlap between customer and supplier interest in this regard.

Value production and coordination

Value production and coordination are made up of organisation structure, stakeholder management and operations management. Stakeholder management is a matching process. Li and Fung customers are delegating their production and logistics coordination processes to Li and Fung and, as a result, release management time to focus on brand, product and customer satisfaction development. Li and Fung 'match' the interests of their customers with those of their suppliers to ensure that all stakeholder goals may be met. These include commercial issues such as profitability, productivity, cash flow and growth and the lifestyle based objectives of end-user customers. This can be difficult because the end-user customers are quite different, depending upon the marketing strategies of Li and Fung customers, and this has resulted in the customer-centric organisation structure favoured by the company.

The operations management aspect of organisation structure has four distinct, but nevertheless well coordinated component processes. Clearly an efficient procurement process is a fundamental feature of value production. Li and Fung's extensive knowledge and expertise in managing some 7500 suppliers are crucial to the efficient management of the procurement component. It could be argued that this aspect is a key process. Without supply market management expertise, the quality and cost objectives could not be realised. This expertise has resulted in 'assortment packaging', a process in which sourcing expertise results in multi-sourcing to optimise cost/quality value.

Production management has two important features. Production design is a process by which retail customer product range strategy and design can be implemented and a production plan formulated. Li and Fung start with designer concept sketches and then research supply markets for appropriate materials and production methods to ensure the value proposition may be transformed through a relevant production process. Borderless manufacturing involves Li and Fung in identifying and using the specialist manufacturing skills and resources that reflect the value offer their customers are seeking to deliver. Borderless manufacturing extends throughout Asia; garments may be manufactured in a number of countries. The important concern for Li and Fung is that the finished product meets the value (style, quality and cost) objectives decided by its client customer base.

Logistics was described earlier as being possibly the most important process of strategic operations management. Logistics is responsible for managing much more than inventory flows. In the Li and Fung business model, it is clearly responsible for inventory management but also manages the flow of information within the value chain (particularly the supply chain component). A primary function of inventory is to manage the economics of logistics through unitisation – the management of customer specific assortment requirements – which saves time and costs by 'delivering' the exact needs to value chain members and eliminating conventional consolidation activities.

Service for Li and Fung is the core offer to its customers. While service processes pervade their organisation, the customisation of value chain operations, from working on design and development issues with customers, to the matching processes involved in procurement and production (through distributed/borderless manufacturing), the unitisation of logistics and delivery to customer distribution centres, is Li and Fung's core competency and distinctive competitive advantage feature.

Value drivers are a central focus

Value drivers are the '... things that are so important to customers that they are willing to pay premium prices or switch suppliers' (Slywotzky and Morrison, *op cit*). It will be recalled (Chapter 10) that value drivers are also cost drivers and consequently should be evaluated from two directions: the impact on value delivered and customer perceptions of the value *and* the cost of providing the value influence. For Li and Fung, five value drivers emerge as important. They are time-to-market, close-to-market, flexibility, dispersed manufacturing, and supply market knowledge. No information is available concerning the cost of these value drivers, but clearly, they are cost-effective.

Li and Fung's processes and decisions

Implementation of the Li and Fung value strategy is made up of a number of decisions within a process model and these are shown in Figure 11.6. The

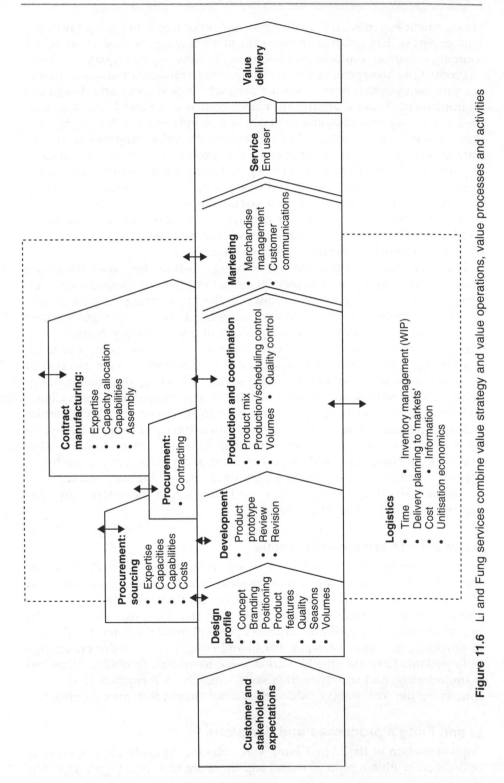

Figure 11.6 Li and Fung services combine value strategy and value operations, value processes and activities

design profile process is usually a customer responsibility because customers know their own markets well and therefore, concept decisions, branding, positioning and related specific decisions are made by the customer. Similarly, *marketing* and *services* processes are managed by Li and Fung customers.

Procurement is two processes. *Procurement sourcing* is an ongoing knowledge based process which identifies expertise, cost profiles and capacity potential throughout the Li and Fung resource market. This particular process is part of Li and Fung's core competency base, not so much its existence but the use of the knowledge base developed by the company. *Procurement contracting* is another important process for Li and Fung because it is closely associated with the *development* process. Given a concept by a customer, the company uses its knowledge of suppliers to *develop* the concept into a product prototype. Implicit in the prototype development is the knowledge that quality and quantity at budgeted costs can be delivered and that once customer approval is obtained, procurement contracts can be issued.

Production and coordination involve Li and Fung in its assortment packaging and distributed/borderless manufacturing activities. As described in previous paragraphs, Li and Fung coordinate the production activities across company and international boundaries. Again the knowledge of resource markets, an understanding of manufacturing product and process technologies and the trust developed from a long period of operating in these resource markets, are part of the Li and Fung competency base and a primary reason for their success. The process outputs here are quality, quantity, time and budgeted cost.

The logistics process is used by Li and Fung to drive their business. Fung is on record as saying '. . . inventory is the root of all evil' (Magretta: 1998), and a standardised, fully computerised operating system manages order processing and progressing. The coordination role of the logistics process is indicated by the arrows linking other processes into the logistics function. The logistics process 'connects' customers' design processes with their marketing process, from a product concept to a delivered finished product following the quantity and quality schedules required by the customer.

The Li and Fung activity provides the company's customers with an extensive part of the value chain. By offering a management service for the development, procurement and production processes, the customers are able '. . . to focus on the product development without worrying about where to source it . . . We're able to develop products smarter, faster and with cost efficiencies' (Avon Products, press quote 1999).

The acquisition of Inchcape's distribution, retailing and contract-manufacturing operations has extended Li and Fung's value chain capability. The company is now using its expertise to offer a pan-Asian distribution facility for international business.

SUMMARY

This chapter has considered the activities involved in implementing value strategy. It has reviewed earlier contributions to the topic such as the move towards modular production in a number of industries and returned to the original concept of Coase (1937) whose work predicted the importance of specialisation and its impact on the economics of production and logistics.

A conceptual model of strategic operations management was developed in which three activities were described as important: identifying and delivering customer value, coordinating partners' objectives, and doing so by coordinated process management. A number of examples were offered in which customer value expectations and customer acquisition costs could be identified and production implementation solution options considered.

The value chain models introduced earlier were revisited with emphasis being placed upon the relationship between value positioning and value production and coordination and value driver identification and cost analysis. Both models were explored using a 'generic' approach and the roles of knowledge technology and relationship management in both developing value positioning and strategy were discussed. Reference was made to core competencies and the relationship between these and value decisions. Value production and coordination were explored with the coordination or management of stakeholder interests and 'physical' processes of operations management being discussed.

The 'process and decisions' model discussed the notion of co-makership and some of its underlying conceptual components. From this a number of system based strategies that underpin strategic operations management were derived. The importance of identifying core processes for the success of both strategy and its implementation were inferred in this discussion.

The chapter concluded by revisiting the Li and Fung organisation to explore how the company effectively manages the implementation components of value strategy. Li and Fung represent the future direction of value chain management in the effective implementation of the strategic operations management concept.

REORFERENCES •••••••••••••••••••••••••••••••••••

Baldwin, C. Y. and K. B. Clark (1997), 'Managing in an age of modularity', *Harvard Business Review*, September/October.

Beech, J. (1998), 'The supply-demand nexus', in Gattorna, J. (ed.), *Strategic Supply Chain Alignment*, Gower, Aldershot.

Coase, H. R. (1937), 'The nature of the firm,' *Economica*, Vol. 4.

Dell, M. with C. Fredman (1999), *Direct from Dell*, Harper Collins Business, London.

Kaplan, R. S. and D. P. Norton (1992), 'The balanced scorecard – measures that drive performance', *Harvard Business Review*, January/February.

Magretta, J. (1998), 'The power of virtual integration: an interview with Dell Computers' Michael Dell, *Harvard Business Review*, March/April.

McHugh, P., G. Merli and W. Wheeler III (1995), *Beyond Business Process Reengineering*, Wiley, Chichester.

Slywotzky, A. J. and D. J. Morrison (1997), *The Profit Zone*, Wiley, New York.

Tedeschi, R. (2000), 'Comment' in *Australian Financial Review*, October.

part two
Existing value chains

Introduction

Examples of value chains can be found for industries and for companies. Two of the next chapters identify value chain structures that have been in existence for some years. They are examples of industry and organisational situations drawn from the literature and were used to present examples of problems and solutions not directly related to the value chain concept. The other two are examples of how the concept is being applied in healthcare and education. Both of these chapters were written with the cooperation of the organisations featured.

Both the industry and the organisation examples share these basic criteria:

- They have a 'visionary' who has identified that 'putting pieces together' can create a more effective business model.
- They have core processes that become inter-organisational rather than intra-organisational.
- They have supporting infrastructure that facilitates integration.
- They view the customer as an integral part of the value chain, as a major stakeholder.
- They have an inter-organisational performance planning system.

What has emerged in this approach are:

- an emphasis on processes rather than functions;
- distributed assets;
- an emphasis on flexible delivery;
- inter-organisational communication;
- infrastructure linkages that are based upon cooperation;
- synchronised networks which create *virtual organisations*.

Bovet and Martha (2000) use the term *value nets* in an argument suggesting them to be '. . . a business design that uses advanced supply chain concepts to achieve both superior customer satisfaction and company profitability';

and: '. . . a value net begins with customers, allows them to self-design products, and builds to satisfy actual demand'. The customer (business unit) is central to the decision process, surrounded by the company (or business unit) which in turn is surrounded by a constellation of providers that perform some or all of the sourcing, assembly and delivery activities. The authors offer five characteristics that distinguish a value net business from the traditional business model:

- *Customer aligned*: customer expectations initiate sourcing, building and delivery activities in the net. 'The customer commands the value net.'
- *Collaborative and systemic*: companies engage suppliers, customers and possibly competitors in a unique network of value-creating relationships. 'Each activity is assigned to the partner best able to perform it.'
- *Agile and scalable*: flexible manufacturing and distribution enhanced by information flow design facilitate responsiveness. 'Everything in the value net, physical or virtual, is scalable.'
- *Fast flow*: lead times are rapid and compressed. 'Rapid delivery goes "hand in hand" with reliable and convenient delivery.'
- *Digital*: e-commerce is a key enabler. However, it is the flow of information and its 'intelligent use' that drives the value net. 'Rule-based, event-driven tools take over many operational decisions. Distilled real-time analysis enables rapid executive decision making.'

Bovet and Martha's value net model does not differ markedly from that developed in our earlier chapters. Their criteria are similar; perhaps the emphasis in value net design is much more on the organisation rather than the structure of the value chain. Strategic operations management differs in this respect; it identifies the process alternatives required to meet customer expectations and considers the social and economic characteristics as part of the value chain decision process.

REFERENCE ●

Bovet, D. and J. Martha (2000), *Value Nets: Breaking the Supply Chain to Unlock Hidden Profits*, Wiley, New York.

12 Industry Value Chains

LEARNING OUTCOMES

The student will be able to:

- identify the value chain structure operating at the industry level;
- construct an industry value chain comprising its organisation profile and its processes.

THE PRATO (ITALY) VALUE CHAIN

Introduction

An example of a successful industry chain, one that has survived for a number of years, is the textile/apparel industry of Prato, a group of towns in the Italian provinces of Florence and Pistoria. Piore and Sabel (1984) describe a situation in which employment in Pratese textile manufacturing remained steady (about 45,000 workers, distributed in roughly 10,000 firms) and exports boomed. At the same time employment in the rest of Western Europe was declining by 25 per cent in France and the then West Germany and more than 35 per cent in the UK. By 1977 Pratese exports totalled about US$820 million (1984 prices), 60 per cent of the output, and increased to 75 per cent, US$1.5 billion in 1982. The authors suggest two factors responsible for this success: '. . . a long term shift from standard to fashionable fabrics, and a corresponding reorganisation of production from large integrated mills to technologically sophisticated shops specialising in various phases of production – a modern *system Motte*': a value chain structure.

Piore and Sabel describe the formation of a value chain that demonstrates the characteristics outlined in the introduction to Part 2. The 'visionary' or co-ordinator is the *impannatore*, '. . . a descendant of the medieval merchant and the early-modern *Verleger* (putter-outer)'. The *impannatore* had survived during the era of mass production and became increasingly important during the move towards mass customisation. During the mass production period the *impannatore* purchased raw materials, organised a network of small 'shops' to produce cloth according to established specifications and then sold the 'finished' product on to a merchant. A move to what became mass customisation increased the importance of the *impannatore*: s/he became a designer, a conduit for responding to (and shaping) fashion as well as for organising production and selling. The *impannatore* encouraged experimentation and innovation with materials (fabrics) and production processes. Success fostered success, increasing the creativity of the *impannatore*, increasing further their activity. Thus the small firms '... coalesced into networks, and these expanded – at the expense of the integrated firms'.

Johnston and Lawrence (1988) use the example as one of a number to explore the notion of value-adding partnerships: '... a set of independent companies that work closely together to manage the flow of goods and services along the entire value chain'. They use the concept of a value-added chain in which '... partnerships first develop between organisations that perform adjacent steps in the chain'. It is suggested that the sequential characteristic is not a necessity within the context of value chains designed specifically to implement strategic operations management decisions. The inference drawn from Johnston and Lawrence's excellent examples is that the structures existed and were used to explore the successful relationships identified, as indeed is the exercise undertaken in this chapter.

Changing customer expectations create a need for a new response from suppliers

Changes in *customer value criteria* such as an increasing awareness of fashion changes and choice were clearly important features in initiating 'market' changes to which the Prato industry responded. Added to this, time-to-market response was clearly an important issue to address, particularly if 'fashion' was of importance to customers. *Customer acquisition* costs did not appear to be addressed either before or after the changes were made. It is clear from both sources that design creativity and specialisation had become *competency requirements*, with coordination skills and response flexibility (in terms of design changes and market volume fluctuations) clear *key success factors*.

Both authors identify the impact of the breakup of the large integrated manufacturing units. Johnston and Lawrence identify a major impact following Massimo Menichetti's decision to end the unprofitable and unproductive trend within his organisation by pursuing a policy of disintegration. The company was large, bureaucratic and slow to respond to the rapidly changing marketplace. The Menichetti's mill was sold to employees through a share transfer arrangement and this dismantling process resulted in a group of specialist shops coordinated by the *impannatore*. As a result shared objectives are derived. *Partner value objectives* consider the impact of the overall need to maintain close links through the coordinating process. The *impannatore* role ensures the value chain operates to optimise profitability, productivity and

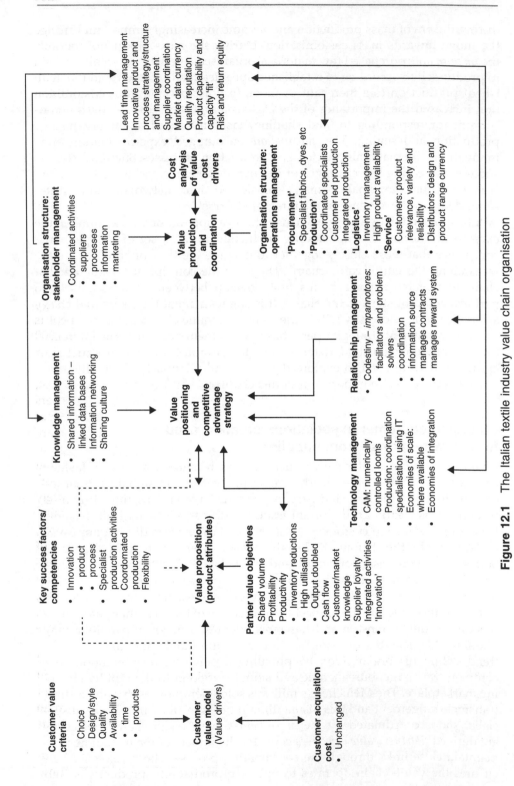

Figure 12.1   The Italian textile industry value chain organisation

cashflow. This is achieved by developing 'market' and 'process' knowledge by being involved in design, materials/fabric purchasing, profiling production capabilities and processes and logistics operations. Being active in markets and processes gives the *impannatore* the information to negotiate with all types of suppliers. The industry's *value proposition* becomes a fashion garment reflecting current style/design, in a range of fabrics relevant to end-user requirements, with a range of choice of styles and colours.

Value positioning strategy: a 'different' approach

The complex of decisions comprising *value positioning and competitive advantage strategy* reflects the role of the *impannatore* in the organisation structure. See Figure 12.1. *Knowledge management* is developed and distributed by the *impannatore*. This varies from interpreting market trends to identifying relevant operations process developments. Johnston and Lawrence report on the application of numerically controlled looms and computer systems that '. . . enhances coordination and boosts the speed and quality of responses to the market, an example of linking knowledge management with *technology management*. The acceptance of the importance of technology management is also commented on by Piore and Sabel: 'In the early 1970s, the area's 13,000 old looms were being replaced by automatic models – costing $100,000 or more – at the rate of 1000 per year'.

Relationship management is clearly demonstrated by the *impannatore* concept, within which codestiny plays a leading role: 'Realising that their partners must also be financially sound, efficient and marketwise if they themselves are to be competitive, the players in the Italian textile VAPs are eager to share information and to cooperate'; and '. . . sharing information is very different from sharing rewards. As a VAP, as in any other industrial or organisation structure, innovation and adaption must be rewarded if they are to be encouraged . . . the *impannatore* can ensure that the rewards are shared appropriately by influencing prices and channelling work only to cooperative members'.

A perspective of *stakeholder management* follows. The *impannatore* ensures, through coordination and knowledge based negotiation, that the interests of stakeholders are maintained. The *impannatore*'s knowledge of market expectations and prices ensures a balanced perspective from which a sense of equity can be seen to be derived. Further (as Piore and Sabel report), local banks, trade unions and artists and industrial associations began to collaborate. Computer based technologies were introduced to increase the flexibility of the inter-firm linkages.

An *operations management* perspective may be concluded from Johnston and Lawrence who report that within five years utilisation had reached 90 per cent for labour and machine productivity and capacity had increased by 25 per cent. And: 'Product variety was increased in each of the eight units from an average of 600 to 6000 different yarns. Average in-process and finished goods inventory dropped from four months to 15 days'.

The customer based *value drivers* can be deduced. Customers were responding to a rapid response by the industry. However, the improved lead times were achieved within budgeted costs. Constant innovation has been met by customer response and loyalty. The ability to match value production processes with customer expectations through capability and capacity 'fit' is essential in this respect. The Prato value chain can only meet customer value expectations if it offers acceptable returns at acceptable risk levels to all members of the value chain.

The Prato value chain processes

A presentation of the value chain processes is made in Figure 12.2. Two sets of *customer expectations* are suggested; end-user or consumer expectations and reseller expectations. The consumer concerns were discussed earlier. The reseller(s)' requirements are for fashionable, fast moving products that have high returns; sell through promptly, thereby ensuring no large inventories (or storage facilities) are required; and they represent price/quality/aesthetic value. *Design and development* is one of the roles involving the *impannatore*. Both Piore and Sabel and Johnston and Lawrence have identified the influence of the *impannatore* in providing guidance in product and manufacturing process design. *Procurement* is also one of the *impannatore*'s functions. However, within the value chain the development of 'fashionable and workable' fabric has been a success factor. The role played by the *impannatore* is to ensure an appropriate fabric selection. The *impannatore*'s role is important at the *production* stage in the value chain and has two characteristics. The first is the coordination of production, which includes a 'matching' activity in which capabilities and capacities are matched with customer product expectations. The second is to ensure that methods and costs are kept current by collecting and disseminating 'knowledge' that updates the technology management of the value chain.

The *marketing* role within the value chain comprises reading and understanding the market, knowing its structure and its workings and identifying the key organisations at various levels of the market. The selling role is one in which the *impannatore* conducts negotiations and manages transactions. *Service*, in the value chain, is provided by coordinating activities and ensuring the flow of work through the value chain. The role of logistics in this value chain is major and without it, or with only a poorly managed logistics process, the flow of materials to specific locations in relevant quantities at appropriate times would not occur. Clearly the value chain would cease to function.

THE AUTOMOTIVE INDUSTRY

Competition, complexity, customisation and excess capacity: messages for change

The automotive industry has a value chain that is constantly changing. In an IBM sponsored article four competitive challenges were identified: competition, complexity, customisation and excess capacity. It was suggested that to be competitive, 'They need to be in every niche of the market to maximise

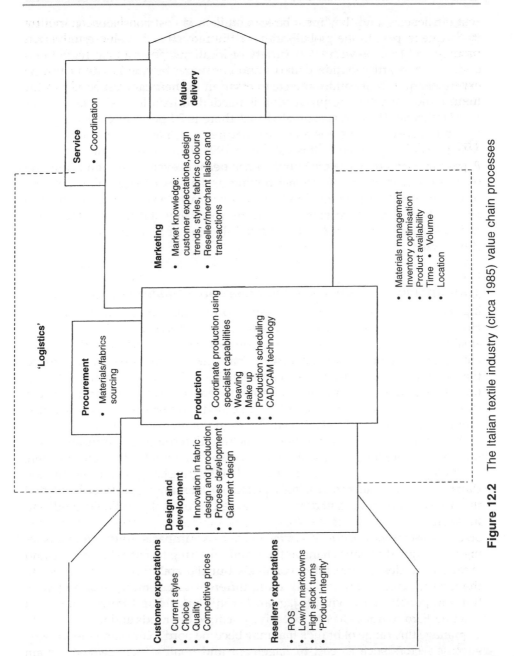

Figure 12.2 The Italian textile industry (circa 1985) value chain processes

cost efficiencies, and they must be lean, agile and cost conscious'. Complexity is due in part to the globalisation of the industry; this has resulted in a requirement to cope with '. . . a variety of locations, government regulations and incentives, distribution patterns and consumer buying habits . . . Buyers are demanding more and more customisation in their cars, especially at the luxury end. Very flexible production is needed to handle this'. (*International Herald Tribune*: 1998). It is estimated that there is 20 per cent excess capacity in the industry and there is a cyclical nature to demand. Two other characteristics could be added to this list. Since 1998 the merger/acquisition activity has intensified, hence *concentration* has become even more significant and *cooperation* in the form of Internet buying exchanges being established, and other collaborative activities. The *Herald Tribune* article was sponsored by IBM as an attempt at identifying the critical role being taken by information technology, but reinforced with additional comment, a value chain can be constructed.

The automotive industry value chain organisation profile

The automotive value chain organisation profile appears as Figure 12.3. The customer value model comprises *customer value criteria* in which customisation and 'features' are dominant. It is safe to say that by and large the 'Friday afternoon/Monday morning' vehicle has been eliminated by improved manufacturing methods: buyers' emphasis is on differentiation and features. Clearly warranty liability and a rapid response from the manufacturer/distributor network is expected – and assumed. Convenience is expected and mobile servicing is well established although not by manufacturer franchises. *Customer acquisition costs* continue to include determining specification and searching (more for the most attractive transaction than for the vehicle). Here technology in the form of Internet based selling exchanges and information databases is becoming increasingly popular. Operating costs (fuel costs) and maintenance are important as is the projected value at the end of its predicted lifespan.

Competencies and *key success factors* have major impacts. Core competencies could be argued to have changed their rank ordering recently. Innovation and creativity in design are still major items but the ability (or competency) to manage a range of brands with quite different target markets is becoming more important. Ford with its Jaguar, Aston Martin, Land Rover, Volvo and existing Ford marques has an extensive portfolio of brands and it is the ability to manage this range of brands that may become Ford's core competence. Key success factors such as cost management and quality management remain important but it could be argued they are becoming secondary issues as technology management and its techniques and processes become widespread.

The *value proposition* offered by the industry is strongly influenced by the extent to which individual companies have the capability to meet customer expectations. For example, Audi have introduced a customer specification facility. A number of dealer outlets, plus five airports, are being equipped with kiosks that enable customers to 'build' a vehicle to their own specification.

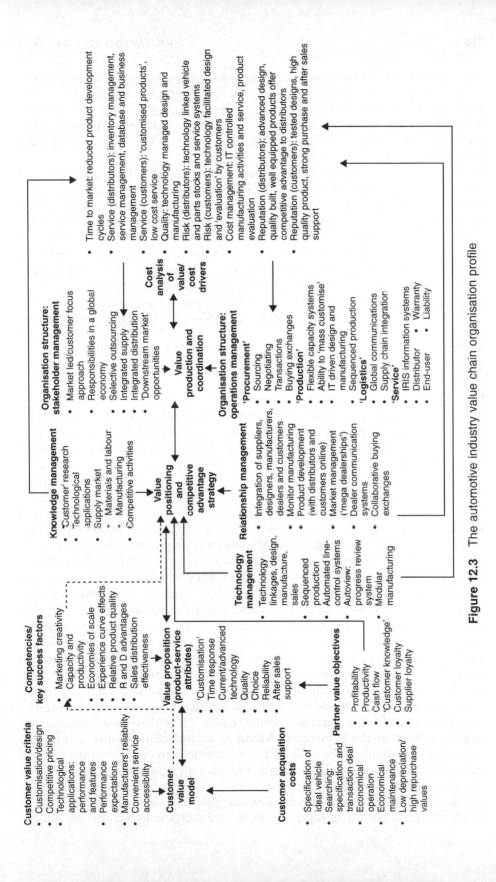

Figure 12.3 The automotive industry value chain organisation profile

Fiat redesigned the Punto using a web based interaction exercise and Japanese motor manufacturers are planning to offer purchasers the facility to make changes to vehicle specification during production. Key attributes are customised products, short lead times, and customer managed choice together with the 'qualifying' attributes of quality, choice, reliability and after sales support.

Supplier and dealer networks continue to be important in the automotive industry but changes are occurring in both networks. The value chain visionary or initiator continues to be the manufacturer and responsibility for *partner value objectives* remains with manufacturers. Clearly their concern is for supplier and distributor profitability, productivity and liquidity (cashflow), but increasingly developing supplier and customer loyalty becomes a network objective. Another, covert objective is the development of customer data; knowledge created from information on customer decision making and purchasing processes is likely to prove to be critical in developing IT networks which access customers rather than being simply databases accessible by customers.

Value positioning strategy

Knowledge management and technology management are driving *value positioning and competitive advantage strategy*, both in turn are being driven by information science. *Knowledge management* demonstrates three primary components: customer decision and purchasing; technological developments (that may be tracked and developed into 'consumer' products (for example ABS braking systems and global (satellite) positioning systems were both in military use long before being applied to automobile design)); and network management systems (Internet, Extranet and Intranet applications) that provide an opportunity to create cost-effective (strategic) and cost-efficient (operational) systems for external and internal relationship management.

It is in *technology management* that many changes are occurring. Computer aided design (CAD) shortens development time and 'sophisticates' linkages among designers, suppliers and users. IBM suggests: '. . . manufacturing processes are now so complex that nothing else can handle them', when discussing the role of IT in resolving design issues. Designers almost universally use 3D digital design tools which eliminate physical prototypes. CATIA (computer-aided tridimensional interactive application) shortens production cycles, lowers costs and results in quicker 'time-to-market'. In addition these systems offer the facility to introduce changes relatively late in the product development cycle as well as introducing the customer into the design process. CATIA also permits 'virtual reality' test drives or specification configuration in the showroom. Modular manufacturing, modularity, has resulted in redefining the cells in the production processes: 'Under intense pressure to reduce costs, accelerate the pace of innovation, and improve quality, automotive designers . . . are now looking for ways to parcel out the design of their complex electromechanical system' (Baldwin and Clark: 1997). The result has been to redesign the cells in the production processes. Rather than attempt to control a network of hundreds of suppliers, maintaining intricate schedules and large levels of inventory as an insurance against unexpected developments, manufacturers 'delegate' the production to suppliers of modules comprising complete units such as the driver's compartment. Baldwin and Clark report that Volkswagen '. . . has taken this approach even further . . . The company provides the factory where all modules are built and the trucks are assembled, but the independent suppliers obtain their own materials and hire their own workforces to build the separate modules'. There are implications here for relationship management.

Relationship management is a critical component of the value positioning and strategy decision. The expansion of outsourcing and the integration currently being undertaken (and considered) in the value chain increases the importance of relationship management. Greater levels of cooperation and collaboration are necessary if the 'virtual organisation' structures in modular manufacturing are to succeed. Other issues are of concern. The extension of IT systems into supplier/manufacturer/distributor/customer communications, negotiations and transactions suggest that cooperation may become conflict. Online sales applications and more recently buying exchanges are expanding for both new and used vehicles. GM have been reported as considering a Net based sales facility that would include other manufacturers' products, and as networks are established by manufacturers, distributors and the 'dot.com' media, relationships begin to come under pressure. For example, the existing dealership structure considers itself under threat as the prospect of direct sales by manufacturers comes closer to reality; commercial market research suggests there to be considerable success for Internet services as 'search' tools. Ford announced its intention to integrate downstream by purchasing equity holding in a number of large, strategically located, dealerships in order to exercise greater control of marketing and to obtain a share of the expanding 'services' markets such as in tyres, exhausts, batteries, and so on. Upstream activities by Ford include brokering mergers among its suppliers (Sutton: 1998).

Value production and coordination

Value production and coordination are strongly influenced by *stakeholder management* concern. Returning to the opening paragraphs of this section (the four competitive challenges confronting the industry), it can be argued that stakeholder management is likely to be more demanding as integration, globalisation and concentration intensify. The expansion of operations throughout the world brings with it responsibilities for not just foreign labour forces but possibly for major impact on fragile economies. The Korean motor industry has been the subject of a number of acquisition possibilities by the large European and North American manufacturers and the recent (November 2000) problems of Daewoo suggest the scenario that they may become an offshore contract manufacturing unit for these large manufacturers. Already Ford has hinted at the possibility of extending its outsourcing activities to include manufacturing. There is a logic to this. Technology management is able to ensure that quality standards in manufacturing are uniform; consequently the large manufacturers may consider there to be very little competitive advantage to be gained from 'bending metal' and focus their capital and management expertise on design, development and brand management. This approach makes downstream markets more attractive as sources of revenue and profit.

Operations management is becoming reliant upon information technology. The recent moves by the major manufacturers to collaborate in the development of web based buying exchanges is an indication of these trends. Industry sources point to the potential for very large savings in terms of cost and time throughout the *procurement* process. This move has been accompanied by divestment of ownership (varying from complete to partial) interests in component subsidiaries. The application of IT to design has been discussed. Other *production* applications are of interest. Sequenced production techniques permit customer ordering for specific motor cars. In principle, the system has operated for some time but has had initial problems. The revised system, a combination of lean production, sequenced production and AutoView (automated line control) customisation, becomes a reality. AutoView has quality checks built in, plus easy-to-change features enabling a manufacturer to individualise production based upon customer requirements. A link is planned with Java which will facilitate Internet working for JIT with suppliers.

Many of the *logistics* applications are integrated with production systems. Mercedes, together with IBM, has created an enterprise wide IT system to support its business processes. The direction of most logistics applications is towards the reduction of lead times and of inventory levels throughout the value chain, but availability remains a primary goal.

Service is also becoming web based. After-sales service has intranet applications. Saab has installed IRIS (intranet retail information system) and aims to increase after-sales support to both distributors and customers. IRIS offers a data management system detailing vehicle servicing records as well as vehicle sales and parts availability. Saab plans to expand IRIS to include links to financial institutions, carriers (vehicle transportation companies – to notify customers of the arrival of a new vehicle), used car information, calendars for online scheduling of service appointments, and online vehicle purchasing.

Value drivers are the link with the customer value model. Figure 12.3 identifies four groups of value drivers. Operational effectiveness (the implementation of strategy) is clearly important and is demonstrated by the response to competitive issues such as product development time, quality and cost management, all of which have an impact on customer product choice through the medium of relative competitiveness. Service offer characteristics to distributors and to customers are clearly important across a number of factors from customisation processes for customers via distributor considerations of inventory and service management and market information. Risk management for customers and distributors considers product performance and reliability (customers) and cost efficient but high levels of performance from service and support systems.

The automotive industry value chain processes

The value chain process example shown as Figure 12.4 uses end-user customer expectations to maintain simplicity. *Customer expectations* provide an information input into the design and development process. Based upon this input, *design and development* consider both long term and short term design issues. Long term considerations concern the future product-market strategy of the organisation and take in 'macro' factors such as target market, product offer and geographical considerations for marketing and production. From this follow product design specifics which increasingly consider the production process itself (or production design). Range coordination reviews the relationships between brands (marques) and the product positioning decisions within brands and product groups. It is not unknown for *specialist design* services to be used to create specific vehicles or styles such as motor sport applications or to achieve a design image. From this process linkages are established with *components* suppliers who may supply proprietary systems or components such as brake systems or 'navigational' equipment and, of course, in-car entertainment. *Production* manages an entire range of related processes. For example, the actual production of the vehicle may be out-sourced entirely or partially. Planning and scheduling of production activities and 'flows' is part of the role as is the negotiation of specifications for manufacturing. Depending upon the capabilities and capacities of the partners to be used, quality and cost control standards are an essential element of the process. Concurrently (with component decisions), production works closely with *procurement* to develop a profile of suppliers at primary (major component) level, secondary (significant suppliers) and tertiary level (material suppliers for interior trim and so on).

One process undergoing change is *marketing*. Vehicle manufacturers have promoted new and used vehicles, service and parts but utilised finance and insurance as services. Now these latter two, together with other related service products, are being seen as increasingly attractive. The increasing amount of information available (and that that can be generated) concerning customer preferences and behaviour makes marketing related services both attractive and relatively simple. Marketing is becoming dedicated to branding and brand management. New channel conduits (such as e-commerce routes to customers) are offering more opportunities for 'branded' products, particularly as vehicle sales become increasingly competitive.

Service processes are, for many vehicle distributors, more profitable than vehicle sales. This has been the situation for a number of years. A number of distributors are using their service infrastructure to expand into a branded *after-market* activity. For some this includes 'seasonal' service packages such as winter and summer holiday checks. Most offer mobile parts services to small vehicle repair shops but none have expanded into a branded 'mobile tune up' service offer.

The *logistics* process is becoming increasingly important. As processes and as process owners become more closely linked through information driven systems, the smooth flow of materials and information assumes a major role.

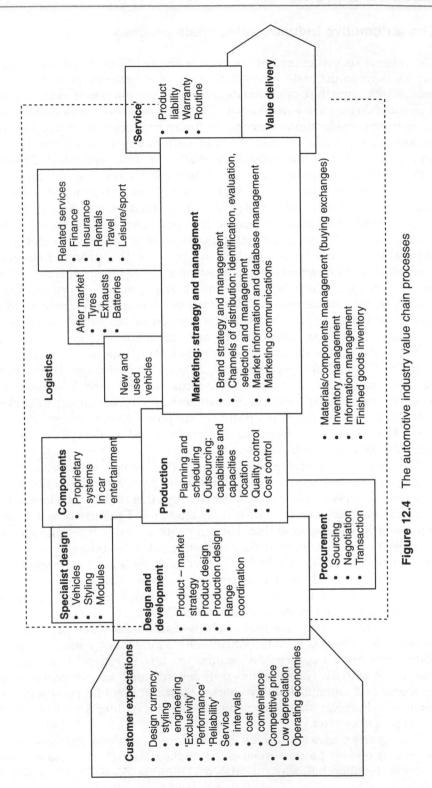

Figure 12.4 The automotive industry value chain processes

Furthermore, the focus on managing time and inventory levels places logistics in a dominant role in the value chain.

SUMMARY

Given the criteria established in the introduction to Part 2, it is useful to review both the Pratese textile industry and the automotive industry examples and to identify how many of the criteria have been met.

In the textile value chain the *impannatore* is clearly the *visionary* or coodinator and it would appear this role has been around in one guise or another for some time. The *core processes* are the fabric production and the wearing processes that reflected the specialisation increasingly required by the market. The processes became *inter-organisational* as the earlier activities 'de-integrated'. Piore and Sabel report that an *infrastructure* of banks, local artists, and so on formed around the value chain and these together with computer based technologies became part of the value chain. A *customer focus* is clearly discernible, indeed it was the absence of this that resulted in the need to establish the value chain. *Inter-organisational performance planning* is coordinated by the *impannatore* who 'translates' market expectations into procurement and production tasks.

What has resulted reflects the characteristics of a value chain organisation structure. Processes have replaced functions and in doing so they have become specialisations. Assets are distributed within the value chain; expensive capital equipment is located at specific process points rather than aggregated in vertically integrated structures. Flexible delivery capability is the very reason the value chain evolved. Infrastructure linkages are managed by the *impannatore* who manages communication and cooperation. The value chain is a virtual organisation; each unit is involved in the overall production only on the basis of the need for its contribution.

The automotive industry is more complex with 'brand' structured organisations. Nevertheless there is clear evidence of a value chain structure. *Visionaries* (rather than one visionary) are apparent. For example, in the Ford organisation Nasser, the CEO, has suggested Ford's future is likely to be focussed on design and development and marketing processes; vehicle manufacturing is likely to be outsourced. *Core processes* are developing through trends such as modularisation and specialist component manufacturing. The very nature of the product requires these to be *inter-organisational*. A supporting infrastructure has always existed but shows very clear evidence of changing as IT applications become important. *Customer-centricity* is strong with the goal of all industry brands attempting to move towards customisation. Product and component manufacturing processes have been accompanied with inter-organisationally linked planning disciplines and performance measurements driven by cost and time metrics.

Processes have clearly superseded functions in this industry; the impact of global operations has been a major influence in this respect. The nature of the production process, as it is now being structured, determines the distribution of assets. Flexibility together with time and cost metrics are becoming essential objectives. Both communication and cooperation are apparent; the nature of the linkages between processes makes this essential. Increasingly the industry is moving towards becoming a virtual organisation. The reality may be a series of virtual organisations that are located strategically and based upon economies of integration.

REFERENCES ●

Baldwin, C. Y. and K. B. Clark (1997), 'Managing in an age of modularity', *Harvard Business Review*, September/October.

International Herald Tribune (1998), 'Business to e-business: automotive', IBM sponsored page, 14 December.

Johnston, R. and P. R. Lawrence (1988), 'Beyond vertical integration – the rise of the value-adding partnership', *Harvard Business Review*, July/August.

Piore, M. J. and C. F. Sabel (1984), *The Second Industrial Divide*, Basic Books, New York.

Sutton, C. (1998), *Strategic Concepts*, Macmillan, Basingstoke.

chapter

13 *Corporate Value Chains*

LEARNING OUTCOMES

The student will be able to:

- identify the value chain structure operating at the company level;
- construct a company value chain comprising its organisation profile and its processes.

THE McKESSON HBOC CORPORATION

Introduction: market forces create an environment for making change essential

The McKesson Corporation was another company cited as an example of a successful 'value adding partnership' by Johnston and Lawrence (1988). McKesson is also an example of a 'visionary' who, because of rapidly changing circumstances in the environment, developed a new business model as a response. In 1988 the company's revenues were US$6.7 billion and it was considered successful. It also enjoyed a reputation for innovative applications to improve customer service. It was, until this point in time, a wholesale distributor with its future tied to the success of the independent drugstores it sought to service.

McKesson became threatened by fierce competition from large, integrated drugstore chains, who were eliminating the independents. McKesson converted this threat into an opportunity. McKesson introduced a 'rudimentary order-entry system' for its customers. The system reduced order processing costs by expediting inventory checking, order transmission and recording, and packing and shipping to customers. Order assembly to meet customer display formats made in-store merchandising more cost-efficient.

More innovation followed. Software was developed to help retailers set prices, design store layout and plan profitable operating activities and financial reporting. In addition McKesson recognised the value of its aggregated information to suppliers. The information was sold to suppliers who used the information to increase their own distribution efficiencies. Computer-computer order enabled McKesson to make significant labour savings. The company also used its systems to help process insurance claim applications for reimbursements. This strengthened links among insurance companies, customers and drugstores by decreasing payment times and administrative problems. McKesson, through its visionary approach, has structured a value chain that includes manufacturer, distributor, retailer, consumer and third party insurer. The success of McKesson's approach to strategic operations management is its innovative leadership in building an inter-organisational structure that leverages the 'assets' of each player. Assets in this context are tangible, such as warehousing, computer systems inventory, and so on, and intangible, such as information and knowledge.

By 2000 McKesson revenues were almost US$28 billion, the EBIT some US$600 million. The business had expanded both revenues and activities considerably from 1988. In its annual report, McKesson suggests it:

> . . . is pre-eminent in the world of pharmaceutical and medical-surgical supply man-
> agement information solutions, pharmacy automation and sales and marketing ser-
> vices to the healthcare industry . . . We deliver unique cost reduction and quality
> improvement solutions to:

- 25,000 independent and chain pharmacies
- 5000 hospitals and integrated delivery networks
- 35,000 physician practices encompassing more than 250,000 individual physicians
- 10,000 extended care sites
- 600 'payor' organisations
- 450 pharmaceutical manufacturers
- 2000 medical surgical manufacturers.

Since Johnston and Lawrence's article in 1988 the company has continued in its visionary role and has focussed on IT applications to reinforce its position in the healthcare value chain. McKesson HBOC's mission is:

> . . . to advance the health of the healthcare system by advancing the success of our
> partners, . . . reflects the commitment of our employees to make a positive impact
> every day on the quality of care experienced by patients.

The McKesson HBOC value chain organisation profile

The McKesson HBOC mission statement 'prescribes' the company's view of its value chain structure. The customer/patient is clearly in focus, employees are important and partner organisations are also considered to be important to the overall success of the value chain.

The customer value model contains criteria that reflect the overall goal of McKesson: '. . . the quality of care experienced by patients', but in Figure 13.1 the more immediate value criteria of healthcare practitioners and organisations are reflected. Given the availability of IT applications, both generally and specifically, the *customer value criteria* reflect benefits (or attributes) that 'enable' practitioners to maximise the time available for patient care. For distributors the concern is for relevant product range offers, high levels of availability and efficient supply chain management by McKesson that minimises inventory investment and maximises space productivity. McKesson customers are also keen to minimise *acquisition costs*. Again these topics reflect time and unnecessary effort such as supplier searching and evaluation and administrative tasks.

McKesson's *core competencies/key success factor* portfolio reflects those necessary for success in the healthcare sector. In terms of skills and resources these are identified as specialist knowledge, development skills and infrastructures capable of 'delivering' value both physically and digitally.

Creating a value proposition

The *value proposition* is made up of a range of systems based products that offer customised solutions. The company annual report suggests this as:

> . . . the nation's largest distributor of pharmaceuticals and medical-surgical suppliers . . . products and services from our comprehensive set of solutions . . . from supply chain management to pharmacy automation, pharmacy outsourcing and a full set of systems and programs for independent pharmacies, drug chains, the pharmacies of food stores and mass merchandisers, and hospitals and long-term care facilities.

And in systems:

> . . . a broad set of information solutions ranging from stand-alone products to comprehensive outsourcing and consulting services . . . including products and services to reduce medication errors and enable compliance with new regulations . . . to use the power of the internet and other innovative, emerging technologies to share information realtime and drive improved clinical outcomes, cost-efficiencies and increased satisfaction for all healthcare participants.

The McKesson product-service portfolio offers an ASP (applications service provider) delivered physician service that includes clinical connectivity, including claims, prescribing, clinical ordering and reporting, and practice management programs. Proprietary 'brands' offer a range of software products such as:

- Pathways HR/Payroll;
- Pathways Financial Management;

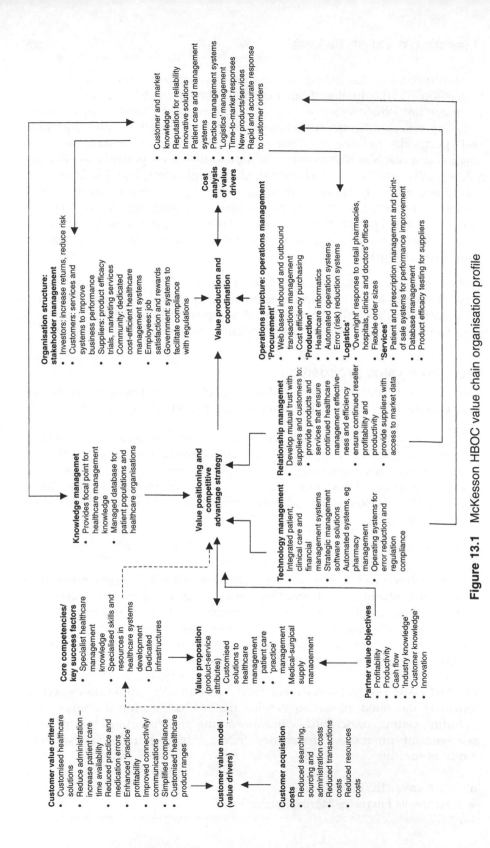

Figure 13.1 McKesson HBOC value chain organisation profile

- Pathways Surgical Manager;
- Pathways Materials Management;
- Pathways Staff Scheduling;
- Pathways Healthcare Scheduling.

These resource management applications help healthcare organisations maximise the efficiency of healthcare delivery through better management of people, facilities, supplies and equipment.

Similarly clinical care information systems offer applications that facilitate and improve the practice of medicine by helping organisations define standards of care and measure outcomes, examine variances, and make necessary changes. Brands here include:

- Pathways Care Manager;
- Pathways Coordinated Care;
- Pathways Healthcare Network Server;
- Pathways Laboratory.

Partners (McKesson suppliers and organisational customers) share a set of *value objectives* that combine market and financial performance with developing a knowledge base. By seeking innovative solutions to healthcare problems the knowledge base enables McKesson and its partners to develop into a learning organisation.

Value positioning

Competitive advantage (through value positioning and strategy) is a complex of knowledge, technology and relationship management, with technology as a dominant influence. McKesson considers itself to be a provider of healthcare knowledge. The company uses *knowledge management* to develop databases from which healthcare management solutions are developed. McKesson's practice management solutions allow physicians and clinicians to build their own knowledge management bases through aggregated patient treatment data. McKesson is developing case management and disease management tools designed to deliver greater patient care at lower cost with improved outcomes. Patterns Review is a knowledge base of physician-developed diagnosis-specific clinical recommendations designed to evaluate both inpatient and outpatient services used by healthcare payors as a utilisation management tool and a cost containment tool.

Technology management is the dominant characteristic of McKesson's competitive advantage. The company has developed IT infrastructure applications that are not limited to a single clinical department or function; rather they provide networking and database applications that offer key elements for integrating healthcare provision across and along the continuum of care. Technology has been applied to routine procedures. Automated Healthcare is a McKesson business unit that has developed a medication distribution system, a medication dispensing cabinet and bedside medication scanning. In addition systems are available to monitor activities to ensure that errors are reduced and government regulations are complied with.

Trust is an integral part of McKesson's value positioning and strategy. *Relationship management* is important in supplier and customer dealings. McKesson's Pharmaceutical Partners Group is '. . . a business designed to help its manufacturing partners speed products to market, design effective marketing programs, drive sales higher through greater market penetration and compliance, and prolong sales through innovative patient support and marketing programs'. The company offers clinical supply and biological specimen management, pharmacy services, patient registries, patient assistance programs and reimbursement services. McKesson's service is based upon an understanding of customers' culture, business objectives and marketplace. This approach enables McKesson to develop and implement creative and measurable solutions that drive market share for more than 100 of the largest pharmaceutical and biotechnology companies.

Value production and coordination: an information/communication solution

Value production and coordination components also have prominent characteristics in the company. *Stakeholder management* concerns appear throughout the McKesson organisation structure. For example: '. . . provides a comprehensive offering of services and technologies designed to help its customers improve asset management and . . . help independent pharmacies and small chains manage their cashflow and businesses more effectively. 'Valu-Rite' and 'Health Mart' franchise programs provide benefits usually associated with chains, such as private-label products, merchandising and marketing tools, nutritional and disease management programs'. The 'coSource' program integrates pharmaceutical distribution with pharmacy automation and pharmacy consulting from Med Management to deliver the lowest total patient cost and improve healthcare quality.

Operations management is made up of procurement, production, logistics and services. *Procurement* activities have been enhanced by the formation of an independent, Internet based buying exchange together with four other large healthcare distributors. *Production* for McKesson reflects the 'market space' concept of Rayport and Sviokla (1994) where, they suggest, the product is replaced by information about the product and information processes are the value for the customer. The Automation Group manufactures and markets automated pharmacy systems and services. Web based products offered by McKesson enable physicians to submit prescriptions, order lab tests (and receive results), maintain patient records, verify insurance eligibility and submit medical claims, electronically.

Logistics is an important characteristic within operations management. Through retail customer operations, the Pharmaceutical Group operates 34 distribution centres and provides websites for its pharmacy customers. The

Medical Group offers a full range of medical/surgical supply logistics and information management to IDN's hospitals, surgery centres, physicians' offices, and so on.

Services are extensive and are integrated with production and logistics. Supply management online is a suite of Internet based applications and services that facilitate customer management of activities such as order entry and management, decision support and supplier payment.

The *value drivers* for McKesson HBOC would appear to be relatively easy to determine. Clearly their extensive customer and market knowledge is important as is their obvious reputation for reliability. The extensive use of IT applications provides what is possibly the most important value driver, that of innovative solutions to patient care, practice management, and 'logistics' management. Being in the healthcare sector requires an ability to respond to market developments and to customers' operational requirements. McKesson HBOC clearly manages the product development aspect and the logistics services well.

McKesson value chain processes

The processes McKesson HBOC manages in achieving successful value delivery are described in Figure 13.2.

Customer expectations are complex 'consumer' expectations that form the basis for those of practitioners and intermediaries. It is these that influence McKesson's strategic operations. Medical practitioners' concerns are for providing cost-efficient healthcare for patients. The acceptance by the healthcare professionals of IT systems based solutions for diagnostics, treatment and practice management facilitates their concern to allocate time and resources to patient care. Healthcare intermediaries provide a conduit for pharmaceutical products. These reseller partners have typical distributor based objectives: access to relevant product range assortments, reliable logistics services and adequate return on their investment in space and inventory.

It follows that *design and development* processes are directed towards applied IT systems solutions for healthcare management and for supply chain management. The output of design and development for healthcare practitioners is a range of managed care software solutions. These include 'managed care', and 'physician solutions'. McKesson merged with HBOC 'to provide customers with a single source for enterprise-wide solutions to reduce costs and improve quality'. The infrastructure applications are not limited to a single department or function, rather they form the foundation of emerging information structures of health enterprises. McKesson HBOC's networking and database applications provide the key elements for integrating healthcare activities. Similarly, the Supply Management Business has responded to user needs by developing a suite of comprehensive Internet-based applications and services. These include web based order entry and management, decision support, receiving and accounts payable management systems.

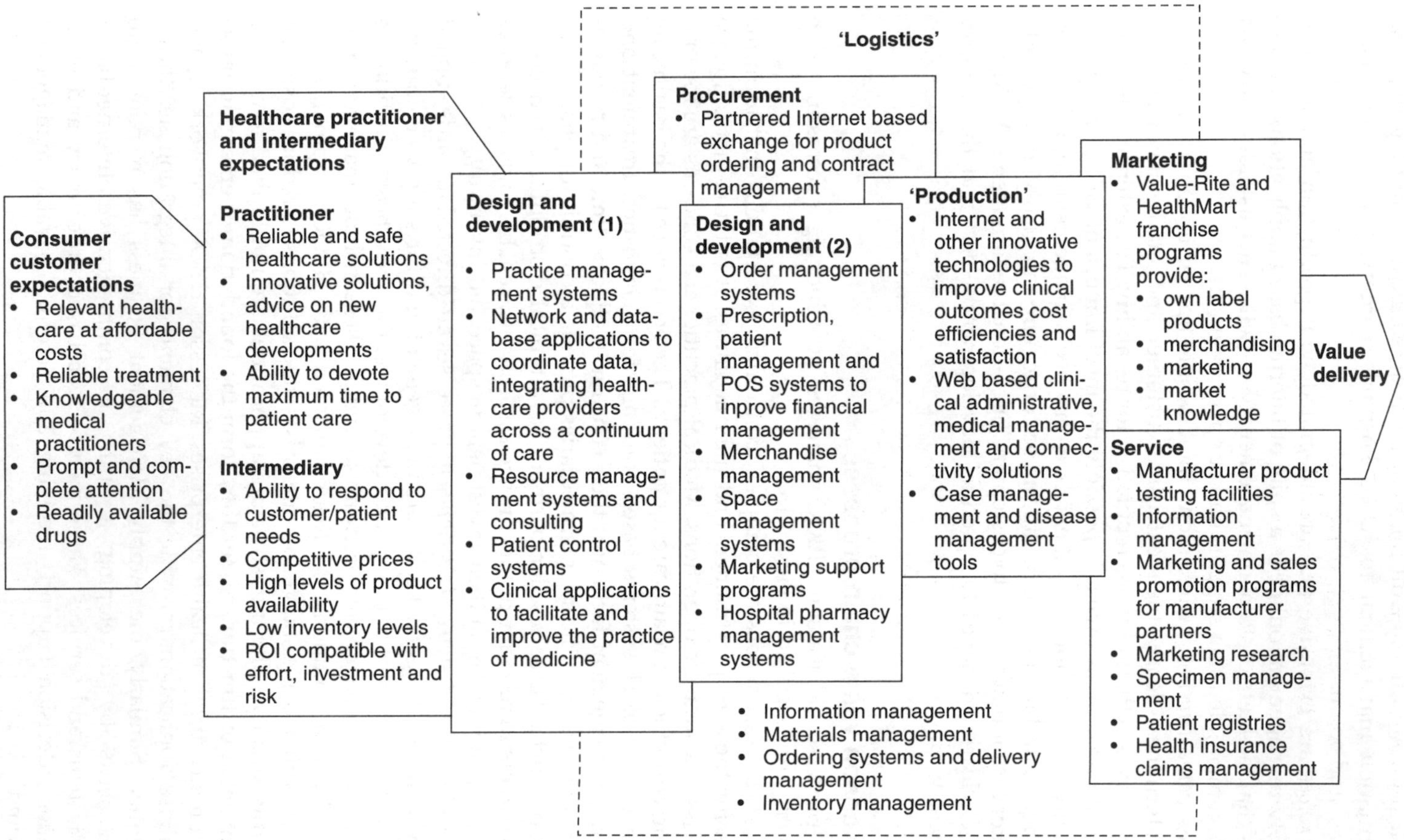

Consumer customer expectations
- Relevant healthcare at affordable costs
- Reliable treatment
- Knowledgeable medical practitioners
- Prompt and complete attention
- Readily available drugs

Healthcare practitioner and intermediary expectations

Practitioner
- Reliable and safe healthcare solutions
- Innovative solutions, advice on new healthcare developments
- Ability to devote maximum time to patient care

Intermediary
- Ability to respond to customer/patient needs
- Competitive prices
- High levels of product availability
- Low inventory levels
- ROI compatible with effort, investment and risk

Procurement
- Partnered Internet based exchange for product ordering and contract management

'Logistics'

Design and development (1)
- Practice management systems
- Network and database applications to coordinate data, integrating healthcare providers across a continuum of care
- Resource management systems and consulting
- Patient control systems
- Clinical applications to facilitate and improve the practice of medicine

Design and development (2)
- Order management systems
- Prescription, patient management and POS systems to improve financial management
- Merchandise management
- Space management systems
- Marketing support programs
- Hospital pharmacy management systems

'Production'
- Internet and other innovative technologies to improve clinical outcomes cost efficiencies and satisfaction
- Web based clinical administrative, medical management and connectivity solutions
- Case management and disease management tools

Marketing
- Value-Rite and HealthMart franchise programs provide:
  - own label products
  - merchandising
  - marketing
  - market knowledge

Service
- Manufacturer product testing facilities
- Information management
- Marketing and sales promotion programs for manufacturer partners
- Marketing research
- Specimen management
- Patient registries
- Health insurance claims management

Value delivery

- Information management
- Materials management
- Ordering systems and delivery management
- Inventory management

Figure 13.2 McKesson HBOC value chain processes

Design and development have been driven through internal development and acquisitions. McKesson has expanded from a drug wholesaling company into '. . . the most comprehensive healthcare services company in the world'. Its design and development processes are clearly focussed, as are supply management and information, information solutions, manufacturer services, and 'iMcKesson', offering web based clinical and management solutions and connectivity solutions.

Procurement processes have been developed with the four healthcare distributor partners through the Internet-based exchange.

McKesson HBOC's *production* processes are taking the direction first suggested by Zuboff (1985) and subsequently developed by Rayport and Sviokla (1994), whereby physically based products become electronically based. Rayport and Sviokla suggested the traditional 'marketplace' (the interaction between physical buyer and physical seller) is being replaced by the 'marketspace', in which physical product content becomes information content, product context becomes an electronic channel or product/service outline, and service/infrastructure is computer based and replaces physical and institutional networks. The extensive range of systems based products for healthcare management and supply chain support is evidence of this.

Marketing processes are structured around the electronic products and are solution focussed. Web based products offer services and technologies designed to help customers improve profitability, productivity and cash flow. The web based products are enhanced by franchise process programs offering own brand product ranges, merchandise and space management for resellers.

Service processes follow the systems approach. A comprehensive range of service products is made available to manufacturer partners. These are based upon McKesson HBOC's intangible asset base, primarily knowledge, but as Figure 13.2 suggests they leverage the database being developed continually by the company. Indeed the expansion of services to partner organisations can only enhance the value of the service products and service infrastructures.

IKEA

IKEA is an acronym of **I**ngvar **K**amprad (the entrepreneur), **E**lintaryd (Kamprad's home farm) and **A**gunnaryd (his home village). The IKEA business model is designed to '. . . offer a wide range of home furnishings with good design and function at prices so low that as many people as possible will be able to afford them. And still have money left'. The IKEA concept can be expressed very simply as: form, function, fit. Kamprad is quoted as saying: 'Simplicity and commonsense should characterise planning and strategic direction'. The IKEA business model is also an excellent example of co-productivity: IKEA *designs* the product and *identifies suppliers* to undertake manufacturing, and *co-opts customers* to select, 'deliver' and complete the production process.

The IKEA mission statement, like that of McKesson HBOC, prescribes the organisation structure of the value chain. See Figure 13.3.

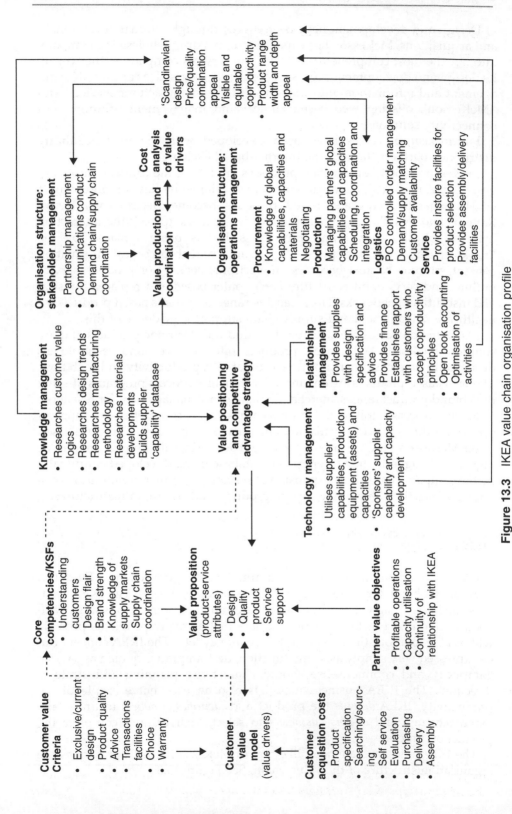

Figure 13.3 IKEA value chain organisation profile

Coproductivity: an important component in creating customer value

Customer value is made up of a trade-off between aesthetic and functional design, the acceptance of a role in selling (self-selection), distribution (transporting a flat-pack product home), and manufacturing (self-assembly). The IKEA concept is a manifestation of understanding the customer value criteria/customer acquisition costs model: the company appears to understand the customer decision/acceptance trade-off process very well.

This intimate knowledge of the customer, an understanding of the customer's value universe, is clearly one of the *core capabilities* of IKEA. Others are its knowledge of supplier markets together with the ability to coordinate the supply chain structure and IKEA brand and the management of the brand itself. Normann and Ramirez (1994) suggest a core competency is the organisation's ability to identify underutilised capabilities elsewhere and to motivate owners into cooperating with IKEA.

IKEA's *value proposition* is not difficult to identify. It is an almost unique customer focussed package of style, quality and price supported by instore services designed to relieve customers of the usual shopping stresses. The value proposition is communicated in realistic and current terms. For example, the San Francisco store layouts are designed as residential apartment-type settings such as 'single mother with infant' instead of the traditional IKEA room settings.

Partner value objectives are of concern to IKEA. Long term profitable and productive relationships are sought. IKEA is aware of the need to match supplier capabilities and capacities with the product characteristics of manufacturing complexity. In this way suppliers' skills and resources can be optimised in terms of profitability and productivity.

The quest for sustainable competitive advantage through *value positioning* has some exclusive points. An aspect of *knowledge management* that is important to IKEA is to understand the 'value creation logics' of its customers prior to purchase, during purchase and in the post-purchase period. Other important characteristics include a continuous monitoring of design trends and manufacturing methodologies. For example, the availability of particleboard in the 1960s was seen as a major benefit for IKEA. Being inexpensive and hard wearing, it was introduced as a basic material input into IKEA products. *Technology management* is also important but clearly is not highly specialised. However, being able to match suppliers to products is an application of the economics of integration in as much as managing capabilities, capacities and materials specifications is clearly essential. IKEA uses quality/cost ratios to make these decisions, which identify the 'minimum' necessary elements for effective coproduction. Other aspects of supplier selection decisions are interesting. One criterion concerns the impact the decision will have on IKEA's subsequent market entry, and another concerns the opportunity to learn about local business conditions (a long term version of coproducing the business's future). These are a mixture of knowledge management and relationship management criteria. Other *relationship management* characteristics include the relationships with suppliers and customers. Agreeing (and working) the 'optimisation of activities' or the division of work formulae is critical to the long term success of coproductivity. Facilitating or enabling factors are the selection process itself and the support given to suppliers in particular. IKEA has franchisees and they are seen as partners.

Stakeholder management has three aspects. Suppliers and the determination to ensure a 'win-win' partnership are clearly important to IKEA. Customers are of concern and the quality/design/price and coproductivity role of customers is closely monitored. A third concern is the environment. IKEA is conscious of ISO 14 001 concerning environmental management. The IKEA catalogue is printed on chlorine-free paper and contains at least 10–15 per cent post-consumer waste. No rainforest or old-growth fibres are used. The company has established minimum requirements for operations and these are closely monitored. Concern for shareholder value is significant but with IKEA being a private company there is no pressure on share prices, dividends, and so forth.

Operations management has some exclusive features. *Procurement* is closely controlled and arrangements with suppliers follow a select protocol (see above). Additional to this is a buying function that is linked to its logistics system. IKEA uses its warehouse system to integrate the components produced by its many suppliers into kits for customer assembly. The principle of coproductivity means that different components of any given furniture item are likely to have been made by different suppliers in different countries. It follows that 'integration' as a process is an essential part of coproductivity success. The company maintains a number of 'buying offices' dispersed worldwide. They pre-select suppliers for a centralised evaluation process. Selection of reliable, quality suppliers is vital to the continuity of the success of coproductivity. The *production* process includes managing supplier relationships, and matching their capabilities and capacities with IKEA's existing and new product programs. *Logistics* (apart from providing a base for integrating components from disparate sources) also provides a platform for territorial expansion. Normann and Ramirez discuss a situation in which a large warehouse in Lyon was opened prior to opening IKEA stores in Spain and Italy. POS controlled order management is essential if high levels of product availability are to be maintained throughout 155 stores in 29 countries and stretching across five continents. Typically an IKEA store will carry some 10,000 items but colour and size choices can increase this to over 80,000 items.

Service is an essential feature of any retailing activity. Offering roof-rack loan services for customer self-delivery continues the co-productivity theme, and for customers not wishing to assemble the products an assembly service is offered by a series of local partner operations. Instore coffee shops and children's' play areas are part of the service offer.

IKEA's value drivers are simple but effective. Its 'Scandinavian' design combined with a price/quality offer is clearly effective. To maintain this offer the product range requires adequate choice through width and depth variety. Consumer risk is reduced by adopting the highest quality standards. But central to success is the understanding and successful implementation of the IKEA policy of coproductivity.

IKEA value chain processes

IKEA'S value chain processes are illustrated in Figure 13.4. *Customer expectations* were discussed in detail earlier but essentially they can be summarised as a desire for style/design, quality, guaranteed by IKEA, at competitive prices, and solutions or ideas for home improvement.

Customer expectations have had a clear impact on IKEA's *design and development* processes. IKEA's designers are conscious of customer expectations of '. . . beautiful, functional and affordable products'. IKEA designers try to carry out product development on the shop floor. They work closely with manufacturers to improve production methods and to decrease costs. The company has co-opted the services of child psychologists and early learning specialists in the development of children's products so as to ensure their motor, social and creative skills development. Designers take into account the capabilities of manufacturers (90 per cent of manufacture being outsourced from over 1700 suppliers). While the 'flat-pack' concept was found by accident, it has become central to the production and logistics processes' cost efficiencies. Consequently the concept is important in the design process.

Essentially IKEA is a design house. Consequently, the design role considers both continuity and conformity and considering the large number of suppliers, brand integrity is a major concern.

Procurement is managed through a worldwide network of buying offices. Procurement has two primary roles. The first is to identify compatible manufacturer/suppliers, who are then evaluated centrally by 'head office'. The other role is to ensure that the materials used meet environmentally acceptable standards. Buying office criteria are established by IKEA head office and were discussed earlier.

The role of *production* is to establish and to ensure that the 90 per cent of outsourced products are meeting IKEA specifications. Advice and often financial assistance are offered to suppliers to ensure IKEA quality standards and delivery output requirements are maintained. Hence production in this value chain is partly a role of ensuring quality/cost ratios are maintained, and partly one of ensuring that politically (or economically) the suppliers meet IKEA's forward expansion plans.

Marketing processes are essentially based around the IKEA catalogue (reinforced by press and television advertising) and instore merchandising. However, underwriting these activities is a very clear understanding of the important value drivers – utility, quality and price. The company is well aware of lifestyle, social and economic differences between markets and product managers take these into account when developing new product ranges.

Service processes need to consider instore needs of customers such as answering their questions concerning size and style compatibility with their domestic situations, and order administration. Another aspect of service is to provide sufficient facilities to enable the coproductivity process that customers engage in to be successful and cost-efficient. Hence colour and size options for products are readily available (as is advice on their use if required) and post-purchase delivery and assembly service availabilities are made very clear.

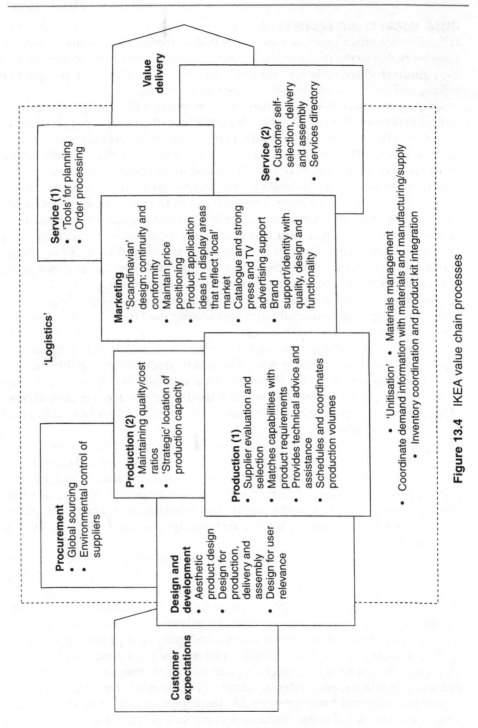

Figure 13.4 IKEA value chain processes

The IKEA value chain processes are based upon the concept of coproductivity with suppliers and customers. Processes are designed with coproductivity as the principal feature and management assumes a coordination role throughout the value chain.

SUMMARY

As in Chapter 12, the two value chains featured in this chapter have been examined against the criteria outlined in the introduction to this part.

Clearly McKesson is the visionary in the healthcare value chain it has created. By a process of organic growth (distribution) and merger/acquisition activities (technology) the organisation has become both a *visionary* and a *coordinator*. By structuring the organisation around customer needs, *core processes* have formed the basis of an inter-organisational healthcare service in which patient care (the end-user *customer*) is central. The nature of the organisation that McKesson HBOC has become has resulted in an *inter-organisational planning system* becoming an essential feature of the operation.

Processes are emphasised and aligned around product delivery to meet customer needs. Assets would appear to be distributed within the range of McKesson HBOC business units. Given the 'marketspace' nature of McKesson's approach to the market, flexibility is built into both the physical product delivery and the information based products. The very structure of McKesson HBOC suggests intra- and inter-organisation cooperation and communications. It could also be argued that this structure is approaching that of a virtual organisation.

Ingvar Kamprad, the IKEA founder, is clearly a visionary who has created a value chain structure around IKEA's design skills. The business is based upon 90 per cent of its products being outsourced so is clearly inter-organisational. IKEA's *core processes* are design and development, production management and marketing. IKEA's *infrastructure* is based upon its suppliers and its warehousing system that undertakes a 'production' role in assembling flat-pack kits. *Customers* are clearly central to IKEA's business. They are involved in product development and numerous aspects of service are customer focussed. The structure of supply requires IKEA to work closely with a mutually agreed *inter-organisational performance planning system*.

Processes are more important than functions, but it would appear these are macro-processes such as customer satisfaction. Clearly assets are distributed among the 1700 suppliers, with appropriate assets owned by IKEA. Flexibility is apparent; the fact that products are sourced as components requires flexibility in supply and customer relationship management. This in turn leads to high levels of cooperation and communication; it is hardly likely that IKEA could operate without this level of cooperation. The claim for IKEA's value chain to be considered as a virtual organisation is somewhat tenuous; however, given the nature of the product and of its manufacturing and distribution, it could be argued that it is.

REFERENCES ●

Johnston, P. and P. R. Lawrence (1988), 'Beyond vertical integration: the rise of the value-adding partnership', *Harvard Business Review,* July/August.

Normann, R. and R. Ramirez (1994), *Designing Interactive Strategy: From Value Chain to Value Constellation*, Wiley, New York.

Rayport, J. F. and I. T. Sviokla (1994), 'Managing in the marketspace', *Harvard Business Review*, November/December.

Zuboff, S. (1985), 'Automate/informate: the two faces of intelligent technology', *Organisation Dynamics*, Autumn.

http://www.mckesson.com

http://www.ikea.com

chapter 14

Value and Value Chains in Healthcare

LEARNING OUTCOMES

The student will be able to:

- identify the value chain structure operating at the company level in a service organisation;
- construct the value chain comprising its organisation profile and its processes.

INTRODUCTION: VALUE CHAINS AND A HEALTHCARE APPLICATION

Healthcare is a market. It shares a number of similarities with conventional markets. It has market sectors (segments) for which common characteristics can be identified. It also has customers – patients. It also has similar problems such as increasingly discerning customers and management structures which are revenue, cost and therefore 'profit' conscious. It follows that healthcare does not (should not) differ in its concern for customer care.

Is healthcare in any way different? Clearly the answer is no. Patients are customers. They have value needs which are met by specific resources and services. Healthcare has 'marketing channels' and has specialist infrastructures that deliver value (or treatment services). In the case study which follows, a model produced by the author was applied to the Queen Elizabeth Hospital (QEH) in Rotorua, New Zealand. QEH is a specialist hospital for rheumatic disease and rehabilitation. It has a clearly defined mission:

> ... to provide the highest quality services for rheumatological care and rehabilitation – achieving standards that ensure such services remain the first choice of patients and customers.

To fulfil this mission they adopt an holistic approach to care for patients living with the effects of rheumatism, arthritis and other locomotor disorders resulting in disability. Patients are of all ages and backgrounds and the objective is to help them articulate and achieve their personal goals. These differ between clients, but include effective self-management of pain and disability, and appropriate use of medication. The aim is to help people achieve personal value and self worth, and achieve their functional potential and contribution within social relationship roles. A 'team approach' to treatment and education makes this possible. Working with QEH staff, patients achieve maximum physical, psychological and social independence.

A range of specialist doctors, nurses, therapists and counsellors offer the highest care in physiotherapy, balneotherapy, occupational therapy, vocational assessment, educational programmes, orthopaedic surgery and orthotics. Specialist rheumatology services are provided, mostly on an outpatient basis by three doctors working closely with rheumatology specialist nurses. Around 2000 new patient sessions and 4000 follow-up visits are provided annually at clinics located at QEH and around the region in outreach clinics. Referrals are also accepted from a wide geographical area for musculoskeletal rehabilitation. The hospital provides residential, day-stay and inpatient services for clients with chronic degenerative and inflammatory arthritis and chronic musculoskeletal pain. These are mostly provided by defined clinical pathways of care (such as a chronic back pain programme) but also by individually customised programmes. Approximately 8000 patient-days of care are provided annually.

A range of elective orthopaedic surgery is also performed with around 500 joint replacements annually. The orthopaedic service is regionally funded and provides community services as well as supporting the primary activities of the hospital. As a major tertiary health service provider, QEH has an active clinical research programme with Government research funding and pharmaceutical industry contracts as well as contracts with tertiary education providers. External funding also comes from charitable research funding agencies. Funding for the clinical activity comes mainly from Government contracts, with a small amount of private health provision for local and overseas clients. Some revenue is derived from the Government's worker compensation scheme and other accident insurance schemes. The market for publicly funded patients is interesting in that neither the patients, nor the general practitioners (who are the main source of referrals and also have needs) are involved directly in paying for the services provided. There is, therefore, a third party payer involved, either a health funding authority or a disability insurance agency that also has specified needs and expectations. This has allowed QEH to develop its own service provision according to 'what seemed best' – what it could provide and what it thought it should provide. This poses a danger to the organisation as it attempts to respond to the demands put upon it without clear definition of what it is being paid to do. This problem is common among publicly funded health providers, but is a real threat to a specialist unit that cannot afford to provide services for which it does not get paid. A value chain study is, therefore, of considerable benefit to the long term viability of the organisation and the continuity of the services it provides.

A VALUE CHAIN STUDY AT QUEEN ELIZABETH HOSPITAL

The QEH value chain organisation profile

The value chain, as a concept, has been with us for some time. Traditionally it started with a view of the assets and core competencies of an organisation and then moved towards inputs and other raw materials, to the delivery mechanisms and finally to the customer. Thus it began with assets and competencies (skilled staff, specialist equipment, supplies and services) then found a way to make the assets into a product or service that fits a template that is important to a customer.

As we have seen, the current approach reverses the process. Thinking begins with customer problems, needs and priorities and identifies options through which these may be met. It reverses traditional thinking. Managers should think of what customer needs are, the most relevant delivery methods suited to satisfy customer needs, the inputs required to create product-services, and then what assets and core competencies (or key success factors) are required to compete successfully. It follows that a comprehensive understanding of an organisation's value chain is essential. This chapter aims to explore the QEH value chain. See Figure 14.1.

Customer value/expectations criteria

During any 'purchase' situation certain aspects or attributes of a 'product' represent *value* to customers. Attributes enhance a customer's situation, resolve problems, offer solutions. Typically they are combined into a *value proposition* that has particular relevance for a response to a particular customer: they appeal to the customer's value criteria.

Customers have costs. *Customer acquisition costs* are incurred when considering a purchase. Customers maximise value when they select the option for which customer value criteria exceed customer acquisition costs. Both the value criteria and acquisition costs are influenced by external features, such as the 'significance' of the expenditure, the strength of the vendor's brand (reputation), the customer's life cycle/style characteristics and their purchasing expectations (the benefits to be delivered).

A *customer value model* for QEH 'customers' is described below:

Customer value criteria
Given the generic criteria below what do customers seek from QEH?

- Security: Safety in procedures?
- Performance: Healthy independence?
- Aesthetics: Status? (association with progressive and successful hospital)

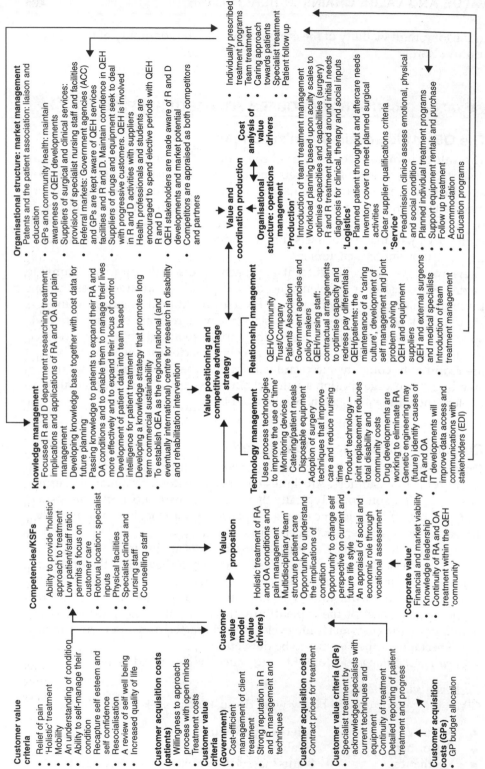

Figure 14.1 The QEH value chain

- Convenience: Time? location?
- Economy: Affordable healthcare?
- Reliability: Acceptance of ability? recommendation?

Customer acquisition costs

- Specification: Diagnosis?
- Search: Identifying expertise?
- Transactions: Healthcare insurance?
- Installation (delivery): Skilled treatment?
- Operation: Skilled support staff?
- Maintenance: Post procedure care?
- Disposal: The return to independence?

QEH has at least three customer categories. There are patients who are the end-user customers, but QEH customers also include Government and general practitioners. Each has a different perspective concerning both value criteria and acquisition costs. The end-users' *value criteria* are clear. They seek pain relief, mobility, functionality and training in how they may better manage their lives. A value benefit that is delivered, of which they may not be initially aware, is the re-establishment of self-esteem and the ability to reaffirm control of their lives. Their *costs* are that of the treatment and the psychological cost of changing their attitudes towards their condition.

The New Zealand Government is an important customer mostly through the Health Funding Authority, but also through the Accident, Compensation and Rehabilitation Corporation (ACRC), New Zealand's workers' compensation scheme. Attempts to deregulate the ACRC have resulted in a number of other insurers entering the market; but this funding remains sensitive to policy changes. Their value criteria are based not only upon delivery costs but also on the basis of a strong reputation for achieving results in the treatment of rheumatic disease and particularly in rehabilitation of the labour force into productive work. Their acquisition costs are controlled by budgets.

General practitioner 'customers' are concerned to obtain the treatment for patients that will offer effective and long-lasting relief. They also require support in managing chronic and incurable diseases that result in a huge burden of physical and financial disability. Value for them extends beyond the knowledge that QEH has a reputation for expertise and patient care; it includes the reporting of patient progress and recommendations for treatment. New Zealand has not yet embraced general practitioner fundholding, but in general GPs feel a responsibility to spend public money wisely. It follows that implicitly they are applying cost-effectiveness criteria.

Core competencies, processes and assets

Any organisation, if it is to be successful, should have a set of core competencies, processes and assets as well as possessing the *key success factors* necessary to compete successfully in its 'market(s)'. Typically these relate to its competencies (described by its capabilities and its capacities); its cost structures (economic characteristics), and the 'technology' it has available. *Core competencies* for QEH are:

- Competency (capabilities):   Specialist expertise
- Competency (capacities):   Response time and facilities
- Economic characteristics: Cost structures which permit
                                  competitive tenders/prices for treatment
- Technological characteristics: Equipment and treatment facilities
                                  (and methods)

Core processes for QEH include: customer centred practice procedures and a 'team approach' to treatment and to patient education. *Core assets* at QEH are tangible and intangible. Tangible assets include its location adjacent to treatment inputs such as balneotherapy, and the facility itself, which is equipped to implement all aspects of the treatment programmes. Intangible assets are the aggregated experience of the staff accrued over many years and, most importantly, the high quality of the staff. All combine to create a QEH brand.

We identified a number of key competencies, process and assets. One was clearly the capability of specialist healthcare providers to offer a complete package of interrelated treatment processes. The second concerns capacity: such treatment does require both skill and time, and accordingly a low patient: staff ratio permits this. QEH is located in an area of geothermal activity, using thermal water from a famous Rotorua outlet, Rachel Spring. Geothermal steam, hot mineral baths, massage therapy and thermal mud packs are seen as beneficial in treatment for some conditions. Specific physical facilities such as physiotherapy and occupational therapy are essential to the holistic approach, as is the input of trained counsellors where specialist training contributes to the recapture of self-esteem and self-confidence. Perhaps the main strength of QEH, however, is the team philosophy that flows through the programmes. Patients become part of the team for a while and are helped to change the way they see themselves and their condition and are led to make positive changes that lessen their disability, dependence and distress. This is a process of empowerment (a current buzzword in healthcare, but rarely achieved).

Value proposition

Customer value expectations *and* the core competencies combine to produce a *value proposition* which identifies *what* is to be delivered to the customer and by *what means*. In other words the value proposition identifies the benefits and costs for the customer and the internal activities (or processes) necessary to produce the benefits (value).

The QEH value proposition is focussed on the holistic treatment of rheumatoid and other types of inflammatory arthritis, multiple joint osteoarthritis and chronic musculoskeletal pain. In almost all cases, the physical state of the joints is only one of a number of factors contributing to the overall loss of quality of life. Just as important is the way in which this proposition is made. The team approach to treatment reinforces the value proposition. Following an initial diagnostic visit, patients are directed towards a team and a specific treatment programme. Thus, the customer is receiving a customised response to their condition. The team approach ensures that patients are 'educated' in the issues and the implications of their condition, together with being given an opportunity to understand how best to adapt to their environment. The final aspect of the value proposition is an appraisal of their potential social and economic role. More often than not, the patient has a negative approach to the possibility of contributing and enjoying such roles; education, support, counselling, physiotherapy and occupational therapy (including vocational rehabilitation) result in a positive outcome. For QEH a value proposition that could be used is:

> *Recovery or relief of specific symptoms within a specified time period. A level of knowledge, self belief and motivation that maintains the health benefits gained from after procedure care in specified surroundings. QEH would therefore identify staff, equipment and infrastructure requirements to meet the customer's value expectations.*

Partner value objectives

QEH needs to be financially viable. Without such success the potential for growth is restricted; hence the normal commercial financial criteria are essential metrics. The exploration and dissemination of knowledge is of importance to QEH. To be seen and recognised as a leading research centre in arthritis and rhuematism will enhance the QEH reputation academically as well as for treatment. In addition it is seen as essential that QEH explores applied as well as pure research. Treatment practices within the community, outwith the hospital, are becoming common practice and QEH recognises the value of this.

No organisation should consider entering a contractual arrangement unless its own value expectations can be met. These typically relate to financial and market viability together with a number of other quantitative and qualitative features. QEH may have criteria which include:

- contribution to financial reserves;
- utilisation of tangible and intangible assets; equipment, staff, and so on;
- development of relationship with referring GPs and case managers;
- target response times;
- reputation for innovation;
- development of integration with medical infrastructure;
- development of 'knowledge';
- capital asset management and development.

Value positioning and competitive advantage strategy

From this we derive a *value strategy and positioning and competitive advantage* statement which simply states what QEH sees as the scope of its business. In other words, what services it will offer, how these will be 'promoted' to its customers (both patients, referring GPs and payers) and how the services will be delivered. There are three influences. These are knowledge management, relationship management and technology management. The context of these for QEH is interesting. In outlining them here, we at the same time recap on what we have said about them in earlier chapters.

Knowledge management is suggested as 'the organisational capability which identifies, locates (creates or acquires), transfers and converts knowledge into competitive advantage'. In other words, what is QEH's knowledge strategy? How does it perceive its research as a contribution to its competitive advantage? What are the capabilities of its information systems? What is the role of knowledge and can QEH become a learning organisation? Knowledge management in healthcare has a number of facets. Research into causes and treatment of specific conditions is an obvious concern. But there are other issues to be considered. For example, developing an understanding of both efficacy and costs of treatment methods is essential for managing current options and for planning future activities (these include facilities, staff and extent of treatment services). In addition, there is a role for knowledge management in patient education as well as that of staff. If the holistic approach is to be maintained cost-effectively and developed further, knowledge resources need to be directed towards this activity and a database detailing treatment and outcomes becomes essential. A knowledge strategy is required if QEH is to work towards a long term commercial and clinical position and, at the same time, build a reputation around its 'knowledge'. Currently QEH is proactive towards this end. Partnerships with pharmaceutical companies that conduct drug trials add financial viability and allow the research department to expand its activities.

We also consider *technology management*, the integration of equipment and processes to meet the value objectives of QEH as expressed in its value proposition. Healthcare technology management includes treatment procedures as well as equipment. Inevitably these overlap. Technology management in healthcare typically focusses on surgical and clinical techniques. There are generic nursing techniques and prosthesis technology. The discipline is also optimistic about the increase in developments in genetics as well as those continuing in pharmacology. Also of note is the use made of process or applied technology, to improve the use of time. QEH staff identified a number of developments in clinical and nursing processes that have released staff from routine activities and have enabled them to spend more time with patients. Developments in information technology have (or will) improve(d) communications within the hospital and with stakeholders (suppliers, GPs and the Government). The introduction of EDI (electronic data interchange) facilities in healthcare is already responsible for expanding both 'richness' and 'reach' of information simultaneously.

Relationship management is concerned with what is required by QEH to identify, establish, maintain and reinforce relationships with customers, suppliers and other partners with *complementary* capabilities and capacities so that the objectives of QEH *and* of their partners may be met. In other words, what does

QEH need to do to work successfully with *all* of its partners to ensure mutual success? QEH has a number of relationships that are important to its success; these are both internal and external. Being a private hospital activity, QEH has a complex management task with its shareholders (the company), the 'Community Trust' and the lease owners of the QEH site. Other important relationships are those with the Patients' Association and the Arthritis Foundation. The former provides an ongoing link with a group who are very loyal (and appreciative) towards QEH, providing some funds and voluntary services. Liaison with policy makers and funding authorities is an important task. Relationships with funding organisations are important on cost-effectiveness grounds as well as on the research front. ACRC's concern is for cost-effective means of returning patients to the workforce or reducing dependency on benefits. QEH should therefore have a productivity focus and through audit and research, develop activities to reduce costs, decrease treatment times, or develop more effective treatment methods. Ongoing relationship management with GPs is important; GPs are crucial to QEH revenues through their referrals. Consequently, specific patient progress information is part of ongoing relationships together with information concerning research activities.

Maintaining relationships with the pharmaceutical industry is also important, as is the efficient and reliable conduct of contract clinical research. This is achieved through performance and networking. The QEH specialists are seen as opinion leaders within the rheumatology community.

QEH has other external relationships that are extremely important. The 'partnership' with orthopaedic surgeons is one such relationship. QEH offers orthopaedic surgeons highly skilled, specialist nursing staff and specialist equipment and is aware of the importance of these to maintaining and strengthening this important relationship from both revenue and reputation considerations. Similarly, it maintains close and open dialogue with equipment suppliers. This ensures both service (prompt deliveries of prosthetics and so on) and information concerning suppliers, suppliers' competitors and relevant research activities.

Possibly it is the relationships with patients (customers) that concern QEH most. Interviews with patients identified a strong bond between physicans, nursing, therapy and counselling staff. They are very vocal concerning their appreciation and this relates to the re-education processes (from which they emerge with a change of attitude, increased self-esteem and self-confidence) as well as the pain relief. This aspect of QEH's relationships with its patients may be regarded as a significant contribution to the hospital's competitive advantage.

Finally the intra-relationships among staff are crucial to success. The introduction of team treatment management has reinforced the strong sense of cooperation among all members of staff. This extends to administrative staff members who see themselves as part of the patient recovery processes.

QEH value positioning and strategy emerge from a combination of these three areas. Its value proposition is one that offers patients/customers both pain relief *and* an education process in which they begin to understand their own role in managing their condition. QEH understands well the need to manage the roles of knowledge, technology and relationship management *and* the interfaces between each area.

Value production and coordination

Value production and coordination is the operational function that ensures that value positioning and strategy decisions are implemented successfully. There are two considerations: the organisational structure for stakeholder management, and an organisational structure for operations management. The organisational structure to cope with stakeholder management for QEH includes important stakeholder groups. These are customers (patients); referral organisations (GPs); suppliers (equipment and drug companies); an internal market (nursing staff and administrators); 'influencers' (patient groups such as the Arthritis Foundation and Patients' Association, local and national Maori health groups, health service agencies); 'recruitment' (medical and nursing recruitment agencies); and 'investors' (Government and other funds providers). Each requires a strategy for managing the interface between QEH and the 'market' component.

QEH has a complex market structure. Its primary market is its patients. A number of patients are loyal customers, they return regularly because of the benefits all or some of the facilities offer. Consequently the 'repeat business customer' is important to QEH. For similar reasons its position with GPs is an important market. They are important sources of revenue continuity. Government sources of business are clearly important, not only because of the contribution towards revenues and revenue continuity, but also because of the 'referral influence' Government holds. The very fact that Government is a customer acts to reinforce the overall market position of QEH, but also makes it vulnerable should its purchasing policy change. Supply markets are important sources of 'knowledge' and can be helpful in promoting the strengths of QEH patient care and research and development activities. Recent Government research grants and an expansion of drug trial activity suggest the important role of QEH in research and development is being increasingly recognised.

QEH actively encourages healthcare professionals and students to spend elective periods with the hospital. QEH considers this an important aspect of 'market management' as it fosters interest in arthritis research and treatment, resulting in increased recognition of the importance of QEH's activities. Competition exists in healthcare just as it does in other commercial markets. QEH has local competitors in both public and private sectors. Competition is keen for patients and funding and some decisions concerning market positioning (based upon core competencies) and capacity utilisation are necessary. It is not unrealistic to expect a value chain solution to emerge in which both capabilities and capacities are focussed on achieving an increase in customer satisfaction.

The second influence on value production and coordination is an *organisa-*

tion structure, which implements operations management tasks and concerns the management of procurement, 'production', 'logistics' and 'service'. *Procurement* management is an important aspect of QEH's operations, particularly as it involves expensive prosthetic equipment. By working closely with suppliers inventory levels are maintained on a 'just-in-time' basis. *'Production'* management is the process by which value is 'manufactured'. It is a process during which decisions concerning what, where, how when and by whom, production processes occur: it identifies options for in-house activities and outsourcing. 'Production' processes are focussed on patient care. Team treatment management (discussed above) is a means by which the management of clinical treatment is made more individual and effective. It is a form of matrix organisation structure. Patients' treatment programmes are partly based upon a physician's diagnosis prior to the program commencing (for example, newly diagnosed rheumatoid arthritis), but mostly on the patient-defined goals of rehabilitation as determined by team assessment on entry to the programme. Surgery 'production' is based upon workload planning in which the available capacity is allocated on the basis of the complexity (and therefore the theatre time required) of the operation. Nursing capacity requirements are planned on the same basis together with a planned patient/staff ratio that will ensure adequate time for patient care. Preadmission clinics are held to ensure that before an admission date is confirmed the patient is emotionally, physically and socially prepared for surgery. Once a date is agreed and the patient enters, QEH staff begin to plan the patient's discharge by identifying tasks that will be required, support and facility needs and administrative requirements, such as GP involvement. The awareness of related technology developments (see earlier discussion on technology management) has resulted in nursing staff assuming more responsibility for patient care. This, together with the fact that QEH is a specialist unit, has resulted in benefits of economies of specialisation *and* cost benefits from an 'experience effect'. These factors contribute to a strong and positive relationship with surgeons who exhibit preferences to work with QEH.

Logistics management considers both material and non-material (service and information) flows throughout an organisation. The 'value added' concept here refers to enhancing the perceived value of the 'product-service' to both the customer (patient) and the referral customer – the GP. Economists consider value in terms of utilities created; these are of form, possession, time and place. The logistics function is concerned with time and place utilities. Time and place utilities add value in a QEH context by allowing medical and nursing staff to provide healthcare and customer care in a cost-effective way and one in which confidence is built.

Logistics in medicine is an interesting management concern because it covers a combination of patient care process, patient logistics (moving patients through the hospital) and materials logistics (the flow of equipment, drugs and information). Logistics is increasingly becoming an area of specialist outsourcing in a number of sectors. For example, in national defence we now see *ab initio* pilot training conducted by civilian organisations, and more recently the UK Government has outsourced in-flight refuelling. Information systems connecting internal and external activities with all suppliers become a major concern, particularly in the control of outsourced activities and services.

Logistics systems relate to progressing patients through QEH facilities, after care needs and administrative procedures. QEH's holistic approach involves a complete range of procedures (discussed earlier). It follows that if high utilisation is to be achieved, then capacity management procedures are important. It must be remembered that QEH's assets are not only in 'plant' but also in specialist staff; it is essential that patient flows are managed smoothly throughout. There is an inventory management concern for QEH as both prosthetic and orthotic equipment is expensive. Strict inventory management control is exercised to ensure that optimum levels of items are matched with the rate of use and the inventory budget. Supplies are appraised against quantitative and qualitative criteria such as product availability, service response, staff training, as well as the essential product quality. QEH has developed a 'just-in-time' approach with its prosthesis suppliers.

There are a number of important *'service'* aspects to the operational structure and management of QEH activities. The preadmission clinics were discussed above within the context of productivity planning. However, they are an important characteristic of the QEH service offer and this is recognised by patients who comment upon the role of the clinics in the overall customer care programme.

Possibly the most visible aspect of QEH service is the individual care for patients undergoing treatment. Patients are full of praise for staff and for the benefits received. The focus on self-awareness and self-help are the most commented upon aspects of the treatment, possibly because pain relief was an expected outcome; the ability to be prospective about the future is, for many, a surprise. This feature is extended into follow-up treatment. An additional service feature is the availability of orthotic equipment through purchase or rental services. QEH's R and R program does not necessarily require patients to be 'in hospital' and the service extends to arranging external accommodation. One final aspect of service is the increasing number of educational programmes provided within and outwith the hospital by QEH staff.

Value drivers

A knowledge of the *value drivers* (and their costs) that influence the extent of success of the value production process is the final but possibly most important consideration. The process by which value is produced and delivered incurs cost. An organisation therefore needs to identify the relationship between customer satisfaction (what creates which levels of satisfaction) and the cost incurred. Thus it is the value drivers which influence the value created for customers (by offering a range of differentiated products and services) and because of the competitive advantage created, value (in terms of profitability, productivity and so forth) for the organisation.

Value drivers (and their costs) have implications for all stakeholders. Clearly unless all stakeholders receive benefits from a 'transaction' then collaboration via partnership or alliance is not worthwhile. For most value chain studies the existence of generic value and cost drivers can be assumed. Adding value implies adding costs because the process of adding value incurs cost; the concern for any organisation is to ensure that the value generates a greater return than the cost of the processes involved.

For QEH there are a range of value drivers. From the customer perspective individually prescribed treatment programmes create value. The patient perceives value and while the process is expensive this customer response exceeds the cost of providing such value. Similarly the integrated team approach and the emphasis on customer care, together with specialist staff, creates strong customer value but costs are significant, surgery costs being a major expense item.

QEH has developed a number of skills that help manage efficient value delivery. QEH achieves a very high capacity utilisation of surgical facilities and staff because it is a specialist orthopaedic centre. Specialisation enables theatre turn-round times to be kept to a minimum and this, together with capacity management techniques (described earlier), contributes towards controlling this cost driver. Another similar consideration is patient mix. A balanced number of treatment programmes, such that facilities requirements can be planned evenly (and staff time for that matter), also helps control the revenue (value delivered) and costs. This also results in QEH being able to offer reliable treatment timetables.

The economies of specialisation can offer both value and cost benefits. Value may be enhanced due to the skills and expertise resulting from specialist treatment and surgery. In other words, QEH can differentiate its product from that of its competitors by offering more advanced treatment, shorter treatment turn-round times, or more patient care. QEH can also benefit from lower costs. The economies of specialisation can be managed to reduce procedure and patient care costs, thereby adding to corporate value.

VALUE CHAIN PROCESSES

The move by business organisations away from traditional functional or departmental structures, an approach to structure that gradually narrowed its focus (see Beech: 1998) and is embracing process management, is encouraging for value chain analysis.

Process management combines the tasks and inputs comprising value delivery and structure required (regardless of ownership) into an effective value delivery system. The six value delivery processes identified earlier are discussed below within the context of QEH. See Figure 14.2.

Customer expectations
There are three components here, and, not surprisingly they are interrelated. Patient expectations are also the concern of referring GPs who, given a patient's condition, seek the most cost-efficient solution to the condition. In

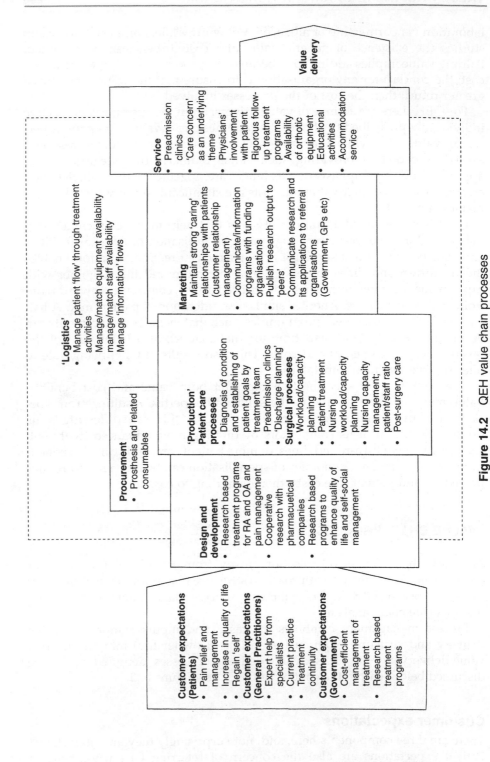

Figure 14.2 QEH value chain processes

so doing they too have expectations that include expert help and the knowledge that the treatment methods their patient is to receive are 'current' and reflect 'best practice'. Government's expectation set is similar but is strongly influenced by its concern for cost-efficient management of treatment contracts and for treatment that will return the 'client' to productivity, or reduces the client's dependence on welfare support and benefits.

Design and development

Healthcare design and development processes are research led and are directed towards improving the effectiveness or lowering the costs of treatment programmes. QEH cooperates with pharmacuetical companies and other suppliers to ensure that arthritis treatment not only reflects current knowledge but that QEH is in the forefront of developing knowledge. The non-medical aspects of QEH treatment are also important and research into methods by which patients' quality of life and self-ability for 'social management' are improved forms part of the design and development process.

'Production'

There are two production processes within QEH. Clearly they are closely linked, but for analytical purposes are separated. Patient care processes relate to the diagnosis of the patient's condition, treatment requirements and their implementation by a treatment team. The importance of preadmission clinics and the notion of discharge planning are two important components within patient care process design and management.

Surgical production is an important outsourced process. QEH provides surgical facilities and nursing staff. Surgical procedures are conducted by independent (private) orthopaedic surgeons. It follows that surgical production process management requires detailed planning to ensure both availability of capacity and the productive use of the capacity. Production planning in this regard has much in common with techniques used in manufacturing management.

Procurement

Both surgical equipment and patient support (orthotic) equipment are subjected to inventory management and procurement routines. Prosthetics are specialist and expensive items, accordingly QEH works very closely with suppliers who have been identified as offering prompt and reliable service at competitive price levels.

Marketing

Customer identification, communication and relationship management are of primary importance and are implicit in every staff member's job specification.

The QEH ethic of caring relationships with patients is integral in all customer liaison.

An ongoing dialogue with funding organisations is an essential role for marketing. This ensures awareness of QEH's current and developing capabilities and its research profile.

Marketing acts as a conduit between QEH and its 'customers', suppliers, 'peers' and competitors to ensure that its research activities are widely recognised. This plays an important role in QEH postioning and therefore its competitive advantage profile.

Service

Essentially service is an underlying process in QEH and serves to link many of the processes in the overall process of value delivery. The preadmission clinics and the continuous contact of all members of staff with patients are a dominant service feature.

Service attributes that enhance the QEH value proposition include the attention to detail in follow-up treatment and the availability of support equipment. Because of the nature of QEH treatment methods, patients are not necessarily 'admitted' in a conventional way. Many can be accommodated in local hotels and self-catering facilities. QEH offers a service that organises accommodation for both patients and, if required, for relatives.

An important service component for QEH is its education activity. QEH undertakes numerous internal and external educational sessions for a range of audiences, from patient groups locally to international seminars with peers and the healthcare industry.

Logistics

As with other value chains, logistics provides a time and materials management process. Efficient logistics management ensures an appropriate matching of facilities with planned patient requirements and, in so doing, enhances system productivity. Clearly this matching process includes both internal and external resources such as 'plant and equipment', clinical staff, support and consumable supplies. Logistics also manages information flows and these are becoming increasingly important, particularly with the role rapidly being undertaken by information technology, such as EDI, that improves productivity *and* provides increasingly useful information for patient care process management.

SUMMARY

This case study demonstrates the application of the value chain concept in a healthcare situation. It offers benefits to healthcare managers because it asks them to disaggregate their healthcare function and question its efficacy, and to identify alternative methods of achieving current results and to explore future opportunities. Value chain analysis permits an intra- and inter-organi-sational review of the cost efficiency of resource application and thus encour-ages medical staff as well as management to explore alternative methods and structures for meeting objectives.

A number of alternatives and opportunities emerged from this study. The prospect of extending partnership arrangements was discussed, as was the notion of using the staff skills to present preventative options to industry and the wider community.

REFERENCE ●

Beech, J. (1998), 'The supply-demand nexus', in Gattorna, J. (ed.), *Strategic Supply Chain Alignment*, Gower Press, Aldershot.

chapter

15

Value and Value Chains in Education

LEARNING OUTCOMES

The student will be able to:

- identify the value chain structure operating at the company level in a service organisation;
- apply the value chain model to service products and organisations.

INTRODUCTION

Since its inception in 1986, International Education in Australian universities has been dominated by an approach that can be described as:

> the recruitment to home campuses of international students via differentiated regional and country strategies, conventional marketing techniques and commission agents.

This paradigm has served universities well. It has been the basis for the development of an industry that has grown from a few hundred thousand dollars in export value in 1986 to over 3.5 billion Australian dollars in 2000. It has also been the basis for the development of a view of internationalisation that includes internationalisation of the curriculum, staff and student mobility, and the formation of cooperative links between institutions. The operation of offshore programmes has also been important, but as a generalisation, and with notable exceptions, has been marginalised at the university level and dominated by faculty interests.

The various facets of internationalisation have been largely treated as separate functions within institutions. Onshore recruitment has dominated and been separate from student mobility, offshore programmes, distance programmes and the development of strong cooperative links.

The recruitment of international students has also changed the financial landscape of universities. In tough financial times there have been for most institutions few if any other sources of resource expansion. There is much anecdotal evidence to suggest that while this has probably been understood by Vice Chancellors, the number of institutions where the investment for expanding international student number targets and outcomes has been understood and implemented is small.

Within the existing paradigm many institutions are beginning to examine ways of integrating their international recruiting strategy with web marketing, online applications and other facets of what has now become generically known as e-commerce or e-business. In some cases this is being tied back to a teaching and learning strategy that is creating online course products. Evans and Wurster (1999) put this approach into context:

> Product suppliers and physical retailers still see the Internet as an arena for marketing and promotion: a new channel for doing old things. If they persist in that view, they will handicap themselves against new competitors . . . that see e-commerce as a business in its own right.

It might be argued that the so called dot.com collapse may have negated this position, but another view is that the collapse was a shakeout of marginal businesses and has only delayed but strengthened the survivors.

Business operates everywhere in an environment that is both dynamic and challenging: markets have globalised (supply markets and customer markets); technology has become all embracing (this includes product and process technology); and relationships with suppliers, customers and competitors are undergoing constant change (often influenced by external forces such as technology). A new *business model* is emerging, one in which competitive advantage is based upon rapid and flexible responses to 'market' change. The new *capabilities* are based upon developing unique relationships with partners (suppliers, customers, employees, shareholders, government and, often, with competitors); an understanding of, and the ability to use and to manage, the new technology; and an understanding of the impact of knowledge creation and its distribution. These influences will inevitably change the ways in which universities think about internationalisation, the recruitment of students and the delivery of programmes. E-business becomes a necessary approach within the new paradigm.

This new model can be described as:

> recruitment of students to a network of regional, global and virtual campuses through the creation of innovative international degree products, relationship and technology management.

In this chapter the internationalisation of Australian universities around this emerging business model and its impact on strategy and operations are described. However, before considering the operational details, a review of the concepts underlying the paradigm is necessary.

A NEW BUSINESS MODEL FOR EDUCATION?

The supply chain on its own is tactical, with a primary mission to provide 'acceptable' service at 'efficient' levels of cost. It works hard to optimise this goal within an environment of dynamic change. Typically it has been built upon conventional supplier-procurement models and relationships. The value chain seeks solutions beyond the old constraints. It is a new form of business design that leverages customer choice and operations decisions to develop sustainable competitive advantage.

In a university, the value chain focusses on what the needs of students and potential students are, how they are to be met, by whom, and where. It identifies the students' value drivers in terms of quality, destination, and cost-benefits, and determines the value proposition that we make in terms of academic reputation, capabilities, products, services and strategies that give us competitive advantage in meeting these customer led needs.

The traditional supply chain approach is designed to meet customer demand with a fixed product line, relatively undifferentiated and with an average service package for average customers.

This is how international offices have operated for more than a decade, using a standardised approach to marketing and recruiting through printed materials, education fairs and largely undifferentiated agreements with recruiting agents (including Independent Development Program), a group largely seen as a 'necessary evil' in undertaking the activity, and whose impact is seen as a cost to be minimised.

A value chain approach considers the uniqueness of customers, or small customer segments. It encourages customers to choose the product-service attributes they value most. It then seeks to construct an organisation structure that effectively and efficiently meets their needs. Design and development, procurement, production, marketing and service processes are driven by logistics management – often coordinated through a multi-enterprise organisation – to meet the different customer expectations and to do so profitably.

As university finances tightened in the mid to late 1990s many universities looked to the international office not only as a source of increased revenue but of greater efficiencies. International offices were 'pulled into' university wide budget models that focussed on contraction of services. Rather than being seen as business units that required continuous investment to succeed, they were caught in a cycle of increasing transactions and cutting costs.

Even where international recruiting operations were within company structures, they faced restructuring to meet overall university strategies oblivious to the cross subsidies and economies of scale that existed within them.

Process management rather than functional management

To be effective organisations need to work together to identify core processes within the value chain. They must explore the implications of locating these core processes within specialist, partnership organisations. Each core process in the demand chain comprises numerous sub-processes, the importance of which varies across industries. Often similar sectors of industry differ in their sub-process infrastructure. Where they do not differ is in the integration of core and sub-processes with the shared goal of maximising strategic effectiveness and operating efficiencies.

An example within many international offices is that of admissions. If thought of as a function, then the efficiencies and control aspects of operating a centralised group might seem to be overwhelming. Looked on as a series of processes, outsourcing all or some of enquiries, applications, offers and the actual enrolment, then becomes a possibility.

Why does a student resident in Malaysia, undertaking an Australian university degree in Singapore, need to have the enrolment function substantially handled by university staff in Melbourne? The traditional answer has been that the technology or regulations or some notion of control, meant that most of the functions would probably be on the home campus under the control of home university staff. The use of technology and partnership relationships backed up by quality assurance allows the processes to be distributed over multiple organisations such as offshore programme partners and agents, to the likely benefit of the student.

Knowledge management

In international education, knowledge management relates to developing an understanding of markets, customers' needs and decision process 'influencers', opportunities and threats, marketing channels, and brand position. It also relates to understanding products and the ability to bring new products, that represent customer needs, into the market in a timely fashion. It is about the extent to which innovation and development are valued.

In the traditional model, quite a bit about all of these things is known, but rarely at a deep level; furthermore new programmes (products) sometimes take years to bring to market, where they could take only weeks. This will be replaced by institutions working under the new paradigm with a much deeper understanding of markets, customers and brand, and institutional processes that are designed to create and discard programmes (products) quickly. In the context of the value chain this is a time-to-market issue being resolved by improving knowledge management among partner organisations.

Technology management

Technology management is more than introducing new computer and e-business systems. It is about integrating processes in appropriate technologies within the organisation (and often between organisations) and includes those that might have strong non-electronic components. As processes go beyond the single organisation then inter-operability (the seamless interconnection of systems) of system components must be seen across organisational lines. It is the mapping of e-business systems such as prospect management across marketing strategy at one end, and application processes at the other, that becomes key to success in international education.

Relationship management

Typically universities have always had a multitude of partnerships internationally; offshore providers, agents, other universities and colleges. In many instances these have been long standing and successful relationships. Most, even the successful ones, have been grounded in a small number of activities and have not been deep. Typical of these have been the relationships between universities and recruiting agents including IDP.

In the emerging model this will change dramatically. Universities are facing the situation where more and more students are being recruited via commission agents. This is costly and is seen often as an undesirable trend. There are two responses. The first is to attempt to limit access by agents, by encouraging direct applications through the web and through the presence of university staff continuously in key markets. The second is to embrace the change and develop a strategy that leverages agent activity for the benefit of the university. The first strategy is bound to fail over a range of markets. Prospective students will seek out information resources from the university and use these to help select a destination, but are likely to look for the security of assistance from an agent.

Furthermore the Pareto (80/20) rule appears to apply. Twenty per cent of the agents will bring forward eighty per cent of the students recruited from agents. When the list of high achieving agents is examined it will include a large percentage of very substantial and professional organisations, increasingly with offices across regions or even globally, and with strategies to develop sophisticated marketing and recruiting electronically to universities they are confident of working with. IDP as a global agent for Australian universities, with extensive English language testing and aid project interests, is perfectly placed to move from providing an 'equal' service to all Australian universities to providing 'favoured' status to clients it can develop strong relationships with to mutual benefit.

IDP will not be alone. IEC in Norway has already extended to Germany and has 'badged' itself there as IEC Online, a portent of what is to come. Working successfully with the new generation of 'super agents' will no longer be a matter of signing a contract, attending a couple of fairs and expecting that students 'will come'. It will be about extending functions across the organisational boundaries, with sophisticated online processes that move decision making away from university international offices in state capitals to where the student is, or to virtual locations occupied by the partner organisation. In this process we stand to lose our ability to market our own products and to control the quality and flow of students. By developing the relationship to tie together electronic and other processes across the boundaries and creating strong brand identification for on-selling through the partnership, we maintain the control and distribute the costs and benefits.

There are many other examples. Three years ago, on the establishment of the new International Office at Macquarie, it became clear very quickly that the physical resources or the technology to handle the management of enquiries, largely by email, were not available. Three years on, outsourcing 'prospect management' to Hobsons, the British based publishers and owners of the *Good Universities Guide* has occurred. This was not a product that could be purchased 'off the shelf'; rather it started as the realisation that no university in Australia had the financial or technical resources to develop a set of electronic processes that were not clearly understood.

To get the 'product' on air took the development of enormous trust between the five university stakeholders and between them and Hobsons. The result is that there is now a stable prospect management system, together with the ability to reinvent it almost continuously. The key to the development has been the creation of a multi-enterprise virtual organisation from the fusing of:

- *relationship management* – the way the universities have worked together and opened up their own organisations and processes to the scrutiny of all, and the relationship between the universities and Hobsons;
- *knowledge management* – our shared understanding of markets, and Hobsons' knowledge of call centre processes, as well as the shared ability to innovate new product variations;
- *technology management* – Hobsons' understanding of the technology needed to underpin the operation and the universities' ability to link the technology to their own systems;

bound together by processes that extend university reach out through the Hobsons-owned technology.

WHAT ARE THE IMPLICATIONS OF VALUE CHAINS FOR UNIVERSITIES?

Whether universities like it or not, the ground rules have changed. They are faced with being part of a globalised set of economies that are doing business in different ways. The only question is whether universities will embrace the changes and use them to their benefit, or see them as new ways of doing the old things.

Competition

For Australia competition has traditionally come from the US and UK and to a lesser extent from Canada and NZ. The emergence of Asian and European destinations will change the dynamic. In Europe, the Bologna declaration moves degree structures to the *British-American model* and a number of countries are looking closely at the success of the UK and Australia in taking an export position. Private providers too will become a bigger factor. Licensed and/or virtual programmes offered through technology partnerships with a global reach will have a significant place in the market. The weak dollar, good quality for price and lifestyle factors that support activities now, may not always be strong competitive factors for Australian universities. By not *embracing* the changes there is the risk of facing a competitive market in which decline is the norm.

Marketing

At the moment, there is a tendency clearly to delineate marketing for different aspects of the business, and see them as different businesses. Integrated marketing across onshore, offshore and online/distance modes is providing a network of choices in delivery mode and location. Student mobility products (incoming and outgoing) now certainly seen as separate will become part of the network and the options. Universities are heading for a delivery network in which the home campus is one, and perhaps not the largest of the delivery network nodes.

The web will replace print media as the dominant marketing tool and the universities will need to develop marketing strategies to funnel prospects to e-business sites. These sites will increasingly be those owned and operated by partners, whether agents, offshore providers, or what Evans and Wurster (1999) call *navigators*, organisations that don't sell anything. In these new relationships universities will begin to lose control over the direct marketing to clients. The task will be to manage the relationships and to brand strongly our institutions to be marketed by intermediaries and network partners including other universities. This branding may have more to do with selling a lifestyle choice than education as it is presently understood.

The essential task will be to funnel large numbers of deliberate and accidental enquiries from the web to virtual and physical sites where these prospects can be converted to enrolments in our network (Lawrence: 2001).

Much stronger and more reliable market research is now available, as is the ability to mine successfully the data available from prospects. Knowledge of markets, the relationships with intermediaries and an understanding of the technology are the key components to manage.

Recruitment

The management of web prospects and their conversion to enrolments in the network is the task of recruitment. The features of the emerging models are:

- multiple purchase channels for buyers. This may include multiple prices within the same market;
- integrated, seamless prospect management strategies based on web tools;
- integrated online application processes based on student centred portals;
- growth of global/regional super agents with sophisticated application systems interfaced to university systems;

- full reliance on intermediaries;
- growth of network nodes to support local agents and offshore programmes;
- global and regional partners contracted to deliver student numbers;
- students also becoming more sophisticated in examining global options.

The key to success will be to quality assure processes and policies that flow across these organisational boundaries. It will no longer be a question of working closely with a single IDP office to ensure the smooth flow of applications and responses, but with working across the entire IDP network, or that of another agent, to deliver students to a network of campuses, sites and modes of delivery in virtual space.

Independent quality reviews, such as the IQR (Intenationalisation Quality Review) will become necessary to provide assurance in a much more complex operating environment than exists presently. The IQR is conducted as a professional service by the European Universities Association, a system that has evolved from the IQRP (Internationalisation Quality Review Process) described by Knight and de Wit (1999).

Admissions

In general admissions processes have been tightly held within university admissions offices or international offices with final decisions being either made by the relevant office according to academic criteria, or the decision passed back to academic units. Even with offshore programmes this has been essentially the case, with some admissions criteria being exercised by partners. Some agents also administer aspects of the process, but very much on a piecemeal, office to office basis.

Online applications systems are now beginning to be used, but are not likely to interface across agent and home system boundaries. The NOOSR qualification recognition handbooks remain an archaic throwback to an earlier age when national university systems could be reviewed every five to ten years and the information they contained remained static and largely correct in the meantime. The new paradigm suggests the following aspects will be important:

- admissions processes distributed electronically to major partners and intermediaries, including the transmission and storage of documents presently transmitted and stored manually;
- certification of programmes and standardisation across trading blocs;
- increased use of standard tests to supplement knowledge about national qualification structures;
- self assessment by students against entry criteria leading to new forms of conditional offers being generated automatically;
- a breakdown of the hegemony of IELTS (a language test similar to TEFL) with the emergence of negotiated English Language agreements with partners, consistent with visa requirements where needed;

- sophisticated double degree, international degree and consortia based articulation and pathway arrangements;
- fast track development of customer driven products.

In a similar way to recruitment, admissions will be about loosening the institutional role to become that of quality assurance and policy based, with processes, strategies and policies moving across organisational boundaries. We will need to concentrate our efforts on this quality assurance within a context of relationship, knowledge and technology management.

Partnerships and strategic alliances

All universities have many excellent international partnerships and strategic alliances. It is how to select key alliances from those that exist and those on offer to drive the universities' future direction that is difficult. What type of alliances, where and for what purpose will be important and is something that all universities will have to offer.

Alliances such as Universitas 21 internationally and the Australian Technology Network are bound in the end to fail, or at least fail to meet reasonable expectations. They will fail because they bring together *like institutions separated only by physical location*. They bring together the same set of capabilities, strategies, course types and student profiles many times, when what is required is to bring together different but complementary capabilities. Cooperation, not competition, will become commonplace.

Universities will need to develop strong alliances with key channel providers: global and regional agents, offshore partners, technology platform companies, web navigation companies, universities and university systems. These relationships will be strategically managed and will open both sets of organisations to crossing boundaries with processes, quality assurance and strategy.

Other alliances will be more transitory and informal: groups coming together to work closely on specific projects and then, as the needs change, to fade away or metamorphose into something new. The older, low level partnerships will continue to exist but will more and more be marginalised.

The changes that international education is undergoing can be represented by the value chain structures that may be seen emerging. These are shown as Figures 15.1 and 15.2.

SUMMARY

Strategy in international education can be seen to be moving towards strong branding that links with the strategies of key global and regional partners and intermediaries. In this way the universities can benefit from the economies of specialisation in areas where this is important (for example, curriculum) and economies of scale (for example, handling enquiries).

The strategy of a university under the new paradigm will be based around the following major components of the value chain.

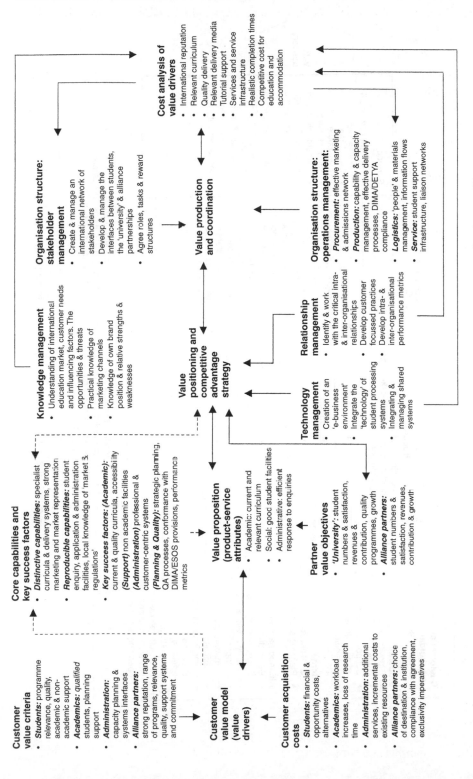

Figure 15.1 The value chain in international education: organisation profile

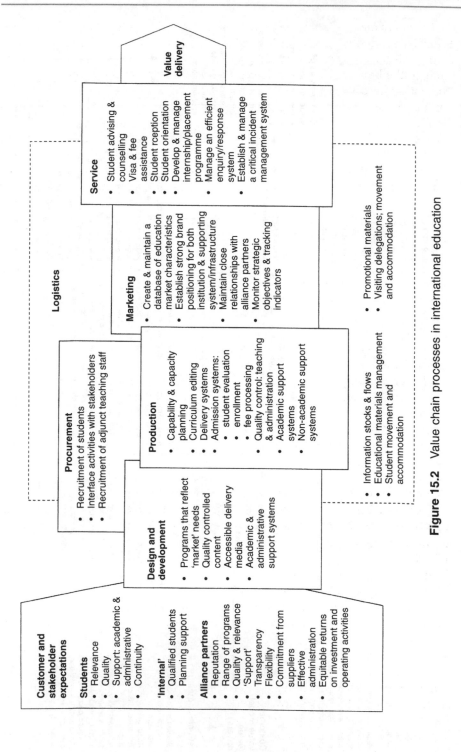

Figure 15.2 Value chain processes in international education

Identifying the customer value model: the costs and benefits that stakeholders: students, academic staff, administrators and partners experience and incur during the selection and purchase process. The universities should attempt to enhance the benefits they perceive as important to their achieving maximum satisfaction, and where possible, work with partners to reduce the costs customers incur when acquiring an educational product, to maximise customer satisfaction.

The value proposition should make very clear the attributes of products and services that are available to customers. This identifies responses to customers' expectations. It also identifies the roles and tasks of employees, partners and other intermediaries involved in the value creation and delivery process.

Value positioning is the unique or exclusive way in which knowledge management, technology management and relationship management are integrated to gain competitive advantage. For example, *knowledge management* may be used to build an exclusive curriculum in an emerging academic area. *Technology management* may be deployed in applying knowledge to programme content as well as the method of delivery. Positioning decisions are increasingly based upon *relationship management:* the development of partnerships with other providers (co-option) is becoming commonplace and in many ways is as important as developing strong and sustainable relationships with intermediaries.

Value production and coordination concern the organisational structure necessary to implement our value positioning and the logistics to make it happen. There are two aspects. One aspect is the management of stakeholder interests; these include those of prospective students (customers) but also the interests of our partners. Other important stakeholder groups are the community (concern here should be to ensure that educational programmes are relevant to their *specific needs* and not some esoteric perceived need on the part of the university academic). Regulatory bodies within the countries where universities operate are also important stakeholders. It is essential that the value proposition is in tune with local needs and that it complements rather than substitutes for local educational offers. Organisational structure decisions include the structure and management of production, delivery and service activities. This is an important aspect of value production and coordination as it ensures the cost-efficient implementation of the value offer.

Cost analysis of value drivers: value drivers are 'the features that customers are prepared to pay a premium for, specific features such that, if they are not available, they will switch to an alternative supplier'. Because these are essential to the customer, they are also essential to the success of the value chain partnership that has been organised to deliver customer satisfaction. Implementation of the value strategy depends upon the cost-efficient delivery of the value proposition. It follows that the value drivers should be monitored constantly to ensure that the costs of production and delivery are within budgeted totals. Furthermore, they should also be monitored to be equally sure they remain relevant to the customers' needs.

This strategy, reviewed on an annual basis, radiates out from the university to link with the strategies of major partners and intermediaries and enables a coherent examination of stakeholder needs.

Strategies, if they are to be effective, require efficient implementation. The new paradigm requires shifts in attitudes towards managing 'international education' as well as behaviour. The 'new paradigm' reflects the many changes that are occurring and suggests the new structures and behaviour patterns that will be required if they are to be successful.

REFERENCES ●

Evans, P. and T. S. Wurster (1999), 'Getting real about virtual commerce', *Harvard Business Review*, November/December.

Knight, J. and S. de Wit (eds) (1999), *Quality and Internationalisation in Higher Education*, OECD/IMHE, Paris.

Lawrence, R. (2001), Personal Interview with Professor Tony Adams, Director of International Programmes, Macquarie University, Sydney, Australia.

part three
Configuring the value chain, structure and performance

Introduction

In this final part of the book the tasks of considering optional value chain structures and the need to consider performance measurement are addressed.

Many of the earlier topics are revisited and reviewed in a process that brings them together to discuss design and performance. During the time that this text has been researched and written numerous additional contributions have become available and those relevant to the topic of the value chain have been included.

The final chapter offers the reader the opportunity to develop further the case studies that are introduced. Caterpillar, Wal-Mart and Dell are well established companies. For each organisation the concepts introduced and discussed in the earlier chapters can be seen working. The reader is offered an opportunity to consider if and how these may be made to be more effective organisations. They are also offered an opportunity to research and explore in more detail and depth their structure and the potential for future development. An additional exercise, concerned with the value chain that operates within European broadcasting, is included.

It is recommended that in order to obtain the full benefit from Chapter 18's case studies the reader first identifies the industry value chain and its component organisations and then moves on to analyse the company value chain. Topics that should be explored include:

Industry value chain analysis:

- Market characteristics
- Customer expectations
- Capabilities
- Processes and activities   Current and
- Added value profile(s)   future trends
- Profit pools
- Competitive value chain structures

312

Company value chain analysis:

- Current market participation
- Current customers
- Current capabilities
- Supplier processes and activities
- Customer processes and activities
- Competitive advantage(s)
  - customer monopolies
  - capabilities
  - processes and activities

that may or may not be transferrable other parts of the value chain

Current and future trends

Beyond these cases the reader is also encouraged to apply the 'audit model' included in Chapter 18 to other organisations.

chapter

16

Configuring the Value Chain: 1

LEARNING OUTCOMES

The student will be able to:

- comment critically on the future directions of operations management and strategic operations management;
- understand the importance of integrating and coordinating knowledge, technology and relationship management for effective value chain development and management;
- develop an appropriate performance planning and control model for application to value chain decision making.

INTRODUCTION: CONCEPTS AND ISSUES FOR THE FUTURE

The evolution of the value chain

Previous chapters have introduced new concepts and have identified a number of issues. The emergence of new business models (or new anything for that matter) will bring controversy concerning scope and territories.

It is clear from the literature that while operations management academics and practitioners argue that operations management has a strategic role in the organisation, the reality is that at present it does not.

It is arguable that 'operations' have never fulfilled a strategic role in any organisations other than in a few exceptions. Hayes *et al* (1998) argue the need for operations to be taking a leading role in competitive strategy development rather than assuming the role of an implementer of strategy. The authors identify small companies that '. . . although lacking the advantages of size, experience, established position, and proprietary technology – take on big companies and in a relatively short time push their way to industry dominance'. They argue that '. . . the key to success is often an operations based

314

advantage'. This advantage is capability related and based upon the organisation's management and staff and its operating processes.

Examples given by the authors illustrate the use of specific capabilities (not necessarily internally owned) to develop competitive advantage. Hayes *et al* refer to the importance of 'positioning' (a marketing concept) in developing operations based advantage. Having established positioning as a decision concerning marketplace differentiation they contend: '. . . having decided what kind of superiority it wants to achieve, the company must configure and manage its operations organisation in such a way that it can provide that form of advantage most effectively'.

Hill (2000) suggests two components to operations strategy: operational and strategic dimensions. The *operational role* is concerned with efficiency, managing and controlling the '. . . wide-ranging tasks involved in making products and providing services and to do this efficiently'. The *strategic role* is to '. . . contribute to the debate about and agreement on the markets in which to compete in terms of retaining customers, growing market share and entering new markets. Operations then needs to develop and invest in the processes and infrastructure to provide these competitive dimensions for which it is responsible – for example, price and delivery speed. In this way operational capabilities are guided by strategic requirements . . .'.

Hill is suggesting that strategy is about effectiveness and doing the right things, while operations is about efficiency, doing the right things right. However, there is an issue concerning the extent of the involvement of operations management in prescribing strategic direction. Increasingly this becomes an important issue as alliances and partnerships are extended. The importance of 'distributed operations' (and therefore assets), the notion that core processes may be inter-organisational rather than intra-organisational, and the increasing frequency of the inclusion of customers in the design, development and production of products, suggest the need to expand the concept and the role of operations management into a planning and coordinating role.

Pilkington (1998) argues that while operations management in the UK automotive industry has applied 'Japanisation' and 'best practice' they appear to have failed in developing strategic competencies and aligning manufacturing with corporate strategy. Pilkington is suggesting that manufacturing managers should consider each of the techniques within the context of their firm's overall corporate strategy. He also argues that Japanisation has resulted in a shift of inventory from manufacturing towards the sales networks: 'The firms that have been the most successful in reducing manufacturing stocks have experienced the largest increase in finished product stocks'. And: '. . . [this] alignment of manufacturing with the rest of corporate strategy has been ignored in many firms pursuing best practices – where, for example, the manufacturing manager has been rewarded for reducing costs when the rest of the organisation has been trying to compete on product differentiation'.

Pilkington concludes that as the strategy literature suggests: '. . . competitive success comes from a strategy that challenges norms and aligns all the business units into a common purpose'.

Organisational considerations in an approach to 'value led' management: the virtual enterprise forces a review of strategy and structure

Organisation structures are undergoing change alongside the changes in managerial philosophy. Figure 16.1 illustrates this change. Any strategy requires an organisation structure within which strategy may be evolved, evaluated and decided upon. It also requires an efficient implementation facility. Figure 16.1 is suggesting fundamental changes. An effective value strategy requires the emphasis on cost reduction and administrative efficiency to be replaced by one which focusses on value creation for customers using innovation in the design, production, marketing, delivery and servicing components of value. Organisation strategy should emphasise empowerment of employees in order to meet customer expectations for product relevance and service. This differs markedly from the production focus all too frequently seen within many organisations. Operations strategy should become proactive rather than be reactive. In many respects we have the growth of supply chain management and operations management techniques sharing the responsibility for this. Just-in-time, quick response, materials requirement planning, and so on are essentially cost reduction activities applied to processes which may be more effective if customer satisfaction maximisation were the primary objective. This is the role of strategic operations management.

The issue for operations managers is to confront the fact that increasingly the question they should be asking themselves is not where the manufactur-

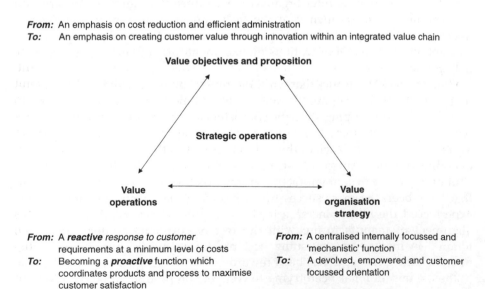

From: An emphasis on cost reduction and efficient administration
To: An emphasis on creating customer value through innovation within an integrated value chain

Value objectives and proposition

Strategic operations

Value operations

Value organisation strategy

From: A *reactive* response to customer requirements at a minimum level of costs
To: Becoming a *proactive* function which coordinates products and process to maximise customer satisfaction

From: A centralised internally focussed and 'mechanistic' function
To: A devolved, empowered and customer focussed orientation

Figure 16.1 An approach to 'value led' management

ing facility should be located and how large it should be, but whether a manufacturing facility is needed at all! The success of a wide range of business organisations (some presented in previous chapters) suggests that for some this question has been dealt with. The answer is no, if expertise and capacity already exists and if a lasting, working relationship can be worked out.

Doz and Hamel (1998) suggest that this is a possibility for an increasing number of organisations. The authors suggest three 'basic logics' of value creation:

- gaining competitive strength through co-option;
- leveraging cospecialised resources;
- gaining competence through internalised learning.

Co-option turns potential competitors into allies and suppliers. Both competitors and 'complementers' need to be co-opted into coalitions. *Cospecialisation* is the synergistic value creation that results from combining separate resources, positions, skills and knowledge sources. 'Partners' contribute unique and differentiated resources – tangible and intangible – to the success of an alliance. They became substantially more valuable when bundled together. Cospecialisation becomes increasingly important and a central feature of a partnership as companies refocus on a narrower range of capabilities (core skills and activities) as opportunities become systems and solutions rather than discrete products. Individual companies become less likely to own all the necessary resources. *Learning and internalisation* are an avenue for learning and assimilating new skills that are tacit, collective and embedded. Often they are learned and transferred beyond the boundaries of the alliance into other activities and businesses.

Doz and Hamel stress the differences between joint ventures and strategic alliances and these have implications for strategic operations management. Strategic alliances form part of a central strategy of an organisation, joint ventures are rarely used to pursue new opportunities, rather they are used to develop economies of scale. Joint ventures are typically bilateral whereas alliances increasingly involve multiple partners that are '. . . forged to develop complex systems and solutions calling for resources from a number of partners rather than coproduce single products'.

To Doz and Hamel's co-option, cospecialisation and learning and internalisation must be added coproductivity, codestiny and prosumerism, concepts identified earlier. It is argued that by doing so the strategic alliance becomes the value chain element of strategic operations management. *Coproductivity*, it will be recalled, is the concept by which the production process is distributed within the value chain and is conducted by members with specific skills (such as initial component manufacture) followed by assembly later in the process chain because of cost advantages that can be realised. *Codestiny* adds an 'adhesive' by ensuring shared values and strategies motivate value chain membership. *Prosumerism* is increasingly important. The involvement of the end user in the design and development process is another feature that differentiates the value chain from both strategic alliances and joint ventures.

The customer becomes involved in design and development as well as production

'Co-opting customer competence' is seen as an interesting challenge of the new economy. Prahalad and Ramaswamy (2000) suggest: 'Customers are stepping out of their traditional roles to become cocreators as well as consumers of value'. The authors identify changes that are occurring.

Customers, once seen as passive buyers with a predetermined role of consumption, are now part of the value production process. 'They are collaborators, co-developers and competitors'. Until recently 'management' regarded the customer as 'an average statistic' that over time became 'a person'. The authors suggest the current view of the customer to be: '... not only an individual but also part of an emergent social and cultural fabric'. Traditional market research that was used to create products without much feedback has been replaced by codevelopment and creation by customers. The traditional one way communication model with customers has given way to an active dialogue in which customers shape expectations and the eventual products.

The customer's involvement in the production process was discussed at length in the IKEA case study in Chapter 14. Prahalad and Ramaswamy take customer involvement a little further by discussing this in the context of customer competencies. They argue: 'Customers are fundamentally changing the dynamics of the marketplace. The market has become a forum in which consumers play an active role in creating and competing for value. The distinguishing feature of this new marketplace is that consumers become a new source of competence for the corporation ... [what they] bring is a function of the knowledge and skills they possess, their willingness to learn and experiment, and their ability to engage in active dialogue'.

REVISITING VALUE POSITIONING AND COMPETITIVE ADVANTAGE STRATEGY

Knowledge management, intellectual property and the learning organisation

It was argued earlier that knowledge management is 'the organisational capability that identifies, locates (creates or acquires), transfers (disseminates or shares) and converts knowledge into competitive advantage'. The current issue of concern is more about applying knowledge management – the development of a knowledge management strategy. Blumentritt and Johnston (1999) identify an important issue for value chain management, suggesting that '... the ability to identify, locate and deliver information and knowledge to a point of valuable application is transforming existing industries and facilitating the emergence of entirely new industries'. Furthermore they suggest that while knowledge is recognised as a key to competitive advantage and is indeed an asset, there are challenges awaiting managers when attempting to 'manage' this intangible asset. The authors debate the difference between knowledge and information, making the significant point that information cannot be substituted for knowledge and to attempt to do so typically results in disaster. However, the transmission of knowledge requires that it be 'translated' into information. The success (or otherwise) of the transfer leads to a retranslation into knowledge.

The authors introduce a knowledge-information cycle to reflect the relationship between knowledge and information. The knowledge side of the cycle has two basic steps: knowledge creation and knowledge use. They argue that knowledge creation involves the interplay of information with an intelligent system.

Of more interest to value chain management is a model representing an organisation's knowledge and information assets. Organisations possess both assets, with the mixture determined by the extent to which activities may be largely routine or innovative, which will require the support of a knowledge capability.

Figure 16.2 develops this model. The arrows that run in counter direction at the top and bottom of the model signify the knowledge/information combination necessary for a specific task. The authors suggest that for innovative

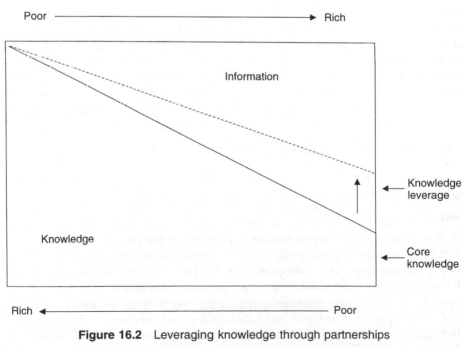

Figure 16.2 Leveraging knowledge through partnerships

Source: Based upon Blumentritt and Johnston (1999)

tasks a larger amount of 'core knowledge' will be required than for routine tasks. The authors make the distinction between mature manufacturing industries (requiring small amounts of core knowledge due to standardised processes) and service industries (requiring larger amounts of core knowledge) reflecting the knowledge needs in creative service companies such as advertising agencies.

A modification to the model (shown as knowledge leverage) illustrates how the knowledge base can be increased within a value chain partnership. A manufacturing organisation seeking to enter new markets would not have the necessary design and development knowledge to enter an innovation led market. A partnership with a design and development company (cospecialisation) would provide the additional core knowledge.

Technology management

Zineldin (1997), considering the impact of environmental forces on business organisation, comments that 'Science is the accumulation of knowledge about human beings and the environment. Technology is the application of such knowledge to practical purposes'. This is in the context of rapidly changing developments that have expanded the availability of products and delivery systems to both consumer and organisational end users.

Zineldin identifies the risk and uncertainty that accompany rapidly advancing technology in terms of the '. . . profitable life of present and future fixed investments, products, production processes and employee skills'. He argues that failure to adapt to change can result in intensive competition from companies that have switched their strategies to more technologically advanced products and services. Companies that do not adapt to technology change clearly face difficulties. Change may not necessarily require reinvestment but rather a change in philosophy. This may involve a new perspective towards technology management: '. . . creating networks, alliances and relationships with other high-tech companies provides the means to create [a] competitive advantage'. Zineldin provides an example of a network of Hughes Aircraft, Electronic Data Systems and General Motors that resulted in a design for General Motors' 21st century production lines.

The management of technology within an organisation has been considered by Irani and Love (2001). They suggest: 'Technology management should be seen as a business process that facilitates the development of a comprehensive and robust technocentric infrastructure, consequently enhancing the delivery of accurate, timely and appropriate services within an organisation, which in turn increases the economic viability of the business'. They refer to a 'technology management gap' that may result in a competitive advantage being jeopardised. The inference they make concerns the efficacy of the evaluation processes used. However, another conclusion may be that the evaluation was made without considering the technology interface issues between suppliers (upstream) and distributors and end users (downstream).

Chanaron and Jolly (1999) advocate that '. . . the management of technology would benefit from a stronger influence of management disciplines such as accounting and control, finance, marketing, human resource management, organisational behaviour . . .'. By adopting such a view: 'Technology becomes more than an idiosyncratic set of resources: it is the common thread of an integrated management perspective'. The authors describe a transitional process based upon an expansion of the discipline from an R and D focus, to the management of technology and eventually to technological management. They argue: 'Technology management's *raison d'être* is using technology to leverage all functions within the company. It perceives technology as an impacting variable and a major resource for all management functions as a producer, a customer or a user . . . it assumes that any management function should take technology as an input shaping both its strategic vision and its operational procedures and methods'. Among their conclusions three are of particular relevance. They suggest technological management should aim at 'capturing and mastering the shaping effects of technological variables on businesses'. And: 'It deals with stakeholders who so far have not employed and are even scared of technological variables, such as accountants and finance experts' (clearly others may be added). A third conclusion suggests that technological management is not only applicable to 'high-tech' businesses, but may have significant impact on 'low-tech' businesses.

The thrust of Chanaron and Jolly's contribution can be extended. They suggest technological management is 'to understand and control the impact of technology on all management functions'. This currently includes all management processes within and across organisations.

Morita (1992) identified the potential of technology transfer (outbound and inbound): 'Borrowing or importing technology, then creating new and better products based on that technology, is Japan's strongest competitive advantage'. It follows that the *integration* of process and product technology within a value chain to address the planning, development and implementation of technological capabilities and capacities can have a major impact on customer satisfaction *and* competitive advantage for the value chain partnership.

Thus the view of Badaway (1998) interpreted broadly, positions the emerging view of technology management: 'The management of technology is the practice of integrating technology strategy with business strategy . . . such integration requires the deliberate coordination of R and D, manufacturing and other service functions'. It is assumed that 'business strategy' includes the relationships an organisation creates with its business partners.

Relationship management

Relationship management is essentially the effective and efficient coordination of the different internal and external parts of a business. Zineldin (*op cit*) cites a quotation from Mikhail Gorbachev: 'Life is making us abandon established stereotypes and outdated views. It is making us discard illusions. The very concept of the nature and criteria of progress is changing. It would be naïve to think that the problems plaguing mankind today can be solved with means and methods which were applied or seemed to work in the past. Today we face a different world for which we must seek a different road to the future'. And look what that comment prefaced!

Zineldin pursues this theme within a business context by identifying recent changes in the business environment (such as globalisation, liberalisation, innovation, market structures, deregulation, resources conservation and competition) each of which have an impact on strategic management decision making. It follows, he argues, that establishing relationships with customers is not the only issue but that relationships within and among organisations based upon a holistic approach become essential.

Jarillo (1993) remarks: 'It is not surprising then that the last few years have seen a plethora of articles and books on topics such as networking, value-added relationships, de-layering, modularisation, the need for companies to nurture long-term relationships in all spheres. All these works point in one direction: companies must look at their boundaries with new eyes – things that have traditionally been "inside" should perhaps be outside, and outsiders might perhaps deserve the treatment of "insiders"'. The current business environment is arguably changing such that an organisation can only grow effectively by developing strategic networks with its suppliers, distributors and customers.

Zineldin argues that a *total relationship approach* requires both *strategy* and *philosophy*. Philosophy is necessary because it can be used to *communicate* the idea that a major goal of management is to plan and build appropriate close and flexible long term relationships with partners who contribute to the organisation's long term success and growth. It guides overall thinking and decision making in the organisation as well as in the execution of decisions. A strategy is required because it *emphasises* maintaining product and service quality of internal and external relationships in order to maintain long term stakeholder relationships.

Håkansson and Sinhehota (1995) agree with Zineldin in a view suggesting that long term and close relationships may not be an appropriate strategy for all organisations. They argue that while there may be benefits, equally there may be severe limitations and burdens. Effective, and therefore strategic, relationship management requires management to get beyond the more descriptive and theoretical level and to develop an understanding of how the different parts of a whole business and its partnerships can be coordinated in a holistic way '. . . that is simultaneously efficient, flexible and conducive to innovation and creativity . . . It is about learning, adopting a new style of thinking, perceiving, showing concern and responding' (Zineldin: *op cit*).

EXPLORING THE INTERFACES

Interface 1: Knowledge management / technology management

An important aspect of the knowledge management/technology management interface concerns the communication role played by information technology. 'Corporate knowledge' is often 'forgotten' unless IT based storage and access systems are designed to prevent this happening. Silver (2000) comments on how Ford 'lost' the 'know how' of developing an international vehicle, and International Harvester 'lost' the knowledge developed when they built a truck assembly plant in Russia when asked to repeat the exercise some years later. Silver contends: 'Companies compete not only on the basis of product, service and operational superiority, but also through enhanced management of their corporate memory and intellectual assets. They are beginning to realise their edge lies in how they manage the efficient flow and transfer of knowledge across the organisation'. Silver is commenting on inter-organisational interface issues but the argument is valid in a value chain context. It is suggested that perhaps the inference implied by Silver is even more important.

Both within an organisation and within a network of collaborative organisations some essential roles exist. For example there need to be clearly stated definitions for both products and processes to enable the value chain to match relevant technology with process and product requirements. Information technology facilitates technological forecasting (and its interpretation) and from this develops response scenarios. The effective management of this interface provides variety/volume/cost forecasts for cost-efficient operations management. A major benefit is also the ability that it gives management to explore the costs/benefits of technology transfer and to leverage R and D expertise as well as partners' assets. Based upon Silver, it can be concluded that certain generic attributes must be present if a 'technology solution' is to be successful. It should be: easy to use, easy to integrate into existing applications, scaleable to the enterprise, easy to access, easy to customise, measurable and secure.

Interface 2: Technology management / relationship management

The technology management/relationship management interface is one in which trust has a major role. Companies entering partnerships for value production are only likely to obtain maximum value from the relationship if process technology and product input properties are shared *throughout* the value chain. The results will be an improvement in product/service value delivery and lower costs throughout the value chain. The coordination of economies of specialisation, scale and integration will ensure the efficiency of value added operations.

Intra-organisational relationships within processes may be improved by working with adjacent process managers within the value chain. The author's research identified a situation in which large productivity improvements were obtained following liaison visits between 'inbound' quality assurance and production control management of adjacent value chain partners. In another intra-organisational problem, distribution centre staff did not fully perceive their role in achieving customer satisfaction. They had not been encouraged to think of themselves as a vital value chain link between suppliers and end user customers. Their perceptions were that enhanced information systems undermined their previous involvement in providing service and their roles were subordinated to enhanced technology.

Interface 3: Knowledge management / relationship management

There are five important features of this interface. Again trust plays an important role as quite often issues of intellectual property assume significant importance. Effective 'learning' can only be achieved if joint learning processes are established and the costs and benefits of shared knowledge bases are identified. An increasing emphasis is being placed on developing operational networks for sourcing and procurement; however, there are problems occurring with legality and competitive fairness (in the USA) as they begin to take shape. If it is assumed that brands accumulate knowledge and that this represents intellectual property as well as customer loyalty there is a need for the responsibility and authority of brand ownership to be acknowledged within the value chain. Integrated (and therefore) shared knowledge will ensure effective management of 'time-to-market' and 'total-cost-of-relationships' throughout the value chain.

The results of a well managed interface will be manifested in such benefits as close and strategic collaboration between suppliers, distributors and customers concerning product development and design (and subsequent changes), production scheduling and management, and customer service. It is also likely that mutually agreed methods for determining costs, margins and return on value added will also result in their acceptance as performance goals for organisational units. Selling activities will be coordinated to help customers derive supply requirements and find optimal ways of meeting their specific requirements. The sales force becomes an essential component of the knowledge database by developing feedback linkages for desired operational and product/service delivery improvements *and* for product development and enhancement ideas.

INTRA- AND INTER-ORGANISATIONAL PROCESSES

A business process is '. . . a set of logically related tasks performed to achieve a defined business outcome' (Davenport and Short: 1990). These authors suggest that a set of processes forms a business system – or a value chain. They also suggest processes have two important characteristics. Processes have defined business outcomes for which there are recipients that may be either internal or external to the organisation. They also cross organisational boundaries; that is, they normally occur across or between organisational (either intra- or inter-) boundaries and are independent of formal organisational structures.

Inter-organisational processes take place between two or more business organisations. The authors comment that: 'Increasingly, companies are concerned with co-ordinated activities that extend into the next (or previous) company along the value added chain'. Davenport and Short explore the role of IT in process redesign, accordingly their examples emphasise this application. One example they use is that of Du Pont's concept of 'effectiveness-in-use' as the major criterion of customer satisfaction and suggest it to be '. . . one leading approach to measuring the effectiveness of inter-organisational processes'. Du Pont goes beyond selling a product to its customers; it links its internal processes for creating value in a product to its customers' processes for using the product. EDI delivered material safety data sheets with the chemicals the company sells, to ensure safe use.

Intra-organisational processes exist within organisations crossing functional or divisional boundaries. These processes achieve important operational objectives, such as new product development, asset management or production scheduling. It is interesting to note that since this contribution first appeared (1990) these intra-organisational processes have, for many organisations, become inter-organisational processes. Furthermore they are becoming commonplace, due primarily to the acceptance of partnership relationships and the increasing role of information sciences and technology as facilitating agents.

Thinking of the business as a number of integrated core processes enables management to focus on streamlining the processes and identifying inter-organisational linkages which result in creating more value for less effort. This is very different to current activities aimed at reducing functions simply to reduce costs, often with no tangible impact on value outputs. Beech (1998) comments: 'It is the linking between enterprises that can lead to the ultimate goal of moving beyond supply chain efficiency to integrating supply with demand. The performance outcome is synchronisation'.

A broader perspective of process management

A similar approach is taken by Srivastava *et al* (1999) by considering marketing, business processes and shareholder value. They are arguing from a marketing perspective, taking a 'macro level' approach and exploring the issues from a customer value creation focus. They contend that customer value creation '. . . necessitated the accomplishment of three central organisation tasks', these being:

- the development of new customer solutions together with the revision of existing solutions;
- continued review and enhancement of inputs and transformation processes;
- the creation and leveraging of linkages and relationships to external marketplace entities, particularly channels and end users.

If these tasks are to be achieved, three core processes are required: a product development management process, a supply chain management process and a customer relationship management process. The authors identify a number of sub-processes for each core process. Srivastava *et al* are concerned with the integration of marketing with business processes and shareholder value. However, they have identified five 'macro environmental and competitive factors' that have implications for the entire organisation. These are as follows.

- A customer function or application focus is replacing the traditional product focus.
- Customisation or at least mass customisation is the dominant feature of differentiation.
- Customer relationship longevity is more important than single transactions.
- Co-ompetition and codestiny are replacing traditional competition. Networked rivalry is increasing and competition is increasingly between value chains.
- Economies of scope are being added to economies of scale. So too are economies of integration as increasingly networks are using 'distributed operations'.

The authors offer a proposed taxonomy of business processes based upon their three core processes. They argue (in the context of a product development management process – but it is an argument that may be used to address each of their proposed processes), that 'often, physical products are only a part, sometimes only a small part, of the overall solution. Rather than largely unrelated relationships with disparate internal and external entities, the organisation develops and leads some networks and participates in others with the intent of spawning, nurturing and devising solutions that otherwise would not be possible'.

An interesting and very valuable contribution considers the impact of their model on shareholder value. They discard currently favoured measures and state preference for economic cash flow, and develop impact scenarios for each of the business processes that are cash flow based. These are accelerating cash flows, enhancing cash flows and reducing risk (seen as the vulnerability and volatility of cash flows). While these measures meet the requirements of the financial analyst they only indirectly address the primary concerns of CEOs which include cash flow but add profitability, productivity and, in the current business climate (as at mid 2001), share price enhancement.

PERFORMANCE PLANNING AND MEASUREMENT IN THE VALUE CHAIN

Adoption of the value chain as a means of evaluating, planning and coordinating strategic operations options requires a hybrid performance measurement model. Chapter 8 discussed a number of performance measures lending themselves to this task. Kay's approach to added value was found helpful, as was the balanced scorecard. Both are useful planning models and the 'scorecard' can be helpful in asking 'what if?' questions. Kay's measure of competitive advantage is another helpful 'what if?' approach.

However, as commented earlier, a CEO's responsibility to the shareholder is often seen as the primary measure of corporate success. The growth of both share price and dividends together with strong positive economic cash flow are seen as shareholder value measures. However, among these it is usually the share price that has priority. Given that the value chain is made up of a collection of organisations involved in a partnership because they assume that their organisation's performance can only improve and be comparably greater, share price remains important. It follows that improved individual organisational performance is the primary motive for involvement and further that, rather than one performance measure, it is a number of measures that we should be seeking to establish.

Enterprise value: a strategic planning model

Slywotzky's (1996) value migration model and the enterprise value model of Knight and Pretty (2000) are relevant approaches to value chain performance planning and measurement.

Value migration occurs as both economic and shareholder value flows away from obsolescent (and obsolete) business models. Slywotzky (1996) argues that new models offer the same benefits to customers but at lower cost by changing the model structure. This change often results in a restructuring of profit sharing throughout the business model. Uren (2001) quotes Schremp (CEO, Daimler Chrysler) who expresses the view: '... within 10 years the price of a car will represent only a quarter of the total value provided to a customer with the balance consumed in maintenance, finance and other services'.

Uren also identifies differences between Qantas and Ansett, suggesting that Qantas with its international networks and travel agency links, together with an investment in services is building a strong advantage. Similarly in the B_2B sector Amcor and Visy (both in packaging) are using IT based e-commerce systems to increase customer service. In each of these examples, four basic issues emerge. First the 'value' of the brand is enhanced by service extensions or additions to the basic product. Second is the increased importance of intangible assets and the shift in investment patterns. Third is the importance of partnerships/alliances in the containment of fixed asset investment and, therefore, increased utilisation, albeit the assets are shared. And fourth is the acknowledgement that business organisation or 'models' have changed. Virtual enterprises have expanded and the principle of outsourcing has expanded such that the maxim of: 'why own it when you can rent it?' has resulted in many businesses opting for a new model.

The basis for adopting the alternative (or new) model is based upon a simple thesis. Some competencies or capabilities are 'distinctive' and as such offer possibilities of sustainable competitive advantage; others, the 'reproducible' competencies/capabilities, offer no such benefits and in fact are readily available in supply markets. Uren's observations suggest that typically distinctive competencies/capabilities are 'intangibles' and substantiate the inference to be drawn from findings from the Brookings Institution that in the US fixed asset ownership of large manufacturing and mining companies is decreasing. Fixed tangible assets fell as a proportion of total assets from 67 per cent in 1982 to 38 per cent by 1992. By 2000 the figure was reported to be less than 30 per cent.

A question arising from this research concerns the reasons for this continuous trend. Two possibilities appear likely. One is that businesses are investing less in fixed tangible assets because they are increasingly benefiting from the 'asset leverage' resulting from partnership arrangements. The other is that more investment is occurring in brands, research and development, knowledge based intellectual property, patents and franchise building. Clearly we need to know if overall total assets are increasing or whether there is a shift in investment. Perhaps both are occurring. The important point would appear to be the strategic implications of such decisions.

Investment by 'high-tech' companies in fixed assets may not be the wisest of opportunities. Technology life cycles are shortening making profit *and* capital recovery difficult. The investment in intangible assets such as R and D strengthens the organisation as does the investment in brands and corporate reputation. Clearly both are important but both have risk issues to be concerned about. The risk with R and D investment concerns time-to-market and eventual success. The risk with building strong brands and a reputation is more difficult to deal with as many of the activities may not be within the direct control of the brand owner. Problems can occur, and are occurring, for many of the international brand owners as their partners come under question concerning ethics and conformity to social responsibility issues.

In a discussion on 'the philosophies of risk, shareholder value and the CEO', Knight and Pretty (2000) offer an interesting model of the business. Their interests were more in the company's valuation than its structure but it is a relevant and valuable contribution to this discussion. Knight and Pretty's contribution represents the view of the business structure adopted by many of the leading multinational companies:

> 'The core value of a quoted company has three components: *tangible value, premium value*, and *latent value*. Tangible value reflects the bedrock of the real and tangible assets which will sustain the company's value in times of crisis. It is usually measured as book value . . . Premium value represents the value in excess of book value at which the company trades in the open market. This element is the source of a company's competitive advantage . . . Latent value represents the potential value within a company. Sources of hidden value might include operating efficiencies yet to be realised . . .'

The authors argue that tangible value has been downgraded as the market valuation of Internet based companies: '. . . with a little or no book value but promises of great wealth outshone their traditional competitors'. The events since June 2000 suggest this not to be the case but it is interesting to note that the emphasis on intangible assets persists and is a major contribution to the growth of virtual enterprises.

The *enterprise value model* described by the authors has a simple structure:

$$
\begin{aligned}
\text{Enterprise value} &= f \left[\begin{matrix} \text{NPV of} \\ \text{returns on} \\ \text{fixed and} \\ \text{working} \\ \text{capital} \end{matrix} + \begin{matrix} \text{NPV of} \\ \text{returns on} \\ \text{growth} \\ \text{opportunities} \end{matrix} + \begin{matrix} \text{NPV of} \\ \text{returns on} \\ \text{latent} \\ \text{value} \end{matrix} \right]
\end{aligned}
$$

Market value =   based upon generating . . .

$$
\left[\begin{matrix} \text{Tangible} \\ \text{value} \end{matrix} \right] + \left[\begin{matrix} \text{Premium} \\ \text{value} \end{matrix} \right] + \left[\begin{matrix} \text{Latent} \\ \text{value} \end{matrix} \right]
$$

from . . .

$$
\left[\begin{matrix} \text{Tangible} \\ \text{assets} \end{matrix} \right] + \left[\begin{matrix} \text{Intangible} \\ \text{assets} \end{matrix} \right] + \left[\begin{matrix} \text{Efficiency} \\ \text{improvements} \end{matrix} \right]
$$

where *market value* is derived by multiplying share price by the number of shares outstanding and adding long term debt.

Knight and Pretty discuss enterprise value from a risk management perspective. They argue that it is the role of the chief executive to identify the risk confronting the organisation and to '. . . first to develop a clear philosophy of risk and then to formulate clear corporate policies to guide the management of risk'. Their thesis is that it is the role of the chief executive to identify and realise sources of value and the risk each presents to the organisation; by doing so an *optimal* growth strategy will be evolved in which returns will be achieved at acceptable levels of risk.

An important observation made by Uren (earlier) is based on a comment originating from McKinsey and Co. They suggest there have always been markets in which a small difference in performance makes a huge difference in rewards. Uren comments to the effect that this offers a large opportunity to the business than can identify the important *customer value drivers* and match them with cost-effective delivery strategies. Given the evidence that partnerships and outsourcing are favoured methods of either reinforcing or adding service based differentiation, value chain analysis becomes increasingly important, as does a model for measuring the value of the inter-organisational enterprise.

The Knight and Pretty model addresses both of these issues. Clearly no approach to valuing the enterprise (albeit one single organisation or the partnership based inter-organisational value chain structures that are becoming commonplace) can avoid the issues of quantifying the components.

Managing the growth of enterprise value

The enterprise value model has obvious attraction. It offers not only the facility to consider the enterprise as a number of individual (but related) components but also the facility to explore strategic growth alternatives. Figure 16.3 identifies the three components and the methods for quantifying the value for each.

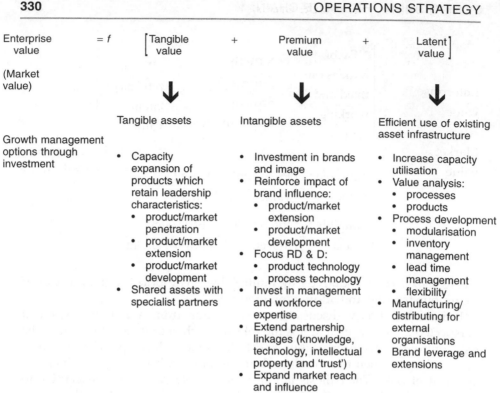

Figure 16.3 Managing the growth of enterprise value

The investment market view, suggested by Rappaport (1983), Reimann (1988), and Copeland *et al* (1994), considers that a business is worth (the enterprise value), the net present value of its future cash flows discounted at an appropriate cost of capital. This approach avoids the inadequacies of traditional financial measurements and recognises the time preference for money and the risk of an investment. This is suggested by Knight and Pretty as a means of measuring tangible value where future cash flows are discounted at a relevant cost of capital. No proposals were made for either premium or latent value. Given the Brookings Institution findings, this is an important consideration, one requiring attention due to either the increasing leverage of partners' fixed assets (the Dell approach) or the increasing importance of intangible assets (such as brand values and innovative RD and D) or clearly the two together.

It follows that given three growth options the innovative organisation will identify an option (or perhaps a combination of options) that offers the highest NPV. Further, the options may require searching for suitable partners to contribute to the required competencies/capabilities. The major benefit of the model is that it encourages the search for strategic alternatives that may create significantly larger opportunities for competitive advantage.

In Figure 16.3 a number of growth options have been identified. The list is not exclusive but is suggested as typical. Options for the growth of tangible value include the expansion of the capacity in products for which leadership can be established or reinforced. The familiar Ansoff product-market strategy options are suggested as a basis for the search for responses to customer value drivers.

The increased efficiency of existing assets also offers growth options. Typically these are low risk and low return options but do offer short term alternatives. Each option can be categorised as a component of a consolidation and productivity strategy which should be ongoing in any organisation. An inter-organisational approach could well result in improved performance within a value chain structure.

Possibly the largest choice of options are those offered by intangible assets for premium growth. Each is based upon an application of knowledge, technology or relationship management, either exclusively or more likely as a combination of two out of three or even all three. Premium value growth is likely to offer the highest return and the highest risk. It is likely to offer high returns because the nature of the resulting competitive advantage will be distinctive and therefore either unique or exclusive to the organisation. However, the risk is high because any action that undermines the factor will impact only on the one organisation. For the value chain the risk and return will be greater; competitive advantage will benefit from synergy effects but failure will impact on all partners.

The examples introduced earlier may help. Strong branding has enabled a number of companies such as Coca-Cola, American Express, Nike (to name just a few) to build international recognition for their products. The benefits are very obvious in facilitating product-market or perhaps more accurately market-product extension and development. Indeed it is often the strength of the brand that has facilitated the development of other *intangible assets*. Certainly strong brands have a very large impact on expanding market reach and influence and will also reinforce customer and supplier loyalty. Shareholders and investors generally have also been impressed and supportive. However, the recent (early 2001) problems experienced by Nike, The Gap and others concerning outsourced manufacturing in the Far East are gathering momentum. Responses have been manifested at a number of 'corporate/consumer' levels, with resistance at the point of sale and by 'ethical investors'.

Growth through *tangible assets* and from the efficient use of the *existing asset infrastructure* has become a less important feature of the equation. The growth of tangible assets has, for most companies, been limited to processes that can be protected and which offer sustainable competitive advantage. The development of partnerships that offer outsourcing facilities for the necessary aspects of business (such as cost and quality efficient mass production) have relieved the large organisations of investment in tangible assets and has enabled them to focus investment on intangible assets offering premium growth.

Kay's measure of competitive advantage, Slywotzky and value migration

Kay (1993) argued: 'Corporate success derives from a competitive advantage which is most often derived from the unique character of a firm's relationships with its suppliers, customers or employees and which is precisely identified and applied to relevant markets'. In the context of a value chain the relationships are between partners comprising all aspects of value creation. One measure of success of the value chain, therefore, is the maximisation of the ratio of added value; the difference between the aggregate added value of the value chain and its aggregate inputs. See Figure 16.4. This approach enables alternative value chain formats to be considered and shares the notion of value migration with Slywotzky (1996). Value migration, it will be recalled, is the shift of business designs away from outmoded designs toward others that are better designed to maximise utility (value) for customers and profit for the company. Slywotzky contends that business designs (similar to products) also have cycles and reach economic obsolescence. Customer expectations have a tendency to change over time but business model designs tend to stay fixed. By combining both, alternative added value structures may be evaluated.

Slywotzky measures the value migration process by using market value relative to the size of the company; size is measured as revenue. Thus we have:

$$\text{Power of business design} = \frac{\text{Market value}}{\text{Revenue}}$$

Where market value is defined as the capitalisation of a company (shares outstanding multiplied by current share price plus long term debt).

Gadiesh and Gilbert and profit pools

It will be recalled that Gadiesh and Gilbert (1998) argued that 'Successful companies understand that profit share is more important than market share', suggesting that by identifying the profit pools within the value creation system the company would understand the 'actors and processes' involved. Their argument continued by suggesting that profit pools differ within segments and by value chain and that profit pools shift as structural changes occur within both segments and/or value chains. They also argued that many companies '. . . chart strategy without a full understanding of the sources and distribution of profits in their industry'. Plotting the revenue profits, cost and productivity profiles of alternative value chain formats enables the options to be identified in the knowledge of critical financial *and* structural criteria.

Measuring value chain performance: profitability, added value and market value as metrics

There are, clearly, conceptual differences between profitability and added value. Kay argues that '. . . the added value statement focuses on the

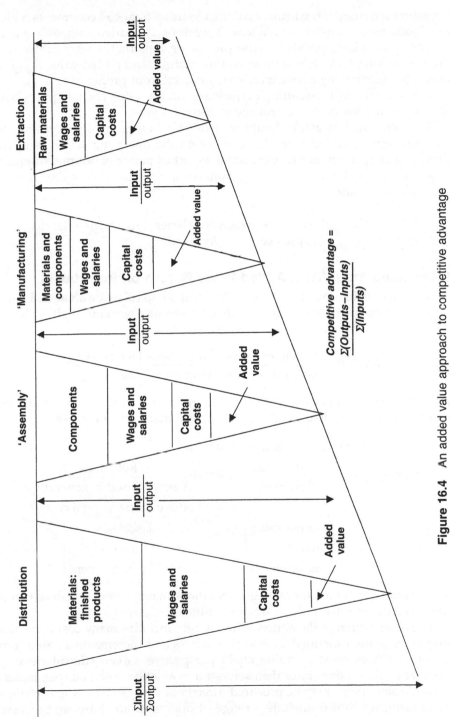

Figure 16.4 An added value approach to competitive advantage

operating activities of the firm, in contrast to usual financial statements which emphasise the returns to its investors'. Therefore: '. . . added value is less than operating margin or profits because profits are constructed after subtracting interest on long-term debt from operating margin, and added value is calculated after subtracting a return on equity capital from profits'.

This suggests that measuring performance in the value chain requires both an operational metric *and* a strategic measure.

An operational measure should consider Kay's argument concerning the measurement of added value (it focusses on the operating activities of the firm) and as such offers the operational aspect of performance measurement required in a value chain context. Following Kay an *added value 'margin'* measurement comprises:

Added value = Revenues − (wages + salaries + materials + services
'margin'   + capital costs) − Dividends

Calculating the AVROI: Added Value Return on Investment

As with the calculation of a return on investment, to calculate an added value return on investment the assets used (fixed assets and working capital) should be considered; therefore the measure becomes:

$$AVROI = \frac{Revenues - Operating\ costs - Dividends}{Assets\ utilised\ in\ generating\ added\ value}\%$$

As with the conventional ROI measure there are profitability or margin considerations as well as productivity or asset management issues:

$$AVROI = \frac{\begin{array}{c}Revenue - Operating\ costs\\ -Dividends\end{array}}{Revenues} \times \frac{Revenues}{\begin{array}{c}Assets\ utilised\ in\ generating\\ added\ value\ (capital\ costs)\end{array}}$$

$$\begin{bmatrix}Added\ value\\ 'margin'\\ management\end{bmatrix} \qquad \begin{bmatrix}Added\ value\\ 'asset\ base'\\ management\end{bmatrix}$$

The advantages offered for strategic operations management decisions can be identified by examining the component ratios.

The composition of the added value margin includes many cost items that may be critically examined against alternatives and therefore evaluated from an internal viewpoint or value chain perspective. Given current trends a number of alternatives offer themselves for evaluation. For example, materials and components may be procured directly or through a buying exchange; manufacturing choices include a range of options from complete processes through to modularisation and assembly. Numerous marketing and service options exist through partnership arrangements.

Similarly, asset base decision alternatives exist. The concepts of asset leverage and distributed manufacturing and distribution offer a wide range of options. An organisation should consider both market and financial objectives alongside the options of value chain structures versus a vertically integrated and owned structure. Issues such as risk, return and control are important considerations. This raises the issue of calculating *capital costs*. Calculating capital costs of the value chain presents difficulties. Clearly the aggregated value of depreciation is one approach but not the most realistic. Kay identifies four methods. The *cash flow basis* treats capital expenditure like any other expense item and is charged against revenues as it occurs. The *historic cost* basis uses the 'useful life' of the asset and depreciates the cost over an accepted period. However depreciation is based upon historic costs and these may bear very little relationship to the current value of assets. Inflation *may* have an impact; technology developments *will* have had an impact. The *current cost* basis is based upon the price of a 'modern' equivalent asset. Typically, IT assets may have lower replacement costs. Current *market value* as a method includes an opportunity cost to the shareholders' funds as well as a depreciation charge. The depreciation charge is based upon historic costs and changes to the market value that will vary year to year, depending upon the market's assessment of the organisation. Simplicity and accuracy are required and this suggests the cash flow method as most suitable for calculating value chain costs. This would comprise:

> Expenditure on fixed assets, *less* disposals
> Replacement expenditure
> Acquisition expenditure
> *plus/minus* changes in working capital

Kay does not include working capital in his appraisal of the alternatives, however given the purpose of the value chain (to develop a cost-effective network structure of 'providers') the alternatives may include significant inventory management, supply and customer account management differences. For this reason the inclusion of working capital may be important. The added value return on investment has profitability, productivity and efficiency implications. Essentially it is the outcome of a strategy decision and reflects the implementation of strategy decisions. Value chain partnership decisions therefore have strategy concerns.

Customer value: quantifying qualitative attributes

The primary objective of strategic operations management is to maximise customer value and, at the same time, ensure that value production partners meet their objectives.

Customer value is maximised by offering greater relative benefits than competitors *and* lower customer acquisition costs. The optimal position for the customer is that in which benefits or attributes, less acquisition costs, are at a maximum and meet with other objectives the customer may have. For example, in a B$_2$B situation there may be issues of social responsibility (local community employment) and environmental issues (pollutant free processes) that constrain the customer. In this context the customer will seek an optimal solution, one offering achievable profitability and maintaining a satisfactory position on its other objectives.

It is in these situations that value chain management offers opportunity. By identifying customer 'objective portfolios' an optimal solution may be reached at lower cost by dealing with the constraints. The value creation 'inhibitors' are converted into value creation 'facilitators'. A systems software company overcame this problem when it created a partnership with a firm offering workforce skills training. Prior to the partnership its service department was receiving costly requests for ongoing implementation and 'maintenance' visits. By considering the customer's acquisition costs and developing a skills package with the partner this particular aspect of customer cost was eliminated and overall value increased. It subsequently proved to be a major feature in the systems company's value proposition.

In another situation a value chain partnership was extended to deal with customers' increasing inventories of serviceable but 'unfashionable' consumer durable products. In order to maintain volume a multiple durables retailer had introduced a trade-in offer that proved to be very successful, such that inventories of used products expanded to embarrassingly high levels. A major supplier, in consideration for an exclusivity arrangement, began a 'recycling' program by identifying small independent refurbishing and resale retail companies who handled the trade-in products. Again the impact of decreased acquisition costs through a value chain innovation improved the 'value' received by all members.

Many customer benefits are difficult to quantify, particularly in B_2C markets. However for B_2B markets where benefits are clearly more tangible the value delivered to the customer can be expressed by the following relationship:

$$\text{Customer value} = \$ \text{ value of benefits } less \$ \text{ value of}$$
$$\text{customer acquisition costs}$$

VALUE CHAIN PLANNING AND CONTROL

The enterprise value model offers a long term planning and control facility, capable of considering both tangible and intangible options for growth. The added value return on investment model considers short term implementation. Both are combined as Figure 16.5.

The model addresses enterprise value decisions by focussing on *effectiveness* and the strategic aspects of profitability and productivity. Enterprise value focusses on both tangible and premium growth. By exploring opportunities for co-option and cospecialisation through value chain holistic networks, not only can tangible growth be increased and expanded into new ventures but asset leverage and distributed operations (manufacturing and logistics activities) can increase *productivity and* contain overall investment. Intangible growth is increased by focussing on brand values and intellectual property. The value chain approach can lower risk for brand leverage by

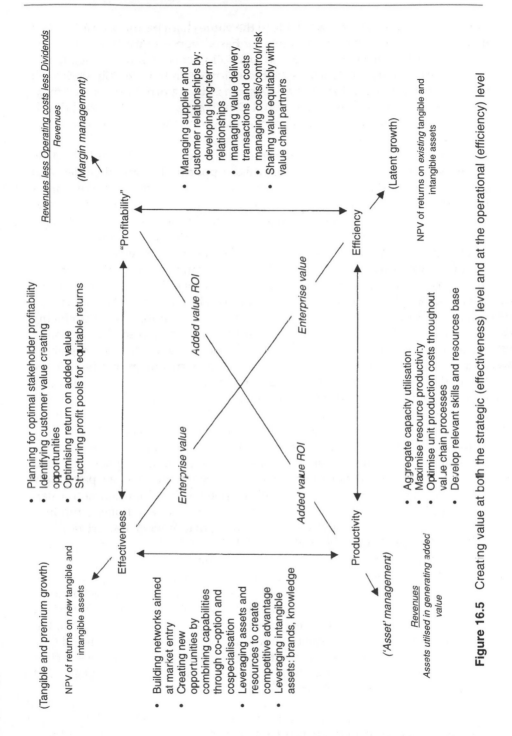

Figure 16.5 Creating value at both the strategic (effectiveness) level and at the operational (efficiency) level

evaluating fully the options available to the value chain partnership and using the most appropriate brand for a market based opportunity. In other words the value chain can deploy its brand portfolio across a range of segments, matching brand attributes with specific customer preferences. Similarly wih intellectual property and knowledge based assets. A portfolio approach maximises opportunities by directing R and D into *appropriate* design and development projects for which it has specific expertise and therefore lowers the risks involved.

The long term *profitability* concerns of the value chain are addressed by ensuring that both profit and added value opportunities are identified and explored and that current structures continue to offer optimal opportunities for profit and added value growth. By monitoring industry and market structures the value chain can identify changes in 'profit pools' and any shift in the roles and tasks of partners resulting in shifts of added value patterns.

The operational or *efficiency* decisions of the model are covered by the return on added value feature of the model. Given a strategic direction operating managers in the value chain are responsible for its efficient implementation. This task includes both the profitability and productivity aspects of efficiency.

The operational aspects of profitability are optimised by introducing customer relationship management techniques reinforced by customer account profitability programmes. Customer relationship management ensures that appropriate steps are taken so that customers receive service levels that are specific to their needs, while customer account profitability management ensures that this is done in a cost-efficient way. Figure 16.5 suggests a number of factors that are important such as liaison, relationship building over time and, in the case of VARs, sharing value equitably.

Relationships with suppliers are also important for margin management. While it may be assumed that materials and components suppliers are practising the supplier/customer techniques described in the previous paragraph, the efficient customer will have an opposite perspective. For example, an alert customer in a B_2B situation will evaluate the impact of a supplier's product, service and price in an objective way, ensuring that other characteristics such as control and risk are adequately covered.

The productivity aspects will require attention to both capacity and resource utilisation throughout the value chain to ensure that product and service value is delivered at affordable cost and maintained at a level of delivery consistent with customer expectations. Both profitability and productivity have a role to play in the expansion of enterprise value through their interplay in developing latent growth. Latent growth is essentially consolidation and productivity. It considers cost-efficiency techniques and decisions such as product range rationalisation, value engineering, and the outsourcing of low volume processes and products.

Exploring value chain structure options

The model described thus far may be supplemented by introducing concepts discussed earlier in Chapter 8. The balanced scorecard and strategy mapping (both Kaplan and Norton innovations) may be combined to produce an analytical planning model. Figure 16.6 combines both concepts to provide a 'what if?' option for strategic operations decisions. The model identifies customer and stakeholder value expectations. Stakeholder value comprises aggregate enterprise value and return on added value – both will be influenced by the performance of the profitability, productivity and cash flow generated by customer responses.

Customer responses are met by managing the value chain processes: design and development, procurement, production, marketing and service. Alternative configurations can be evaluated by looking at trade-off potential and using logistics as a base process. It will be recalled that the logistics process manages materials and information stocks and flows throughout the value chain, acting as a service process that measures the impact of changes in terms of costs and time dimensions.

Given both customer and stakeholder performance criteria, together with the optimal structure of the value chain processes, the capability and asset requirements can then be determined. The decisions required here concern which processes are core to the enterprise and therefore should become investment entities, and which are non-core and should be leased. A further decision concerning which tangible assets should be located where in order that the value chain processes will produce the desired results, and which intangible assets should be developed and by which partner.

Finally the learning and growth perspective components require to be developed and to receive appropriate investment. Decisions need to be made concerning key areas in each of the three components.

For example, *knowledge management* decisions concern the knowledge/ decision making infrastructure, the precise knowledge requirements, where 'stocks' of knowledge exist and to where they should 'flow', and ownership issues concerning intellectual property to be resolved.

Technology management requires a clear and shared understanding of the role of R and D and innovation within the value chain, and clearly defined responsibilities and 'ownership'. An issue that will require early resolution concerns the investment in both R and D and process technology. The implications of shortening technology life cycles, technology transfer and the economics of integration are other issues.

Relationship management decisions start with establishing the key characteristics of relationships in the value chain structure together with the expectations of the partners. The structure of the value flows (added value and profits) and the equity issues are major issues to be resolved as are leadership and coordination roles.

SUMMARY

This chapter has introduced some of the recent and more relevant contributions to value chain analysis and management. An ever-expanding literature based on knowledge management and intellectual property, technology

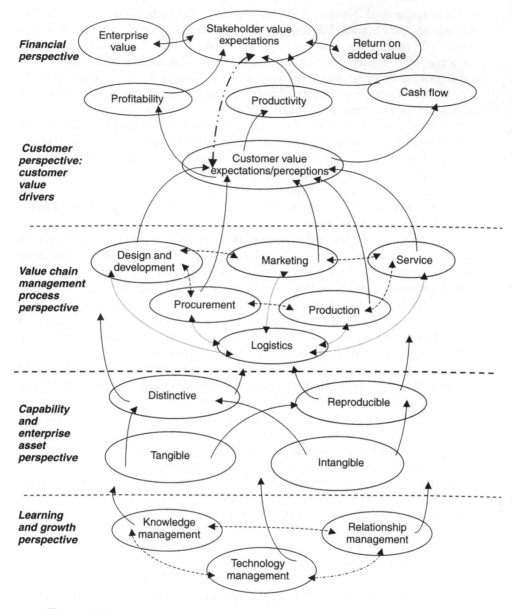

Figure 16.6   Using strategy mapping and the balanced scorecard to plan for customer and stakeholder value delivery

management and relationship management is beginning to offer a firm basis for this new business model.

The chapter has also served to bring together many of the performance and planning concepts discussed in earlier chapters. The result has been to develop a planning and control model for value chain management. By combining concepts of added value, value migration, enterprise value and the ever-useful Du Pont planning and control model, a model can be derived that helps the strategic planning and implementation tasks of the value chain, thereby ensuring effective strategies and efficient implementation.

Strategy mapping and the balanced scorecard add a dynamic element. Given quantitative data concerning customer and 'corporate' expectations the model can determine the roles, tasks and expected performance metrics of the value chain partners. Given these, alternative structures may be explored and evaluated to ensure an optimal performance outcome is achievable.

REFERENCES ●●●●●●●●●●●●●●●●●●●●●●●●●●●●●●●●●●●●

Badaway, M. K. (1998), 'Technology management education: alternative models', *California Management Review*, Summer.

Beech, J. (1998), 'The supply-demand nexus', in Gattorna, J. (ed.), *Strategic Supply Chain Alignment*, Gower Press, Aldershot.

Blumentritt, R. and R. Johnston (1999), 'Towards a strategy for knowledge management', *Technology Analysis and Strategic Management*, September.

Chanaron, J.-J. and D. Jolly (1999), 'Technological management: expanding the perspective of management of technology', *Management Decision*, Vol. 37.

Copeland, T., T. Koller and J. Murrin (1994), *Valuation: Measuring and Managing the Value of Companies*, Wiley, New York.

Davenport, T. H. and J. E. Short (1990), 'The new industrial engineering: information technology and business process design', *Sloan Management Review*, Summer.

Doz, Y. L. and G. Hamel (1998), *Alliance Advantage: The Art of Creating Value through Partnering*, Harvard Business School Press, Boston.

Gadiesh, O. and J. L. Gilbert (1998), 'How to map your industry's profit pool', *Harvard Business Review*, May/June.

Håkansson, H. and I. Sinhehota (1995), 'The burden of relationships or who's next?', Paper presented at 11th IMP International Conference, Manchester.

Hayes, R. H., G. P. Pisano and D. Upton (1998), *Strategic Operations: Competing Through Capabilities*, Harvard Business School Press, Boston.

Hill, T. (2000), *Operations Management: Strategic Context and Management Analysis*, Macmillan Business, Basingstoke.

Irani, Z. and P. Love (2001), 'The propagation of technology management taxonomies for evaluating investments in information systems', *Journal of Management Information Systems*, Winter 2000–2001.

Jarillo, J. C. (1993), *Strategic Networks – Creating the Borderless Organisation*, Butterworth-Heinemann, Oxford.

Kay, J. (1993), *Foundations of Corporate Success*, Oxford University Press, Oxford.

Knight, R. and D. Pretty (2000), 'Philosophies of risk, shareholder value and the CEO', in *Mastering Risk*, Financial Times, 27 June.

Morita, A. (1992), 'Partnering for competitiveness: the role of Japanese business', *Harvard Business Review*, May/June.

Pilkington, A. (1998), 'Manufacturing strategy regained: evidence of the demise of best-practice', *California Management Review*, Fall.

Prahalad, C. K. and V. Ramaswamy (2000), 'Co-opting customer competence', *Harvard Business Review*, Jan/Feb.

Rappaport, A. (1983), 'Corporate performance standards and shareholder value', *The Journal of Business Strategy*, Spring.

Reimann, B. (1988), *Managing For Value: A Guide to Value Based Strategic Management*, Blacwell, Oxford.

Silver, C. A. (2000), 'Where technology and knowledge meet', *The Journal of Business Strategy*, Nov/Dec.

Slywotzky, A. J. (1996), *Value Migration*, Free Press, New York.

Srivastava, R. K., T. A. Shervani and L. Fahey (1999), 'Marketing, business processes, and shareholder value: an organizationally embedded view of marketing activities and the discipline of marketing', *Journal of Marketing*, Vol. 63, Special issue.

Uren, D. (2001), 'To winners go more spoils in rivalry tango', *The Australian*, 10 March.

Zineldin, M. (1997), *Strategic Relationship Management A Multi-Dimensional Perspective: Towards a New Co-opetive Framework on Managing, Marketing and Organizing*, Almqvist & Wiksell International AB, Stockholm.

chapter
17

Configuring the Value Chain: 2

LEARNING OUTCOMES

The student will be able to:

● explore market led opportunities that can be met with value chain structures;
● evaluate alternative value chain structures;
● decide upon an optimal value chain design that meets customer and corporate stakeholder expectations.

INTRODUCTION

The value creation and production processes are revisited in Figure 17.1, which superimposes these value processes on the value strategy and structure model developed in Chapter 16 (Figure 16.1). *Value strategy* decisions consider the interpretation of customer value expectations and include the consideration of both product and production process R and D. *Value organisation* is concerned with value creation and production and its interpretation to end users and intermediaries. The issue of who is the 'brand master' is an important organisational issue, as are the decisions concerning value delivery structures. *Value operations* decisions determine the value delivery and service infrastructures necessary if the value strategy is to be implemented efficiently.

This chapter provides the methodology for constructing industry and corporate value chains. The issue confronting managers is to decide at what level to conduct the analysis, bearing in mind that they must first identify the industry in which they operate and its competitive scope. They must then explore the structural options available. The exercise is based upon an understanding of customers' expectations and a thorough knowledge of the capabilities and capacities that exist within the industry and from which a value chain can be constructed.

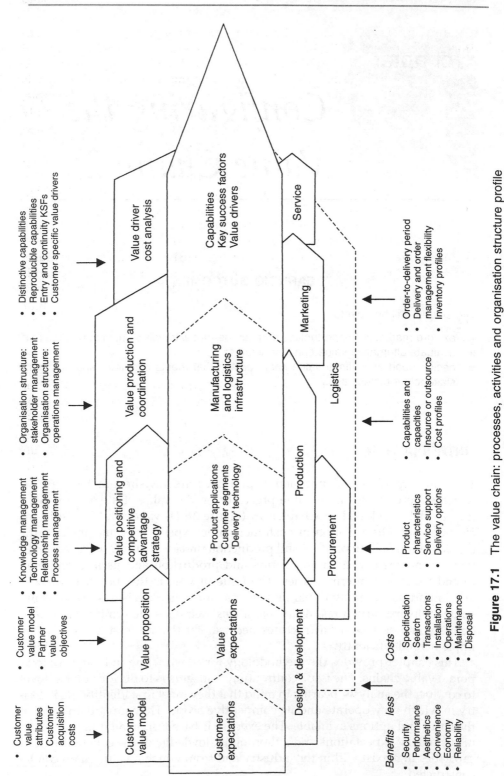

Figure 17.1 The value chain: processes, activities and organisation structure profile

Before any design work can be conducted an analysis of the market environment is necessary. This should include a review of both consumer and supplier practices. There exist numerous cultural differences that may require quite different approaches to value chain organisation decisions. This is particularly important in an age of global business relationships. For example, Harrison (2000) reports an interview with Hau Lee (director of the supply chain management executive programme at Stanford University Business School) in which Hau Lee comments on basic differences that exist between countries and which often require a very different approach to be considered when constructing the value chain. Hau Lee identifies a significant difference in the low number of credit card holders in Japan compared to the number in the US. This difference resulted in an exclusive e-commerce model for Japan. The company 7dreams.com is an organisation between 7-Eleven stores and a diverse group of companies selling a range of varied items such as concert and airline tickets and Sony products. Japanese customers purchase products online; but instead of using a credit card to pay for the purchase and the products being delivered to homes, customers pick up the items from the nearest 7-Eleven store and pay for them in cash. Taiwan is considering a similar model.

Hau Lee advocates a three 'S' approach to implementing e-commerce. The first step concerns the 'substitution' of existing technology (faxes) by Internet based procedures to perform transactions and ordering communications. The second step is 'scale' in which the Internet is used to increase the scale of service, such as by increasing order frequency or perhaps reducing order response times. The third step (one that is emerging) is a 'structural' development in which direct shipments are made without intermediaries being involved, using Internet technology. Lee gives software companies as an example but consumer audiovisual products are making rapid progress with this approach.

Revisiting the value chain

The example of basic differences in consumer attitudes and behaviour patterns does not negate the basic value chain structure. It does in fact strengthen the argument for the value chain approach: an analysis of consumer behaviour identifies fundamental differences that should be understood prior to structuring the processes that will ensure the value chain's success. Figure 17.1 combines the organisational profile with the management processes necessary for effective implementation. In the Japanese example, cited in the previous paragraphs, the importance of specific consumer expectations is considered. For example, the 'security' concerns of Japanese consumers (the preference for cash transactions) are reflected in the management of transactions and product delivery. In this example some 'coproductivity' is evident as the customer is involved in the delivery process. Furthermore the logistics process is tasked with ensuring that delivery schedules are met as customers may make specific visits to the 7-Eleven stores to receive and pay for purchases.

However, the point is that the basic value chain structure and its processes are the same; it is the activities that differ.

CREATING A VALUE CHAIN DESIGN

According to Hagel and Singer (1999) the traditional organisation consists of three basic kinds of business: a customer relationship business, a product innovation business and an infrastructure business. The authors suggest each of these differs concerning the economic, competitive and cultural directions. They argue that as more and more information is exchanged and 'digitisation' occurs through electronic networks, the traditional structures will become 'unbundled' as the need for flexible structures becomes an imperative (see Figure 16.1) and 'specialists' offer cost-effective strategy options in each of these 'basic businesses'. They also suggest this is likely to lead car manufacturers to adopt outsourcing models for manufacturing operations or to enter the after-market through partial acquisitions or partnerships, or fully acquiring downstream activities. This move is evident in companies such as Ford and Volkswagen.

The argument underlying Hagel and Singer's model concerns a conflict of production economics. They argue that *customer relationship businesses* are essentially driven by the need to achieve economies of scope and do so by seeking to offer customers a wide range of products and services. By contrast *product innovation* is driven by speed: by minimising its time-to-market, the company increases the likelihood of capturing a premium price and a strong market share. *Infrastructure businesses* are dominated by economies of scale. They are typically characterised by capital-intensive facilities which entail high fixed costs. Given the relationship between throughput and fixed costs, it follows that large volumes of product throughput are essential.

The authors argue that '... these three businesses ... rarely map neatly to the organisational structure of a corporation. Rather than representing discrete organisational units, the three businesses correspond to what are popularly called "core processes" – the cross functional work flows that stretch from suppliers to customers and, in combination, define a company's identity'. The solution for Hagel and Singer is to 'unbundle the organisation' and to restructure based upon maximising the effect of the economics of the individual businesses. Product innovation will occur in the *design and development* process of the value chain and is increasingly likely to be the province of small creative units often outwith the organisation, and if within it, free of the bureaucracy typical of large organisations.

Customer relationship management responsibilities are shared by the *marketing* and *service* processes. Marketing identifies and communicates with intermediaries and end user customers, providing an opportunity for economies of scope to operate efficiently. Service creates strong loyalties by offering product knowledge and post sale service. This process may well be divested. Many durables manufacturers have outsourced service in order to provide a more responsive service to customers and to reduce the high fixed costs of facilities and inventories. Service companies, banks and other financial products providers use call centres to manage customer services with similar motives – to benefit from economies of scale. Chapter 15 gave an example of the application of call centres in international education.

Aspects of infrastructure businesses have been outsourced for some time. Third party distribution service companies have offered economies of scale through consolidation of inventories and deliveries. Manufacturing/production processes are increasingly becoming outsourced. The automotive industry is one in which an increasing proportion of the product is manufactured by outside suppliers while the manufacturers restructure their organisations around processes and activities offering greater added value return on investment.

Hagel and Singer conclude: 'The secret to success in fractured industries is not to unbundle but to unbundle and rebundle, creating a new organisation with the capabilities and size required to win'. This requires identifying and understanding fully the economies of scale, scope, specialisation and integration.

Bornheim (2001) shares these views and proposes a customer-centric model for the automotive industry in which value-creating activities are reorganised around customer needs. The elements of the model '... are highly specialised, intensely inter-linked, and aim at synchronisation of resources and information flows with true customer demand'. Bornheim predicts a future automotive business model similar to that of Dell's built-to-order model: '... in which customised demand nearly exactly matches supply and which revolves around a digital order processing, inventory management, and manufacturing system, that removes the assets from an asset-intensive process'.

Both Hagel and Singer and Bornheim take a similar perspective to that of Doz and Hamel (1998). They suggest gaining competitive strength through co-option, leveraging cospecialised resources and gaining competence through internalised learning. Within value chain design and management, learning should be across processes and across organisations.

Identify the value cycle: a 'market sensing' approach

Day (1999) argues that market sensing means that 'Market-driven firms ... stand out in their ability to continuously sense and act on events and trends in their markets. They are better equipped to anticipate how their markets will respond to actions designed to retain or attract customers, improve channel relations or thwart competitors ... [they] also excel in their ability to make sense of the information that they draw from the market ... turn this information into knowledge and then share it across the organisation'. If market sensing is to contribute to competitive advantage it should provide input into interactive marketing: '... the use of information *from* the customer rather than *about* the customer'. Thus market sensing interacts with each process of the value chain. Day uses the notion of a value cycle to demonstrate this; his value cycle is shown in a modified form as Figure 17.2.

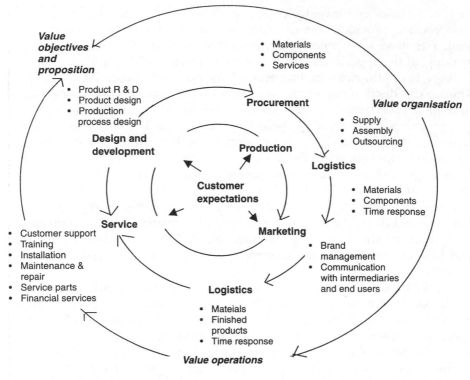

Figure 17.2   The value cycle: components of value strategy, structure and
operations

'Audit' the value chain and value chain characteristics

Effective market sensing is a customer-centric activity and part of an added-value strategy. Essential questions to be asked are concerned with market trend characteristics, competitors, suppliers, value criteria and acquisition costs, customer led opportunities that are emerging and latent, the competitive criteria for competitors (capabilities and entry KSFs), and the characteristics of value production and delivery. These 'who', 'what' and 'where' considerations are addressed in Figure 17.3. The 'how' concerns are also included but serve as an introduction to Figure 17.4 which continues to examine specific value chain design and management characteristics.

A thorough review of the existing value chain is necessary prior to making revisions. This entails mapping each value chain operating within the industry, both the organisation structure and the processes and associated activities. With these identified revenues, process costs and cash flows can be estimated together with the fixed assets and working capital involved. Together this information will provide sufficient detail to calculate the aggregate added value return on investment for the value chain and for each process.

Another important concern is to identify the core capabilities that are necessary to compete in the marketplace *and* for market leadership. Clearly

Who
- is the target market?
- are the different customer groups?
- are the suppliers?
- are the competitors?

What
- are the customers' value criteria?
- are the customers' acquisition costs?
- uses and applications are made of products?
- other related needs do these customers have?
- are the needs and applications not yet met?
- capabilities, capacities and KSFs are required to meet these emerging needs? Are they available? Where?
- are the strategic value drivers necessary for long-term competitive advantage?

Where
- is value added in the value chain?
- is value migration occurring?
- can value be enhanced? At what point and by whom?

How
- is the current value offer delivered?
- can the basic value characteristics be maintained/enhanced more effectively and efficiently?
- do competitive value chains deliver value?
- can the value chain configuration be restructured to implement effectiveness and efficiency decisions?

Identify the value chain configuration alternatives
- What is the current configuration, value positioning and competitive advantage strategy?
- Are value chain customers receiving optimal returns?
- Are value chain stakeholders receiving adequate returns on resource investments?
- Can changes be made to resource investment and ownership structures that could improve customer value delivery and/or stakeholder returns, that is:

  - Can costs be reduced while value delivery remains constant?
  - Can value be increased at the current level of costs?
  - Can resources be restructured to improve value delivery?
  - Can resources be reduced and value delivery maintained?

- Would changes result in strengthened competitive positioning?
- Are there processes and activities that customers can perform more efficiently?
- Are there processes and activities that competitive value chains perform more efficiently?

Figure 17.3   Identify the value cycle: what value for whom? where? and how?

these are unlikely to be the same. The review should also consider the KSFs necessary for market entry. These should be evaluated from an entry barrier perspective as well as simply an entry necessity.

The review should build upon the 'who', 'what', 'where' and 'how' analysis of Figure 17.3. A critical look at the value chains operating within an

---

Identify the value chain and its performance profile

- Identify and map each of the value chains operating within the industry
- Profile their organisation structures, processes and activities
- Identify fixed and variable costs and the added value
- Determine revenues, process costs, cash flows and assets
- Determine the AVROI at each process stage using revenues and transfer prices
- Have these changed? How? To what extent?

Identify value chain capabilities and KSFs

- What are the core capabilities (distinctive and reproducible) necessary to compete?
- What are the core capabilities (distinctive and reproducible) necessary for market leadership?
- What are the entry KSFs?

Identify the value chain's served market characteristics

- What is the value chain's value proposition?
- What is the customer response?
- How does the value chain's value proposition compare with that/those of competitive value chains?
- What is the customer response?

Figure 17.4   Review the value chain and value chain characteristics

identified served market will identify each value proposition and match each of them with the relevant customer response characteristics. A comparison of competitive value chains may then be made. Further, an investigation of non-competitive, but successful value chains can provide very useful design points.

An analysis of alternative value chain configurations concludes the analysis. Particular attention should be given to performance. Successful value chains are those that deliver customer satisfaction and optimal returns (AVROI) to the value chain partners. Consideration should also be made of the alternatives available. Changes in resource investment and ownership structures may result in performance improvements, either in customer value, AVROI for partner stakeholders or in an overall reduction of costs. The objective is to reach a design or format that maximises competitive advantage in such a way as to offer long term market competitiveness. Figure 17.4 summarises the topics for review.

Value chain structures: deciding on objectives

The advantages offered by value chain structures (McHugh et al: 1995) reflect the objectives that should be set when considering the appropriate design for a value chain. Among McHugh et al's suggestions, the following are particularly relevant:

- asset leverage: increased utilisation from distributed operations through synergy;
- speed: specialist inputs enhance time-to-market;
- flexibility: the ability to meet requests for product and service changes within existing response times;
- faster growth and increased profitability, through improved response (time) rates;
- increased customer loyalty: longer and more profitable customer relationships;
- shared assets and lower total capital investment: investment by partner organisations is limited to its core processes and working capital requirements are influenced by a 'just-in-time' approach;
- shared risk at reduced levels: risk is reduced by being dispersed among network members *and* because of the high aggregate level of expertise that is deployed.

It follows that value chain design should reflect these advantages. To do so will result in:

- increased AVROI (and therefore aggregate profitability);
- lower investment in fixed costs and working capital;
- lower operating costs due to optimal economies of production and increased customer response (reducing customer acquisition costs and increased transaction values);
- reduced business risk, defined here as fluctuations in planned market volume (and market share(s));
- reduced financial risk, defined as the probability of failure to achieve a target return on net assets;
- decreased response times (both time-to-market, a strategic consideration and operationally, the order cycle time);
- an optimal enterprise value for corporate stakeholders.

Value chain structures: processes, decisions and outputs

Given customer expectations, together with the corporate stakeholder objectives, it is possible to identify the decisions and outputs required from the value chain processes. This exercise precedes decisions concerning the organisation structure of the value chain because it is essential that tasks be identified and that the specific outputs necessary to meet the objectives of enterprise value, AVROI and operational performance be determined. By identifying the decisions and outputs required by each process a number of other decisions may be resolved. The first concerns the *performance metrics* for each process (see Figure 17.5), and the second concerns the impact of the decisions of downstream processes on their upstream partners. For example, 'production' may set cost/budgets, TQM, time-to-market performance measures that for production are essential to meet marketing and service process requirements, which in turn are based upon planning performance levels to satisfy

Design and development

Decisions
• Target market
• Forecast volumes
• Product uses and applications
• 'Delivery' methods: time-to-market response
• Product life span and life cycle cost profile
• Product performance range profile
• Product range dimensions
• Production process: assembly (modularisation, components and so on)
• 'Service' infrastructure
• Capital requirements

Outputs
• Product and service specification: characteristics, volume, quality, variety and flexibility
• Production design specification
• Procurement tasks
• Service support specification
• Performance metrics:
    • AVROI   • Time-to-market   • Enterprise value

Procurement

Decisions
• 'Ownership' and partnership options
• Format for supply: raw materials, components, modules, and so on
• Substitutes
• Number of suppliers: tiers, tier structures and responsibilities
• Location of suppliers
• Supplier relationships: responsibilities and responses
• Quality control: accountability
• Inventory management: accountability
• Capital requirements

Outputs
• Procurement schedules
• Quality levels
• Costs/budgets
• Continuity
• Conformance
• Performance metrics:
    • AVROI   • COGS/gross margin   • Costs/variances
    • Supplier service times   • Enterprise value

Service

Decisions
• Customer service expectations
• 'Branding'
• Product knowledge support
• Product and service liabilities
• Service advice infrastructures

Figure 17.5 Value chain processes: decisions and outputs

- Service intermediaries and partnership options
- Delegated responsibilities
- Capital required

Outputs
- Service response times
- 'Warranty' costs per customer and/or per product
- Performance metrics:
  - AVROI
  - Customer retention costs (service costs/customer)
  - Time response
  - Customer perceptions
  - Enterprise value

Logistics

Decisions
- Customer service expectations
- Order-to-delivery period; time response
- Inventory profiles; availability response
- Delivery and flexibility requirements
- Capabilities and capacities required
- Role of logistics in the capability set: distinctive or reproducible
- Control required; extent of involvement in the logistics process
- Cost structures: fixed and variable cost relationships
- Capital required

Outputs
- Volume throughput
- Scheduled throughputs
- Inventory locations
- Time response targets
- Performance metrics:
  - AVROI
  - Inventory availability
  - Customer proximity
  - Response time
  - Delivery frequency(ies)
  - Flexibility
  - Customer perceptions
  - Enterprise value

Production

Decisions
- Capabilities and capacities required
- Control required
- Partnerships and co-option
- Role of production in the capability set: distinctive or reproducible
- Extent of involvement in production process
- Flexibility requirements
- Cost structures: economies of scale, scope, specialisation and integration
- Cost structure: fixed and variable cost relationships
- Order-to-delivery and time-to-market
- Capital required

Outputs
- Volume throughput
- Production schedules
- Quality
- Performance metrics:
  - AVROI
  - Costs/budgets
  - TQM
  - Time-to-market
  - Enterprise value

Figure 17.5 *Continued*

Marketing

Decisions
- Target customer profile
- Market forecasts: potential, available, penetrated and potential markets
- Value proposition
- Brand ownership, development and management
- Market management: role of intermediaries and channel management, 'corporate control'
- Capital required

Outputs
- Customer and market penetration
- Product specification
- Intermediaries: roles and tasks and liaison roles
- Pricing and margin targets
- Customer/end user communications and liaison
- Performance metrics:
  - AVROI • Cost of acquiring customers • Cost of retaining customers
  - Market share • Customer loyalty • Brand equity • Time-to-market
  - Enterprise value

Figure 17.5 *Continued*

customers. However, unless the performance metrics are developed sequentially, starting with customer expectations, and potential conflicts resolved, overall success is unlikely. Furthermore a 'reverse sequential approach' offers the potential for increased performance (either enhanced customer satisfaction or lower operating costs, or perhaps both). It follows that by identifying the value cycle (see earlier section and Figure 17.2) the task is made a little easier. Figure 17.5 identifies and classifies typical value chain process decisions and outputs.

Value chain structures: configuration options

The value chain concept offers the facility to explore alternative ways of structuring a business and its alliances and partnership arrangements. A number of considerations operate. Figure 17.6 identifies a starting point for choice. Market characteristics may suggest that coordination rather than integration (ownership of assets) is preferable. The reasons (discussed earlier) may be because of fragile demand, rapidly changing customer expectations or technology, the extent of the required investment that would make the option of shared assets and lower individual capital investment more attractive, and the implications of time responses (both time-to-market and order cycle contraction) for competitive advantage. Closely associated is the capital cost of fixed assets and working capital. Again if these are high the preference for distributed assets (or manufacturing) will prevail. A third influence may be the nature of labour inputs. If the required labour input is for a high level of skills

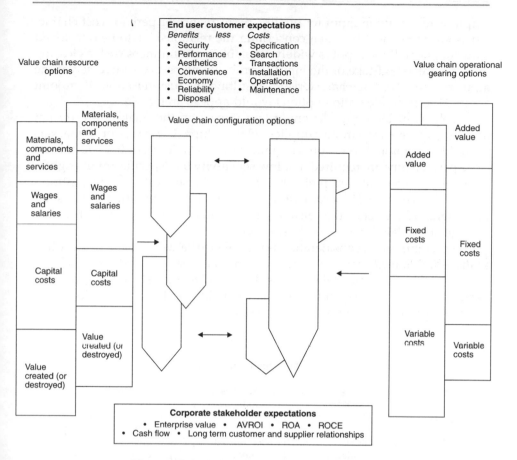

End user customer expectations

Benefits   less   Costs

Benefits	Costs
• Security	• Specification
• Performance	• Search
• Aesthetics	• Transactions
• Convenience	• Installation
• Economy	• Operations
• Reliability	• Maintenance
• Disposal	

Value chain resource options

Value chain operational gearing options

Value chain configuration options

Materials, components and services

Materials, components and services

Materials, components and services

Wages and salaries

Wages and salaries

Capital costs

Capital costs

Value created (or destroyed)

Value created (or destroyed)

Added value

Added value

Fixed costs

Fixed costs

Variable costs

Variable costs

Corporate stakeholder expectations
• Enterprise value • AVROI • ROA • ROCE
• Cash flow • Long term customer and supplier relationships

Figure 17.6   Value chain configuration options

and/or training a preference for capital equipment rather than labour may be decided, or the use of outsourced specialists.

These options are illustrated in figure 17.6. Generic customer expectations are suggested together with important objectives for the corporate stakeholders. Labour availability and/or cost and the cost of capital influence the value chain resource options. These are linked to the operational gearing options (the relationship between fixed and variable costs). Market characteristics and the cost of capital equipment, together with working capital costs are strong decision influencing factors.

Selecting partnerships is critical in value chain decisions

Two other sets of relationships are important to the final decision. The first of these is the availability of specific resources and the sensitivity of the output to the resources. Figure 17.7 explores this important relationship. If the final output is reliant upon input for quality, performance or perhaps cost characteristics, a view must be taken concerning the relationships to be developed with suppliers. If the input is widely available a commitment such as leasing or a guaranteed off-take of the input is probably necessary. Conversely if the input requires specific characteristics resulting in 'customisation' then joint venture/vertical integration options would appear preferable.

Widely available inputs having a low impact on the final output do not usually require such strong supplier relationships. Clearly supply markets should be monitored to ensure continuity of availability but beyond this no close partnerships are required. For low sensitivity but 'specific' inputs tighter supplier arrangements are preferable. Figure 17.7 suggests leasing contracts or some form of vertical coordination (a low level equity investment) as a solution. Figure 17.7 extends the consideration of alternative arrangements across a range of availability/sensitivity situations.

Another important consideration is the balance between business risk (fluctuations in planned market volume (and market share(s)) and the capability profile of the corporate stakeholders. Figure 17.8 suggests a range of partnership options that depend upon the capability profile of the value chain members and the perceptions of business risk.

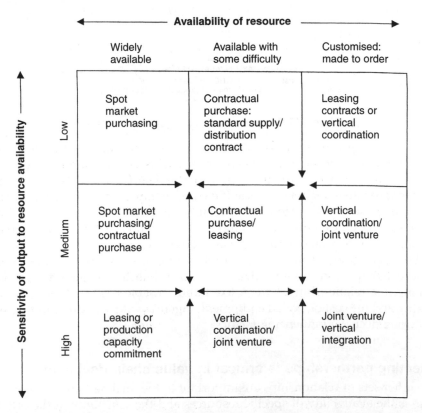

Figure 17.7 Guide to selecting partnership options in value chain decisions

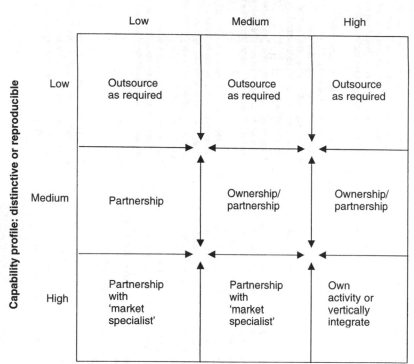

Figure 17.8   Identifying business risk in partnership options

Distinctive capabilities that have a high impact in situations where business risk is high should be owned or integrated into the value chain if ownership is difficult (due to patents or other exclusivity situations). If business risk is low then a partnership with a market specialist would appear to be the solution. For capabilities that have low impact and are reproducible, outsourcing arrangements should be satisfactory across the range of likely business risk conditions. As with Figure 17.7, Figure 17.8 extends the discussion across a range of alternative combinations.

The importance of selecting a relevant structure can be seen from Figures 17.9 and 17.10, which offer examples of value chain alternatives to meet both customer expectations and customer acquisition costs. Each alternative and example can be fitted to the model described by Figure 17.6. The reader is encouraged to consider alternatives for the examples.

SUMMARY

This chapter has revisited many of the concepts discussed earlier. It has also introduced recent contributions that identify the holonic network or

Customer benefits Expectations	Value expectations	Value chain alternatives	Examples
• Security	• Warranty • A/s service delivery/continuity • Insurance • Product liability (recall/recovery) package	• Strong brand/franchise a well known brand • Customer service/service organisation • R and D – product design (product platforms) • Establish an emergency product recall network	• Mercedes/BMW/Caterpillar have developed strong brands and strong service organisations to reinforce their product reputation with end users. Resellers and service organisations are incorporated
• Performance	• Quality • Consistency • Continuity • Variety/suitability } 'Solutions' relative to existing market offers that are currently available (product and service)	• TQM throughout operations (manufacturing and logistics/use inputs/components with strong identity) • Partnership arrangements with high VA resellers • Use partners' information systems to customise value proposition	• Computer manufacturers use 'Intel' in hardware manufacturing and 'Microsoft' software as partner organisations • Reseller reputations (Harrods, Nieman Marcus, etc) 'endorse', recommend and support products
• Aesthetics	• Styling/design • Image/'appearance'	• Develop prestige brands/franchise prestige brands • Partnership arrangements with prestige resellers and service organisations • Leverage the reputation of well known customers	• Motor vehicle manufacturers (and other industrial product producers) use design services for 'exterior', design performance
• Convenience	• 'Product formulation' flexibility • Time availability • Location availability • Information availability	• 'Multimedia' distribution • High 'access' distribution } 'supported by 'easy access' information facilities • Increase physical availability through increased field presence using service organisations with specialist service attributes	• Manufacturers and distributors are using telecommunications networks for order processing and progressing and service distribution companies to provide location availability (Telstra, Australia)
• Economy	• Competitive pricing of original equipment • Competitive pricing: service parts • Competitive pricing: service activities • Ownership alternatives	• Product design (product platforms, value engineering), coproductivity with suppliers and customers • Develop industry standards for common or similar replacement parts • Reduce, reformulate ownership/transaction costs using finance specialists	• Consumer durables manufacturers design 'standardisation' into products, resulting in cost-efficient and time-efficient servicing
• Reliability	• Availability (time) • Availability (product and services formulation) • Availability (location) • Conformance • Continuity	• Leverage suppliers' and resellers' fixed assets and working capital • Integrate operating technology • Product development and design 'committees' which incorporate suppliers, resellers and end users	• Computer manufacturers coordinate manufacturing and supply chain activities to offer customised products within advertised delivery lead times and contain costs (Dell)

Figure 17.9 Examples of a range of customer expectations

Customer acquisition Costs	Value expectations	Value chain alternatives	Examples
• Specification	• Information and technical advice on product-service suitability (relevance of input) • Assistance in developing input performance criteria for NPD	• Communicate through multimedia networks, such as Net based systems, direct technical representation or VA intermediary (distributor or 'consultant' operation) • R and D based upstream and downstream working with suppliers, resellers, relevant intermediaries and end users to develop longitudinal perspective of all needs	• Fiat product development using Internet on Punto • Electronics manufacturers working on problems with customers in partnership R and D ventures • Industrial designers are used to advise on 'packaging' • 'Turnkey' consultants offer IT specification services
• Search	• Supplier competence profiles: capabilities, capacities, location	• Maintain web based information on products, services and NPD • Close liaison with key and development customers	• Computer components manufacturers using websites to communicate problem solving abilities, manufacturing capabilities and capacities
• Transactions	• Ownership requirements	• Customise ownership packages (owned, leased, financed options) • Use partner organisations to develop finance/ownership packages	• Sale and leaseback facilities permit customers use of capital in core company activities. Examples are extensive in airlines
• Installation/delivery	• Minimum time to full operations	• Skilled installation personnel • Ongoing training programmes for staff	• Consumer durables manufacturers and retailers use specialist companies for this essentially labour intensive activity
• Operations	• Standardise inputs • Minimal operating costs • Simplify operations	• Online technical support • Ongoing training programmes for staff	• Computer and photocopier companies offer integrated services which manage installation, operations, maintenance and copy paper replenishment. Elements of these processes are outsourced. IT services are also commonplace.
• Maintenance	• Minimise service intervals/parts costs • Maximum productivity	• Maximum service coverage • Service parts availability • Planned maintenance	• Military operations and maintenance (RAF) are increasingly managed by specialist service companies
• Disposal	• Maximum terminal value (ROI) • Repurchase options/price • Removal and resale	• Remove and dispose of replaced equipment • Develop resale markets • Planned replacement/finance packages	• Commercial aircraft are recycled using 'reseller' specialists

Figure 17.10   Examples of a range of customer acquisition costs

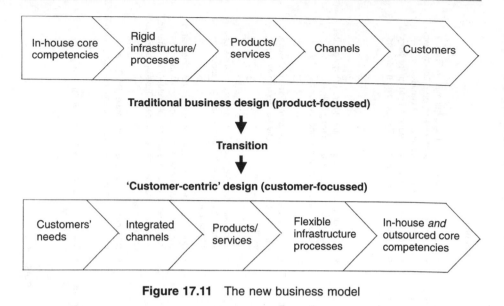

Figure 17.11 The new business model

value chain approach as a viable model to cope with the changing business environment.

The notion that the organisation consists of three basic kinds of business reinforces the argument that cost-effective strategies and their cost-efficient implementation are increasingly becoming inter-organisational decisions. The concepts of co-option, coproductivity and specialisation when coordinated into a virtual organisation not only offer greater competitive advantage but also broaden the market opportunity. Furthermore this approach offers the 'organisation' an opportunity to apply knowledge and technology management more effectively by working closely together through relationship partnerships. A number of issues in this context were addressed in the chapter.

Probably the most controversial issue the value chain approach offers is that of performance expectations. The approach suggested using both ROVA and enterprise value does address this concern. However at the end of the day there are some searching questions for the corporate stakeholders: do my customers gain additional benefits and can we lower their costs? And does participation in a value chain increase the value of my business?

Figure 17.11 was previously used in Chapter 7 to introduce the value chain concept. It is used again to close this chapter and is relabelled to suggest that it is a viable 'new business model'.

REFERENCES ●

Bornheim, C. P. (2001), *e-roadmapping: digital strategising for the new economy*, Palgrave, Basingstoke.

Day, G. (1999), *The Market Driven Organisation*, The Free Press, New York.

Doz, Y. L. and G. Hamel (1998), *Alliance Advantage: The Art of Creating Value through Partnering*, Harvard Business School Press, Boston.

Hagel, J. and M. Singer (1999), 'Unbundling the corporation', *Harvard Business Review*, Vol. 77, No. 2.

Harrison, S. (2000), 'US models out of step with Asia reality', *Morning Post*, October 3, Hong Kong.

McHugh, P., G. Merli and G. Wheeler III (1995), *Beyond Business Process Reengineering*, Wiley, Chichester.

chapter 18

Case Study Exercises

INTRODUCTION

This chapter introduces a number of case studies for which the research is not complete; the reader is encouraged to complete the value chain structure for each organisation. Each case is introduced with information gathered from published sources and the exercise task is to research further each organisation to identify additional, relevant data. To help the activity an 'audit model' is offered.

[*Note*: In this chapter, references are listed after each case study.]

A VALUE CHAIN 'AUDIT MODEL': QUESTIONS REQUIRING ANSWERS

The value chain organisation profile

Customer value

- What are the *key* customer value attributes?
- Which of these are supplied by your organisation?
- Which of them do you not supply?
- Which does the customer 'insource'?
- Which of these attributes can the organisation claim to meet *better than* competitors?

Customer costs

- What are the *key* cost processes for customers?
- Which of these are addressed by your organisation?
- Which are addressed by your competitors?
- Which are insourced?

Core customer value drivers

- What are they?
- What are the priorities?
- What are the implications for differentiation and therefore customer loyalty and retention?
- What are the implications for cost structures?
- Is there potential for *tradeoffs* among value chain partners either to increase customer and/or partner value, or to reduce costs of either?

Core competencies/capabilities

- What skills, resources, 'technologies' are required for leadership in the sector? Which offer a strategic competitive pathway for future activities?
- How many, and which of them, does your organisation possess?
- Which of them are unique (or at least exclusive) to your organisation?
- Are any unique/exclusive to your competitors or any other organisations?

Core processes

- *Competitive necessity*: which processes are critical to value production, delivery and service if the value offer is to be considered credible?
- *Competitive advantage*: which core processes will move the value offer into a *preferred* position?
- Specify *distinctive capabilities* and develop and reinforce them.
- Identify *reproducible capabilities* and find partners.
- Monitor capability profiles for change, market needs and competitive threats.

Core assets

- Which assets are required to meet market (often specific customer) determined value specification? (the *capability and capacity issues*)
- Form utility (performance, quality and quantity)?
- Time utility (delivery frequency and reliability)?
- Place utility (convenience)?
- Flexibility utility (the ability to change the utility specifications at short notice)?

Key success factors

- What are the characteristics, conditions or variables that when well managed have significant impact on the success of an organisation competing in your industry, sector or market?
- Which do you have?
- Which do your competitors have?
- Which are available to you on an inter-organisational basis?

Partner value objectives

- Market value objectives?
- Financial objectives?
- Shared objectives?

Value proposition

- What are the benefits and costs for the customer?
- What 'value' is delivered to the customer?
- By what means?
- What are the resource requirements?
- Brand/reputation
- Knowledge
- Technology
- Relationships/networks/alliances
- Human resources
- Financial resources

Value positioning and strategy: competitive advantage

- How does *knowledge management* (the organisational capability which identifies, transfers, converts knowledge into competitive advantage) contribute to delivering value?
- What are the key elements of *technology management* (the integration of inter-organisational technological capabilities) that contribute to delivering value?
- Which aspects of *relationship management* (partnerships with customers, suppliers, even competitors with complementary capabilities) are important to delivering customer value?
- What are the competitive advantage characteristics/objectives to be generated?

Value production and coordination

- What are the key functions?
- What is the role of the visionary or integrator?

- What are the key *operational roles* and who fills these roles?
- What are their specialisms?
- What are their core capabilities?
- What *support* processes are critical in producing customer value?
- What *production* processes are critical?
- What *service* processes are critical?
- What is the role of *logistics* in value production?
- Who are the *resource providers* and what are the key resources?
- Specialist labour
- Information
- 'Customising' facilities
- Management services

Value drivers

- What are the things that are so important to customers and reflect their priorities such that they will pay a premium for them or switch suppliers?
- How are their costs analysed?

Value chain processes and decisions

Design and development

- What are the key design and development processes in the value chain?
- Which of these processes are managed by the organisation?
- Which are outsourced?
- Are customers involved in design and development processes; if so which processes?
- Are suppliers involved in design and development processes; if so which processes?

Procurement

- What is the role of procurement in the value production process in the value chain?
- Is this a major or a minor role?
- Are any of the procurement processes outsourced?

Production

- What are the key production process activities in the value chain?
- Which of these activities are undertaken by your organisation?
- Where are the other activities located?
- Do customers become involved?
- Do suppliers have any major role in the process activities?

Marketing

- What is the role of marketing in the value chain?
- What are the key marketing activities?
- Where are these activities undertaken?
- What positioning characteristics are central to the value proposition?
- How are these decided and by whom?
- Who in the value chain owns the 'brand'?
- Are intermediaries included in the value chain and what are the roles/processes/activities they undertake?

Service

- What are the key service elements in successful value delivery?
- Where are these performed in the value chain?

Logistics

- What is the customers' involvement in determining the importance of the logistics service outputs?
- What are the key logistics activities?
- Who performs these activities?
- Who coordinates the activities?
- How is logistics performance monitored?

CASE STUDY 1: CATERPILLAR INC

Caterpillar is a well known international brand. While generally assumed to be successful it admits to feeling the impact of Japanese competition between 1982 and 1992. Fites (1996), the company chairman and CEO, describes Caterpillar's response to the Japanese challenge; his description maps the Caterpillar value chain. While the thrust of Fites' article is aimed at the role played by distributors in the industry, there is sufficient material to be able to construct a value chain.

Fites identifies the KSF requirements of a major industry participant in his description of the factors that were used defensively. They are: a strong brand; responsiveness to customers; efficient, flexible operations; strong distributors who are loyal and responsive to the company's leadership; and a product that is innovative, of high quality and well supported in the field. Fites identifies the role of distributors as conduits for information to the end user, often acting as 'consultants'. This adds another KSF: investment, in product development *and* in the distribution network.

There are numerous examples of how Caterpillar uses information management and relationship management to construct an effective value chain through the dealer network. Given the commitment to the distributor organisation, many decisions are simplified. For example, product design includes this: 'A critical design criterion for our machines is that they can be repaired economically and conveniently. And our highly integrated manufacturing and distribution systems are designed so that we can replace a part in any machine anywhere in the world within 48 hours'.

Fites argues that Caterpillar competitors' customers typically wait four or five days for a part, suggesting: 'One possible reason for the disparity is that few companies have integrated their dealers into their business systems to the degree we have'. Here is an example of making supply chain and logistics management an important component of relationship management.

The role of information to create market knowledge comes from the learning aspects of the manufacturer/distributor partnership relationships. Another aspect of information management concerns the productivity of Caterpillar and distributor inventories and customer equipment. The remoteness of many applications implies serious problems when parts of equipment begin to deteriorate. Caterpillar has begun to resolve such problems by installing sensors on each machine that automatically spot a problem which may occur and send an electronic alert to the local dealer's field technician through their portable computer. A technician who determines the necessary actions validates the symptoms and diagnosis. The computer program identifies exactly the parts and tools required to effect repair. This done, the technician can then use another feature of the program to identify sources of parts, availability and a delivery date. Beyond this, an integrated replenishment program retrieves parts from storage and issues replenishment orders as and when required. The computer program contains best-practice repair procedures and, on completion of the repair, will update the equipment's service record and issue an invoice. It can also handle electronic payments.

The supply chain and logistics management implications are major. Caterpillar in 1996 invested in the expansion of the remote monitoring system and the worldwide sharing of inventories by the company, suppliers and distributors. Already the company maintains 22 parts facilities around the world, with in excess of 10 million square feet of storage. Caterpillar services 480,000 SKUs of which 320,000 are stocked. Caterpillar dealers stock between 40,000 and 50,000 items. The remote sensing facility permits the company to deliver a part *before* a customer realises the need for it.

Linkages with both customers and distributors are maintained in order to monitor product performance and, subsequently, product development. Both dealers and customers are involved in programmes on product quality, cost reduction and other manufacturing issues. More recently the company has reported a major e-business initiative to: '. . . be industry leader where e-business is concerned and strengthen e-business capabilities to drive consistency, efficiency and velocity throughout the entire value chain'. A strategic alliance has been formed with i2 to combine i2 expertise with Caterpillar's experience: '. . . to transform Cat's supply chain, logistics, planning and customer management business processes'. The project includes a facility to make it easier for existing customers to go online and to encourage online customers to visit the online Cat Dealer Storefront which allows customers electronic access to detailed product information useful in making important purchasing decisions. More than 1000 internal intranet websites offer Caterpillar engineers real-time online dialog with counterparts anywhere in the world.

Measures of the strength of relationships between Caterpillar and its distributors are the actions taken to ensure the longevity of the partnerships during periods of difficulties. During recessions and foreign exchange fluctuations the company undertakes whatever financial actions are necessary to insulate the dealers from financial difficulties. The company shares dealer support such as financial assistance for customers' purchases, and it supports the dealers with inventory management and control, logistics, equipment management and maintenance programs. Many of these aspects are reinforced by Caterpillar-designed software programs. Dealer staff are trained in technical and managerial techniques and technical literature is constantly updated. Business management programmes to improve profitability, productivity and cash flow ensure dealership performances.

The structure of the Caterpillar value chain organisation profile is shown in figure 18.1. It includes both customer and dealer perspectives. Each of the attributes has been derived from the material provided by Fites (1996). As with previous examples the role of information and relationship management can be seen as influencing the structure and operation of the value chain. The role of integrated supply chain and logistics management has been expressed both explicitly *and* implicitly. Figure 18.2 illustrates the value chain processes.

Caterpillar's vision is to 'be the global leader in customer value'.

The Caterpillar Mission states that:

- 'Caterpillar will be the leader in providing the best value in machines, engines and support services for customers dedicated to building the world's infrastructure and developing and transporting its resources. *We provide the best value to customers.*
- Caterpillar people will increase shareholder value by aggressively pursuing growth and profit opportunities that leverage our engineering, manufacturing, distribution, information management and financial services expertise. *We grow profitably.*
- Caterpillar will provide its worldwide workforce with an environment that stimulates diversity, innovation, teamwork, continuous learning and improvement and rewards individual performance. *We develop and reward people.*
- Caterpillar is dedicated to improving the quality of life while sustaining the quality of our earth. *We encourage social responsibility.*'

REFERENCES •

Fites, D. V. (1996), 'Make your dealers your partners', *Harvard Business Review*, March/April.

www.caterpillar.com

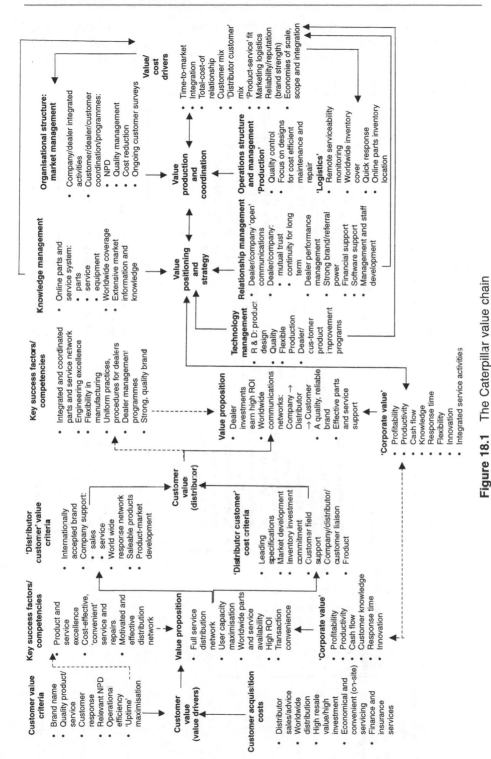

Figure 18.1 The Caterpillar value chain

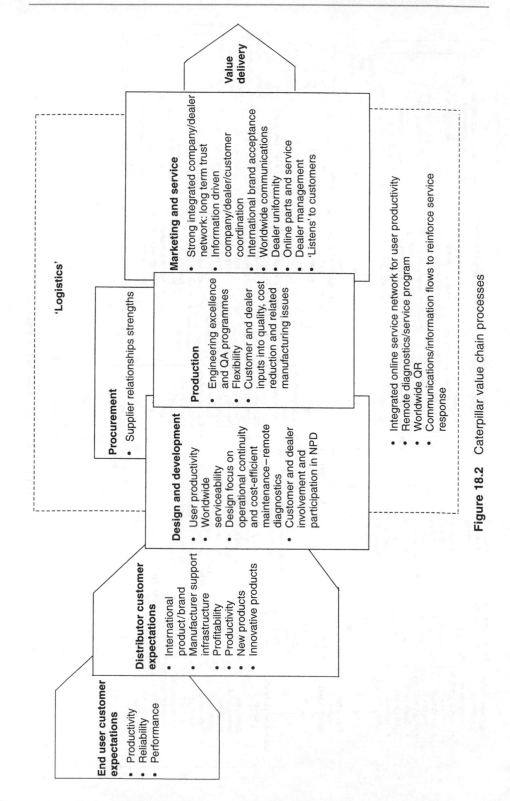

Figure 18.2 Caterpillar value chain processes

Exercise

Glen A Barton, Chairman and Chief Executive Officer stated in April 2001:

> Caterpillar enters the new millenium as a growth-oriented, high-tech global leader and competitor . . . strong, diversified, resilient and forward thinking. We're dedicated to pursuing strategic investments and taking tough action to improve our long-term cost structure. We continue to bolster our leadership in the industries we serve, progressing with a clear focus on well-defined initiatives and renewed strategic planning efforts. We remain committed to realizing profitable growth, fully leveraging the benefits of e-business, aggressively reducing costs and dramatically improving quality – all in an effort to strengthen business processes and improve efficiencies throughout the value chain. We intend to continually advance our ability to cost-effectively serve customers while enhancing profitability and shareholder value. We will continue to raise the bar, building on traditions of excellence based, as always, on the knowledge, creativity, commitment and passion of Caterpillar people worldwide.

- Review and update the Caterpillar value chain organisation profile and the value chain management processes.
- Given the strategic intent expressed in Glen Barton's statement, is the existing value chain relevant to these tasks or could changes be made?

CASE STUDY 2: VALUE CHAINS IN BROADCASTING

In Chapter 16 the notion that '. . . co-option turns actual or potential competitors and "complementers" into partners' was discussed. Doz and Hamel (1998) suggested that '. . . co-option is a means of reaching the critical mass needed for effective competition'. They also discuss alliances in the context of 'enablers' – the means by which a company may take a leadership role in a network (or value chain) from which it can lead and coordinate development activities. This is a similar role to that suggested by McHugh *et al* (1995), where holonic nodes fill four different roles within the value chain; an *operational* role (a complementer), a *support* node (a service function), a *resource provider* node (providing specialist skills and resources such as information or technical expertise or technology) and the *integrator* node (innovator or visionary role).

Doz and Hamel provide an example of co-option in digital broadcasting. They use the development of digital television in Europe as an example. In this value chain broadcasters have allied with content providers (the owners of movies and televised events). The broadcasters have also allied themselves with companies that control the distribution 'channels' (cable television companies and major retailers) to gain rapid access to mass markets.

The broadcasters needed alliances with content providers in order that they might build customer (viewer) acceptance and loyalty. The alliances enabled broadcasters to differentiate their programme offers (their value proposition) from that of their competitors. The authors suggest that the broadcasters staved off competition from traditional communication companies, such as print publishers and content owners. An essential feature is the need for speed in creating critical mass volume due to the fact that most customers are likely only to purchase one subscription. Figure 18.3 uses the notion of co-option alliances to construct a value chain process map for the digital television broadcasting industry in Europe.

REFERENCES •

Doz, Y. L. and G. Hamel (1998), *Alliance Advantage*, Harvard Business School Press, Boston.

McHugh, P., G. Merli and G. Wheeler III (1995), *Beyond Business Process Reengineering*, Wiley, Chichester.

Exercise

● Research this industry in detail and construct an organisational profile for the value chain.
● Research the pharmaceutical or biotechnology industries to identify their holonic network structure and develop a value chain organisation profile and a process map.

CASE STUDY 3: WAL-MART – A MODEL FMCG RETAIL VALUE CHAIN?

Introduction: a simple business model

The secret of successful retailing is to give your customers what they want. And really, if you think about it from your point of view as a customer, you want everything: a wide assortment of good quality merchandise; the lowest possible prices; guaranteed satisfaction with what you buy; friendly knowledgeable service; convenient hours; free parking; a pleasant shopping experience.

We're all working together; that's the secret. And we'll lower the cost of living for everyone, not just in America, but we'll give the world an opportunity to see what it's like to save and have a better lifestyle, a better life for all. We're proud of what we've accomplished; we've just begun.
Sam Walton (1918–1992)

The first Wal-Mart store opened in 1962. By 2001, Wal-Mart Stores Inc employed more than 1.2 million associates in some 4203 stores and offices across the US. The company has expanded internationally with more than 1000 stores overseas. It has also expanded online with Walmart.com.

Wal-Mart's growth has been supported by its international activities. Wal-Mart's global expansion has been achieved through a combination of building retail outlets as well as by acquisition. The company has found that its 'retail culture' is transportable. It is a 'global brand' with recognition as a

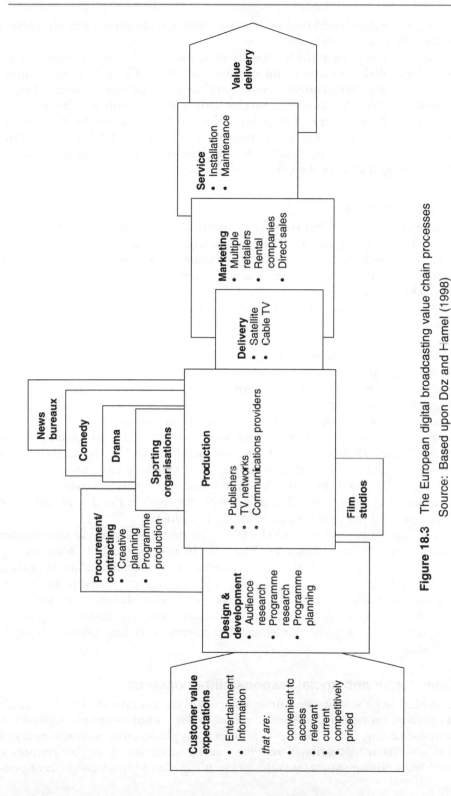

Figure 18.3 The European digital broadcasting value chain processes

Source: Based upon Doz and Hamel (1998)

value proposition based on low cost, best value, wide choice and high levels of friendly customer service.

The company has transplanted its business model(s) to its international operations; Wal-Mart stores, supercenters and SAM's Clubs all have the most advanced computer technology, with standard goals for sales, inventory, gross margin objectives and customer service dedication. Not only has the company transferred its retailing concepts but it also has taken its emphasis on adapting to local cultures and to community involvement. Globally, Wal-Mart responds to local needs, merchandise preferences and local suppliers in the same way as it does in the US.

Customer focus

The key to understanding Wal-Mart's competitive advantage is its strong customer focus. 'Every day low prices' reinforced with wide choice and visible service is a reflection of Wal-Mart's response to customer expectations. The Wal-Mart value proposition continues to reflect Walton's original, but simple, business model.

Among a number of consumer oriented value strategies that support the value proposition are its own label product strategy and its extensive customer loyalty programme.

Wal-Mart's own label products are offered as a range of brands. Products in the range include pet foods, garden fertilizer, soft drinks, delicatessen, dry groceries, meat and produce, pharmacy and health and beauty aids, and vitamin healthcare products. There is a clear view of the expected role of own label products: 'We don't create private-label brands to improve our profit margins; we create them to improve value to customers, which builds customer loyalty' (Bob Connolly, Executive Vice President, Merchandise). Own labels are used to fill a value or pricing void that may have been neglected by the well known brands. This approach may include buying a brand abandoned by a supplier. This policy was exercised in the diaper and toilet tissue product range as well as in apparel products.

The loyalty programme, SAM's Club, has both customer and shareholder value as its primary objectives. The introduction of the Elite Membership package offers '. . . a valuable, convenient array of benefits' to its 38 million card members. The new Elite service offers emergency roadside assistance, discounted business insurance, Internet and long distance service, auto brokerage, member cheques and a pharmacy card. The membership offers a 'special rate' for telebank membership offering excellent rates on deposits and so on.

Community and social responsibility concerns

Wal-Mart has a strong commitment to each of the communities within which it operates. Projects include underwriting college scholarships for high school seniors; raising funds for local children's hospitals; environmental concern and associated 'educational' activities; and a 'matching grant' programme – joint fund raising efforts by Wal-Mart staff together with a non-profit organisation. The company is a sponsor of the Missing Children's Network, a cooperative project with the non-profit National Centre for Missing and Exploited Children.

Supplier partnerships

One of the reasons that Wal-Mart can maintain its value proposition can be found in the relationships built between the company and its suppliers. There are a number of aspects to be considered.

Wal-Mart has built a high level of mutual trust with its suppliers. A *supplier agreement* identifies the structure of alliances, infrastructure requirements, performance expectations and conformance expectations (compliance and equal opportunity practices). Wal-Mart has some fundamental expectations of its suppliers: their keenest prices, innovative ways to maintain service and lower costs, and time-to-market performance.

Potential suppliers are directed to a web based vendor pack that requests detailed information concerning product and service performance abilities together with financial status and insurance guarantees. They are subject to scrutiny to verify capabilities, capacities, quality control, people management and culture. This review compares the potential vendor against Wal-Mart criteria.

Sharing information

A key feature of being a Wal-Mart supplier is a willingness to share information. Information exchange allows both Wal-Mart and its suppliers to be proactive. Shared information develops and strengthens the long term partnerships. It includes sharing replenishment and forecasting data that improve service and lower inventory holding costs, and optimise the cost-efficiency of promotions. Wal-Mart aggregates supplier data input for planning purposes to meet joint goals.

The Wal-Mart relationship with Proctor and Gamble is legendary and is often cited as an example of a manufacturer/retailer relationship in which the cooperation between the two organisations has resulted in a relationship in which the exchange of detailed POS data has enabled P&G to manage inventory for Wal-Mart, and the two companies have managed to work together to lower costs and maintain 'every day low prices'.

Time-to-market

A distinctive competence that can be claimed by Wal-Mart is its aggressive product development activity. The company works closely with suppliers' NPD activities to ensure a 'first-to-market' with new products. A notable success has been the natural health categories (vitamins, herbal cure aids and dietary supplements). The company took full advantage of the passage of the Dietary Supplement legislation to build a strong proposition in the category and develop strong market share.

Technology management

Wal-Mart has taken advantage of almost every viable application of technology relevant to its business. Sales are monitored automatically to ensure on-time replenishment. Suppliers are linked to the facility and are able to monitor sales on a store-by-store basis. The satellite system also links the company's communications activities and is used for the transfer of administrative data and for the exchange of promotional ideas and results.

Information technology is to play an important role in the trading exchange being tested by Wal-Mart. The hub is intended to consolidate global purchasing and to bring suppliers online to compete for contracts in a similar way to that of a public electronic marketplace. It will be integrated with the existing supply chain infrastructure, Supplier Link, comprising EDI networks and an extranet used by Wal-Mart buyers and some 10,000 suppliers to aggregate information detailing sales and inventory levels in every store. Wal-Mart considers that savings will be derived mutually and that forecasting and planning accuracy will be improved. Suppliers will benefit by participating in online bidding for new lines of merchandise.

REFERENCES/FURTHER READING • • • • • • • • • • • • • • • • • •

Carr, M., A. Hostrop and D. O'Connor (1998), 'The new era of global retailing', *The Journal of Business Strategy*, Boston, May/June.

Eder, R. (2000), 'How Wal-Mart takes OTC share: true partnerships and speed to market', *Drug Store News*, New York, 12 June.

Hennessy, T. (2000), 'Wiring the produce patch', *Progressive Grocer*, New York, September.

Kaufman, L. (2000), 'As biggest business, Wal-Mart propels changes elsewhere', *New York Times*, 22 October.

Mahler, D. Q. (2000), 'An American century of retailing', *Chain Store Age*, New York, April.

Whitehead, M. (2000), 'Store wars', *Supply Management*, London, 7 September.

www.walmart.com

Exercise

Clearly Wal-Mart is a successful company and one for which growth is important. Using Figures 18.4 and 18.5, explore the implications of future growth on Wal-Mart's value chain. Identify changes likely to occur.

CASE STUDY 4: DELL COMPUTER CORPORATION

Dell has become a major organisation in a very short space of time. Dell's *direct business model* has created major advantages other than a substantial cost

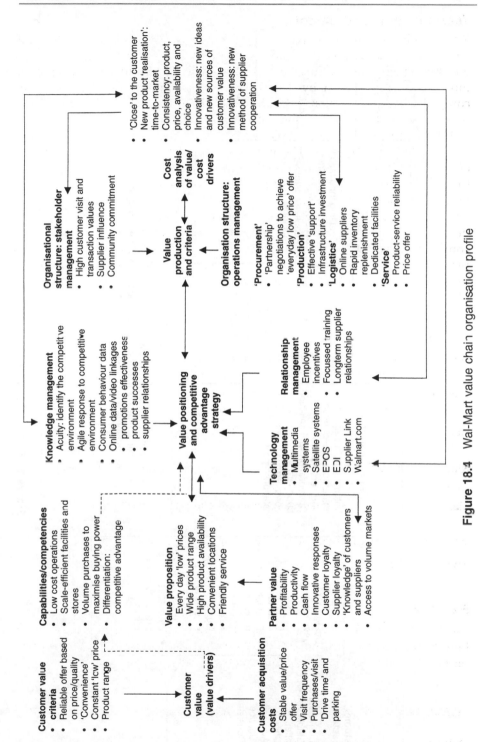

Figure 18.4 Wal-Mart value chain organisation profile

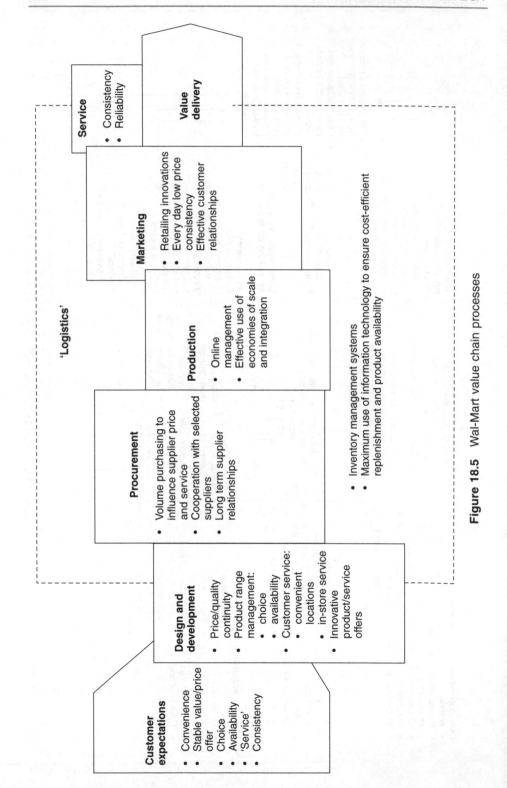

Figure 18.5 Wal-Mart value chain processes

advantage. 'You actually get to have a relationship with the customer . . . and that creates valuable information, which in turn, allows us to leverage our relationships with both suppliers and customers. Couple that information with technology, and you have the infrastructure to revolutionise the fundamental business models of major global companies'. (Dell: 1999)

Dell's business model

Traditional value added resellers can add value in a number of ways. They act as a conduit for suppliers to a market; they can create and/or expand a market; they can hold inventory to offer availability to customers; they can be delegated all or part of the customer service management processs; and they can be a source of market knowledge. Dell's direct business model achieves each of these but adds customisation, and rapid and convenient delivery.

Customers' orders are assembled to meet their specifications, with the software required and ready to ship within hours of receiving the order. There is no risk such as that existing with *speculative* systems, and the customisation that *postponement* affords reduces obsolescence risks (Bucklin: 1966, see Chapter 6). Using JIT-type replenishment systems reduces this risk further. By working with component suppliers who assume responsibilities for inventory management, Dell can also obtain an immediate benefit from any cost reductions their suppliers may realise from design or operational efficiencies.

Direct marketing eliminates a proportion of the distribution margin. It eliminates stocks of finished computers held by distributors and, therefore, the loss of margin on products that become obsolescent.

Dell's demand chain management processes

Dell's competitive advantage is its management of supplier relationships. The postponement model uses information management (the Internet) to communicate component needs and to complete transactions with both suppliers and customers. Essentially Dell is managing a *value chain* because the order process, assembly and delivery, are initiated by the customer.

The Dell approach is a 'pull' system for assembly and distribution rather than a preassembly 'push' system. Once an order is completed and payment cleared (or arrangements confirmed), a production invoice is electronically forwarded to the production facility and the required parts are ordered from suppliers' nearby distribution centres. Dell subcontracts mainboards from the closest regional suppliers; finished computers are then inspected, packed and despatched directly to the customer or to a system integration contractor.

Logistics management is an important feature of the Dell value chain. Logistics efficiency is essential throughout the production and delivery processes. Not only is it essential that components are available as and when they are required, but some items (for example monitors) are despatched from supplier locations to be matched up (by the distribution company) with the remainder of the order prior to delivery to the customer.

E-business developments are an essential feature of the Dell business model. The integration of assembly with its global supplier network also integrates its direct transaction marketing process with procurement and production into a virtual organisation. Individual elements of strategy, customer focus, supplier partnerships, mass customisation, and lean production technology are all coordinated across individual corporate boundaries to optimise productivity.

Supplier partnership

Dell created a customised web page for each of its primary suppliers who can log onto a secure, personalised site to view demand forecasts and future order patterns. This facilitates production scheduling and eliminates unnecessary inventory – they make what is needed only when it is required. Dell makes available data concerning defect rates, specification and engineering changes, and product improvement details. Online communication reduces both error and waste.

Quality assurance is enhanced; parts that fail to meet expectation are 'tracked' on the extranet and the data are 'directed' towards the supplier. Dell insists on knowing suppliers' assembly line rejection rates. Both Dell and the suppliers benefit by manufacturers addressing the quality problem in the early stages of production.

The service process (conducted by contracted service partners) is also based upon a web model. Dell's SMART software is able simultaneously to alert internal systems managers and its service partners when a failure occurs at a customer site. The failure can also be logged on a customer's record, giving a service engineer information concerning the symptoms of the problem. For more serious problems the engineer can be despatched prior to a call from the customer.

Suppliers are required to share sensitive information with Dell. Quality problems, production scheduling failures and so on are important to Dell, because knowledge of these problems can be used for current and future scheduling and forecasting plans. Furthermore it has an impact on the quality and price offer to the customer.

Dell is using the Internet to create bulletin board facilities for its suppliers. Websites have links to bulletin boards to enable partners to exchange experiences with Dell and the Dell value chain. Constructive comments improve both the product and the production process, and therefore customer satisfaction.

Project management tools are also web based. Dell's partners are able to collaborate in real time on product development and enhancement through this facility. Dell's design and development process relies heavily on input from its suppliers to refine design elements and component manufacturing. This is supplemented by personal meetings and video conferencing, to maintain product performance, quality and cost profiles.

Customer relationship management

Dell has used the Internet to increase its links with its larger customers, the business users. 'Premier Pages' contain approved specifications, pre-negotiated prices and new workflow capabilities. When a customer company employee requests a new computer, the order is automatically routed into the appropriate buying area for approval and action. Large companies report significant cost savings using Premier Pages. Ford saved some $2 million in initial procurement costs.

The website offers non-business users a product search facility which can also be used to 'design' their own computers and systems; there is also a parts ordering facility. Dell uses this information to identify and to understand customer buying patterns, replacement needs and operating/decision making directions.

Premier Pages provide data that is useful for customer segmentation and customer profitability analysis. They also provide a basis for creating significantly different service packages for addressing specific customer needs.

Dell and VARs

Dell's customisation, delivery lead times and price competitiveness have created a significant competitive advantage. However, the channel intermediaries that work with Dell to add value providing installation and service, report receiving little or no support from the manufacturer. This suggests a weakness. Dell appears not to understand fully the role of VARs and their capabilities and capacities. This could prove difficult in the future as Compaq continues to expand its direct marketing activities. It would suggest a need for Dell to reappraise its relationships with VAR intermediaries and perhaps develop a strategy for their involvement.

REFERENCES/FURTHER READING ● ● ● ● ● ● ● ● ● ● ● ● ● ● ● ● ● ●

Aragon, L. (1998), 'Dell's channel secret revealed', *VAR Business*, 20 July.

Bucklin, L. P. (1966), *A Theory of Distribution Channel Structure*, University of California Press, Berkeley.

Currey, J. and M. Kenney (1999), 'Beating the clock: corporate responses to rapid change in the PC industry', *California Management Review*, Berkeley, Fall.

Dell, M. with C. Fredman (1999), *Direct from Dell: Strategies that Revolutionised an Industry*, Harper Collins, London.

Gillmore, D. (1998), 'Michael Dell's perdiam', *MC Technology Marketing Intelligence*, New York, December.

Greengard, S. (2000), 'Design to go', *Industry Week*, Cleveland, 15 May.

Joachim, D. (1998), 'Dell links virtual supply chain', *Internet Week*, 2 November.

Kirkpatrick, D. (2000), 'Please don't call us PC', *Fortune*, New York, 16 October.

Morris, B. (2000), 'Can Michael Dell escape the box?', *Fortune*, New York, 16 October.

Stewart, T. (1999), 'Larry Bossidy's new role model', *Fortune*, New York, 12 April.

www.dellcomputer.com

Exercises

- Construct value chain organisation profile and process maps for Dell.
- Construct similar maps for the computer industry.

Index

accurate response 87–8
acquisition costs *see* customer acquisition costs
activities 129, 131, 137, 146–50, 165–6, 344, 345–6
  value strategy 234–8
added value 40–3, 51, 52, 138–9
  performance measure 160–2, 163, 332–4
added value return on investment (AVROI) 334–5, 336–8
admissions, university 305–6
aesthetics 27, 185, 358
alliances 101, 159 60, 306, 317 18
American System of Manufactures 63–4
assets 8, 10–11, 285–6, 363
audit model 135–8, 348–50, 362–6
automotive industry 99 101, 211, 347
  industry value chain 254–63, 263–4

balanced scorecard 159–60, 162–5, 238, 338–9, 340
  performance planning and control 165–74
barriers 180
benefits, costs and 31–2, 106, 107, 182, 183
broadcasting 371–2, 373
business environment 2–5, 13–19
business plan 115, 116
business processes *see* processes
business risk 356–7
buying organisations 180–1
buying process 176–7, 178–82

capabilities 8, 33, 201–9, 215–17, 222–4, 363
  capability balance sheet 205–7
  capability profile 356–7
  decisions 115, 116
  as economic rent 203–4
  see also core competencies
capacities 33
  capacity planning profile 115, 116
capital costs 335
cash flow 109–13, 135, 157, 158
Caterpillar Inc. 366–71
codestiny 66, 317–18
codification 73–4
co-makership 234–8
competency/capability balance sheet 205–7
  see also core competencies
competition 2, 3, 303–4
  effective value strategy 48–9, 50
  key success factors 211–12, 213
competitive advantage 41, 160–1, 332, 333
  see also added value; value positioning and competitive advantage strategy
configuration options 354–5
consumer durables 101–2
consumer surplus 28, 36–40, 41, 138–9
consumption chain 30–1, 176–7, 178–9
control
  and coordination 148–50
  planning and 106–9, 165–74, 336–9, 340
convenience 27, 185, 358

co-option   317
coordination   15–16, 148–50
coproductivity   65–6, 275–6, 317
core assets   8, 10–11, 285–6, 363
core competencies   137–8, 141, 142, 144,
    200–25, 363
    competency/capability balance sheet
    205–7
    corporate value chains   267, 268, 274,
    275
    education   307
    healthcare   285–6
    industry value chains   251, 252, 256,
    257
    key success factors, value drivers and
    215–17
core processes *see* processes
corporate value chains   248, 265–80
cospecialisation   317
costs and benefits   31–2, 106, 107, 182,
    183
creativity   113
cultural differences   345
customer acquisition costs   307, 359,
    363
    corporate value chains   267, 268, 274,
    275
    customer value   182–4, 185–7
    healthcare   283–5
    industry value chains   251, 252, 256,
    257
    organisation profile   141, 142
    value profile   229, 231, 232–3
customer-centric thinking   21, 95–6
customer expectations   8, 17–19, 148–50,
    151, 157, 158, 308
    corporate value chains   271, 272, 277,
    278
    healthcare   283–5, 293–5
    industry value chains   251–3, 254,
    255, 261, 262
    and the value proposition   27–8, 193,
    194
customer experience   176–7, 177–8, 179
customer focus   117–18, 374
customer involvement   318
customer perspective   164, 167–76
    passim
customer relationship   346–7
customer satisfaction index   189
customer value   105–7, 176–99, 362

components   182–8
    quantifying qualitative attributes
    335–6
    value delivery gap   188–92
customer value criteria   27, 141, 142,
    184–5, 307, 358
    corporate value chains   267, 268, 274,
    275
    healthcare   283–5
    industry value chains   251, 252, 256,
    257
    value profile   229–32
customer value expectations   201,
    228–33
customer value model   27–8, 31–4,
    178–88, 307, 309
    end-user and intermediary   196, 197
    organisation profile   141, 142
    purchasing decision   178–82
    qualitative components   184–5
    quantifying   182–4
    see also customer acquisition costs;
    customer value criteria

Daiichi   29–30
Daimler-Chrysler   78, 101
decisions   144–8, 151, 365–6
    value chain structures   351–4
    value strategy   234–8, 241–3
Dell Computers   56, 63, 76, 118, 212,
    376–82
demand   14–15, 59
    analysis of   212, 213
    derived   196–8
demand chain   87–9, 379–80
    integration with supply chain   5–7,
    98–9, 122–3, 130–5, 219–20, 221
demand life cycle   207–9
derived demand   196–8
design and development   352, 365
    activities   147, 148, 151
    corporate value chains   271–3, 277,
    278
    decisions   144, 145, 151
    healthcare   294, 295
    industry value chains   254, 255, 261,
    262
    Li and Fung   242, 243
differentiation   48–9, 50
digital broadcasting   371–2, 373
disposal   186, 233, 359

distinctive capabilities 203, 357
dollar defence 160
Du Pont control model 106–9

earnings, cash flow from 109, 110
economic rent 202–4
economies of integration 66, 74–6
economists' model 28–9, 36–40, 51, 52
economy 27, 185, 358
education 298–310
effectiveness 20, 46–9, 315, 336–8
efficiency 58, 315, 336–8
e-lance economy 61–2
employees 157, 158
enterprise value 169, 327–31
   managing growth 329–31
   planning and control 336–8
entrepreneurial rents 204
environment, changing 2–5, 13–19
equity funds 110, 111–12
exchange value 28–9, 36–40, 49–53, 54
expenditure 182
experience based value 18–19
exploration 190, 192
external perspective 167–74 passim

financial perspective 164, 167–74 passim
fixed asset requirements 110, 111
flexibility 15–16, 138
flexible specialisation 68
fmcg service products 101–2
food processing industry 211
Ford 23, 78, 99–100, 129, 256, 259
Four Quadrant Value Propositions
   (FQVP) hypothesis 194–5
functions 6, 218–19
   see also processes
Fung, V. 195
   see also Li and Fung

General Motors (GM) 78, 99–100, 129,
   259
generic value chain 124–35, 136
Glynwed 101, 108, 122–3
growth
   enterprise value 329–31
   stakeholder expectations and growth
      rate 157, 159

healthcare
   corporate value chain 265–73, 279

value and value chains 281–97
Hewlett Packard (HP) 123–4

IKEA 40, 53, 65, 97, 273–9, 279
impannatore 103, 250–1, 251–3, 254, 263
implementation 190, 192
Industrial Revolution 63, 64
industry value chains 248, 250–64
information 29–30, 177–8, 375
information systems 177–8
infrastructure 219, 220, 346–7
innovation 15–16
innovation and learning perspective
   164, 167–74 passim
installation 186, 187, 359
intangible assets 118–20, 204–5, 331
integrating processes 219, 220
integration 15–16
   economies of integration 66, 74–6
integrator 155, 189
   see also impannatore; visionary
intellectual property 318–20
internal perspective 164, 167–74 passim
internalised learning 317
international education 298–310
Internet exchanges 78, 99–100
inter-organisational processes 324–5
interorganisational systems 155–6
interpretation 190, 192
intra-organisational processes 325
investment management 45, 106–9
investment requirements 139, 140
Italy 68
   Prato textile industry 62, 103, 250–4,
      255, 263

joint ventures 317–18

key success factors (KSFs) 141, 142,
   144, 209–12, 213, 307, 364
   and core competencies 212, 214,
      215–17
   corporate value chains 267, 268
   industry value chains 251, 252, 256,
      257
   Li and Fung 222–4
Kingfisher 102
knowledge management 7, 339
   core competencies 208–9, 210
   corporate value chains 268, 269, 274,
      275

education   301, 303, 309
healthcare   284, 288
industry value chains   252, 253, 257,
   258
knowledge management focus   72–4
Li and Fung   239, 240
management interfaces   65–8, 71, 82,
   83, 322–3, 324
organisation profile   142, 143, 233–4,
   235
value positioning and competitive
   advantage   53–4, 55, 318–20
virtual organisation   79, 80

Lastminute.com   78–9
latent value   169, 328–9, 330–1
learning
   innovation and learning perspective
      164, 167–74 passim
   internalised   317
learning organisation   318–20
Li and Fung   162, 195–8, 222–4, 239,
   240–1, 242, 243
   core competencies and key success
      factors   222–4
   implementing value production   238–43
   value proposition   195–8
life cycle   207–9
lifestyle   181–2
logistics   32–3, 366
   activities   147
   decisions   145, 146–8, 151, 353
   generic value chain   133, 134, 135,
      136, 236, 237
   healthcare   284, 291–2, 294, 296
   industry value chains   254, 255, 261–3
   Li and Fung   239, 241, 242, 243
   operations management   142, 143,
      257, 260, 268, 270–1, 274, 276

maintenance   186, 187, 359
management interfaces   65–8, 70, 71,
   322–4
   virtual organisation   82–3
   see also knowledge managment;
      relationship management;
      technology management
market driven organisations   17, 19
market management   57, 143
   see also stakeholder management
market-product strategy   117–18

market sensing   347–50
market turbulence   13–19, 59–60
market value   332–4
market volume, analysis of   114–16
marketing   237, 238, 346–7, 366
   activities   147, 237, 238
   corporate value chains   272, 273, 277,
      278
   decisions   145, 146, 151, 354
   education   304
   healthcare   294, 295–6
   industry value chains   254, 255, 261,
      262
marketing value chain   124, 125, 126
Marks and Spencer   91–2, 101–2
mass customisation   65
mass production   64–5
McKesson HBOC Corporation   265–73,
   279
modularity   226–7

network organisation   60–3
new business models
   education   300–3
   response to changing environment
      2–12
   value chain   124, 360
Nike   18, 63, 75

objectives   350–1
operational effectiveness   20–1, 46–9
operational efficiency   58, 315, 336–8
operational processes   45
operations
   cash flow from   109–11
   customer acquisition costs   186, 187,
      359
operations management   57–8, 314–15
   corporate value chains   268, 270–1,
      274, 276
   healthcare   284, 290–2
   industry value chains   252, 253, 257,
      260
   Li and Fung   239, 240–1
   organisation profile   142, 143–4
operations strategy   5, 119–20
   profile and definitions   7–11
organisation profile   139–44, 362–5
   case studies   369, 377
   combined with processes and
      activities   343, 344, 345–6

corporate value chains 266–7, 268, 274, 275–6
  education 307
  healthcare 283, 284
  industry value chains 251–3, 256–8
  Li and Fung 238, 239
  value strategy 233–4, 235
organisation strategy 119–20
organisation structure 119–20, 142, 143–4, 316–18
  corporate value chains 268, 270–1, 274, 276
  healthcare 284, 290–2
  industry value chains 252, 253, 257, 259–60
  Li and Fung 239, 240–1
  operations management see operations management
  stakeholder management see stakeholder management
  see also virtual organisation
organisational alignment 45–6
organisational value 106–9
outputs 351–4
  sensitivity to resource availability 355–6
outsourcing 60–1, 129–30, 148–50, 156, 167

Pareto rents 204
partner roles 194
partner value objectives 157, 158, 307, 364
  corporate value chains 268, 274, 275
  healthcare 284, 287
  industry value chains 251–3, 257, 258
partnerships 306, 375, 380
  selecting partners 238, 355–7
performance
  customer value criterion 27, 184–5, 358
  expectations 139, 140
  measurement 159–65
  planning and control 165–74, 336–9, 340
  planning and measurement in the value chain 326–36
personalisation 73–4
perspectives 159–60, 164, 167–74
Philips 76–8
planning, and control 106–9, 165–74, 336–9, 340

planning processes 220
positioning
  strategy 45, 46
  value proposition 193–5
potential market 114–16
Prato (Italy) 62, 103, 250–4, 255, 263
premium value 169, 328–9, 330–1
price 13, 31–2, 36–40, 182–4
process quality 182–3
processes 6, 8, 57, 165–6, 365–6
  and activities 137, 148–50
  case studies 370, 373, 378
  combined with organisation profile 344, 345–6
  conduit for value chain operations 217–22
  corporate value chains 271–3, 277–9
  decisions 144–8, 151
  education 300–1, 308
  generic value chain 129, 130, 131
  healthcare 285–6, 293–6
  industry value chains 254, 255, 261–3
  inter-organisational and intra-organisational 324–6
  Li and Fung 241–3
  value chain structures 351–4
  value strategy 234–8
procurement 236–8, 365
  activities 147, 236–8
  corporate value chains 272, 273, 277, 278
  decisions 145, 146, 151, 352
  healthcare 291, 294, 295
  industry value chains 254, 255, 261, 262
  Li and Fung 239, 240–1, 242, 243
  operations management 257, 260, 268, 270, 274, 276
producer surplus 37–40, 112, 138–9
product characteristics 33, 34
product innovation 346–7
product life cycle 207–9
product-service-attribute value matrix 187–8
product use 176–7, 179
production 365
  activities 147, 148, 237, 238
  corporate value chains 272, 273, 277, 278
  decisions 144, 145, 151, 237, 238, 353

healthcare   284, 291, 294, 295
industry value chains   254, 255, 261,
    262
Li and Fung   239, 241, 243
operations management   142, 143,
    257, 260, 268, 270, 274, 276
productivity   38–40, 135
planning and control   106–9, 336–8
stakeholder expectations   157, 158–9
value based strategy decisions   46–8
productivity frontier   20–1, 22, 48–9
profit pools   81–2, 135, 332
profitability   28, 37–40
and management interface areas
    82–3
measuring value chain performance
    332–4
planning and control   106–9, 336–8
stakeholder expectations   157, 158
value based strategy decisions   46–8
prosumer/prosumerism   18, 75–6,
    317–18
purchasing process   176–7, 178–82

Queen Elizabeth Hospital (QEH),
    Rotorua   281–97

recruitment   304–5
recycling   233
relationship management   7, 339, 381
core competencies   208–9, 210
corporate value chains   268, 270, 274,
    275–6
education   302–3, 309
healthcare   284, 288–9
industry value chains   252, 253, 257,
    259
Li and Fung   239, 240
management interfaces   65–8, 71,
    82–3, 323–4
organisation profile   142, 143, 233–4,
    235
profit pools   81–2
value positioning and competitive
    advantage   54–6, 321–2
virtual organisation   76–8, 80
relative competitive positioning   193,
    194
reliability   27, 185, 358
rent, economic   202–4
reproducible capabilities   203, 357

resource availability   355–6
revenues   135
review of value chain   348–50
reward systems   160
rigidities   178–82
risk barriers   180

Sainsbury's   92
scenario evaluation   169–74
search   186, 359
security   27, 179, 184–5, 358
semi-conductor industry   211
served market   135
service   346–7, 366
activities   147, 148
corporate value chains   272, 273, 277,
    278
decisions   145, 146, 151, 352–3
healthcare   284, 292, 294, 296
industry value chains   254, 255, 261,
    262
integral component of value   32–4
Li and Fung   237, 238, 239, 241
operations management   257, 260,
    268, 271, 274, 276
organisation profile   142, 144
service processes   220
7dreams.com   345
share price   160
shareholder value management   106–9
shareholders   156–8
social responsibility   374–5
specification   185–6, 359
speed   15–16
Sport Obermeyer   87–8
stakeholder expectations   8
performance planning and control
    167–9, 170
virtual organisation   156–9
stakeholder management   57
corporate value chains   268, 270, 274,
    276
industry value chains   252, 253, 257,
    259–60
Li and Fung   239, 240
organisation structure for   142, 143,
    284, 290
stakeholders   155–60
strategic alliances   101, 159–60, 306,
    317–18
strategic cashflow   110, 111–12

strategic effectiveness 20, 46–9, 315, 336–8

strategic management 94–5

strategic operations management 226–45
  integrating role 228, 229
  model format 227–33

strategy 20
  enterprise value and strategic planning 327–9
  and structure in the virtual enterprise 316–18
  value chain as a basis for planning 21–2
  value as a component of strategic planning 128
  value creation 96–8
  value strategy *see* value strategy (main entry)

strategy mapping 169–74, 338–9, 340

structural factors 14–15, 59–60

success factors 15–16, 60
  see also key success factors

supplier parks 100–1

suppliers
  influence 179–80
  partnerships 238, 355–7, 375, 380

supply chain 22–3, 86–92, 130–5
  advantages and disadvantages 89–90
  integration with demand chain 5–7, 98–9, 122–3, 130–5, 219–20, 221
  processes, components and structure 90–2
  vs the value chain 112–13

supporting infrastructure 219, 220

surplus value 160

tangible value 169, 328–9, 330–1

technology life cycle 207–9

technology management 7, 339, 376
  core competencies 208–9, 210
  corporate value chains 268, 269–70, 274, 275
  economies of integration 74–6
  education 301–2, 303, 309
  healthcare 284, 288
  industry value chains 252, 253, 257, 258–9
  Li and Fung 239, 240
  management interfaces 65–8, 71, 82–3, 322–3

organisation profile 142, 143, 233–4, 235
  value positioning and competitive advantage 56–7, 320–1
  virtual organisation 80, 81

textile industry 62, 103, 250–4, 255, 263

time 29–30

time-to-market 375

traditional organisations 19, 84, 120

transaction costs 61–2, 186–7, 227–8, 359

transitions 16–17, 60

translation 190, 192

turbulence, market 13–19, 59–60

Unilever 23

universities 298–310

usage barriers 180

use value (value-in use) 25–7, 28, 36–40, 49–53, 54, 105–7

utility 17–18, 27

value 2
  approaches to defining 28–34
  emerging emphasis on 20–1
  perspectives of 25–35, 36–46

value barriers 180

value based organisations
  changing business environment and virtual organisations 59–85
  value chain approach 105–21

value chain 2–5, 22–3, 92–103
  adding value 138–9
  audit model 135–8, 348–50, 362–6
  application 99–102
  basis for planning overall strategy 21–2
  business processes as conduit for value chain operations 217–22
  configuration options 354–5
  configuring 314–61
  core competencies and 204–5, 206–7
  decisions *see* decisions (main entry)
  design 346–57
  early perspectives and characteristics 92–4
  evolution 314–15
  generic value chain 124–35, 136
  integrated demand and supply chains 5–7, 98–9, 122–3, 130–5, 219–20, 221

organisation profile *see* organisation
 profile (main entry)
performance planning and
 measurement 326–36
planning and control 336–9
principles 150–2
processes *see* processes
review of 348–50
strategic management perspective
 94–5
strategy and management 130–5
structures 338–9, 350–5
value based organisations 105–21
value chain integrator 155, 189
 see also impannatore; visionary
value creation 19–22, 57–8, 165–7
 strategy/structure model 96–8
value curve 44
value cycle 102, 124–7, 347–8
value delivery 19–22, 57–8, 165–7
 gap 188–92
 integrating value strategy and
  227–33
 managing 188–90
 style 190, 192
value drains 32
value drivers 8, 212–15, 363, 365
 core competencies, KSFs and 215–17
 corporate value chains 268, 271, 274,
  276
 education 307, 309
 healthcare 284, 292–3
 industry value chains 252, 253–4,
  257, 260
 Li and Fung 241
 organisation profile 142, 144, 234,
  235
 stakeholder value drivers 157, 158–9
value exchange model 44–5, 51–3, 54
value-in-use (use value) 25–7, 28,
  36–40, 49–53, 54, 105–7
value innovation 44–6
value migration 96, 98, 327–8, 332
value nets 248–9
value positioning and competitive
 advantage strategy 8–9, 53–7,
 318–22, 364

corporate value chains 268, 269–70,
 274, 275–6
education 307, 309
healthcare 284, 287–90
industry value chains 252, 253–4,
 257, 258–9
Li and Fung 239, 240
organisation profile 142, 143
value production and coordination 9,
 57–8, 364–5
 corporate value chains 268, 270–1
 education 307, 309
 healthcare 284, 290–2
 industry value chains 257, 259–60
 Li and Fung 239, 240–1
 organisation profile 142, 143–4
value profile 228–33
value proposition 8, 193–5, 234, 364
 components 193–4
 corporate value chains 267–9, 274,
  275
 customer expectations and 27–8
 education 307, 309
 healthcare 284, 286–7
 industry value chains 252, 253,
  256–8
 Li and Fung 195–8
 organisation profile 141, 142
value strategy 46–58, 102–3, 119
 decisions 46–9
 integrating with value production
  227–33
 model 49–58
venture/'market in' approach 234–6
virtual organisation 11, 60–3, 69–70
 emerging characteristics 78–83
 organisation structure 84, 120
 performance measurement 159–60
 relationship management 76–8
 stakeholder expectations 156–9
visionary 5, 155, 265–6, 279
Volkswagen (VW) 101

Wal-Mart 372–6, 377, 378
Whirlpool Corporation 77–8
wine industry 4
working capital 109–11